ADVANCED TOPICS
IN SCIENCE AND TECHNOLOGY IN CHINA

ADVANCED TOPICS
IN SCIENCE AND TECHNOLOGY IN CHINA

Zhejiang University is one of the leading universities in China. In Advanced Topics in Science and Technology in China, Zhejiang University Press and Springer jointly publish monographs by Chinese scholars and professors, as well as invited authors and editors from abroad who are outstanding experts and scholars in their fields. This series will be of interest to researchers, lecturers, and graduate students alike.

Advanced Topics in Science and Technology in China aims to present the latest and most cutting-edge theories, techniques, and methodologies in various research areas in China. It covers all disciplines in the fields of natural science and technology, including but not limited to, computer science, materials science, the life sciences, engineering, environmental sciences, mathematics, and physics.

Zheng Qin
Jiankuan Xing
Xiang Zheng

Software Architecture

With 161 figures

ZHEJIANG UNIVERSITY PRESS
浙江大学出版社

Springer

AUTHORS:

Prof. Zheng Qin,
School of Software,
Tsinghua University,
100084, Beijing , China
E-mail: qingzh@ mail.tsinghua.edu.cn

Jiankuan Xing
School of Software,
Tsinghua University,
100084, Beijing , China
E-mail: xjk05@ mails.tsinghua.edu.cn

Xiang Zheng
School of Software,
Tsinghua University,
100084, Beijing , China
E-mail: xiangmyself@ gmail.com

ISBN 978-7-308-05453-9 **Zhejiang University Press, Hangzhou**
ISBN 978-3-540-74342-2 **Springer Berlin Heidelberg New York**
e-ISBN 978-3-540-74343-9 **Springer Berlin Heidelberg New York**

Series ISSN 1995-6819 Advanced topics in science and technology in China
Series e-ISSN 1995-6827 Advanced topics in science and technology in China

Library of Congress Control Number: 2007937689

Springer is a part of Springer Science + Business Media
springer.com

Cover design: Joe Piliero, Springer Science + Business Media LLC, New York
Printed on acid-free paper

Preface

Building software nowadays is far more difficult than it can be done several decades ago. At that time, software engineers focused on how to manipulate the computer to work and then solve problems correctly. The organization of data and implementation of algorithm were the crucial process of software designing then. However, more and more tasks in low level, such as memory management and network communication, have been automatized or at least can be reused with little effort and cost. Programmers and designers, with the help of high level programming languages and wieldy development tools, can pay more attention to problems, rather than bury themselves into the machine code manuals. However, the side effect of these utilities is that more complicated problems are given according to the requirements from military, enterprise and so on, in which the complexity grows rapidly day by day. We believe that software architecture is a key to deal with it.

Many people become aware of the existence of software architecture just recently. Nevertheless, it in fact has a long history, which may surprise you. Before the invention of C++ or even C, some computer scientists had begun to notice the concept of software structure and its influence to software development. In the 1990s, software architecture started its journey of bloom, when several communities, workshops and conferences were hold with a great amount of published articles, books and tools. Today, software architect, the job of taking software designing, analysis and dealing with different concerns and requirements from different stakeholders, is considered as the center of development team.

But there is an ironical problem that most existing architects in fact do not take any study or training in this field, some of whom even do not realize that software architecture is a kind of realm requiring academic effort, just as artificial intelligence or data mining. The reason is that software architecture has no widely-accepted definitions and standards of basic theories and practical methods, which leads to that there are almost no universal course about this subject. Meanwhile, the rapid growth and division of software architecture result in too many branches and sub-fields, most of which still keep non-dominant and unified. These changes aggregate the trouble in learning even a subset of software architecture area. In this book, we will provide an overview among the classic theories and some latest progresses of software architecture and try to touch the software architecture's essence.

This book is a collaboration of three authors: Zheng Qin, Jiankuan Xing and Xiang Zheng. More particularly, Professor Qin is the primary author who decides the contents and issues what you can see in this book. And Jiankuan Xing organizes the work of writing, and facilitates the cooperation with authors and other contributers.

Targets

This book aims to give an introduction to the theory foundations, various sub-fields, current research status and practical methods of software architecture. In this book, readers can acquire the basic knowledge of software architecture, including why software architecture is necessary, how we can describe a system's architecture by formal language, what architecture styles are popular for practice use and how we can apply software architecture into the development of systems. Study cases, data, illustrations and other materials which are released in the recent years will be used to show the latest development of software architecture. This book can be used as the learning material for touching software architecture.

How to Read This Book

We target to give readers an inside-out understanding of software architecture, therefore this book is divided into two parts (not shown explicitly in content):
- Basic Theories: Chapter 1—Chapter 5
- Advance Topics: Chapter 6—Chapter 9

In detail, we give the overview descriptions for each chapter as follows:

Chapter 1: Introduction. The theme of this chapter is the basic introduction to software architecture, where readers will see why we need it, how it emerged and what its definitions look like. We hope to give readers a clear vision on it, considering a great many misunderstanding and arguments' presence. In addition, with the development of research, concerns and usage of software architecture have become different, which we will mention at the last section of this chapter.

Chapter 2: Architectural Styles and Patterns. Initially, the research on software architecture emphasized the categorization of software in architectural level. Some systems share the common structure and properties are classified into one set in which the same vocabulary and similar models for representing these systems can be used. Each vocabulary and models specified for a category is called "architectural style". What's more, we abstract and represent some representative structure and reuse them with style. Each structure is called an "architectural pattern". Architecture styles and patterns are very precise utilities for constructing complex systems. In Chapter 2, we provide descriptions, study cases and comparison of them.

Chapter 3: Application and Analysis of Architectural Styles. After characterizing several popular styles, we continue to offer a few study cases, each of which combines more than one architectural style. Academically, this is called "heterogeneous style constructing". As a matter of fact, applied software always uses multiple styles simultaneously, no matter how simple they are. The goal of this chapter is to tie the abstract styles to practice use.

Chapter 4: Software Architecture Description. How to describe software architecture is the centric subject of architecture realm, because it is the foundation to represent software's design, perform effective communications among stakeholders and measure systems' behaviors according to requirements. In this chapter, we pay attention to architectural formal description, which stands on the mathematic basis. However, for UML, the language widely used as architecture representation in practice, you can find excessive materials about it.

Chapter 5: Design Strategies in Architecture Level. This chapter gives you a chance to touch the concept of architectural design with formal foundation. In contrast to practical software development processes, such as RUP (Rational Unified Process), formal architectural design strategies stress the relationship and calculus of function space and structure space, both of which abstract the development process performed in the real world. To get through with this chapter, a fair capability of set theory and automata theory is required.

Chapter 6: Software Architecture IDE. Although software architecture is useful for software development, using it with pure handwork incurs too much overhead, and then time and cost, to the development process, which may obliterate its benefits. That's the key why software architecture was not popularly accepted in the 1990s. Now, we have the handy assist, software architecture IDE. The purpose of IDE is to enable an organization to manage its software architecture and other related actions and processes in a way that meets business needs by providing a foundational utility upon which design, communication, framework code generation and validation can be carried out automatically.

Chapter 7: Evaluating Software Architecture. After the initial architectural design is finished, any stakeholder would finger out whether this design is good or not, whether it will contribute to a successful development and then output the satisfying production or doom to crush resulting from the design defects. That's the evaluation's task. In this chapter, currently widely-used evaluation methods are discussed and compared. However, evaluation methods still lack the formal foundation, and more focus on the experience and capability of participators. Therefore, the description here will bring you the practical architectural methods and technologies, based on which evaluation is performed.

Chapter 8: Flexible Software Architecture. Flexible software architecture means the structure of a system which can metamorphose during runtime according to users' instructions, executing environment's changes or other requirements and the related actions and processes. That's crucial for systems' needs of self-healing and self-adaptation abilities. The systems with these needs before normally mix the structure metamorphosis code and application code, which insults more trouble in maintaining and improving procedures. What's more, failing to divide this confusion causes the system as conceived and the system as built to diverge over time. In this chapter, we give an introduction to what flexible software in architecture level looks like and what the principles and organization patterns of constructing it are.

Chapter 9: A Vision on Software Architecture. This is a chapter far away from theories, methods and technologies, in which the applications of software architecture in current software industry and in other fields, such as medicine, electronic engineering and military are presented in general. After that, we will provide several future research directions of software architecture at the end of this book.

·   Considering the relative independence of each chapter, readers can choose several chapters they are interested in. But we recommend Chapter 1 should be read carefully since it can help you understand other chapters easier and better. In addition, you can find more detail and deeper description about some topics through the reference materials we give.

Who Should Read This Book

The graduates and undergraduates whose majors are elated to software design and development will benefit much from this book. Also, other people who are interested in software architecture would be guided to this field by reading this book. Then, experienced software designers and project leaders who want to adopt architecture as the centric concerns and utility of their software development process are our target readers, too. But they may suffer pain for a moment when converting their original mind to the new world, from which they will at last benefit. We assume our readers should have simple experience as follows. (Each capability may only be involved in several chapters rather than the whole book)

- Programming using C++, Java or C#
- Software design (even a simple project would be fine)
- Software project management

Acknowledgements

It is a great pleasure to acknowledge the profound and original work of Software Architecture Group of Tsinghua Univ., especially Jiankuan Xing (Chapters 1, 5, 7, 8) and Xiang Zheng (Chapters 3, 4). Their insights, collaboration and diligence have been a constant source which gestates the publication of this book.

For the current years I have been considering the problems of software architecture. During the book's writing, we have profited greatly by collaboration with many people, including Kaimo Hu, who prepares lots of materials for Chapters 2 and 9. Meanwhile, he often inspired us with wide knowledge and ideas; and Juan Wang who buried herself into various software architecture IDEs and taught us how to use them in a great detail, which contributed much for Chapter 6. She is also participating the XArch project focusing on ADL parsing and model generating. And many thanks to Hui Cao, a nice reader who has inspected most manuscript and offered valuable criticisms and comments.

Beijing   Zheng Qin
June 2007

Contents

1

Introduction to Software Architecture

Compared to the traditional software several decades ago which were simple machine instructions or the combination of data structures and algorithms, current software are more complicated and harder to control and maintain. Normally, software systems are constructed through the assembly of components, whatever those which are developed according to new specifications or those which are stored in the libraries. In this circumstance, a team is needed to face different facets of the system. Some of them deal with the necessary functions to be implemented or reused in components, while others have to focus on how the work from different divisions can be coordinated and communicated correctly. Meanwhile, in this process some qualities of software must be guaranteed in order to approach the success.

Software architecture is a rising subject of software engineering to help people solve problems mentioned above. With it, designers or project managers have the chance to oversee the status of software in a high level. In addition, software architecture can be reused, resulting in the saving of huge cost and the reduction of risks within the development processes and the activities after them, including designing, modeling, implementation, test, evaluation, maintaining and evolution.

However, tracking software architecture is difficult, because it always hides itself behind what you can touch. Visualizing it requires a deep grasp of global information of systems as well as excellent skills and methods. People from different organizations or enterprises use different strategies to handle it, but most of them have something in common. Abstract and summary of these experiences have become the foundation of software architecture science today.

In this chapter, we start from the history of software development, trying to uncover the origin of software architecture. Then we discuss the definitions and meanings of architecture and other related activities. At last, we focus on what benefits we will gain from it.

1.1   A Brief History of Software Development

Revolutions in software development paradigm are not singular since the word "software" was approximately born in the 1940s when the initial stored-program computers emerged. Each shift, along with development methodologies, patterns and tools, occurred to meet new environment and requirements. We believe that software architecture is the next revolution. Many people have begun to follow this trend, while, however, many others do not care about it, just as several years ago the people who were reluctant to change their habits and use new development technologies. Upon history level, we can get more clear sight of how software architecture gradually becomes crucial for current software industry and why we should change our manner of work to follow it.

1.1.1   The Evolution of Programming Language—Abstract Level

Abstract is the process that simplifies the real systems, activities or other entities by ignoring or factoring out those trivial details without missing their essential running mechanisms. To construct a solution with a computer, we abstract it and implement it with programming language, in which the target model of abstract greatly affects what programmers see that problem. The progress of programming languages so far regularly increases their abstract level, transforming the emphases on from machine manipulating to problem solving.

In the 1950s, stored-program computers became popular and thereby monopolized programmers' work manner at that time. Programmers used machine instructions which can be executed directly by their computers and data with naïve categories such as byte, word, double word to express their logic. The layout of instructions and data in memory had to be controlled by hand, that is, programmers must keep in mind where the beginning and end positions of each constant and variable exactly are. When the program needed update, programmers spent a lot of time to check and modify every reference for data or code position that needs a movement to keep program's consistency.

Soon, some people were aware of that these functions could be automated and reused. Therefore, symbolic substitution and subroutine technology were created. The great thing about these was that they liberated you from those trivial but important works for the machine. However, commonly useful patterns, such as conditional control structure, loop structure, evaluation of numeric computation expressions, still had to be decomposed to simple control and computation instructions that machine was able to carry out, which drew programmers' much attention to the computation's realization rather than the problem itself. This improved the high-level programming. In the middle of the 1960s, FORTRAN from IBM became the dominant programming language in scientific computation for its convenience and high-efficiency.

In the latter part of 1960s, Ole-Johan Dahl and Kristen Nygaard created Simula, a superset programming language of Algol, introducing the object-oriented paradigm. The data type in FORTRAN serves to construct a map between FORTRAN types to machine primitive data types. On the contrary, object-oriented paradigm considers data type as the abstraction of entities from real problems. Although FORTRAN and C also have the utility such as "structure" and "union", they are just the accumulation of data in that data type and operations specific to this type are separated, and object-oriented rules, including encapsulation, implementation hiddenness, access control and polymorphism are not touched. With the growth of C++, a widely accepted object-oriented language, the programming world was thoroughly changed.

The prime goal of C++ or other contemporary object-oriented languages was to put class as the basic reuse unit. However, the design and realization themselves of these languages doomed to fail. On the one hand, absence of class meta data ruins the promise of the update capability of a class's implementation; on the other hand, disregard of the separation between the communication contracts among classes and classes' implementation limits their capability of reuse. We can see that majority of reuse performed in C++ stand on source code level, while reuse in binary level may introduce more problems than its benefits. You can find more details about this subject in (Joyner, 1996). When people find that software can be assembled by several independent parts and thus can reduce the cost and time in building larger system, it is clear that finding a proper reuse unit or establishing principles for this kind of unit is crucial. (Ning, 1996) gave the first complete picture of component-based software development model.

Component further raises the design level by increasing the concept size of building block in software. The great thing about this is that it permits designers to construct a system by using interindependent components, under the premise of that strict communication contracts are defined and followed. Object-oriented paradigm is a good basis for component development model, but not each component must be implemented by objects. After the middle of the 1990s, COM and CORBA became popular because they extended C++ or other languages to meet component model's requirements and principles. Java and Net platform support development and deployment in component level since their birth, with the help of explicit utility of interface and meta information. What's more, the design model created by UML can be easily converted to the source code in these two platforms. UML combines concepts, advice and experience of countless designers, software engineers, methodologists and domain experts to provide a suit of fundamental notations, with which people care only components and the relationships, constraints among them. In other words, UML achieves the peak of abstract level so far.

We believe software architecture will bring next shift in software development paradigm. But just as the relation between high-level programming languages and UML, software architecture will not exterminate old methods and tools, but to complement them to deal with large-scale, rapid-changing software intensive systems.

1.1.2   The Evolution of Software Development—Concerns

Along with the evolution of programming language, the focus of software development also keeps changing. It is a commonly held belief among software industry that getting victory needs competitive time-to-market while guaranteeing products' qualities to meet customers' requirements. Most of concerns pay much attention to uncover and annihilate the bottlenecks in the development processes, which depends on the enhancement of development utilities and toolkits.

In the age when machine code or assembly language dominated, the process of designing was to express problem solution with primitive instructions and data. Without the help of automation, programmers needed to track codes according to their physical memory layout. If anybody did a poor job in organizing their codes, he ran the risk of making everything a mess and letting update almost impossible in which every reference of codes and data needing modified had to be changed purely by hand. A good design could suppress a resulted tangly program finally because it tried to clear the programming logic, although in a low level. Some tactics and methods created by designers became the sprout of architectural idea improved later on.

The next shift in concern was how to organize codes and data to avoid the difficulty in reading, tracking, debugging and maintenance, which is now called structuring. Unstructured program can be considered a whole block of continuous code list, allowing the execution point to jump everywhere you want. Assembly language is the typical example of constructing that kind of program. Nevertheless, unlimited use of jump control statement will introduce server consequences. You can find a famous criticism of GOTO statement from "Go To Statement Considered Harmful" (Dijkstra, 1968a). To get structured program, the entire program is split into smaller procedures whose executions depend on invoking among each other. By using structured organization strategies, software designers began to adopt the top-down paradigm, that is, to decompose the large-scale software system into smaller modules and perform detailed design respectively. The relationship among these procedures is simply invocation. One procedure calls a series of sub procedures, each of which repeats this process until the atomic procedures are reached. The top level procedures can be considered as the construct parts of the whole system. The design at that time was commonly a control flow diagram indicating that how a task was performed step by step, and guiding how the program was executed in a sequence.

However, structured paradigm does not mirror the real world very well and thereby easily bring traps and pitfalls. Designers still need convert the problem model to structured model and decompose it into modules, which is not thus natural. Continuingly, code reuse will not be carried out easily because to reuse a procedure, one must take a series of related data structure, which always not be implemented in a single artifact.[1] Therefore, the data-centric organization became a new attracting trend within which action belongs to entity, rather than the vice versa just as what we can see in the structured paradigm. More and more designers preferred to package data type and its proprietary operations in order to provide the basic construction and reuse unit. Object-oriented (OO) languages support this paradigm explicitly and extend it greatly with derivation and polymorphism capabilities. Since the middle of 1980s, modeling entities and their relationships in the problems have turned to the new design methodology. Software designers can directly use vocabulary in the problem space by thinking of their system's structures.

However, unfortunately, OO paradigm is not panacea. For example, pure OO cannot meet needs that concepts cross with each other. For example, the instance of class "Customer" and that of "Transaction" in a business system may couple tightly, resulting in that the modification of one class forces modification of another. If more new classes have to cross existed ones, taking class "Log" for example, boring update work that is commonly considered disappeared comes back. Recent Aspect-Oriented Programming (AOP) tries to remedy this problem. In AOP, designers divided entities into two categories: independent ones (such as "Customer") and crossing ones (Such as "Transaction" or "Log"). By just indicating cross points and controlling the cross styles, AOP interpreter helps deal with the cross work. In my opinion, AOP is a good complement of OO, but still stands in the same level with it.

Upon a higher level, object-orientation itself cannot solve the problem of complex interaction among objects. Unlike software decades ago, software systems increase their complexity drastically according to their execution styles, which are transforming from stand-alone to cooperation. Therefore, methods and technologies of interaction and data exchange draw much attention. Some interaction paradigms, including invocation, point-to-point message transmission, publish-subscribe, are getting their popularity when they are used in all kinds of implemented communication protocols. From the almost all large-scale systems we can see that software behaviors can be split into two categories: computational behaviors, which handle business computation and architectural behaviors, which focus on the integration of system. Whether structured or OO paradigm does not support this separation explicitly since their concerns. Although OO gives people a great building block in design time, it is reluctant to express the runtime structure clearly. (For instance, the runtime structure of C++ programs is identical to that of C program while Java and Net platform only store simple meta-information in execution.) In addition, "interface" implemented by OO is too naïve in that it only regulates methods' signatures but ignoring a rich amount of other items of contracts, such as a method's performance or its memory usage. Interface in the design world has a more generic meaning to handle semantic-understanding and manipulation of a

---

[1] Artifact means the physical entity where implementation or information is placed, such as an executive file, a library or a database table.

service which is referred by that interface. All in all, to get these interaction mechanisms, we have to construct them by ourselves and we need something to express them.

Another important concern in this level is how to evaluate the influence of systems' structure to their qualities. Functionality comes from the computational modules we implement, while others, such as availability, usability, and testability, are attached to system's runtime structure. You can imagine that we create a redundant copy of crucial data in order to achieve performance or we interweave the encryption function with computational components to keep security. Simply speaking, functionality is mostly decided by customers' requirements, while non-functional qualities are the result of how a system is organized in its runtime. What's more, after getting a structure that has several benefits to current domain, how can we record, adjust and reuse it? Domain-suitable architecture is crucial for the survival of any software manufacturer because it is the basis to apply software product line construction, which produces software by slightly modifying domain architecture according to requirements and implementing mainly through assembly. Essentially, it drastically reduces the cost and time-to-market.

When we place our concerns to points mentioned above, we find that a foundation, for designing, recording, evaluating and reusing is extremely required. And we believe that software architecture is the solution.

1.1.3   The Origin and Growth of Software Architecture

The well-defined software architecture began its life in the 1990s, as most people believe. However, its origin can be traced back to the late of 1960s, when software crisis dragged public's attention. At that time, the success of software started to dominate the success of the whole system because, compared to hardware, system designers had more freedom in selecting or organizing software structures. But the process of software development differs greatly from that of other artifacts, such as a building, a car or a machine in that it is hard to figure out several clear phases to layout it. Meanwhile, simply increasing programmers cannot increase the productivity, but rather incur the failure of a project very easily (Brooks, 1975). Software development is more than just to assembly a bunch of parts. Rather, behind the entire process stand extreme complex relationships, which are not yet uncovered today. In the 1968, NATO software engineering conference was held in Germany, starting software engineering as a well-accepted scientific discipline, which aimed to solve the problemsn mentioned above.

The first record touching the concept of architecture used in software development can be found in "*The Structure of the 'THE*[2]*' Multiprogramming*

---

[2] THE is an early multitasking, but not multi-user, operating system whose development was led by Edsger Dijkstra. In fact, THE is the abbreviation of "Technische Hogeschool Eindhoven", the then-name (in Dutch) of the Eindhoven University of Technology, the location of this system was developed.

System" authored by Edsger Dijkstra, which was published in 1968 (Dijkstra, 1968b). He discussed about how to use layers in construing a large-scale system and then led to a design with more clear structures and better maintainability. A deeper understanding of architecture was given by Brooks, who defined it as "the complete and detailed specification of the user interface" in (Brooks, 1975). In addition, David Parnas made great contribution in the architecture's fundamental. His insight included information hiding and usage of interface (Parnas, 1972), structure separation (Parnas, 1974) and the relationships between software structure and its quality (Parnas, 1976), all of which have become the golden rules of architects and programmers nowadays. You can find a more detailed outline of Parnas' work at the end of the chapter of *Software Architecture in Practice* (Bass, 2003).

Since the 1990s, a series of papers, workshops and communities pushed software architecture into popularity. More formalized models to explain architecture were released, setting up the architecture's academic research. In 1991, Winston W. Royce and his son Walker Royce used "software architecture" in the title and as the main topic in their article (Royce, 1991). Two papers (Garlan, 1993) and (Perry, 1992) were widely referred for their fundamental contribution to this field. Later, (Shaw, 1996), an early book containing and organizing a suit of related papers, became the most popular tutorial and premier of software architecture research.

During the middle of the 1990s, two of the most notable results of architecture research were how to model software system with architecture used in general and in single practical use. For generality, we mean architectural styles and patterns, which aim to guide a satisfying design under a certain context. In initial days, architectural styles, including their modeling, representation, categorization and reuse, dominated the architecture research, thus resulting in a deeper understanding of software design's essence as well as more efficient development processes. This subject will be discussed in Chapter 2. For single practical usage, we mean methodologies on architecture descriptions for a specific system. Especially, Architecture Description Languages (ADL) plays a crucial role in this sub-area. ADLs try to formalize document or even visualize a system's various structures and organizations from various aspects. Some of them provide calculus models to help designers to figure out the problems such as deadlock detection, consistency, compatibility check and so on. In some ADLs involved the process algebra, such as Communicating Sequential Processes (CSP) and π-calculus, to support the description of systems' behaviors and evolution. WRIGHT, ACME, Darwin, C2 are the typical ADLs and luckily become members of survivors among hundreds, if not thousands, of their relatives. More information about ADLs will be accessed in Chapter 4.

From 1994 to 2000, the institutions in this field got more and more mature. Lots of communities, workshops and conferences were held when architecture's importance became gradually dazzling. In 1995 International Workshop on Software Specification and Design provided a space for architectural researchers. And the

First International Software Architecture Workshop was held at the same year, marking the bloom of this field. Latter in 1998, the Working IEEE/IFIP Conference on Software Architecture started its life and still continues until today. Moreover, after 1995 more and more conferences and workshops about software engineering and design created several sections specifically on software architecture. During this period, contributions from industry and academia become richer, most of which started a revolution of software development processes and methodologies, including architecture evaluation methods (such as SAAM (Kazman, 1994)), multiple views description (such as Rational 4+1 views (Kruchten, 1995)).

After 2000, software architecture finished converting its position from design phase to the center of the whole development process. And product line architecture (Bosch, 2000) has become the most powerful weapon for any software enterprise's survival. Meanwhile, we get the first standard of software architecture in IEEE 1471-2000, recording the most comprehensive insight about research and practice of this field. In the middle of 2003, UML, an initial modeling language designed for OO development, evolved to its second edition, enhancing the semantic support for architectural vocabulary, followed by a series of automatic design tools, including IBM Rational Software Architect. At the same time, ArchStudio, an open source tool for architecture design drew public's attention, which is introduced in Chapter 6.

Architecture really became popular, not only limit in its research and its usage, but in the interest of people. The SEI series books, including *Software in Practice* (Bass, 2003), *Documenting Software Architecture: Views and Beyond* (Clements, 2003a) and *Evaluating Software Architectures* (Clements, 2003b) became the ones of the most popular books in their years. Courses and seminars are started in many universities or colleges. And many guys now consider software architect as the most attracting career in a software corporation.

But the path of software architecture is far from the end because more challenges come and need to conquer. For example, we need strategies to evaluate architecture automatically and then keep the consistency between architectural designs and implementations. Also, we need to use architecture as the guidelines to perform software tests. Is it possible to realize the software factory in which products are simply assembled? Or even is it possible to automatically design according to users' requirements? While exploring these areas, we in fact are touching the essence of software as well as the principles of human's thinking, which are extremely hard to touch.

What's more, software's shape keeps changing, from the programs designed specially for mainframes to the ones for operating systems on PC, from standing alone to distributing among several nodes in the networking, from inflexible to dynamic. 30 years ago, it was very tough to handle the project such as a compiler, in which may involve the work of tens of top programmers working for one or two years. However, nowadays anybody can make use of Lex and Yacc to generate a compiler within several weeks. We still have some kinds of software that are at present considered as rather complex and difficult to develop. What will they be in the next decade? Along with the change of software, software architecture will follow it and evolve further more.

1.2 Introduction to Software Architecture

In this section, we will introduce software architecture more precisely. Unfortunately, different experts tend to define architecture and its model in their perspectives and scopes, which leads to a mess of fundamental theories. But later we will see that IEEE 1471-2000 standard tries to cover all the theories with which most definitions and models can coexist without severe conflicts. We do not want to create a "brand-new" doctrine of software architecture. Instead, we hope to give readers a better understanding of its meanings and values by tidying up existed theories. Also, detailed explanations will be followed to avoid possible misunderstanding. All in all, we believe that an appropriate thinking in architecture is far more important than catching the rigid definition from certain articles.

1.2.1 Basic Terminologies

Before touching architecture's definition, we will firstly discuss some concepts used in it, which are standing in a high abstract level, thus resulting in easily confused comprehension. The first concept is model. In software development, model means the simplified and closed abstraction of reality, especially the problem to be solved. First, model is the simplification of reality, which means that model only expresses part of reality's mechanism or behaviors. Obviously, it is impossible to concern all the aspects of a system together because too much information interweaved together will incur chaos. A well-defined model will focus on the elements which have important influence and omit those which have little relationships with the specified abstraction level. Second, model is a closed abstraction, which means that model has independency and use the vocabulary and constraints prominently different from their models. A good example is the car's structure, where you can model a car's motility system, electronical system or sculpture. Model can become the blueprint of a project, with which engineers can more easily find where the strong points are and where the shortcomings stand. The reason why I pay much attention to model is that in essence, software architecture is a model.

Modeling can be categorized as informal, semi-formal and completely formal. When modeling a software system, you can choose which one is best suitable for your need. The purpose of formal modeling is to enable the strict calculus and formal check with mathematic theories, such as state machine, to provide a foundation upon which automatic evaluation are made possible. However, the completely formal modeling of a system will introduce a great amount of design information, which may be even more than the final implementation. Therefore, software architecture in academia uses the completely formal style while in industry, semi-formal or informal architecture is adopted. A notable academic case is in (Garlan, 1993), where software architecture is defined as:

$$SA = \{Components, Connectors, Constraints\}$$

As we discussed in Section 1. 1. 2, software architecture concerns only interactions among the units in a system. The units here are defined as "components", indicating any unit that performs predefined services and can communicate with other components. Connectors defined the communication protocols and strategies. And constraints define the rules which the system must conform to. In this model, software architecture can be considered as the decomposition of several related and constrained components. Unlike the class in OO paradigm, which just gives the basic building blocks in design phase, components reflect the status during runtime. Similarly, the relationship such as inherence in OO is not connector, which represents runtime communication. Of course, components and connectors are not necessarily implemented with OO. Instead, all kinds of programming languages, including assembly language, can be used. The point is that components and connectors are elements in architectural level.

However, is that enough to describe a system's architecture? Can only components and connectors along with their constraints contain all the information about system's interaction mechanism? The answer is of course no, because the above model concentrates on runtime structure of a system only, ignoring the static relationships among building blocks, which are also crucial to system's constructing. No matter which structure, runtime or static, servers for the targets of system building, including users' functional requirements and the explicit and implicit needs on non-functional qualities. Architectural information has to cover all of these, in order to help designers' decision making by showing structures which are necessary to designers. For static information, we can use class diagram to show classes' interrelationships in OO development, or adopt Entity-Relation diagram in database design. Or even, how the source code files are organized? How each executive program is deployed to its corresponding physical nodes? All these concerns play roles in the development process of various software projects. Regarding their importance, we have to take them into the realm of software architecture.

Then let us see another definition from (Bosch, 2000):

> The architecture of a software system is concerned with the top-level decomposition of the system into its main components.

In this definition, software architecture is handled as the unique decomposition structure of a system, which poles apart from the first definition, concerning only and single static structure. In addition, the term component has a different meaning, which can be thought of module, the basic unit for implementation. The distinct perspectives are visualized as follows.

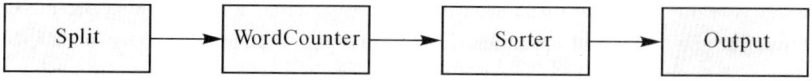

Fig. 1. 1   Component and connector SA model of WordCounter [3]

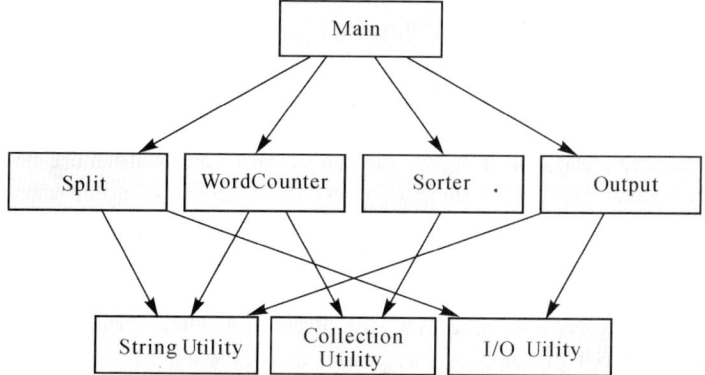

Fig. 1. 2   Decomposition SA model of WordCounter

Clearly, the former tells us how the program's components cooperate by regulating the communication mechanisms while the latter one tells us how programmers cooperate by dividing the whole work into relative independent pieces. Later we can find that they are both views of software architecture, belonging to a series of views used by architecture documentation.

Another definition of software architecture comes from (Gacek, 1995), where the author gave the concept as below:

$$SA = \{Components, Connections, Constraints, \\ Stakeholder\ Needs, Rationale\}$$

In this definition, requirements of functionality and other qualities are taken into account. In practical use, components and connections are the consequence of design decision-making according to various stakeholders' needs. Here, stakeholder means that anybody who has concerns or goals in a specific software system project, including project managers, programmers, marketing sellers, customers, end users, etc. Any decision on architecture constructing needs to take a trade off among numerous concerns, some of which may be entirely conflictive while some of which have intrinsic links. Rationale is the strategies where trade off exists. This definition reflects the practical influence to runtime structure, in order to integrate the research of software architecture in academia and practice in the real world.

Of course, there are far more architectural models than what we mentioned above. However, they can be considered as the typical and representative examples

---

[3] WordCounter reads a textual file and output "word-frequency" pair for each appeared word in frequency order

which are handy to help understanding of this field. In order to meet different concerns, handle different problems in different contexts, or to attempt new methods, a bunch of architectural models have been published during the recent years. But they should not be the gap blocking our paces in learning software architecture, as soon as the essential concerns are followed tightly that how to deal with the troubles in system interaction, decision-making of design and implementation, communication among stakeholders and architectural reuse.

1.2.2   Understanding IEEE 1471—2000

In the September, 2000, the first standard about software architecture was released. This recommended practice targeted to mend the status that no reliable consensus on what software architecture precisely is, including its various elements, links among these elements, organization principles, as well as when and where they can be applied, in the circumstance that architecture and activities in architecture level have been widely accepted and taken into research and industrial practice. We use architecture more out of our habits and experiences, instead of unified standards and consistent foundations, taking formidable risks in our usage. Maybe it seems a childish mission to gather existed theories and integrate them to produce the final result. However, the difficulty is how to make it clear that software architecture captures the complicated features of systems by synchronizing numerous architectural theories and practical experience. There is a similar example that with approximate 5,000 years' effort, architecture of civil engineering still cannot get its precise and unified definition.

There are four kernel principles provided in this document, generalized as follows:

Every system has its own architecture, but they are not identical.

Just as a stone has its own weight, which, however, is just a property for that stone, software architecture can be viewed abstractly as an aspect of the whole system, containing much crucial information. Stakeholders can acquire the general information related to their concerns from architecture, but it is impossible to get everything from it, especially those in small granularity and particular details, which, for example, are expressed in the term of primitives of programming languages. System can be designed, built and run, which means it is a concrete product, while software architecture is the high-level abstraction attaching to the existence of system.

Software architecture and its description are different.

Just as what mentioned above, the existence of software architecture is decided only by the existence of system. But its description is the artifact created in some phase of software development, following the desire to represent system's constituent elements and their communication methods. You may have the questions that when a system stands in its design phase (which means it does not exist), where its architecture is? In my perspective, the design architecture is an expectation to which, in normal cases, system's implementation conforms.

In this recommended practice, software architecture is defined as:

The fundamental organization of a system embodied in its components [4] *, their relationships to each other, and to the environment, and the principles guiding its design and evolution.*

While architectural description is expressed as:

A collection of products to document an architecture.

From these definitions, you can find that software architecture is always invisible. But those you cannot see can help you, if and only if it is visualized, that is, documented. You can use any documenting techniques, including the combinations of several diagrams in UML, a segment of textual code in ADL or even the simple box-line diagrams, with the premise that meaning of each notation has been taken into agreement by people needing to see them.

Nevertheless, architectural description is not obligatory. An example indicating this is legacy system, which might be constructed far before the start of well-awareness or research of software architecture. A sub field of this, called Architectural Reconstructing, aims to extract information in architecture level from those systems without elaborate architecture documents, facilitating their maintenance and evolution. In addition, if a system is rather small or it is a prototype to experiment some algorithms, architectural documents are likely to be simplified, or even completely omitted. However, in these cases architectures still exist, although they might be weak, ugly and easy-to-crash.

Software architecture, architectural description and development process are separated, both in research and in application.

In general, software architecture is what a system's structures look like; architectural description is how these structures are shown, with what notations, formats and organizations; and development processes are a series of activities which might use architectural description. There are no strict restrictions among them, meaning that you can choose any documenting techniques in presenting invisible structures and adopt any development process model in using those architectural documents. IEEE 1471 only defines what software life cycle is, but not assumes nor prescribes a specific life cycle model. Meanwhile, it defines the concepts of view and view point, but does not make it clear that which views and viewpoints are necessary in representing architecture.

But it is worthwhile to highlight that the suitability of architectural description for a specific development process model. For example, UML is the best companion with Rational Unified Process (RUP), which calls for 4 + 1 views, fitting for unleashing of UML's diagrams' capability. For Model Driven Development (MDD), however, a highly formalized architectural model must be built because it is

---

[4] The "component" used here has a different meaning with what we defined exactly in the previous section, which can be considered as part of software in general meaning.

necessary for code-design synchronization. In domain software development, the documenting issues may be distinct by adding the support of domain specific concepts and concerns, which is best suitable for its own development process. Therefore, the generic relations among these three provide the foundation for clearing up the job of architecture, but we should select congruent methods in practice concerning our purposes and contexts.

Space should be leaven facilitating the customization of detailed architectural models for researches and practices.

This recommended practice defines several guide principles for applying software architecture, indicating the range of its basic concepts and related activities, rather than prescribing everything fixedly. Organizations or individual users, then, have the chance to combine these fundamental rules to their own context and provide their own architectural models. Most concepts are introduced as "what should they at least contain", but not "what is that exactly". For instance, the identification of stakeholders is defined as:

> At a minimum, the stakeholders identified shall include the
> following:
> a) Users of the system
> b) Acquirers of the system
> c) Developers of the system
> d) Maintainers of the system

While stakeholders are explained as:

> At a minimum, the concerns identified should include the following:
> — The purpose or missions of the system
> — The appropriateness of the system for use in fulfilling its missions
> — The feasibility of constructing the system
> — The risks of system development and operation to users, acquirers,
>   and developers of the system
> Maintainability, deployability, and evolvability of the system

In this way, expansion can be performed in meeting special situations or solving different problems while misuse is avoided to a great extent.

In addition, concepts view and viewpoint are accessed to indicate how to express an architecture from multiple perspectives. The purpose of a view is to enable system understanding focusing on a few specific concerns. Viewpoint, in addition, defines the vocabulary allowed to use in a view. "Decomposition Architecture" or "Component-Connector Architecture" involved in some articles, in fact, is identical to "Decomposition Viewpoint" or "Component-Connector Viewpoint". Every architecture description should be documented in single or multiple architectural views.

Nevertheless, the appearance of an international standard cannot eliminate most problems in software development, because it does not depict the detailed steps and activities of development in architecture level. Only can it be considered as the meta reference model, guiding us to figure out which models, guidelines and constraints of architecture are suitable, through which we are able to create our own development methodologies.

1.2.3   Views Used in Software Architecture

We discussed systems, architecture, models and views, as well as their interrelationships, which build the basis of understanding of software architecture's shape. Architecture hides itself behind the implementation or the design blueprint of a system, simplified by a number of models, which concerns their perspectives only. Views, through predefined viewpoints, visualize models and then facilitate architecture description and communications among stakeholders. They are generalized as Fig.1.3.

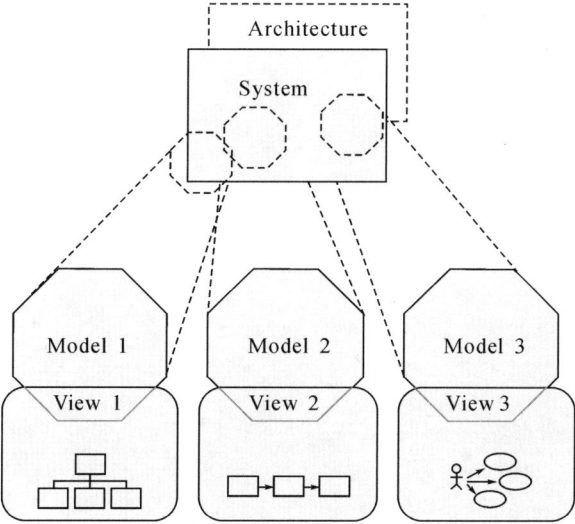

Fig. 1. 3   System, model and view

A rather tough problem about defining a view is how to define semantic of notations clearly and get them public accepted. What Kruchten said in (Kruchten, 1995) gets this point:

> We all have seen many books and articles in which a single diagram attempts to capture the gist of a system architecture. But when you look carefully at the diagram's boxes and arrows, it becomes clear that the author are struggling to represent more in one diagram than is practical. Do the boxes represent running programs? Chunks of source code? Physical computers? Or merely logical groupings of functionality? Do the arrows represent compilation dependencies? Control flow? Data flow? Usually the answer is that they represent a bit of everything.

Similar to the definition of architecture application methodologies, there is also no world-unified views to represent software architecture. Although UML attempts to achieve this goal, architectural puritans do not acknowledge it as a language for architecture, for its lacking of mathematical foundations. But we can find disciplines in categorizing common views which are suitable for most system development. Here we provide some useful view types as follows.

At last, we must declare that view is not necessarily a picture or something of that sort, although it commonly is. The view what we define here is the visual or readable representation of a model, including picture styles, formal textual specification or something mixed by them.

Component & Connector View

In my perspective, Component & Connector View (C&C View) is the most important view for software architecture. As a matter of fact, many researchers only take components, connectors and their annexes (such as their properties, constraints, etc.) as main elements in their architectural models, and thus C&C view becomes the solo representation of them. The reason for this situation is that we can deduce excepted quality attributes from information extracted from this view in the very early phase of software development, which, in turn, decrease development risks.

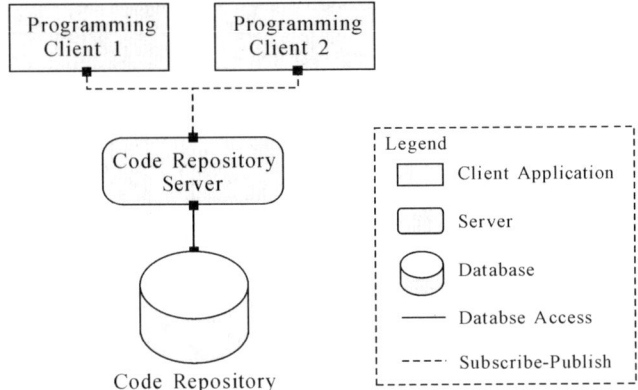

Fig. 1. 4   An example of C&C view

Fig.1.4 is an example of C&C view indicating the structure of a source code version control system. The elements of C&C view are instances of components and connectors, whose types are defined in other places (such as decomposition view or specific views for software building vocabulary). You can find that there may be multiple instances of the identical type appearing in a view simultaneously. C&C view abstracts the runtime scene of a system, including its main functional units, communication methods, data flows, etc. Each element has runtime meaning, rather than building blocks. For instance, in Fig. 1. 4, code repository server may be implemented through several classes in OO, or functions with C.

Each element of C&C view should have clear and non-equivocal meanings, which normally reflected by a notation specification or a legend. The worst thing of view is drawing with notations following habits and hobbies, which will introduce severe mess and misunderstanding, evil enough to counteract all the benefits brought by C&C view. Unfortunately, we often see figures, drawn by boxes, lines, arrow lines, etc. with various colors, in many articles, reports and even design specifications, which are called by their authors as "architecture".

In C&C view, components are functional units which interact with outside through a series of predefined interfaces (not identical to the interface used in programming languages such as Java or C#), which are organized as ports. Through this limited access method, components encapsulate themselves, and thus become independent and replaceable. Connectors are far more complex than what they look like in C&C view, where they abstract the communication protocols. Compared to the simple and basic communication mechanisms, such as invocation, message transmission or asynchronous communication, connectors always represent more complicated interaction systems. The access channel between client and a database is a case of that kind. Different from components, connector itself often does not have code, whose realization needs help of each component involved into connection, where connectors' initialization, reply, interaction control may be located. The interactive points of connectors are named roles, defining exactly how users can manipulate connectors. For example, the connector "pipe" has roles "reader" and "writer", both of which have the privilege just as their names indicating. Only compatible ports and roles can be linked together, which is guaranteed through compatibility validation, as Fig. 1.5 shown. At last, we should make it clear that connector may contain more than two endpoints.

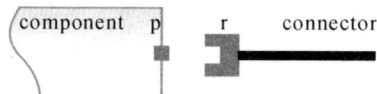

Fig. 1. 5   Connection of component and connector

Experienced architects use architectural tactics to handle necessary non-functional requirements. Assuming we need high security, encrypted access channels will be used; if high availability [5] is crucial, redundancy is employed. Several tactics can be combined and construct architectural styles to meet common design problems. Architectural styles define necessary vocabulary for describing system's runtime structure, and provide the foundation upon which architectural patterns are built, which solve specific problems under a certain context. Architectural tactics, styles and patterns can be represented through C&C view and then enable architectural evaluation, because they can reflect the influence that design makes to system's expected quality attributes.

C&C view and the runtime model it shows are so important that they are believed as an alternative of software architecture. In Chapters 2 and 3, we focus on

---

[5] System availability means the extent to which a system resists against exceptions or errors. For instance, how long will the system take to recover from its database' crash?

architectural styles and patterns; while in Chapter 4, we tend to discuss more deeply about architectural description emphasizing on runtime model.

Decomposition View

Compared to C&C view which reflects dynamic information during runtime, decomposition view, however, supplies more static information. In practice, you may get two kinds of support from decomposition view, as follows.

The first feature is to define the vocabulary of system and construct its logic model. Here, we decompose the whole system into several logic concepts in top-down style. This process of divide and conquer can be carried out recursively, gradually showing system detail more and more clear, until the pieces which enable personal development, test and management are reached. Through this activity, useful and reuse-possible concepts are picked out and extracted. Then concepts are interconnected according to their relationships in the real world, including use, generalization, association, aggregation, composite and so on (generalization is the special case of use, while aggregation and composite are special cases of association). More advanced relationship properties, including multiplicity and association direction, are also used if necessary. In addition, we can define types of components and connectors facilitating C&C view. Concepts and their relationships construct the logic model of a system. Logic model is especially useful for domain software development because building blocks based on the model reduce the work needed in similar development time and time again, because we can reuse existing blocks implementing those concepts and relationships, or purchase them from market.

For example, if a courses-register system is under design, we may define concepts such as student, department, course, and schedule. More concepts will be added if runtime is concerned, such as course repository. Examples of relationships may be that "each department are composed by many students, but each student has to attach to a single department", or "students are categorized as undergraduate, graduate and PhD." During the decomposition process, concepts and behaviors are divided. For example, student may be considered as the combination of ID, name, age, department, address, email and phone number, in which ID may be then divided into several sections regulated by a regular expression. The behavior of register can be described as a number of steps, such as logging in, searching course information, checking course availability, updating course information and logging out. For an explicit example of decomposition view, you can see Fig.1.2.

When development is being performed, architects cluster several concepts, as well as their relationships, into an implementation or test unit, called module, within which elements should work together in common ways to provide cooperative behaviors that are bigger than all of its parts. It is a ubiquitous confusion and misunderstanding between component and module, since they have some link hazily. But they do not stand in the same perspective. In fact, they contain different meanings under different concerns. Component is the logic abstract of functional unit of runtime, while module is the cluster benefiting design, implementation, test and management. It is possible that a module contains exactly the code executed as a single component, but this relationship is not of necessity.

Another feature of decomposition view is to divide developers' work, making cooperation feasible. After decomposition, pieces or modules can be mapped to organizations or teams of developers, which own responsibility to perform management, detailed analysis, implementation and test. Meanwhile, the decomposition structure has benefits to system's learning and understanding, because it avoids the possibility that novices are trapped into a mess of detailed codes and navigates them in top-down style gradually.

There are two bans in decomposition views. The first one is that no loop should exist in decomposition view, considering the recursive decomposition process needs an end point; the second one is that no decomposition piece or module should be contained in more than one parent module, since confusion of responsibility may be bred.

Allocation View

Aside from software's logic structures, development teams finally have to face the physical problems. No matter what the logic units are, e.g. modules, classes or functions, they needs concrete carrier absolutely. For example, we must record our program into source files, and these files need compilation, optimization, link and final code generation. In this process, some libraries might participate. At last binary executed files are finished, which, in turn, are deployed on one machine or several machines if a distributed system is under construction. Allocation view provides us the sight how software architecture are projected into their relationships with its external environments, which mostly contain file structures and hardware. Through this view, we have a chance to perform development management (e.g. source file version control or configuration) and can track the performance and system's bottleneck. What's more, in dynamic distributed system, allocation view helps us follow the location change of logic units.

Two kinds of allocation view should be paid much attention. The first one is called implementation view, or artifact view, focusing on that which source file is used to implement which logic unit, and what the relation among source files is. An implementation view of a calculator is shown as Fig.1.6.

Any source files may contain part, one or multiple modules' implementation. These files include executed code files, declaration files (C++'s header file, for example), build configure files (Java ant script file, for example) and so on. Besides them, configure files, resource files (such as icon, skin or bitmap files) or even data files stored in the format of database table, might be crucial to current development. All of these need organization, commonly in hierarchical styles with the help of folder (or directory), to facilitate the management and configuration of the whole project. Through this view, on the one hand, programmers and testers are easy to understand what they are doing and what influence they are making to the system. On the other hand, managers feel comfortable to configure, build and publish an executive system by easily tracking the dependency among a bunch of files explicitly, if version information is added to implementation view.

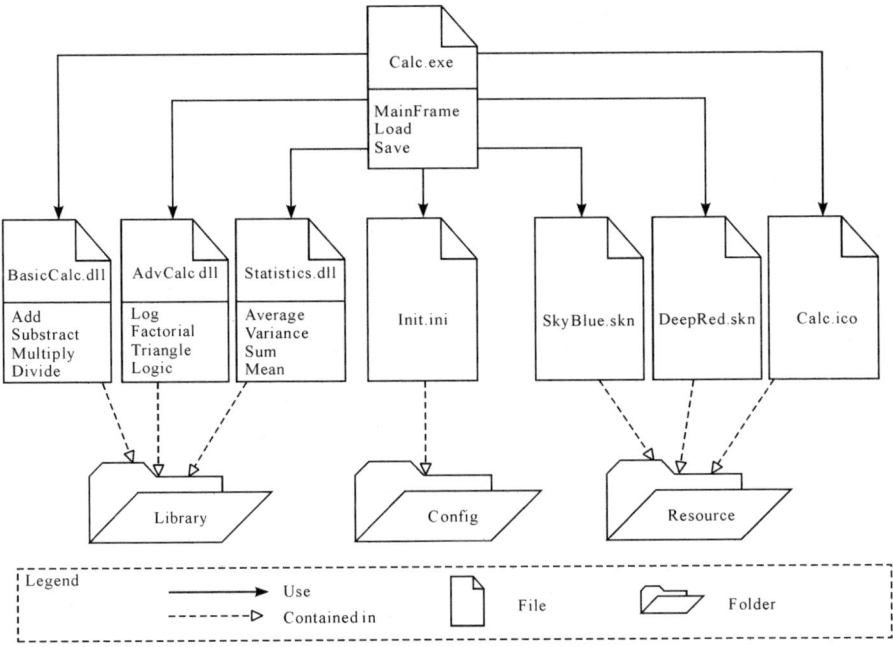

Fig. 1. 6   Implementation view

The second one is deployment view, leading to fill the chasm between software and hardware. The software elements of this kind of view include modules, objects if OO is in use, components or execution processes. The hardware elements are called in general "nodes", which may be a client workstation, a mainframe, a server, a router or mobile device. They are expressed in various forms, from visual icons to strictly defined notation in a formal language, and everything in between.

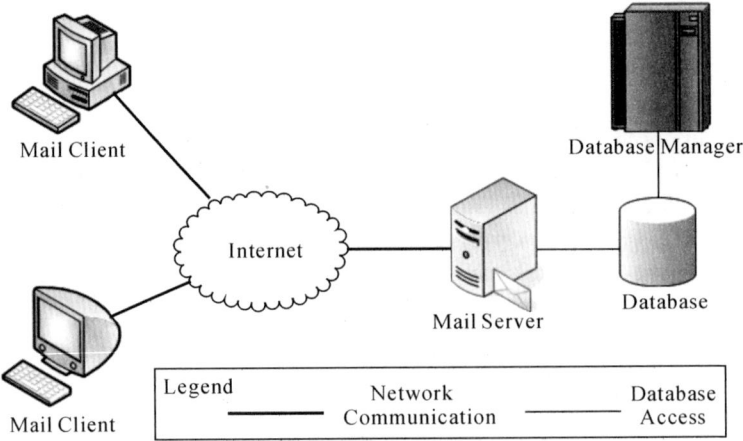

Fig. 1. 7   Deployment view

Through analyzing information brought by nodes' properties, such as CPU features, memory capability, network's bandwidth and so on, many of the problems with current design in architectural level will be exposed. For example, we can calculate and track which part of the whole system slow down the overall performance due to the hardware reason, and then simplify the algorithm implemented there. If too many overloaded modules are put into a single node, which is beyond the capability of CPU or networking, a schedule component may be necessary to allocate limit resource among these competitors, or they are simply distributed into multiple nodes.

Another feature of deployment view enables tracking of component's mobility (Fuggetta, 1998), if dynamic distributed system is under concern. In this case, code is thought of special data resource which can be transmitted and executed in different locations. In order to build the model which is capable of scouting the relation between mobile code and its referred data, abstract of hardware and mobile software unit must be employed.

A common mistake is that people always take deployment view as the solo representation of software architecture for the reason that it is so intuitionistic and "comprehensive" (including software components or modules as well as hardware nodes together) that they are an overall snapshot of a system. It is very often that pictures of this kind exist in a client's user guide document, a public conference or a software production show. But as we mentioned in Section 1. 2. 1, software architecture does not mean a system's arbitrary overview; and it is impossible for deployment view to reflect detailed information in any other perspectives.

Behavior View

All above views are organized in the term of the relationships among a collection of view's structural elements. You can get a deep insight of what the system should look like, what part of the system you are working for, or what a series of influence you will make if you modify something. Some quality attributes can be evaluated through these views, far before the start of system's realization. But to perform more detailed analysis, we need know about the system elements' interaction detail and their internal behaviors which are related to their interactions. For example, when we connect two components through a predefined connector by joining components' ports and connector's roles, if behavior information is available, it is possible to check potential to anomalies, such as unexpected message that will incur crush, or necessary signal is missing which leads to a deadlock. Sometimes, we need specify the order of interaction's rules and orders, the chaos of which might destroy system's usability, even if every component is well established. In addition, if time-crucial system is in design phase, such as an attack control system for military, behavior is the most important one of few cues to track and control the process time of system's certain function.

There are so many types of behavior views with various concerns and usage. We generalize them with three categories:

• Message-Centric Behavior

This style emphasizes the collaboration among a collection of elements under exchange of messages, including invocation, signal transmission or asynchronous communication. While the direction, order, arguments and other detailed information of messages are both shown in view of this style, elements' internal activities are omitted. Typical examples are UML sequence diagram and collaboration diagram, both of them can be converted into each other with little loss of semantic detail.

In UML sequence diagram, time order is shown vertically while involved elements horizontally. Message is considered as the stimuli that activate elements' certain behaviors. In Fig.1.8, a case of successful purchase from a vendor machine which is capable of getting payment from bank account automatically, Mr. Anderson invokes "Buy" message to start the purchase process, which then communicates with his account. We can add time constraints to some steps, just as {<2s} indicated. UML collaboration diagram does not only have similar power to sequence diagram, but has its benefits in checking whether the architecture is valid to run the behaviors necessary because the designed links among elements are exposed.

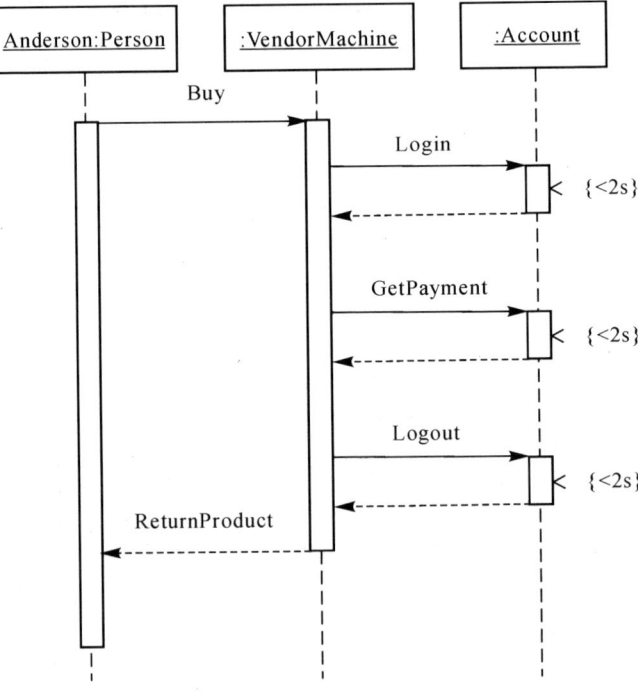

Fig. 1.8   UML sequence diagram

• Overall Activity Behavior

Behavior view of this style can tell us mainly that how a task can be processed, through which we can make clear of every step needed to implement. Overall activity behavior means that it does not care which part of software is responsible

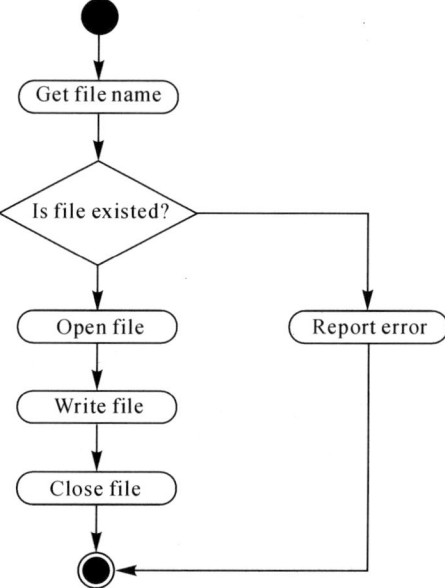

Fig. 1. 9   Control flow chart

for which sub-missions and how these missions are completed. The purpose of it is just to decompose the whole task into several pieces, each of which may become the foundation of system decomposing that constructs decomposition view. The representative examples include normal flow chart, SDL (Specification and Description Language) flow chart and UML activity diagram.

Flow chart is a venerable visualization mechanism, reaching its flourish in the age of structured program paradigm because notation can be easily converted to functions or modules and control structure code, such as conditional expression and loop. Flow chart has been expanded to track the control flow and the update of data structure.

However, some of current software is constructed by the abstract data type style, where functions are not the unique bricks. Therefore, nowadays, flow chart is often used in description of crucial path of work flow. A popular alternative in construction industry of flow chart is Gantt chart, which models what flow chart models plus the period of each overall activity.

As a matter of fact, overall activity behavior view is based on simplified state machine. However, the trigger event is always the complete of previous activity. Each activity is a nonautomatic operation, within which a collection of detailed behaviors are performed.

- Single Element Behavior

Single element behavior view owns the power to show the comprehensive suit of a single element's behaviors. State machine is a perfect abstract which considers behaviors as the events that trigger the transmission among states. UML state diagram enhances the basic state machine by providing primitives of concurrency, state nesting, history record and deferred event. The example of vendor machine is adopted here:

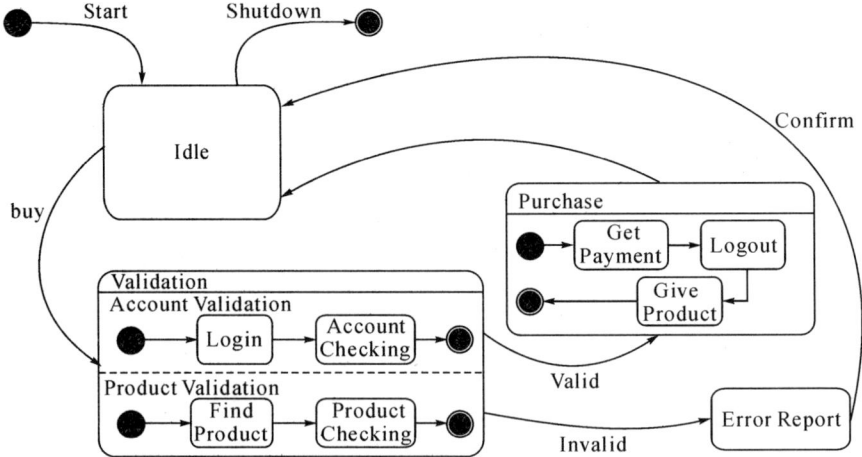

Fig. 1. 10   UML state diagram

We have seen the sequence diagram of this system before, which show the interaction among user, vendor machine and bank account, but ignoring product validation. Here, we can see the behavior of vendor machine more clearly. Everything is set up to the idle state, if "start" event occurs. Validation and purchase are two composite states, each of which is consists of several sub-sstates. Entering a composite state means current state jumps to the start state of it, then sequential states are passed until sub end state is reached. Especially, validation is a concurrent state, which represents multiple processes run simultaneously. Concurrency is visualized by several regions separated by a dash line. The "buy" event triggers the state transmission from idle to validation, where concurrent executions are activated, that is, the validation on account (to see whether the customer gives the correct account ID and its password) and product (to figure out whether there are enough products that customers demand) begin to run. If something wrong during validation, "invalid" is sent to result in error report. If everything is fine, the purchase process is started, enabling the execution of its internal operation, represented by three sub-states. Here, we assume that customer's account always afford his demand to avoid the mess of handling that exception with another error report state which contains logout sub-state. No matter whether the customer gets what he wants or confirms the error information, idle state is reached, ready for next deal. At last, we can shutdown this vendor machine when it is idle to terminate this program.

Although powerful in representing software elements' behaviors, behavior view is not limited within programs' interaction only, but also includes human's or other related systems' stimulation to the current system and the resulted response. This technology, publicly known as "use case", has got its popularity in capturing user's requirements and analyzing interaction between system and its outside environment, to which the making of system's test plan refers.

The key point of use case view is considering the system as an independent entity, sealing everything realization detail. Just as a common talk, user can initialize a command or message and expect the observable response from that system. An example of use case view by UML is shown in Fig.1.11.

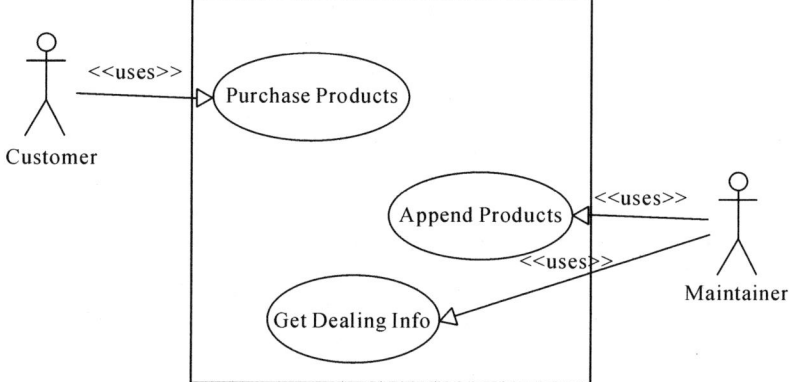

Fig. 1. 11   Use case view

1. 2. 4   Why We Need Software Architecture

A great many beginners of software architecture, especially the ones that take several courses of programming or computer science related mathematics, feel rather confused that whether it is really useful, even though they can repeat the definition of it very accurately. It is the typical phenomenon of lacking experience and suffering of the large-scale system development. Experienced designers, project managers or members of evaluation will get the point of architecture's importance after understanding what it is and how it can be represented. But for beginners, we generalize and give its powerful features explicitly as follows:

Representing system's initial outlines, allowing the analysis and evaluation of system's quality in the early phase of development

Software architecture reflects the earliest design decisions of the whole system, which has the most crucial effect to system's implementation and is almost impossible to change. Every primary requirement, both explicit and implicit, should own its corresponding resolution in it. In software architecture, system building blocks, their behaviors as well as interaction methods among them are described clearly. The purpose of them is to provide a chance to perform the check of potential defects or problems with formal calculus or experienced disciplines, and analysis of system's expected qualities. Meanwhile, if multiple architecture candidates are given, which is a common case in the development of large-scale system, evaluation will be carried out by collecting various stakeholders to select the most suitable one or generate advice for modification.

The reason why these check, analysis and evaluation are feasible is that software architecture comes from the combination of experience tactics to meet certain needs. For example, if you want high-security, the communication and data exchange should be encrypted and components should limits their access point tightly; if you want it to be reused, you must decrease the coupling among elements; if modifiability is your target, you have to limit the affected range when change occurs.

Providing constraints to system's implementation

Decades ago, programmers and designers began to be aware of the disaster consequence of coding without any limits. They try to figure out what should not be done and what should be encouraged, considering targets of the whole system. But experience was the mainstream tool then.

Today experience is still handy, but compared to the amount of members in a team nowadays, it is not realistic to guarantee every developer not to do anything that designers believe harmful, especially in some areas that designers do not describe in detail (It is very common that designers will not do that). Therefore, constraints are crucial and necessary to software development. Luckily, we can use software architecture to convey this information, mainly in two facets.

On the one hand, software architecture decides the decomposition structures, runtime structures and communication mechanisms, some of which can be used in achieving certain non-functional requirements. Under this context, programmers only have freedom in the private parts of their own missions. We will see in the below that this freedom is not absolute. They cannot add a component they believe funny or ignore the implementation of some interface they do not like or are lazy to take. If the architecture is considered as questionable, then a reevaluation will be performed, rather than tampered by programmers. In this case, the latter is almost impossible to happen because strict review, discussion and evaluation have been carried out during architecture's construction.

On the other hand, software architecture may contain explicit constraints about multiplicity, memory usage or processing time. Noticeably, architecture patterns provide great templates to fill a variety of constraints. Constraints are commonly expressed through properties or annotation comments if it is difficult to describe. Any implementation must conform to these constraints in order to contribute to system's expected quality. The precondition of this kind is, of course, constraints' feasibility. This problem can be avoided through an architecture evaluation process taken by the existent programmers or delegates of them as the stakeholders.

Contributing to the reuse and the realization of software product line

Reuse is the fundamental of industrial production, which mark the revolution of our world. Manufacturing has shown us that the production efficiency is extremely increased by the components with unified physical size or unified electrical interface. Due to the standard, there is no need that workers build every product from nothing. Each process of building becomes the assembly of components completed before. What's more, the unification brings us convenience. Imagine that how you can use mini electrical devices without the existence of standard-sized batteries, or that how you will feel if you cannot find the second tire which can be installed on your lovely car.

In software industry, we also need reusable parts just as in other areas. However, before using components, we must identify components first. Architecture has this ability to help us figure out which part of the system can use an existed component, and which part can be possibly reused later, and then implemented as a component. For example, in business information system, it is a good idea to divide the whole system into several layers. Separated persistent storage layer allows the quick switch among various database systems, such as Oracle 10i, IBM DB2 or MySQL. After all, it is unsafe to bind the whole enterprise into a single component provider, considering they may increase price, or stop technique support for some reason.

The reuse in higher level is the reuse of architecture itself. If you are designer of a company focusing on business information system, you will find it is very similar in the design of the system for other companies, educational organizations or governments. They seem to be the variation on a theme, resulting in the similar architecture. We call this "reference architecture" for a specific domain. Owning the reference architecture, cost and time for discussing on the design about basic functions are saved, which, in turn, increases the competitive capability. The more important point is the reference architecture is abstracted from a great amount of practical application, collecting thousands of thousands of people's wisdom and holding many perfect qualities. Is there any other more valuable guarantee than using this in constructing a new system? The answer is obvious.

Reference architecture can be implemented into an adjustable framework. In fact, lots of these have surrounded IT world. Take Web-based business information system for instance, the dominant framework today are EJB (Enterprise Java Bean) and Microsoft Net platform. Services about life management of objects, networking, transactions and others crucial to distributed systems, have been constructed in a flexible manner. Users will gain a complete system only through configuration and writing codes specific to their own business.

With the reusable architecture and the reusable components, software product line becomes feasible. The general idea of product line is to assembly software.

In software production line, part of developers is "assembler", who is responsible for searching and adjusting required reference architecture, as well as assembling components into the final system according to architecture.

Facilitating the communication among stakeholders

Different perspectives from different kinds of stakeholders are obvious. No matter which role they are, including managers, programmers, maintainers, customers and users, they want their concerns to be reflected in system's blueprint. Architecture is just the media by which different voices will get their response.

Architecture is not the language for describing requirements. Some-body who wants to do that may try the "planguage" created by Tom Gilb (Gilb, 2005) or other more classic methods, such as use case or scenario. However, architecture gives you the chance of finding the solution to those concerns, or taking trade off among

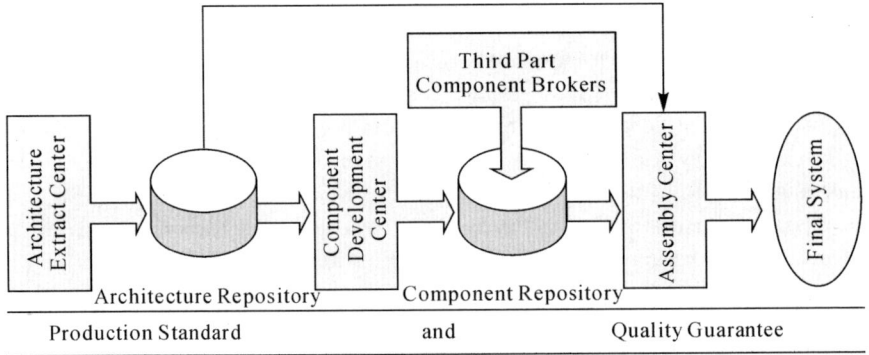

Fig. 1. 12   Software production line

the conflict ones, for the reason that any concerns are affected, more or less, by certain aspects of architecture. This means that architecture is the stand point upon which discussion, trade off, or even debate are carried out. Without architecture, it is nearly no other mechanism to convert the advice from stakeholders to the final design.

What's more, some architecture description allows users to proof their opinions by reasoning. For example, WRIGHT, based on CSP, owns the ability to detect the potential deadlock problems by analyzing the behavior description automatically, which enables you to persuade others, rather than argue endlessly just according to experience or instinct that may be thought of nonsense.

Deciding how to organize team members and allocate tasks

Generally speaking, the structure of system always becomes the reference to which how a development team is divided and organized. In this way, each group focuses on its own mission. The grouping, then, decides the style of management and work. Group becomes the unit of scheduling, test plan, interaction and configuration. For example, team leader may add CVS accounts for different groups with different access permissions, regarding to security concerns; groups must finish the integrated test for their production before any of the whole system scale tests is performed. Architecture defines the interface through which system's primary elements interact. This is just the mechanism that different groups should realize and conform to.

In addition, grouping further erects the future path of team members. After experiencing several projects, a developer pays attention to a more specific area, touching something so deeply that no other guys have ever done. For example, some developers are very good at creating graphic user interface by profoundly understanding users' habits, while some others do extremely well in configuring the database due to their clear comprehension about how a database works. In this way, developers with similar skills, such as programming, eventually become fellows expertized at their own domains, together supporting the development team.

But the grouping according to software architecture will suffer from architecture's change. Any minor fluctuation will severely disturb developers' focuses, hurt their initially zealous emotions. Manner of management and work may be given up and reconstructed, incurring a waste of cost and time. In conclusion, without considerable reason, the architecture resulted from cogitation and agreement should never be changed.

1.2.5 Where Is Software Architecture in Software Life Cycle

Today, software appears rather distinct as what it did several decades ago, that is, the simple combination of algorithm and data structure. It has a life, from the emerging of an idea about "we should develop it" to software's abandon, during which include requirement acquirement, design, implementation, test, maintenance and possible evolution, which means the next loop of processes mentioned above. Architecture can be used among these processes, and if applied skillfully, the positive effect is obvious. On the contrary, the feedback improves our experience and insight about architecture's power.

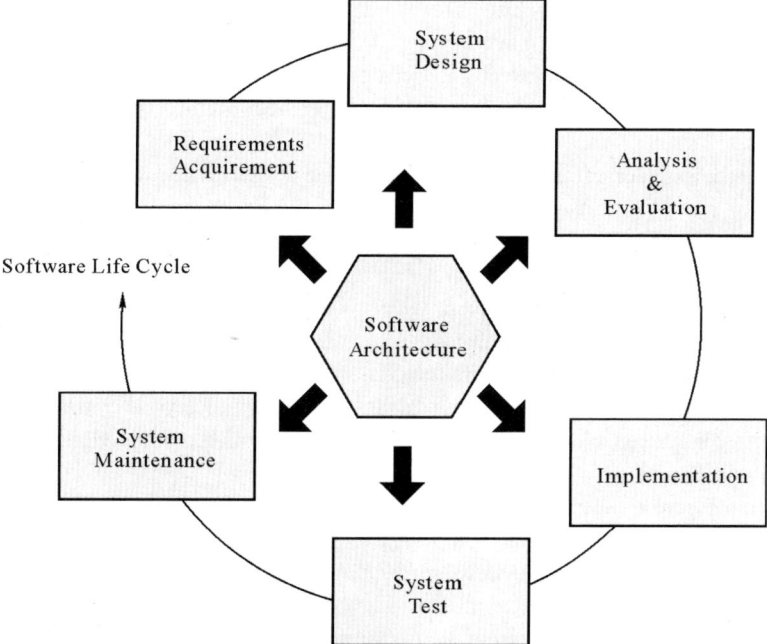

Fig. 1. 13   Architecture centered software life cycle [6]

How we use architecture in software life cycle is represented as architectural activities. A common standpoint hold by architectural beginners and some experts is taking architectural activities as part of architecture's definition. But in this book we distinct these two concepts since we insist that architectures are attached to software system themselves, just as every stone has weight, while how to use it

---

[6] This figure does not represent what the actual situation is exactly. For example, test commonly starts before implementation's finish.

depends on developers' awareness of architecture's importance and skill and creativity of applying it. Common architecture activities include:

- Creating suitable architectural model
- Choosing architecture according to requirements
- Documenting architecture
- Discussing with architecture documents
- Performing architecture analysis and evaluation
- Implementing conforming to architecture
- Testing system with architecture guide
- Reconstructing architecture from legacy system

This book does not target to introduce practical architecture in very detail, so we will not provide comprehensive explanation for the topic above. Nevertheless, this list transmits a message that it is possible to create an architecture-centered development process. In fact, some experimental processes of this kind have been provided, such as ABC (architecture-based component composition) (Mei, 2001). Maybe you insist that you have never touched or heard of architecture before, but in fact you are using architectural activities like methods implicitly, or adopt frameworks whose implementations hide reference architecture or the similar thoughts.

Nevertheless, sometimes, we must omit some activities considering development context or status. The key point is to compare the profit and the cost brought by architectural activities, where profit contains economic benefits and software quality. For example, the architectural description generated by certain ADL may be much longer than its implementation, which is a routine critique by those pessimists of architecture. Or, the evaluation may incur extreme increment of development cost because it needs gathering of numerous stakeholders, possibly distributed at different locations in the world, which, then, may delay the time-to-market. Managers must keep clear that architecture in practice is a double edged sword. You cannot gain benefits by paying nothing.

But software is keeping growing in size and complexity, especially with regard to its integration from several components. This trend increases the necessity of putting architecture into your development process. The real question is the degree to which you should depend on it. For example, it is wise to create an architectural model by inspecting your system's special needs and features; it is a good idea to limit the refinement level, avoiding your system description falling in a detailed trap; it is also very nice to localize a formal description and analysis within several kernel components and their configuration by following, for instance, the 80/20 principle.

In conclusion, software architecture can locate in almost any position in the software life cycle, but you have to make the decision that where and how to apply architectural activities by figuring out whether it is worthwhile. In this perspective, software architecture seems more like a methodology or a philosophy guided by leading principals, rather than a formula, which, given an input, always outputs a clear result. This may be the essential reason why software architecture is so hard to understand, and why its theory system is so hard to found.

1. 3 Summary

A correct initial understanding helps to clear the rugged path of further learning. But for any beginner to software architecture, trouble in how to depict the first figure of it is inevitable. In this chapter, we start with the motivation and growing of software architecture, trying to present clearly why it comes to our world and how it can be used.

Different experts will define software architecture of their own. After all, it is the tool to solve practical problems in various domains and contexts, thus various architectural models or definitions have been released. We can find something in common among them, and summarize several principals in identifying them. Precise definition of software architecture may be important, but as far as I can see, it is not so much necessary, just like the missing of precise definition of human does not affect us to identify whether something can be categorized as human. The key point is to grasp the essential principals and motivations which stand behind the appearance, such as architectural model, ADL, or architectural activities.

This chapter gives a reference understanding of software architecture, under which existed theories and models appear more harmony. We conclude them as follows. But we encourage any creative idea that can improve our insight, which is the engine with which software architecture keeps moving until today.

- Software architecture is the inherent property of software system, no matter what it is.
- Software architecture is the abstract of software system, focusing on a collection of related structures and communication mechanisms among elements as well as between elements and their environment.
- Software architecture and its description are separated. Architecture description has to be generated by some people participating in the development, such as designers or employees concentrating on architecture documenting. You may choose graphic notation or textual language, such as ADL, in description, as soon as they are precisely defined and accepted by development team. Also you can choose a formal description, an informal description or everything between them, considering your real development situation.
- An architectural view is the simplification of a single perspective of software architecture, which contains a collection of related elements, relative independent to the ones in other perspectives. Some view has dominant importance in the architecture analysis, for example, component & connector view. View may not be a graphic representation, although it commonly is.
- Software architecture and architectural activities are separated. Before applying any architectural activity, you'd better to evaluate the benefits and

cost brought by them. What's more, you can model architecture in your own way, if the innovation helps to solve the characteristic problems in your development.

In this book, we concentrate more on the theories behind software architecture and how these theories are integrated to the practice. In the next chapter, we turn our attention to architectural styles and patterns.

References

(Bass, 2003) Bass, L., Clements, P. & Kazman, R. Software Architecture in Practice, 2nd ed.: Addison-Wesley/Pearson. 2003.

(Bosch, 2000) Bosch, J. Design and Use of Software Architecture: Adopting and Evolving a Product Line Approach: Addison-Wesley. 2000.

(Brooks, 1975) Brooks, F. P. The Mythical Man-Month: Essays on Software Engineering: Addison-Wesley. 1975.

(Clements, 2002) Clements, P. & Northrop, L. Software Product Lines: Practices and Patterns: Addison-Wesley. 2002.

(Clements, 2003a) Clements, P., Bachmann, F. & Bass, L. Documenting Software Architectures: Views and Beyond Addison Wesley/Pearson. 2003a.

(Clements, 2003b) Clements, P., Kazman, R. & Klein, M. Evaluating Software Architectures: Methods and Case Studies: Pearson Education. 2003b.

(Dijkstra, 1968a) Dijkstra, E. W. The Structure of the "THE" Multiprogramming System. Communications of the ACM 1968a(18).

(Dijkstra, 1968b) Dijkstra, E. W. Goto Statement Considered Harmful. Communications of the ACM 1968b(11): 147-148.

(Fuggetta, 1998) Fuggetta, A., Picco, G. P. & Vigna, G. Understanding Code Mobility. IEEE Transactions on Software Engineering, 1998(24): 342-361.

(Gacek, 1995) Gacek, C., et al. On the Definition of Software System Architecture. Proceeding of the 1st International Workshop on Architectures for Software Systems, New York.1995:85-95.

(Garlan, 1993) Garlan, D. & Shaw, M. An Introduction to Software ArchitectureAdvances in Software Engineering and Knowledge Engineering. World Scientific.1993.

(Gilb, 2005) Gilb, T. Competitive Engineering: A Handbook for Systems Engineering, Requirements Engineering, and Software Engineering Using Planguage, Butterworth-Heinemann 2005.

(IEEE, 1998) IEEE. IEEE Standard for a Software Quality Metrics Methodology. 1998.

(Joyner, 1996) Joyner, I. C++: A Critique of C++, 3rd ed.: http://burks.brighton. ac.uk/burks/pcinfo/progdocs/cppcrit/.1996.

(Kazman, 1994) Kazman, R., et al. Saam: A Method for Analyzing the Properties of Software Architectures. Proceedings of 16th International Conference on

Software Engineering, Sorrento, Italy.1994:81-90.

(Kruchten, 2006) Kruchten, P., Obbink, H. & Stafford, J. The Past, Present, and Future of Software Architecture. IEEE Software, 2006(23): 22-30.

(Kruchten, 1995) Kruchten, P. B. The 4+1 View Model of Architecture. Software, IEEE, 1995(12): 42-50.

(Mei, 2001) Mei, H., Chang, J. & Yang, F. Software Component Composition Based on Adl and Middleware. Science in China (F) 2001(44): 136-151.

(Ning, 1996) Ning, J. Q. A Component-Based Software Development Model. Proceedings. The Twentieth Annual International Computer Software and Applications Conference (COMPSAC '96) (Cat. No.96CB35986) 1996(389-394).

(Parnas, 1972) Parnas, D. L. On the Criteria for Decomposing Systems into Modules. Communications of the ACM 1972(15): 1053-1058.

(Parnas, 1974) Parnas, D. L. On a "Buzzword": Hierarchical Structure. Proceeding of IFIP Congress 1974, Amsterdam, North Holland.1974:336-339.

(Parnas, 1976) Parnas, D. L. On the Design and Development of Program Families. Software Engineering, IEEE Transactions on 1976(SE-2): 1-9.

(Perry, 1992) Perry, D. E. & Wolf, A. L. Foundations for the Study of Software Architecture. SIGSOFT Software Engineering Notes 1992(17): 40-52.

(Royce, 1991) Royce, W. E. & Royce, W. Software Architecture: Integrating Process and Technology. Quest 1991(14): 2-15.

(Shaw, 1996) Shaw, M. & Garlan, D. Software Architecture: Perspectives on an Emerging Discipline, Prentice Hall.1996.

2

Architectural Styles and Patterns

2. 1　Fundamentals of Architectural Styles and Patterns

One of the most important features of software architecture is the abstraction of system construction patterns; these patterns are the experiences of system designers. In the long process of developing some certain software, they have explored some regular things, summarized, and got lots of general construction patterns. In this chapter, we will bring forward some widely-used design patterns; we hope to provide plentiful reference materials for readers' system analysis and design.

It is common to use design patterns and develop methods based on patterns in many engineering fields. A well-designed universal design pattern is often the sign of a mature engineering fields techniques. The general technical nomenclature and rule have already been written into the engineering techniques handbooks and professional course materials.

At present, people's understanding about software architecture is not uniform. In the early days of software architecture, Dwayne E. Perry and Alexander L.Wolf defined software architecture as: the software system family defined by software system's structure organization. Software architecture styles represent the relationships between components and components through the restriction of component application and the composition and design rule relative to components. In nowadays, the consensuses of people about software architecture styles are: a certain style or a class of styles are abstracted from the successful software system's organization structure, and can be used in different software development fields.

But before the beginning of this chapter, it is necessary to distinguish two important concepts: architecture styles and architecture patterns, just as shown in the title of this chapter. Many researchers think these two concepts refer to the same thing, while others consider they are different. The debate is still continuing. In our opinion, before the clear classification of style and pattern, we should first consider at what level we will describe the system. As described in many books, we will consider they refer to things on different abstract levels. In the book "The Timeless Way of Building" written by Christopher Alexander, the concept of pattern language is built. The concept of software architecture is borrowed from the architectonics field, so we can define: a pattern is a design solution in the relative problems' context for a certain problem (Albin, 2003). A single problem can not be solved lonely; they must be solved in the environment which is full with conflicts and hindrances. Hence, a pattern is a solution for a certain problem to balance the benefit and cost so that the optimal result is achieved. Generally speaking, pattern is not only the objects that exists in the real world, but also tell us the rules that when and how to create this certain object; pattern is not only process, but also things; it is not only the description of live things, but also the description of the process of building these things.

But we consider the architecture style as a solution to solve a certain class of problems which have common quality attributes requirements. There is no architecture style that is proper for all systems, because every system have different quality attributes requirements. Some systems attach importance to the security attributes, whiles others emphasize much on real-time attributes. Architecture styles always benefit some attributes at the cost of losing some other attributes. In the following parts, readers will find each of the architecture's disadvantages and advantages, in fact, the disadvantages and advantages are just the benefited and lost quality attributes. In this sense, we can consider style as the framework of the solution, but not framework, comparing with the patterns which are in fact a solution for the concrete problems. The choices of styles constraint the scale of solution space, so that the complexity of finding proper patterns' process is reduced.

Pattern is a concrete solution just as described above, but at different abstract level, they have different content. For instance, at the architecture level, for the pipes and filter style, they have many forms: if the filters are strictly constrained to have only one input and one output, the system is called pipelines, it is composed by linear sequences of filters and pipes which lay between these filters; if the max amount of data is limited on every pipes, these pipes are called bounded pipes, the whole system is another type in the pipes and filters style; if the data types that will be input into the pipes are defined, we say that the pipes is data strongly typed, which forms another type in the pipes and filters style; if the data streams are not incremental, we call the system is batch sequential. If it is permitted, we would like to call each of the above types architecture patterns in the pipes and filters style. Reader should not think there are some standard criterions which can classify different patterns. In fact, the patterns are abstracted from different perspectives. For example, if a system is build in the style of pipes and filters, the filters are constrained to have only one input and output, and the max data amount is specified, we call the system is not only a pipelines, but also a system that has bounded pipes. In a word, different patterns can be composed.

Behind the concept of architecture style and patterns, we think there are two other concepts that have similar relationship with architecture. We will describe the two concepts in the following parts.

The first one is the control principle. It describes how to activate each component to process information, and how to transfer information between components. For example, in the dataflow systems, components read data from their input port, and send it to their output port, controls are sealed in the low layer transfer mechanisms. In the call and return systems, application structure's controls are explicit, there exists a main instance and thread that call all the other components, and the inner control in the independent components is similar to dataflow system; the components and objects can communicate with other components and objects through messages. The virtual machine control is also different with the other styles. So in this sense, we think that control principle is the main characteristic of each style. In another word, we can say the control principle is the criterion to classify software architecture style.

Control principle describes how to activate a component, or describes how the logic is processed. In the book "The Art of Software Architecture: Design Methods and Techniques", the author think control principle can be classified into two layers: technique layer and design layer. In technique layer, the method call and method execution's match in run-time layer are described. This technique can also describe how middleware activate the remote objects through remote methods or message sequences. Readers must know, in the programming language C, method call and method execution are bind together; but in the language such as Smalltalk, method call and method execution do not match. The client object can send a message to another object, and the corresponding methods may be executed in another control thread. That is to say, method call in the client may not lead to method execution in the same control thread. In design layer, the control principle in run-time layer can be simulated. In nowadays, the object-oriented programming languages all have these abilities, such as C# and Java. The concepts of event and message are frequently used in object-oriented analysis and object-oriented design, even object-oriented systems' implementation. In this layer, the communication pattern can be classified into synchronous, asynchronous and authorized. The synchronous communication means that the client component activate a server component, then wait for the response. Generally speaking, when an operation is called, the calling program is always waiting until the response values are returned. The asynchronous communication between components means when the client component call a server's component, it need not wait for the response. It can be doing other tasks while waiting for response. At last, the client retrieves the response. If the response is not ready, client can continue to waiting for the response or do other things while checking the validity of response in certain intervals. The asynchronous communication is a strong pattern to build high performance distributed application, but the cost is the more complicated applications that have poor error-tolerance. The third is authorized pattern, the client components call the server components and pass an address to which response will be sent. The authorized pattern is similar to asynchronous communication, the sole difference is the called component need not wait for the response, in another word, the response can be sent to other client component and the event can be processed in another thread.

In a word, the activate model, which also can be called control principle, can compare the difference between different architecture style. Exact comprehension about the requirement of sub-system's activate model is of helpful to choose, or to describe better, design a proper architecture style, or design better combination of architecture style. As we will describe in the end of this chapter, in most of application systems, multiple architecture styles are combined to achieve certain quality attributes, this is the concept of heterogeneous architecture style integration.

The second concept is quality attribute. Generally speaking, every architecture style has its history and certain context, this means that each architecture style is proposed in a certain environment, and can solve certain key problems or satisfy certain requirements, but at the cost of debasing another set of quality attributes. For example, the pipes filters style has good reusability, but suffer from the data representation's modification, and sacrifice system's maintenance. Object-oriented system is proper for data representation's modification and system's maintenance, because they encapsulate data's inner representation detail. But, because of designer's objective preference, and they may design classes in their own habits. The lib based systems are good for system's adaptability and performance, but for the algorithm and data representation's modification, they do not have high reusability and maintenance.

Software designers are clever, to build good system that balance the quality attributes, and they combine styles in different fields together. For instance, they may combine the lib method and object-oriented methods.

Using architecture style can benefit much: first, we can improve design reuse. When solving new design problems, developers can improve develop efficiency through using proper style. Second, the extraction about style brings general communication form for developers. The vocabulary about design element facilitates developers' understanding and communications. For instance, if we use vocabulary such as client/server, pips-filter styles in system design, design and develop personnel can easily know the application range and design restraints. Third, using style can improve codes' reuse. When used in different systems, the basic framework code style needs not to be modified; it can be shared in different systems.

In software architecture, the continual summarization and abstraction for software style leads to the research of style classification. For example, Mary Shaw and Clements classified architecture from two aspects: data and control. After that, Mary and Garlan classified style as dataflow system, call-return system, independent component, virtual machine, central repository. In these styles, dataflow system includes sequence-batch process and pipes-filter styles; call-return system includes object-oriented system, layered system; dependent component includes communication process and event driven system. Virtual machine includes interpreter and rule based system. The repository style includes database, hypertext and blackboard, etc., but these classifications do not list all the styles. New styles will continually appear as the development of software techniques. For instance, the rising agent-oriented research does not appear in these classifications. In some fields of the software architecture, which has special style, such as network, web services, peer-to-peer structure, we must research them specially.

In this chapter, we will list the main software styles. For each style, we first describe its basic characteristics, and then give some instances to illustrate the style. After introducing these styles, we will give some general conclusion about each style. Then we describe a virtual system that uses many architecture style meanwhile, so as to introduce the integration of heterogeneous styles.

2.2　Pipes Filters

2.2.1　Style Description

In Pipes-Filters style, each processing step has a set of input and output. A processing step reads a stream of data from the input set, and generates a stream of data to the output set. That is to say, components in the system compute one data set to generate another data set. In the Pipes-Filters style, function modelers which process data are called filters; connectors between function modelers can be treat as the channels between input dataflow and output dataflow, so it can be called pipes.

One of the features of pipes-filters style is the independence of filters, this means, filters implement their function independently, they need not communicate with each other. In addition, each filter need not know the existence of input pipes and output pipes which connect to it, the only thing they need do is to restrict the input data, and guarantee there are proper data in the output pipes, but they do not know the implementation details of other filters existed in the system. At the same time, the final output of the whole pipes-filters has no relation to the operation sequence of each filter. One of the pipes-filters' graph is as follows:

If we give some restriction to the Pipes-Filters style, we can get a variety of Pipes-Filters sub-Style. For example, if we restrict the topology structure of Pipes-Filters in a linear sequence, we call it Pipelines; if we restrict the data amount stored in the filters, we call it Bounded Pipes; if each filter processes all the input data as a single object, this architecture become sequence batch process system. These are also described in Section 2.1.

Pipes-Filters style has the following advantages:

First, Pipes-Filters style decomposes the whole system into a set of filters that connected by pipes. The independent of filters reduces the couple between

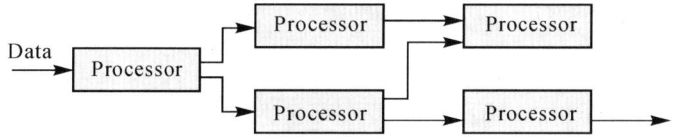

Fig. 2. 1   Pipes-filters style

components, hence, it support the function modular level reuse. Existed filters in the system can be easily applied to new systems which are to be designed. Second, the system that composed by pipes and filters can be easily maintained and extended. The maintenance is mainly incarnated a system's evolution. The filter only needs to consider components' input, output and inner implementation, and not needs to consider the filter's maintenance and modification. If we want to replace a certain filter, we only need to design a filter that has the same input, output with the original one. The extension mainly incarnate on the system functions' expansion. For instance, if we want to add a new function to the original system, add new data output, we can finish it by adding new output port to the original filter. Third, in the Pipes-Filter style, the independence of filter component provides convenience for system's performance analysis, such as data throughout, deadlock analysis and computing accuracy, etc. Fourth, it supports concurrency computing. Systems based on Pipes-Filters style may have many parallel filters; these filters can run concurrently, so that the whole performance of the system improved.

Meanwhile, the Pipes-Filters style has some disadvantage:

Filters may have some restrictions to the input and output data, so this style is not proper for interactive systems. In fact, when the pipes-filters style is brought forward, the applications does not have high interactive requirement. In the early days of computer design, this type of style met the requirement of processing multiple tasks. For some application design that needs sharing much data, it is not proper to use this type of style. The exchanging of data between filters needs large data access space, and the transmission of data will occupy much system running time.

2. 2. 2   Study Case

In this part, we will give a typical example about digital communication system, and introduce in detail how to organize each component using Pipes-Filters style. From this, we can obviously know that software architecture is production produced when system analysis, creation and management technologies have got many research results. Software architecture does not only limit to computer software or other concrete subjects, it has strong general utility.

The goal of communication is transferring information. Messages have a variety of forms, such as symbols, text, voice, music, graph, image, etc., according to the difference of messages. We can classify the communication operation into telegraph, telephone, fax, data transferring and visible telephone, etc. In fact, the basic peer to peer communication is always transferring data form one point to another point. So, this type of communication can be summarized by the model showed in Fig.2.2.

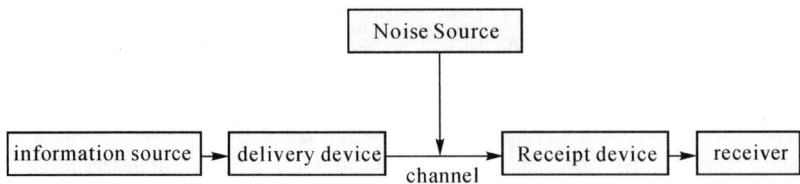

Fig. 2. 2   The glancing model of digital communication system

Fig.2.2 has four filters and pipes that connect them. The function of information source is to transform all possible information into original electric signals; the delivery device changes the original signals in some way so that the original signal can be transferred in the channels. The channels not only can be treated as pipes (because its goal is not to realize some function, but the transferring of signal), but also can be treated as filters (because after each channel, the signals may have some change). At the receive port, the function of receive device is opposite to the delivery device, and it recoveries the received signals to the original signals.

According to the types of signals in the channel, we can classify the communication system into two types: simulative communication system and digital communication system. In this book, we only take digital communication system as example. In digital communications, there are some typical problems.

First, when the digital signals are transferred, the error generated by channel noise can be controlled by error control coding. So we must add an encoder to the delivery port, and add an according decoder to the receipt port. Second, when secrecy needed, we should encrypt the base band signal, so as to avoid the information damage or communication destroy. At this time, we should decipher in the receipt port. Third, because in the digital communication system, the digital signal units are transferred one by one, the receipt part must receive it in the same time. Otherwise, the disaccordance of receiving time may cause confusion; this may leads to receiving ineffective data. In addition, to represent message content, the base band signals are organized by message content, so the rule of delivery port and receipt port's organization must be the same. Otherwise, the original signals can not be recovered even if they are correct. In the digital communication systems, we must have synchronism control components.

As described in this part, the peer to peer digital communication system's Pipes-Filters model can be represented as Fig.2.3.

In Fig.2.3, we do not explicitly represent the synchronism control components, the main reason is that the position of synchronism control components are not fixed. They are flexible, and are different in different concrete systems. Of course, the real digital communications do not necessarily include all the filters showed in Fig.2.3, and they also can include filters that are not showed in Fig.2.3. For instance, whether to use the modulation and demodulation, encryption and deciphering, encode and decode components, depends on the concrete design methods and requirement, and it is this that shows the mightiness of Pipes-Filters. For example,

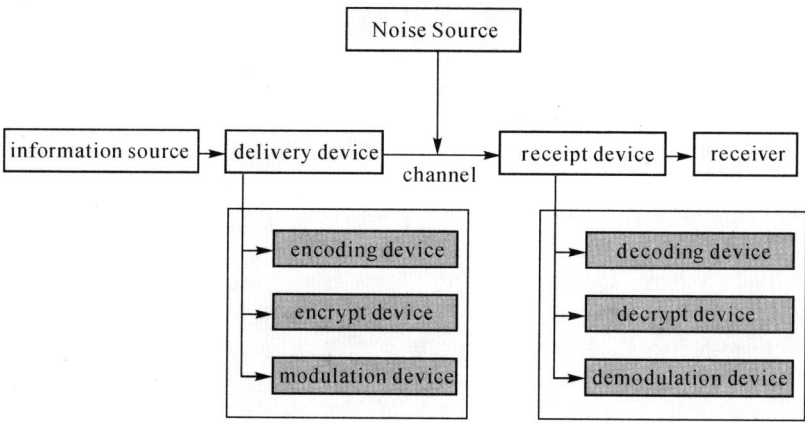

Fig. 2. 3   The detail model of digital communication system

in a digital base band transfer system, the modulation and demodulation are not included; in addition, if we add an ADC to the information source, add a DAC to the receiver, then the digital communication system can process analog signals, this is also called the analog signals' digital process system.

In the systems that use the pipes filters architecture, the filters need not to be atomic. A filter can be divided into many sub-filters, and these sub-filters can be connected together using connectors. We will introduce a simple example. In this example, a string can be splited into an array of words, and then the words can be combined in certain rule to form new strings. At last, we can sort the new negated strings alphabetically, and output them. The architecture model is shown in Fig.2.4.

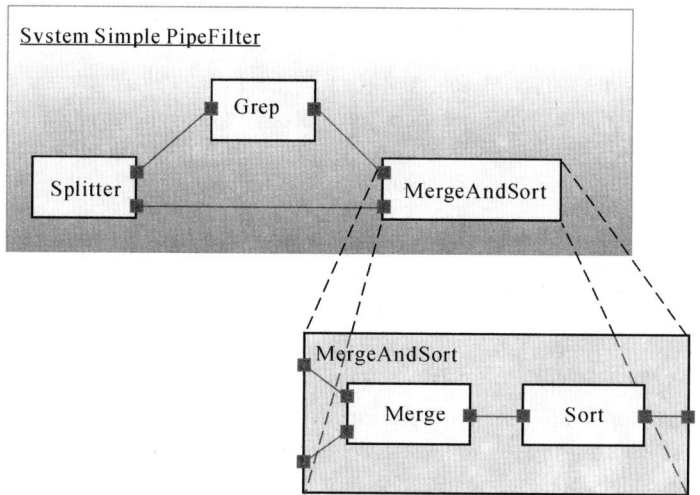

Fig. 2. 4   A simple PipeFilter example

Generally speaking, the whole system can be divided into two filters: The

Splitter filter and MergeAndSort filter. If we input a string into the filter, it will split the string into a set of words, and output them. Then the MergeAndSort filter can accept the output data from Splitter filter, and generate the sorted strings. In the designers and analysts' perspective, they do not care how this MergeAndSort filter works; they only care about the interfaces in the filter, and they consider the filter as an atomic filter. But in fact, if we are in charge of this MergeAndSort subsystem or must implement the filter, we will certainly decompose it into two sub-filters: Merge and Sort. The Merge sub-filter can merge the words in a certain rule to generate new strings, and the Sort sub-filter can sort the new generated strings in alphabetical order. So we do not consider the MergeAndSort filter as an atomic filter. In another word, we can say a filter can be either atomic or combined. I think even a filter can be any type of system as long as the whole system conforms to the Pipes Filter style's constraints.

2.3   Object-oriented

2.3.1   Style Description

The object-oriented style integrates the data abstraction, abstraction data type and class as an incorporate object, and makes the principle of modularization, information hiding, abstraction, reuse implement in the object-oriented style. The ultimate goal of object-oriented pattern design is to seek the natural description and solutions about problems in real world, that is, to seek the consistence of seek problem space and software system space structure. It treats all the resources, such as data, modular, as objects, and it abstracts the problems and their elements through class; it encapsulate its own data structure and function implementation, to realize the information capsulation and data abstraction.

A set of objects that have the same attributes and operations can form an object class. The programs that are defined to describe object operations are called methods, the objects contact with each other through messages between objects; this is the sole way to implement the relationships between objects. The class inheritance makes the subclass be capable of inheriting all the characteristics and abilities of super class. This hierarchy relation can describe the application problems in real worlds easily, it conforms to the reuse goal of software, so it became the main characteristic of object-oriented system.

To construct systems based on object-oriented style, we should first find objects in the problem, so that we can construct proper class to represent different objects, we then solve the problems through message transferring between objects and the inheritance mechanisms of classes.

The object-oriented systems doe not only encapsulate information and segregate system's modification, but also includes methods. These methods encourage us to treat the concept of real world as object, and to model them directly, because users can design classes and packages as they wish. This is similar to the entity-relation modeling in database systems; in fact, the E-R model is another instance in computer field that can simulate human's thought. In dataflow systems, their main view is process but not data. In the object-oriented or data abstraction systems, data view is emphasized, at the same time, the detailed process view is also permitted, and this view is represented by the certain data operation's form and hiberarchy structure between classes, methods overload is also permitted.

With the rapid development of software engineering, the design styles and design patterns are continually increasing, and the new architecture permits us to compose a variety of systems using user-defined objects.

Languages such as Java are object-oriented; programming in such a language is called object-oriented programming (OOP), it allows designers to implement the object-oriented design as a working system. Languages such as C, on the other hand, are procedural programming languages, and programs in this type of languages tend to be action-oriented.

We will see that, when software is packaged as classes, these classes can be reused in future software systems. Groups of related classes are often packaged as reusable components. Just as real-estate brokers tell their clients that the three most important factors affecting the price of real estate are "location, location and location", many people in software community believe that the three most important factors affect the future of software development are "reuse, reuse and reuse", this is just one of the most important characteristics of object-oriented architecture style.

Indeed, with object technology, we can build much of the software we will need by combining "standardized, interchangeable parts" called classes. With the rapid development of object-oriented technology, many related technologies appear and develop quickly, such as object-oriented analysis and design (OOAD). OOAD is the generic term for the ideas behind the process we employ to analyze a problem and develop an approach to solve it.

Pseudo code can suffice small problems, but as problems and the groups of people solving these problems increase in size, methods of OOAD become more involved. Ideally, a group should agree on a strictly defined process for solving the problem and on a uniform way of communicating the results of that process to one another. Although many different OOAD processes exist, a single graphical language for communicating the results of any OOAD process has become widely used. This language is known as the Unified Modeling Language (UML). UML was developed in the mid-1990s under the initial direction of three software methodologists: Grady Booch, James Rumbaugh and Ivar Jachbson. We will not describe the detail of OOAD and UML language; readers can refer to other special books.

2.3.2 Study Case

In this section, we will describe a system instance based on object-oriented style; this model's core idea is component thought, which is the hot research problem in nowadays. We will understand the open distributed system from the component perspective, and then analysis the model.

With the rapid development of computer software and hardware, computers' application and popularization have got good results, and the import of Internet injects new fresh things to the computer system application. At present, a standard computer application system includes: computer operation system (including application software system), database management system and network environment (including network hardware device and protocol, network services). This kind of system is called Open Distributed System, we often call it ODS for short. ODS is the basic form of computer application system in nowadays and future, and is the production of digitalization, information, networking.

In the following parts, we will introduce CBA method, which is the short form of component based analysis. A component is a function unit that encapsulates its design and implementation, it provides interfaces for outer classes, and the interconnection of multiple components' interfaces can form an integrated system. The advantage of component is: we can provide standard technology service framework, implement the position transparence of language and component, and the good reusability based on attributes and events. Just because the good characteristics of component in the modeling process, we take the CBA method as example.

CBA method has three basic modeling concepts: collaboration, type and refinement. On this basis, we can generate a variety of design and style, from the simple component model, to design patterns and architecture description, to the solution of final system's reliability problems. (1) Collaboration. According to different roles that the components take on, the collaboration defines a set of action between components. They can abstract the detail of multiple components' communication and the session models between components. (2) Type. Type defines its function it takes on in the system through the description of components' outer action. Type is not the implementation of according component, but just the outer characteristics that any correct implementation must incarnate. (3) Refinement. Refinement incarnates two different description relations for the same thing. Abstraction description is the basis, the realization description can be treat as the concrete form of abstraction description. These two descriptions are mainly against the different detail degree for the system.

Based on these three concepts, we can use the component thought to uniform the whole system, and to define component, relations between components and refinement of abstract description. The CBA based system is similar to the composite patterns in design patterns; it has the characteristic of recurrence, it can satisfy the requirement of increment development, it has good quality attributes such as maintenance and extensibility.

In this part, we will introduce the components, connectors and configuration's model in ODS system. It is obviously that only having architecture is not sufficient to solve real problems; we must have more concrete method to refine the framework, to incarnate the three concepts of modeling. To achieve this goal, we introduce component, connector and configuration, as showed in Fig.2.4. We will introduce them in detail in the following part.

(1) Component. Component is the basic element to describe Open Distributed System; we can describe a component from the following six aspects: The first one is interface. Interface is the interactive point between components and outer environment; it defines services that a component provides (such as message, operation and attributes). The second one is type. Type is a reusable function modular; a component type can be instantiate any times in the architecture. The third one is semantics. Semantics is the advanced modeling of components' activity. Using this model, we can do system analysis, fix the constraint condition, and make sure the architecture's consistence of transition from one abstraction description to another abstraction description. The fourth one is constraint. Constraint condition is the attributes of the system or one part of the system, and violating constraint condition may leads to system crash. Constraints fix the constraint condition, boundary, and the dependency relationships between components. The fifth one is evolution. In the run time of ODS, components will evolve all the time. The evolution of components can be simply defined as the changes of components' attributes, such as interface, activity and implementation. We can use the component type figure or characteristic refinement to incarnate the dynamic style of ODS. The sixth one is nonfunctional property. This characteristic is mainly in charge of security, privacy, high performance and mobility.

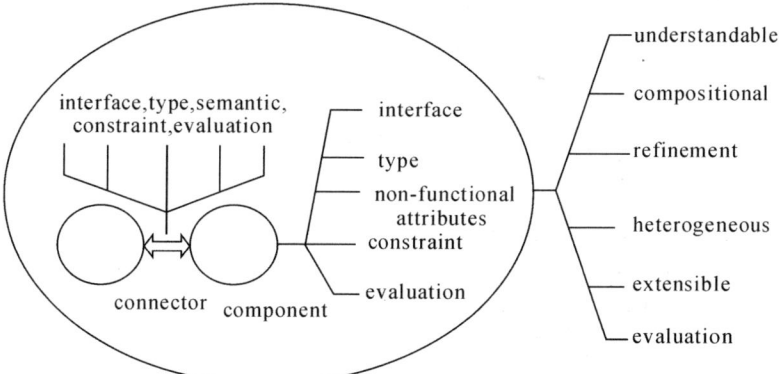

Fig. 2. 5   ODS system framework

(2) Connector. Connectors are used to analysis the interactive model between components, and define the interactive rule. Connectors need not to be a editable unit in the ODS, it may appears as shared variable, table entrance's index finger, buffer area, dynamic data structure, etc. We can describe connectors from the following five aspects: The first one is interface. These interfaces are between connectors and components. Connector does not take part in the network computing, its interface provides component's service to outer environment. Connectors provides the connector between components and interaction, it can

provide necessary information for software architecture's configuration. The second one is type. Connectors' type is the encapsulation for components' communication, coordination and mediation decision. Open Distributed System's inner interaction need complicated protocols to support, and type just provides description of these protocols. The third one is semantics. Semantics define the rule of communication protocol, it can be used to analysis the interaction between components, to maintain the consistence between different abstraction levels, to make sure the constraint conditions of components' communication are satisfied. The fourth one is constraint condition. Constraint conditions are used to make sure connectors' communication protocols are correct, it can also build the dependency between components, and make sure the boundary is used. The fifth one is evolution. Similar to components' evolution, connectors' evolution is also defined as the modification of attributes, such as interface, semantics and constraint condition. Components communicate with each other through complicated, extensible and dynamic protocols; both single component and architecture configuration are continually evolving. To adapt this evaluate characteristic, we can modify or refine connector.

(3) Configuration. Configuration is also called topology, it is the architecture graph composed by components and connectors. The configuration can be used to judge four problems: Are the components suitable? Are the connectors matched? Are the communications of connectors normal? Do the semantics of component connection satisfy the design requirements? On the base of components and connector, the description of configuration can be used to describe system's concurrency, distribution, security, to implement the reliability of Open Distributed System.

In this paragraph, we will introduce the description method of component. Using UML and ADL (Architecture Description Languages), we can describe the components and their relationships in the Open Distributed System. Using the auto generation tools of GUI architecture structure, we can accomplish these function:

(1) Generation of component model;
(2) Construction of connectors, including protocols, attributes and implementation;
(3) Abstraction and encapsulation of architecture;
(4) Validation of type;
(5) Provision of design guide;
(6) Support of multiple view to show different views for different users;
(7) Generation of implementation, including how to reflect components to classes with object-oriented technologies;
(8) Dynamic reflection of modification to system implementation dynamically. The system modeling based on components provides hard base for the analysis of Open Distributed System, a variety of application fields can easily build themselves on this base.

To guarantee the efficient and reliable communication between components, and to provide real-time, synchronous and concurrency communication ability, we must design some connector models that have adaptive steady characteristics. This mainly includes the following two aspects:

(1) The communication protocol stack in connectors

The communication protocol stack is composed by a set of communication protocols which have different functions, and each protocol is in charge of a part work of components' communication. In this system, we mainly use the following basic protocols:

The first is component naming and addressing protocol. The architecture models of ODS system are built on the base of component, and formed by components' composition. Components are their basic elements and the main body of communication, we must build a mechanism to name and address ODS.

The second is component communication transferring protocol. Once the naming and addressing mechanisms are built, communication relationship between components can occur. At this moment, the main problem is the data type definition and routing of communication content. This is similar to the IP protocol in network layer in TCP/IP.

The third is component communication transferring control protocol. The construction of component communication transferring control protocol provides basic function guaranty for the communication between components. But only simple data package transferring is not sufficient for the communication between components, we must have advanced protocols to control transferring of data package, which provide resend mechanism, dataflow control and component/connector management mechanism. This is similar to the transfer layer of TCP/IP.

The fourth is component communication management protocol. Based on the first three protocols described above, communications that have some fault-tolerant techniques are possible, but system manager may hope system to have more control function, such as judgment of components' reach ability, the source suppression of dataflow control, redirector and respond, etc, to provides these extra control ability, the component communication management protocol is introduced. This protocol is on the same level with component communication transferring protocol; it can provide services for the component communication transferring control protocol. This is similar to the ICMP protocol in network layer in TCP/IP. The communication protocol stack in connector model is showed in Fig.2.6.

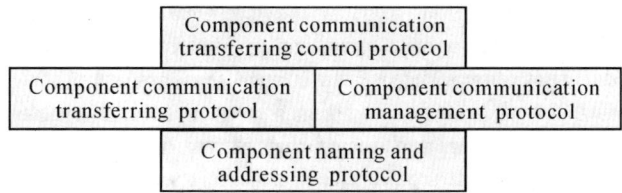

Fig. 2. 6 Communication protocol stack in connector model

(2) The adapted steady algorithm of connectors

To improve the steady of communication protocol stack in component communication process, it is necessary to design some adaptive steady algorithm; so as to repair errors that occur when components are communicating with each other. We can use math methods such as fault-tolerant neural networks and genetic algorithm to design algorithm, implement the robust communication protocol stack. We can encapsulate the designed algorithms to communication management component or connector models' communication protocols, so that the adaptive steady connector model is built.

In the part mentioned above, we have only introduced the basic principle of object-oriented system, including components, connectors and configurations, and the communication protocols between them. In fact, the object-oriented architecture style has a certain activation model, which is similar, or the same to the activation model of event driven architecture. Some reader may ask, since these two architecture styles have the same activate model, and the author said the activate model is the main criterion to classify architecture style, why not treat these two styles as the same one? The main reason is: we think these two styles do not describe a problem from the same perspective. The object-oriented style mainly describes systems from their static model, and emphasizes the data encapsulation and abstraction, which is of great help to system's modularization and extension. But the event driven style mainly describes systems from their dynamic activity, and emphasizes the relation between event generator and event processor. In fact, most of the object-oriented systems have the event driven activate model, as readers will see in the following parts of this chapter. In the following part, we will give a typical application of object-oriented architecture style. In this example, readers will also find some typical characteristics of event driven style. Readers may do not know the definition and description about event driven architectural style. It doesn't matter, because after reading Section 2.4, you will certainly find the answers, and then can go back to review this example.

The problem statement is: a company intends to build a two-floor building and equip it with an elevator. The company wants you to develop an object-oriented software-simulator application that models the operation of the elevator to determine whether it will meet the company's needs. The company wants the simulation to contain an elevator system. The application consists of three parts. The first and most substantial part is the simulator, which models the operation of the elevator system. The second part is the graphical user interface or model on screen so that the user may view it graphically. The final part is the graphical user interface, or GUI, that allows the user to control the simulation.

A system is a set of components that interact to solve a problem. In our case study, the elevator-simulator application represents the system. A system may contain "subsystems", which are "systems within a system". Subsystems simplify the design process by managing subsets of system responsibilities. System designers may allocate system responsibilities among the subsystems, design the subsystems, and then integrate the subsystems with the overall system. From problem statement, we can see the overall system will include three main part (or can be called subsystem): the first is simulator model (which represents the operation of the elevator system), the second is the display of this model on screen (so that users may view it graphically), and the third one is the graphical user interface (that allows users to control the simulation). This is a simple instance of MVC, which is a popular pattern in software architecture design (Note: do not treat MVC as a kind of design pattern, the MVC pattern is on a higher level). The mechanism of MVC is just an instance of event driven architecture style; we will describe it in later section.

The main aim of this example is to make readers understand the principle of object-oriented architectural style; hence we will only describe the analysis and design of first part: simulator model. In this subsystem, many entities are recognized and the relationships between them are identified.

We often choose nouns that perform important duties in our model, for this reason we omit several nouns that do not play important roles. For example, we need not to model "company" as a class, because the company is not part of the simulation; the company simply wants us to model the elevator. We do not model the office building, or the actual place where the elevator is situated, because the building does not affect how our elevator simulation operates. We determine the classes for our system by grouping the remaining nouns into categories. We discard "elevator system" for the time being——we focus on designing only the system's model and disregard how this model relates to the system as a whole. We can identify the group of nouns as these following: model, elevator shaft, elevator, person, floor (first floor, second floor), elevator door, floor door, elevator button, floor button, bell, light. These categories are likely to be classes we will need to implement in our system. Notice that we create one category for the buttons on the floors and one category for the button on the elevator. The two types of the button in the elevator inform the elevator to move to the other floor.

We can now model the classes in our system based on the categories we created. The UML enables us to model, via the class diagram, the classes in the elevator system and their interrelationships. Fig.2.7 shows the complete class diagram for the elevator model. We model all classes that we created, as well as the associations between these classes.

Class diagrams model the structure of the system by providing the classes, or "building block", of the system. In a class diagram, each class is modeled as a rectangle; a solid lien that connects classes represents an association. An association is a relationship between classes. The numbers near the lines express multiplicity values. Multiplicity values indicate how many objects of a class participate in the association. From the diagram, we see that two objects of class FloorButton participate in the association with one object of class ElevatorShaft, because the two FloorButtons are located on the ElevatorShaft. Therefore, class FloorButton has a two-to-one relationship with class FloorButton. We also see that class ElevatorShaft has a one-to-two relationship with class Elevator and vice versa. Using the UML, we can model many types of multiplicity. Readers who are not familiar with UML may refer to some special books.

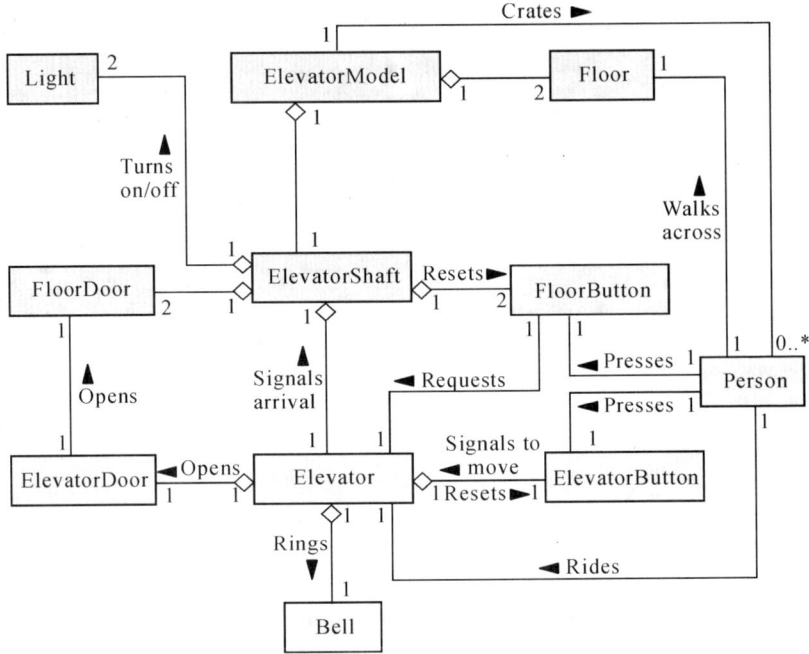

Fig. 2. 7   The class diagram of elevator simulation

An association can be named. For example, the word "Requests" above the line connecting classes FloorButton and Elevator indicates the name of that association—the arrow shows the direction of the association. The diamond attached to the association lines of class ElevatorShaft indicates that class ElevatorShaft has an aggregation relationship with classes FloorButton and Elevator. Aggregation implies a whole/part relationship. The class that has the aggregation symbol (the hollow diamond) on its end of and association line is the whole (in this case is ElevatorShaft), and the class on the other end of the association line is the part (in this case, classes FloorButton and Elevator). In this example, the elevator shaft "has an" elevator and two floor buttons. The "has an/has a" relationship defines aggregation.

Class ElevatorModel is represented near the top of the diagram and aggregates one object of class ElevatorShaft and two objects of class Floor. The ElevatorShaft class is an aggregation of one object of class Elevator and each object of classes Light, FloorDoor and FloorButton. Class Elevator is an aggregation of classes ElevatorDoor, ElevatorButton, the association name Presses and the name-direction arrowheads indicate that the object of class Person presses these buttons. The object of class Person also rides the object of class Elevator and walks across the object of class Floor. The name Request indicates that an object of class FloorButton requests the object of class Elevator. The name Signals to move indicates that the object of class ElevatorButton signals the object of class Elevator to move to the other floor. The diagram indicates many other associations, as well.

In this part, we only model the class diagram. The most important principle readers should remember about object-oriented architecture is: always treat system as a collection of objects and the relationship between them. On the analysis mentioned above, we introduce the associations and aggregation; they all are kinds of relationship between objects. When the system is running, objects communicate with each other through sending and receiving messages between them. Generally speaking, nearly all of the programs in nowadays are object-oriented; this is why the object-oriented technologies are developing so quickly. For system designers, the most important thing to do is to design the system using object-oriented analysis and design, so as to make designed system easier to understand and evaluate. As an object-oriented architecture style, it has much relation with event driven style. We will continue to introduce this example in the event driven part's case study.

2. 4   Event-driven

2. 4. 1   Style Description

Event-driven style is also called Publishing-Subscription style in many books. Its basic viewpoint is that a system's behave to outer environment can incarnate from its processing method to events. If we want to understand a system, we can simply input an event to it, and then watch its output, so as to analyze a system. The conceptual event-driven system is shown in Fig.2.8.

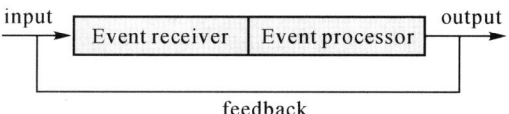

Fig. 2. 8   Conceptual model of event-driven system

Event-driven system has the following characteristics: (1) system is composed by many subsystems or elements, but we consider the subsystems in event-driven architecture style are different from that in the object-oriented systems; they describe system's decomposition from different perspectives. For instance, the subsystems in event driven system can be classified into operation system and management system, but components in object-oriented systems are not classified into operation system and management system in general cases; (2) systems have certain goal, under the control of some message mechanism, subsystems collaborates with each other to achieve system's ultimate goal; (3) under some certain message mechanism control, system adapts and collaborates with environment as a single object; (4) among these subsystems, one of them plays the leading role, and other subsystems are on the subordinate status; (5) any systems and any elements in the system have an event collector and a event process mechanism, it communicates with outer environment through this mechanism.

From the above characteristics, we can get the following conclusions: (1) any subsystem of the system certainly has its own dependence, it communicates with other subsystems through message mechanisms; (2) from this viewpoint, the structured, modularized parts can not be called subsystem. (3) the object-oriented event-driven system design methods treat software system as a single object, and classify it into subsystems to implement.

Fig.2.9 shows a sample of the event-driven based system.

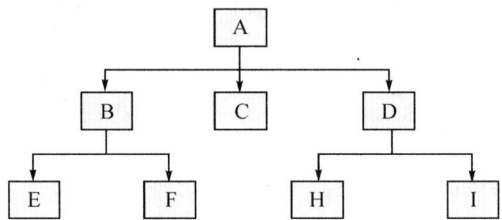

Fig. 2. 9   Event-driven software system

This event-driven system is composed by elements A, B, C, D, E, F, H and I. Please do not treat A as sub-modular or sub-program, and do not treat B and C as A's sub-modular or sub-program. In the event-driven system, we just treat (B, E, F), (D, H, I), A, C as the system's subsystem. A is on the dominate position, it is the coordinator of other systems, and is also their leader. A makes system run correctly through sending messages to B, C, and D, and collecting messages from B, C and D to subsystem (B, E, F) and (D, H, I), the dominate subsystem are B and D respectively.

In the design of event-driven system, we must consider the integration and independence of every subsystem. We will not depend on a certain subsystem absolutely, the collaboration and management between systems are through the transferring and collection of messages. This mechanism is similar to society. Everyone in the world can be treat as a subsystem. He is independent to others, but mankind can collaborate life and work through message transferring, compose family and society, form new system. Just as man is the opposite body, the event-driven based system must treat every subsystems in it as opposite body of general character and individuality, we must not only consider each subsystem's social characteristic, but also its personality.

The design of event-driven based system has the following principles: (1) We always treat the described objects from the system perspective, so we must decompose system properly, guaranty the dependence and society of every subsystem. (2) No matter how the system complicated, how different the subsystems are, any subsystem can be classified into management system and operation system. Operation system has no subsystem, but management system has subsystem, its subsystem not only can be management system, but also can be operation system. (3) To reach the overall system's goal, every subsystem cooperates with each other through message transfer and message operation. Generally speaking, subsystems that lay on the same level do not transfer messages directly, but they transfer messages through their parents system. This mechanism can depress system's coupling, and collaborate actions. (4) Any subsystem, either operation subsystem or management subsystem, has an event processor, to process the events given by its parent system. The management subsystem must also have an event distribution mechanism and event collection mechanism, can judge the event given by parent, and give it to children to operate, and can collect events given by children. (5) In an integrated system, we must have such a system; it has no parent, and collects outer events and subsystems' events. (6) Generally, the management subsystem does not do concrete operation, its main function is to complete tasks through guiding their children; the functional operations are generally completed by operation subsystem. In another word, the management subsystems mainly do conceptual operation, not concrete operation. (7) In general condition, exclude the advanced management subsystems, subsystems respond only when there are some requests.

From the previous description, readers can find, event-driven system has the recursive characteristic in some meaning, and forms the "part-whole" hierarchy, and can be represented by attribute structure. Users can compose many simple subsystems to form a larger subsystem; these large subsystems can form larger subsystems recursively. A simple represent method is to define a class for operation system, and define the container class for these operation subsystems, which is called management system.

But this method has some faults. Using these classes' codes, we must treat operation system and management system respectively; the real cases for uses are the same in most cases. Treating these two systems respectively will make the implementation and usage of the whole system more complicated. To simplify event-driven based systems' design, implementation and usage, we can draw the composite pattern in design patterns theory, to define, organize and manage event-driven system's operation subsystem and management subsystem. The key point to simplify it is to define an interface (abstract class), it can not only represent operation subsystem, but also represent the operation's container (which is called management subsystem). In Fig.2.10 we show the basic structure of the event-driven system's class view.

From the figure above, we can find in the event-driven system, clients communicate with event system, the event system can be classified into two types: execute system (also can be called operation system in the previous part) and manage system, each of which has its own event process methods.

The event-driven style has the following advantages: (1) Event-driven style is suitable to describe system families, in any systems that belong to the same family, the description of system's advanced management subsystem is completely similar, so it can be reused. (2) Because the advanced management subsystem has the control power, and subsystems that in the same level do not communicate with each other directly, it is easy to implement concurrent process and multiple tasks' operation. (3) The event-driven based systems have good extendibility, designers only need to

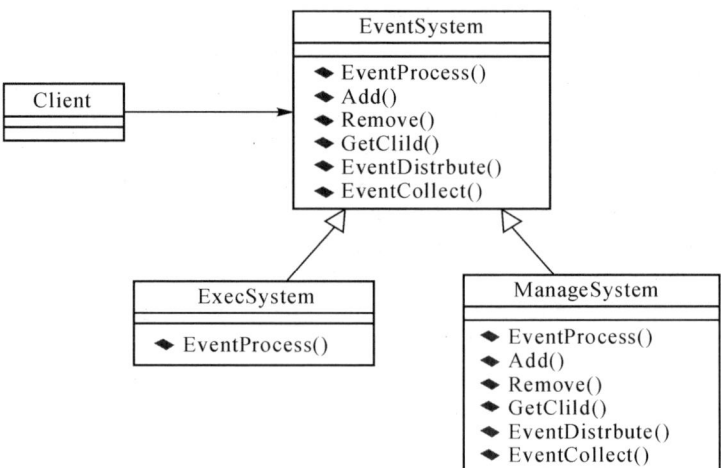

Fig. 2. 10   Basic structure of event-driven pattern

register an event interface for an object to bring this object into the system, and this do not impact other system objects. (4) It defines the class hierarchy structures that include both operation subsystems and management subsystems. The subsystems in the event-driven system can be composed to form a more complicated management subsystem, and this subsystem can also be composed. It is recursive. In customer code, any quote citation to operation subsystems can be replaced by a management subsystem, and the transparence to users is implemented. (5) Simplify users' code. Users can call the operation subsystem and management subsystem using the same way. In most cases, users do not know, and do not care about whether they have called an operation subsystem or a management subsystem. (6) This kind of style can make system design more general. We can easily add new subsystem. But at the same time, there may be some problems: it is hard to constraint operation subsystems in management subsystems. At some times, system designers hope a management subsystem can only have some special subsystems, but using recursive structure. We can not achieve this goal, we must check it in the running time.

The event-driven based system also have the following disadvantages: (1) the most deadly disadvantages of event-driven based system is: the components weaken the control ability to system computing. When a system publishes an event, it can not make sure this event will certainly be responded by system's other objects. Even if it can make sure the event will be responded by other objects, it can not make sure the sequence that the objects will respond. (2) Another problem in event-driven system is the data sharing. In many cases, system designers must define some shared buffers, so that objects in the system can exchange data. In this case, how to guaranty shared data can be visited properly becomes a key problem. The data consistence applications' results in database theory may provide beneficial methods. (3) The logical relationship in systems becomes more complicated. Because the call relations between objects are not fixed, in different cases, the same object may generate different results when activated, that is to say, the object implementation is context dependent, it is impacted by the current status when activated.

The event-driven architecture style often requires independent components. Independent components are a form of distributed system, so they may exist the potential performance loss. In the design of architecture structure level, the performance attribute is processed in the boundaries between components (this is just opposite to optimization's implementation). The communication pattern may depress performance; so, when designing independent components, we must consider the cost of communication itself. If we use authorized communication or asynchronous communication, the communication between components may be less, but each communication may includes more data. For the interactive systems driven by users' command, the communications between components may be frequent but each communication includes small size of data.

Some reader may ask: what is the difference between event-driven style and object-oriented style? Are they the same? From the OOP's view, event-driven and object-oriented concepts are the basic concepts in object-oriented languages, such as Java, C# . Just as described above, the object-oriented based systems are composed by many encapsulated objects, objects communicate with each other through message transfer, and event-driven is just an implementation of message transfer mechanism. Hence, the event-driven based systems generally are object-oriented, but the objects in systems do not only include member variable and member methods, but also include a series of events, which are called objects' event interfaces.

The event interfaces define events that some objects must process. When these events occurred, the process program about this object's event will be activated, thus forming the event-driven mechanism. Obviously, objects in system do not only receive and process events passively, they may generate some events. At this moment, we may associate this mechanism with Fig. 2. 11. Events' generation process and trigger process run round and round, the whole system are running in this way. This is basic characteristic of event-driven based system.

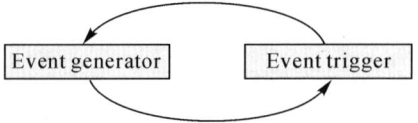

Fig. 2. 11   Event's generator and trigger

2. 4. 2   Study Case

Event-driven is the core of JavaBean architecture. In this part, we will take event-driven in JavaBean as example, to provide a reference real system for readers.

JavaBean system treats some components as event source through event-driven mechanism, these component can generate events that can be received by description environment and other components. So, different components can be composed together in the container tools. The components transfer information through events, so application is formed. In conceptual level, event is a transfer mechanism that exists between "source objects" and "listener objects". Events have many different usages. In Windows applications, we must process mouse events, window boundary events and keyboard events. In Java and JavaBean, a general, extendible event mechanism is defined, this mechanism can: (1) Provide a common framework for event type, transfer model' definition and extension, which is suitable for wide application. (2) The high integration with Java language and its environment. (3) Event can be captured or triggered by description environment. (4) Make other construction tools control events, events' resource and events' listeners' relationships directly using some technologies. (5) The event mechanism itself does not dependent on complicated developing tools.

Besides implementing the basic functions described above, the event-driven mechanism in JavaBean can realize the following special functions: (1) can find events that specified object classes generate. (2) Can find events that specified object classes listen. (3) Can provide a general register mechanism, which permit the dynamic operations to the relationships between event source and event listeners. (4) Can implement without other virtual machine and language. (5) Event resource can transfer events efficiently with event listeners. (6) Can accomplish the neutral reflection mapping from JavaBean's event model to other relative components architecture's event model.

In the following parts, we will describe the mechanism of JavaBean in short. Events' transition from event source to listeners is through the call of Java methods to listening objects. For each explicitly generated event, we define according explicit Java method. These methods are integrated in the event listener interface, this interface must inherent abstract class java.util.EventListener.

The classes that implement some or all methods defined in event listener interface are event listeners. Along with the generation of events, the according states are encapsulated in the events' status object, this object must inherit java.util.EventObject. Event status object is transferred into the response event listeners as the parameters.

The identifier of event source that gives out certain event is: to define register method for event listeners conforming to the design patterns' rule, and to accept the reference of event listeners interface instance.

At some times, event listeners can not directly implement event listener interface, or there are other extra actions, we must insert an event adapt class instance between source and other listeners, to build the relationships between them.

Event state object: the state information that is relative to event generation is generally encapsulated in an event state object; this object is the subclass of java.util.EventObject. In accordance with convention, this event state object class' name is ended with Event, such as "MouseMovedExampleEvent".

Event listener Interface and event listener: because Java event model is based on method call, we must define and organize the patterns of event operation methods. In JavaBean, event operation methods are defined in the EventListener interface that inherits java. util. EventListener class. Conforming to the rule, the EventListener must end with Listener. Any class that wants to operate with the methods defined in the EventListener interface must implement this interface. This type of class is called event listener.

Event listeners' registration and cancellation: to make the possible event listener register itself into the proper event source, and build the event flow between source and event listener, event source must provide registration and cancellation method for event listener. In real cases, the event listener uses standard design patterns to implement its registration and cancellation.

We will introduce a type of class: adaptive class. Adaptive class is a very important part in JavaBean event model. In some applications, the events' transfer from source to listeners must go through the adaptive class to retransmit. For instance, when event source send an event, many event listeners can receive this event, but only one specified object response. We must insert an event adaptive class between event source and event listener, and this adaptive class specifies listeners that must response to this event.

The adaptive class is event listener. In fact, event source register adaptive class behaves as listener into the sequence of listener, but the real event responder does not response in the sequence. The action that event listener must do is fixed by adaptive class.

At last, we will continue to introduce the elevator example. If you do not understand the problem statement, you can refer to Section 2.3, which will make you easier to understand the content of this part.

In object-oriented languages, an Event is a message that notifies an object of an action that has already happened. For example, in this section, we modify our simulation so the Elevator sends an elevatorArrived event to the Elevator's Door when the Elevator arrives at a Floor. The Elevator opens this Door to determine the actions to take when the Elevator has arrived, such as notifying the Person that the Door has opened. This reinforces the OOD principle of encapsulation and models the real world more closely. In reality, the door—not the elevator "notifies" a person of a door's opening.

In our simulation, we create a super class called ElevatorModelEvent that represents an event in our model. ElevatorModelEvent contains a Location reference that represents the location where event was generated and an Object reference to the source of that event. In our simulation, objects use instances of ElevatorModelEvent to send events to other objects. When an object receives an event, that object may use method getLocation and method getSource to determine the events' location and origin.

For example, a Door may send an ElevatorModelEvent to a Person when opening or closing, and the Elevator may send an ElevatorModelEvent informing a person of a departure or arrival. Having different objects send the same event type to describe different actions could be confusing. To eliminate ambiguity as we discuss what events are sent by objects, we create several ElevatorModelEvent subclasses, as shown in Fig.2.12. So we will have an easier time associating each event with its sender. According to Fig.2.12, classes BellEvent, PersonMoveEvent, LightEvent, ButtonEvent, ElevatorMoveEvent and DoorEvent are subclasses of class ElevatorModelEvent. Using these event subclasses, a Door sends a different event (a DoorEvent) than does a button (which sends a ButtonEvent).

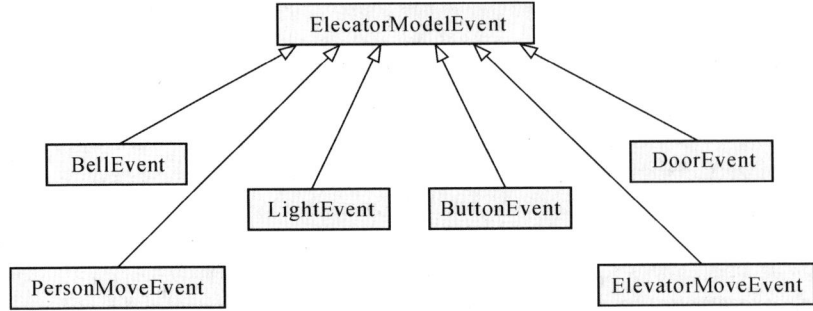

Fig. 2. 12   Class diagram that models the generalization between ElevatorModelEvent and its subclass

The concept of event-driven in software architecture style is similar to the concept of event handing in Java. In Java programming language, the Event handling consists of an object of one class sending a particular message (which java calls an event) to objects of other classes listening for that type of message. The difference is that the objects receiving the message must register to receive the message; therefore, event handling describes how an object sends an event to other objects "listening" for that type of event—these objects are called event listeners. To send an event, the sending object invokes a particular method of the receiving object while passing the desired event object as a parameter. In our simulation, this event object belongs to a class that extends ElevatorModelEvent.

We now present a collaboration diagram in Fig.2.13 to show the interactions of two Person objects—waitingPassenger and ridingPassenger—as they enter and exit the Elevator.

According to messages 1, 2, 3 and 4, the Elevator performs only one action—it sends elevatorArrived events to objects interested in receiving those events. Specially, the Elevator object sends an ElevatorMoveEvent using the receiving object's elevatorArrived method. Fig. 2. 13 begins with the Elevator sending an elevatorArrived event to the ElevatorButton. The ElevatorButton then resets itself (message 1.1). The Elevator then sends an elevatorArrived event to the Bell (message 2), and the Bell invokes its ringBell method, accordingly (i.e., the Bell object sends itself a ringBell message in message 2.1).

The Elevator sends an elevatorArrived message to the ElevatorDoor (message 3). The ElevatorDoor then opens itself by invoking its openDoor method (message 3.1). At this point, the elevator is open but has not informed the ridingPassenger of opening. Before informing the ridingPassenger, the ElevatorDoor opens the

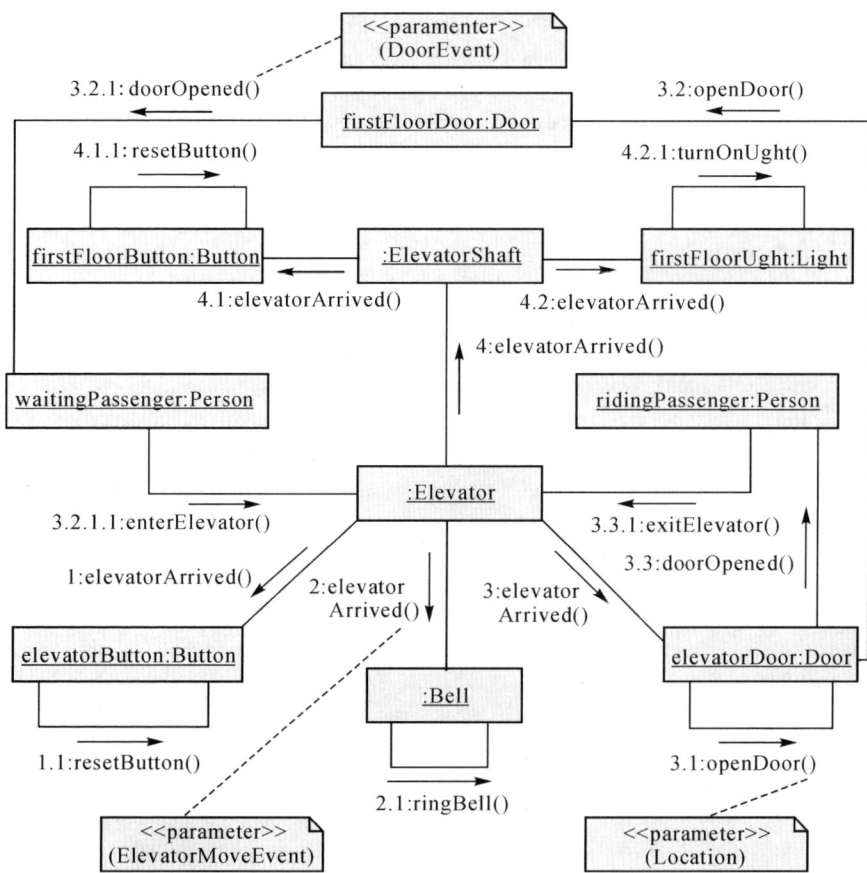

Fig. 2. 13   Collaboration diagram for passengers entering and exiting
the Elevator on the first floor

firstFloorDoor by sending an openDoor message to the firstFloorDoor (message
3.2)—this guarantees that the ridingPassenger will not exit before the firstFloorDoor
opens. The firstFloorDoor then informs the waitingPassenger that the
firstFloorDoor has opened (message 3.2.1), and the waitingPassenger enters the
Elevator (message 3.2.1.1). All messages nested in 3.2 have been passed, so the
ElevatorDoor may inform the ridingPassenger that ElevatorDoor has opened by
invoking method doorOpend of the ridingPassenger (message 3.3). The
ridingPassenger responds by exiting the Elevator (message 3.3.1).

According to messages 1, 2, 3 and 4, the Elevator performs only one action—it
sends elevatorArrived events to objects interested in receiving those events.
Specially, the Elevator object sends an ElevatorMoveEvent using the receiving
object's elevatorArrived method. Fig. 2.13 begins with the Elevator sending an
elevatorArrived event to the ElevatorButton. The ElevatorButton then resets itself
(message 1.1). The Elevator then sends an elevatorArrived event to the Bell (message

2), and the Bell invokes its ringBell method, accordingly (i.e., the Bell object sends itself a ringBell message in message 2.1).

Lastly, the Elevator informs the ElevatorShaft of the arrival (message 4). The ElevatorShaft then informs the firstFloorButton of the arrival (message 4.1), and the firstFloorButton resets itself (message 4.1.1). The ElevatorShaft then informs the firstFloorLight of the arrival (message 4.2), and the firstFloorLight illuminates itself (message 4.2.1).

We demonstrated event handling between the Elevator and object ElevatorDoor using the modified collaboration diagram of Fig. 2. 13—the Elevator sends an elevatorArrived event to the ElevatorDoor (message 3). We first must determine the event object that the Elevator will pass to the ElevatorDoor. According to the note in the lower left-hand corner of Fig.2.13, the Elevator passes an ElevatorMoveEvent (Fig. 2. 13) object when the Elevator invokes an elevatorArrived method. The generalization diagram of Fig.2.12 indicates that ElevatorMoveEvent is a subclass of ElevatorModelEvent, so ElevatorMoveEvent inherits the Object and Location references from ElevatorModelEvent.

For an event-driven architecture style, the Event handling is one important part. In this example, the ElevatorDoor must implement an interface that "listens" for an ElevatorMoveEvent—this makes the ElevatorDoor an event listener. Interface ElevatorMoveListener must provide methods elevatorDeparted and elevatorArrived that enable the Elevator to notify the ElevatorMoveListener when the Elevator has arrived or departed. An interface that provides the methods for an event listener, such as ElevatorMoveListener, is called an event listener interface in java programming language.

Methods elevatorArrived and elevatorDeparted each receive an ElevatorMoveEvent object as an argument. Therefore, when the Elevator "sends an elevatorArrived event" to another object, the Elevator passes an ElevatorMoveEvent object as an argument to the receiving object's elevatorArrived method.

The example's basic events sequences are described above. Generally speaking, the event-driven mechanism is necessary for every object-oriented system. Because every object must communicate with other objects through messages, and messages can be treated as an event sent to other objects. The return value for a method call can also be treated as a kind of event. After receiving the return value, the original object can do some according actions, isn't it an event driven?

We will give another example. In the Turbo Pascal 6.0 developed by Borland Company, an object-oriented event-driven programming tool package named Turbo Vision is provided. Turbo Vision classifies visual object on the screen into two types: one is operation object, the other is management object. They are called TView and TGroup respectively. Yet TGroup and TView have some common things, so TGroup is inherited from TView. In the Turbo Vision, TGroup's object do not do real action, do not show itself in the screen, but show it through its subclass' object. All of the real actions are done through the TView class.

Turbo Vision well incarnates the soul of object-oriented method and event driven programming design. Tapplication is a runable interactive programming. Except starting and exiting, it does not provide any function. Using Turbo Vision, users can develop the high quality application program effectively and quickly. Fig.2.14 shows the objects' structure in the Turbo Vision software package.

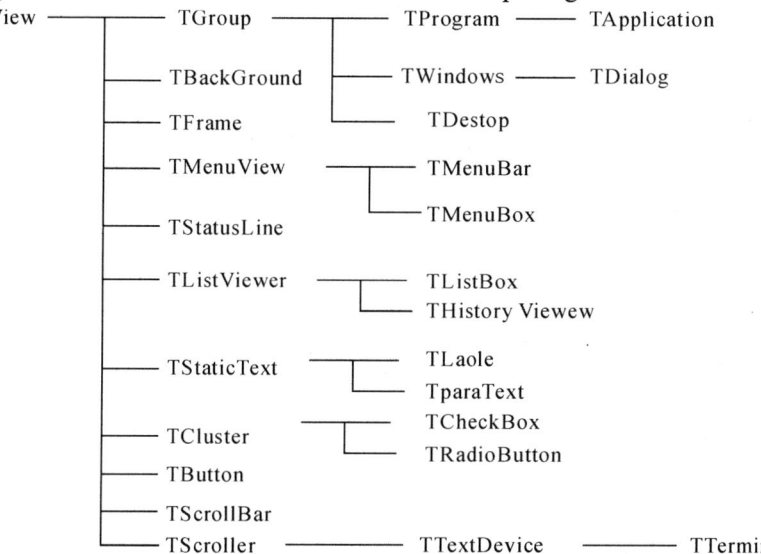

Fig. 2. 14   Objects' structure in Turbo Vision

Generally speaking, Tapplication has three sub-object called TMenuBar, TDeskTop and TstatusLine. The TDesktop has its own sub-object TBackGround. In the practical run time, Application creates a variety of TWindows classes and TDialog classes, and delegate DeskTop to manage. The DeskTop objects' installation is changed with the running of program. The Twindows object and TDialog object also modifies with the difference of application, the typical TWindows and TDialog objects' installation structure are shown in the Fig.2.15.

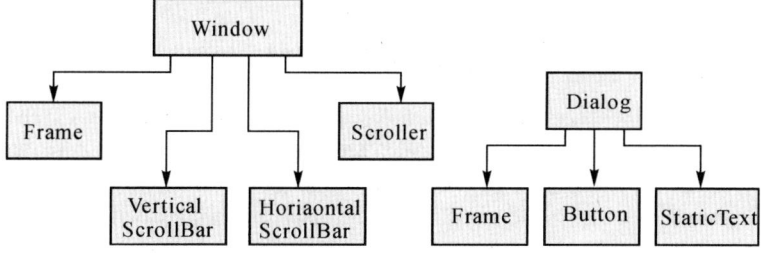

Fig. 2. 15   The structure of TWindows and TDialog's object

Turbo Vision abstract events into three types: location event, aggregation event and broadcast event. The typical location event is mouse event, TGroup class view brings the location event to sub-view that manages this field; the typical aggregation event is key event and command event. TGroup class view brings this event to the low level view that is in the aggregation status; broadcast event is the event that the management view do not know whom to bring it to, for this kind of event. The TGroup will bring it to all its views.

When the Turbo Vision program is running, the object of Tapplication will collect mouse events, key events and all other events, then bring them to the low level objects to deal with in certain rule. For instance, for the mouse events, if it occurs in the menu bar, then it will bring the event to the menu bar to deal with; if it occurs in the status bar, then it will bring it to the status bar to deal with; if it occurs in the DeskTop, then it will bring it to the DeskTop to deal with. In a word, the detailed problems are always dealt with by the low level object. The task of status bar and menu bar is to translate the key events and the mouse events in its own place into command events, then hand in them to Tapplication.

2.5   Hierarchical Layer

2.5.1   Style Description

A layer system uses the hierarchical organization. In this type of system, every layer must take two roles. First, it must provide services for the upper layer in the structure. Second, it must call the lower layer's functions as the customer of the lower layer. Besides these two roles, any layers in the whole system must satisfy these two requirements at the same time. At the meantime, the highest layer has no higher layer, it need not provide any service; the lowest layer has no lower layer, and has no function to call. In some layer systems, inner layer only communicates with the adjacent outer layer in the system, and is transparent to other layers. In some special conditions, for the requirement of processing, inner layer may open some service for other layers to call. In this case, the layer system's components in different layers form virtual machines that have different function level, every virtual machine communicates with each other according to the protocols fixed when the system was designed, but for the layers that are not adjacent, the communications between them are constrained. A conceptual layer system model is shown in Fig.2.16.

In Fig.2.16, three layers are shown. The core level is the basis of the whole system, the lowest level's function calls are implemented by the core level; the function level is on the middle level of the whole system, which is adjacent to the lowest level and the highest level. It not only visit services provided by core level, to implement its own function, but also provide functions that the highest level will use; the highest level is an interface to the outer environment for the whole system, users can visit functions that the whole system provides by visiting the highest level. In these three levels, there are many function components, every level is a virtual machine composed by a component. Every virtual machine communicates with each other through system design's protocols (they may be standard protocols

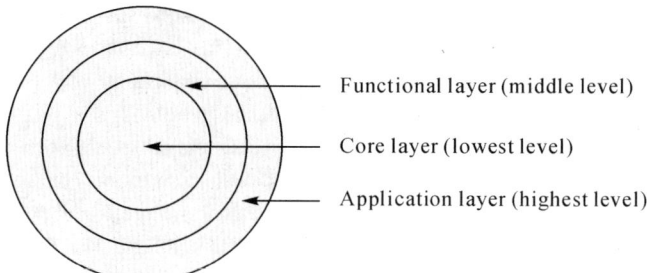

Functional layer (middle level)

Core layer (lowest level)

Application layer (highest level)

Fig. 2. 16 Layer model

or completely personal protocols), the communication manner is incarnated by procedure calls.

Of course, the shown layer model figure is only a sketch map. In real applications, the function level is not composed by only one level. It may composed by many levels, which collaborate with each other, form an integrated system that has powerful functions.

The layer style has some advantages that system designers can not reject:

(1) Layer style supports the gradual abstraction in system design process. When the system designers design the system, they can decompose the complicated functions that the whole system must implement into many different levels, for these levels themselves, they can pretty simple, their functions are increasing. That is, the original problems are decomposed by designers using layer style pattern. We divide system from its function, and incarnate the changes in function by system design; at last, the complicated software architecture is formed. (2) The layer system has good extendibility. Just as we described in pipes filters style, if a system has good extendibility, when one part of the functions or their implementation changes, the whole system will not be influenced much. Combining with layer style's characteristics, this advantage can be described as: If system's function or implementation on one level changes, these changes are only relative to their adjacent levels, that is to say, at most, two levels in the whole system are influenced. If the modifications on this level are only some functions' concrete implementation technologies, and the interfaces for outer environment are not modified, then the adjacent levels almost have no influence. Because the concrete implementations in every level are transparent for other levels, and the adjacent level only communicates with each other through procedure calls, conforms to the communication protocols between layers, the details about services are independent to the called layers. (3) The layer style support software reuse. This characteristic about the layer style is similar to the object-oriented style, that is, if the interfaces are consistent, the different implementation on the same level is used alternately. Because of experiences, technologies, develop time and economic benefits and so on, when the system is first designed, some levels' implementation may not be ideal. With the changing of the constraint, system designers may modify the original design blueprint about these levels, or they may improve the original levels'

implementation. At this time, the second, third versions of these levels' design appear. But if we can guaranty that all these versions have the same interface, then these versions can replace with each other without constraint, and the replacement will not influence systems' other layers or the whole system's function. At present, many standardization organizations use the layer style methods to define the standard function level interfaces, but do not constraint the implementation methods. So, if the different software manufacturers conform to the standard interfaces, they can develop the production themselves, and the finished software production can be integrated with production developed by other software manufacturers. This is very important for computer system integration companies.

In Stephen T. Albin's view in "The Art of Software Architecture: Design Methods and Techniques", hierarchical layer is not a real architecture style. He considers layer as the basic attribute of large complicated software architecture. In Stephen's view, all of the complicated systems have different layers, this means there exists a basic architecture structure view that represents system's composition. So, Stephen did not describe the hierarchical layer in single part.

But in our opinion, not all systems are suitable to be designed using layer style. For some systems, though we can divide system's function into different levels conceptually. We have to combine the high level function and the low level implementation together for the performance reason; this enhances the coupling of different levels. In addition, which level is suitable for the abstracted functions? This is also a headachy problem for system designers, especially. If we want to build a standardization general layer structure, the problem is especially serious. The advantage of layer style is the abstraction of function level and the low coupling between them. This is just the implementation difficulty. So, system designers have to find a balance between the concept design and concrete implementation.

2.5.2 Study Case

In the design of computer networks, we use the layer style methods. Similar with mails' sending process, the data transfer also has many steps, and each step is finished by one or many special layers. So, network protocol designers divide every parts of computer networks into many layers according to their function. Each of these layers can be treated as an independent black box, a close system. Users only care about the outer characteristics of each layer; they need to know the input, output and data process' definition of each layer; they also need to know what to do with data, and which data is suitable to transfer into the lower layer. Every layer in the network is built on the basis of its higher layer, it only receives data from the higher layer, and only need to be in charge of the provision of services for the lower layer.

In network application design, customers only care about the outer characteristics of each layer, but do not care about the details in each layer. This makes each layer becomes an isolation, when one layer' detail change, the functions in other layers will not be influenced. Hierarchy design is the basic methods to describe network architecture, and the architectures that designed using this method always have the characteristics of hierarchy.

In the following part, we will describe the ISO/OSI reference model as example, so as to show the application of layer style.

ISO/OSI uses the 7-layer hierarchy architecture. From the highest level to the lowest level they are: application layer, representation layer, session layer, transfer layer, network layer, data link layer and physical layer, as showed in Fig.2.16. The highest layer is the seventh layer—application layer, which is used to exchange data with application service; the lowest layer is the first layer, physical layer, which is used to connect physical transfer medium so as to implement the real data communication; the associations between layer and layer are implemented through the interfaces between layers. The higher layer requests services to the lower layer through interfaces and the lower layer provides services for the higher layer. When two computers communicate through network, only the two physical layers can implement the real data communication through medium. The direct communication relationship about the other layer that is on the same layer does not exist. The layers that are on the same level can only implement virtual communication through protocols of their layers.

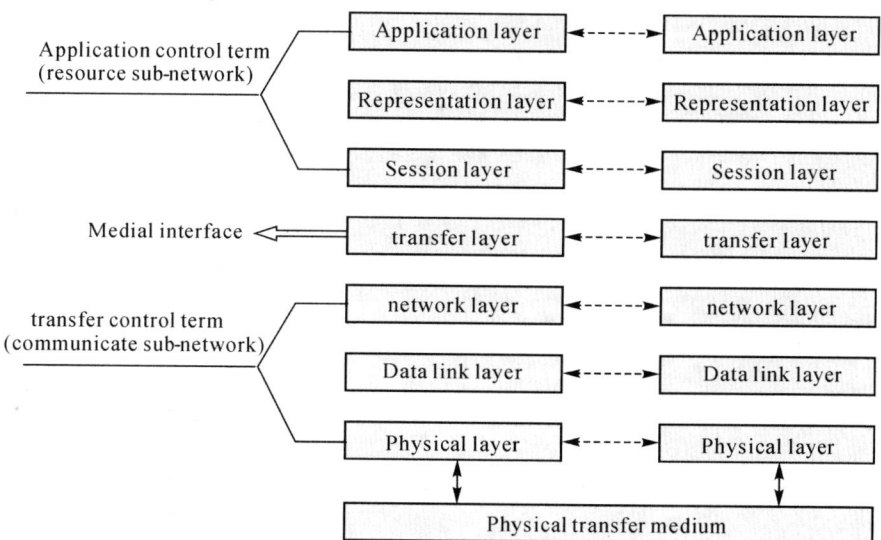

Fig. 2. 17 ISO/OSI network 7-layer architecture

To understand the function of every layer in ISO/OSI, we will take the transport company's goods transport as example in this part. This familiar example is helpful for you to understand the abstract concepts. The 1st ~ 3rd layers in the ISO/OSI reference model are similar to the transport details, the concrete operation methods of the goods transfer process in transport company; the 4th layer is similar to the interface between transport company and customers; the 5th to 7th layers are similar to the prepare work that the customer hands in goods to transport company.

The first layer is physical layer. It is in charge of the transport of original bit flow on the physical channels. It should provide the mechanical, electrical, functional, and rule requirement for the building, maintenance and demolishment of physical data link. This is similar to: the transport cars only need to pick up goods, and transport them to the destination, but these cars do not need to know the goods' detail, and how these goods are encapsulated.

The second layer is data link layer. Its main function is error correction and data flow control, to provide the errorless transfer on the physical layer that may suffer form errors. It must build the data link between the adjacent nodes on the basis of physical layer, provide frame's errorless transfer through the error control mechanism, and control the data flow of each link. This is similar to the transport management and quality supervise department, which must guaranty the finish of task on the transport lines that may have some problems.

The third layer is network layer. Its main function is routing control, congestion control and data package. It must provide building, maintenance, and cancellation of network methods for the higher layer's data transfer, divide data from higher layer into packets, transfer them among nodes, and be in charge of the routing control and congestion control. This is similar to: transport company need to divide goods into many packages, find a line from the source address to destination in the current traffic network. When finding the proper line, they must consider whether this line can reach the goal address, whether this line is congested, whether this line is secure and reliable, and how much the cost of this line would be, etc.

The above layers all belong to the details and concrete operation that the transport company must be in charge of when goods are being transported. But the 4th layer is similar to the interface between Transport Company and customers.

The 4th layer is transport layer. It is an interface for its higher and lower layer. It must provide the peer to peer (end user to end user), transparent, reliable data transfer service for the higher layer. The so called transparent transfer is: when communicating, higher layer can treat the lower layers as a close black system; the transfer layer shields the transport system's details for the higher layer. This characteristic is similar to: Transport Company often sets up the business contact office in many places, these offices are in charge of building a bridge for goods' handing over and taking over between customers and company, so that customers need not to take care how the Transport Company transport these goods to destination, that is to say, the business contact offices shield the goods transport details from customers.

The 5th layer is session layer, its main function is in charge of the handover work for data sending and receiving. In addition, it also organizes and manages data. It must provide functions of building, maintenance and session cancellation for representation layer, and provide session management service. This is similar to Customer Company's mail room; it communicates with Transport Company, finishes mail transition services, and then organizes the goods to be mailed in Customer Company.

The 6th layer is presentation layer. Its main function is providing the concrete style and normal form for data's sending and receiving. It must provide the information representation style for application layer, such as the exchange of data patterns, the text compression and encryption technology. This is similar to person who is in charge of goods' sending and receiving in the Customer Company. It communicates with the department or person in the Customer Company who want to send or receive goods. When gathering goods that are to be sent, he will tell customers how to fill in the tables; when sending goods, he will tell customers what must be done, etc.

The 7th layer is application layer. Its main function is to provide a variety of mail patterns for data. It must provide a variety of application services for network customers and applications, such as file transfer, e-mail, distributed database and network management. This is similar to: when the inner departments or people in the Customer Company want to mail something, they must conform to the relative rules in the Customer Company, and can only use the way in which the Customer Company permits to mail goods. On the other aspect, Customer Company also must provide a variety of mailing ways for its inner departments and people, so that the departments and people in the Customer Company know which way they can use to send or receive goods.

In the above paragraphs, we described the ISO/OSI hierarchy in detail. The ISO/OSI network functions can be classified from two different aspects:

The first aspect is from the data process division, it can divide ISO/OSI 7 layers into 3 terms: the first and second layers solve the problems about network channels; the third and fourth layers solve the problems of transfer services; and the fifth, sixth and seventh layers deal with the visit to application process.

The second aspect is from the data transfer control, it divides ISO/OSI 7 layers into 3 terms: the lowest three layers (the first, second and third layer) can be treated as transfer control term, this term is in charge of communication sub-network, and it solves the problems of communication in network; the highest three layers (the fifth, sixth and seventh layers) are in application control group. This group is in charge of processes that are relative to resource sub-network, and solves the information transformation problems between application processes; the middle layer (the fourth layer) is the interface between communication sub-network and resource sub-network, this layer is the bridge that connects transfer and application.

The second term classification method is just mutually agreed with the goods transport example. The transport control term is similar to the Transport Company's concrete details and operation style in the goods transport process; the application control term is similar to Customer Company's preparing work for the goods transportation; the interface in the middle layer (the 4th layer) is similar to the interface between transport company and customers, generally, we call this contact office sets in distinct places by Transport Company.

As readers know, the active webpage technologies develop quickly in nowadays, and are used widely. In 2003, Microsoft published the Visual Studio 2003, one of its new products is asp Nct. Using asp Net, developers can develop active desktop quickly, and the process is pretty simple. In Microsoft's demos, the active website is a system that includes several layers. Generally speaking, the system may include web layer (also called representation layer), the business logic layer, and the data access layer. Each layer has its own task, it provide service for the upper layer and call the lower layer's function to implement its own function. This is just the characteristics of layer architecture style. We will describe one of its demo called Duwamish 7. 0. Through learning this example, users will know how layer architecture style is widely used, and know how the layer architecture style's theory is used in practical user cases. So, you may understand why in the book "The art of software architecture", the author does not treat layer style as a architecture layer, but an attribute of complicated system; you will also understand why the author thinks you should not judge whether the system must be divided into layers, but how the system should be divided into layers.

Duwamish Books Inc. is a virtual company that sells books on the internet. In this virtual company the typical B2C pattern is current electronic commerce. The basic information flows in B2C pattern are implemented, such as user login, account management, category view, search, shopping cart, etc. Duwamish 7.0 provides deep-rooted analysis and help for the developers who want to design, develop and deploy the software product that based on NET technologies. Based on this system, users may understand how to generate reliable, extensible and high performance applications.

In Duwamish 7.0, many new technologies are used, such as Windows XP server, ASP NET, Web-based windows, Server controls, C # programming language, Internet information service, ADO NET, etc. But in this example, we will not introduce these technologies respectively. Instead, we will give an overview of the whole system's layer, so as to make readers know how the layer architecture is widely used in typical systems.

The main functions in Duwamish 7.0 include six modules. The first is category overview. Users can search books by category. System provides 18 categories, including: anthropology, art, biography, commerce, computer, etc. The second is book search. Users can use dropdown list or other relative text boxes to search the books they want. The key fields to search book include: book name, ISBN, authors, and subject. The third is shopping cart. In the shopping cart, the books user has already bought are shown. It also provides the function to modify the count of this type of book for user. The fourth is user login. Before entering the account management or clearing, users must login Duwamish 7.0 through email and password. If one user has not registered new account, a "create new account" button is provided to create a new account. The fifth is account management. System can show user's account information, and also permit users to modify the account information. But, before modifying account information, users must first have registered accounts and login the system. The sixth is order process. After choosing books, users can make order and finish the transactions. In Duwamish 7.0, the whole system is organized as Fig.2.18.

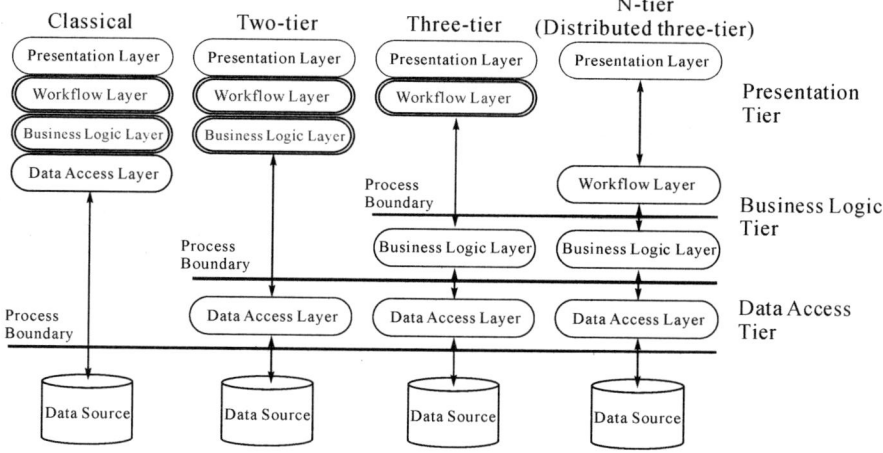

Fig. 2. 18　　The architecture structure of Duwamish 7.0

From this figure, we can see that the whole system is combined by four layers. The first layer is web layer, it is also called client. It provides the access to application, and is composed by web-based windows and corresponding code file. The web-based windows only provide operations for users using HTML, and the code file implements the event processes of controls that lay on the web-based windows.

The second layer is called Business Façade. This layer provides interfaces for accounts process, categories overview and buying books. The Business Façade layer is in fact an isolate layer, it isolates the user interface and a variety of operations' implementation. Besides the low level system and support function, all the calls to database server are through this layer. That is to say, all the user commands are processed by this layer's program. And in this layer, all the functions are implemented by calling the methods in Data Access layer.

The third layer is Business Rule layer. This layer is in charge of the implementation of operation rules and operation logic. For example, the operation rule will finish the tasks such as the validation of user account and book orders. Why do the system designers abstract this layer from the second layer? Their goal is to make the system more flexible. For instance, if customers want the designers to evaluate this system so as to meet new requirements, we only need to modify the Business Rule layer. But in some systems, the Business Rule layer is not an independent layer. Readers must know, the more layer the system has, the more flexible the system is, but the more complicated and lower performance at the meantime.

The fourth layer is Data Access layer. This layer provides data services for operation rule layer. For example, if the operation rule layer wants to search all the books ordered by a certain user, it will call the methods in data access layer. Data access layer is the only layer that knows the tables' attributes and the entity relationship of the whole database. Then data access layer will generate proper SQL, and get returned value from database, or call the stored procedure. Database is transparent for the other layers, so other layers can vary respectively as long as the Data Access layer's interfaces are not modified.

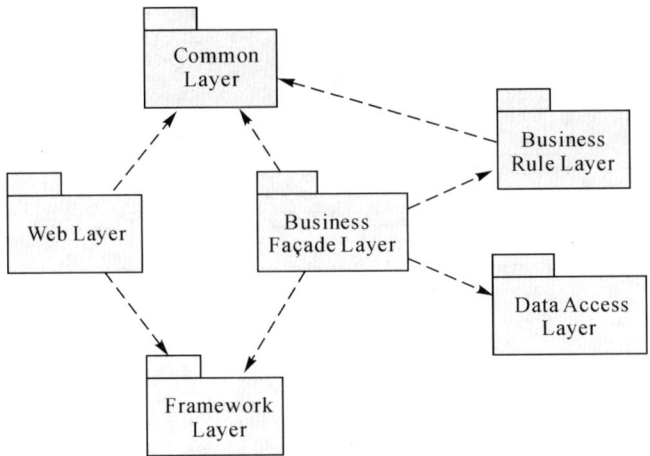

Fig. 2. 19   The package structure of Duwamish 7.0

Besides these four layers, there are two another special layers: the Common layer and Framework layer. Why do we call Common layer a special layer? The reason is: all other layers will use this layer's classes. In fact, the Common layer do not do any real work, it defines the entities and datasets that must be translated between different layers. For example, in Duwamish 7.0, we must define User entity, Book entity, Order entity, etc. The Framework layer has the information of program's configuration and tracking. For example, if we want to make the Session unable, we only need to modify the file "web.config" in the framework layer, but not do other work in other layers. If we want to record errors when system is running, we only need to modify the file that is in charge of recording logs. The relationship between these layers can be described as Fig.2.19.

2. 6   Data Sharing

2. 6. 1   Style Description

The data sharing style is also called repository style. When designed by this style, system often has two distinct functional components: the first one is central data unit component, it represents every state in the current system; the other is the set of some relatively dependent components, these components can operate the central data unit. In this case, the information exchange between central data unit (which is also called repository) and outer components set becomes the first pivotal problem in the system that is based on data sharing style. Because of the differences of functions the system must implement, information exchange patterns are also distinct from one another.

The differences of information exchange leads to the difference of control strategy. Here are two main control strategies. Just because of the difference of the control strategies, systems based on repository style can be divided into two sub-classes. If a system is driven by information services of input data flow, that is, the input data flow's information services can trigger the running of system's according process, this system can be called application system based on traditional database type repository style. On the other hand, if system is driven by current state of the repository, that is, the system runs different processes according to the different states in the current central data units, to response to state change of repository, this system can be called the application system which is based on blackboard type repository style. The blackboard type repository model is shown as Fig.2.20.

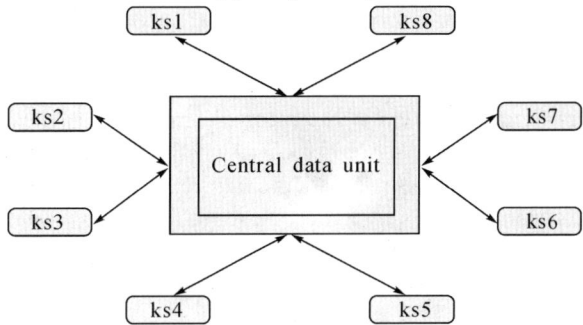

Fig. 2. 20　Blackboard type repository style system

From the figure mentioned above, we can clearly find that, a typical blackboard type repository style system is composed by three parts:

(1) Knowledge source. System that is based on repository style absolutely relies on the change of repository states. In this case, the build of knowledge base, which is also called knowledge source, becomes the first problem to be solved in system design. In Fig.2.20, "ks" represents knowledge source, and is the main information source in repository. These knowledge sources are all independent in logical and physical aspects; they are only relative to the applications which generate them. The multiple data sources cooperate with each other through the coordination of central data unit, they are transparent for outer environment.

(2) Central Data unit. Central data unit is the core component of the whole system, it defines and analysis the problems that system must solve at first, then summarizes the multiple states that may appear when the system is running, and design the according procedure to deal with the desired states. Hence, the data in the central data unit is not only pure data, but also represent some system status which belongs to status data. These data are provided by data source, organized together by some data structure style, and are

modified by the change of data source information, so the functions of the system are implemented.

(3) Control unit. The drive of control unit is completely directed by the state change of repository. The knowledge source inputs the information that system must process into repository continually, this leads to the state information modification of knowledge; when the modification of states matches some predefined control strategies, the according control operations are triggered, so the function control of system is implemented. From Fig. 2. 20, we can not find the explicit representation of control unit, because the control unit is not a independent unit in the system based on repository style, it can appear in the knowledge source or repository, or exist independently as an independent component. Control unit has no fixed style; designers must design it according to the concrete conditions.

2. 6. 2   Study Case

In this part, we will give the Expert System as example, to show the application instance of repository style. A typical Expert System is a good application of data sharing style.

Artificial Intelligence is one of the three most cutting-edge technologies in current world, and Expert System is the most mature field in Artificial Intelligence applications. It combines with pattern recognition, intelligent robots, and becomes the three most active fields in Artificial Intelligence technologies. We are proud to say, repository is just the basis of Expert System, and Expert System is a perfect instance of repository style. In fact, Expert System is a set of programs. From the functional aspects, we can define it as "a program system that has the expert problems solving ability in a certain fields." This system can work like fields experts, using the fruitful experience and expert knowledge, giving high level solution for a special problem in short time. From the structure aspects, we can define it as "a problem solving program system composed by a special fields' knowledge base and a component that can acquire and apply the according knowledge." The research of Expert System creates a new subject, which is called knowledge engineering, whose key research topic is knowledge acquisition, knowledge representation and knowledge consequence.

Expert System works as follows: it acquires knowledge in a special field and the experience that summarized by people in long time, imitates human experts' thinking law and process patterns, using certain consequence mechanisms and control strategies, to perform and reason by computer, so that the experiences of expert become shared resource, and the difficulty of expert lack is overcome. The core content of expert system is knowledge base and consequence mechanism. Its main components includes: knowledge base, consequence machine, work database, user interface, interpreter program and knowledge acquisition program. Expert System's general structure is shown as Fig.2.21.

In the following part, we will introduce the main components in ES in brief.

The first component is man-machine interface. Man-machine interface is the

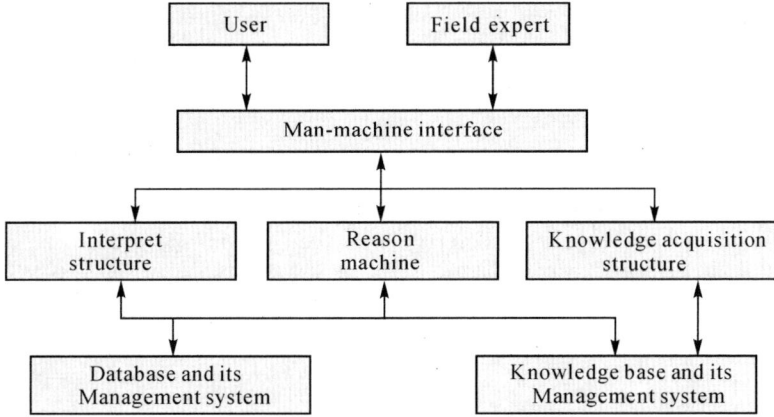

Fig. 2. 21   The basic structure of ES

interface between expert system and field expert, knowledge engineer and general users. It is composed by a set of program and the according hardware, and it finishes the input and output work. Through man-machine interface, field expert or knowledge engineer inputs, updates and perfects the knowledge base; through man-machine interface, general users can input the problems to be solved or ask questions to the expert system; system can output the operation result through the man-machine interfaces, answer the questions or ask for further facts from users.

In the process of input and output, man-machine interfaces must change information representation from inner style to outer style. For instance, when input something, they may transform the field expert, knowledge engineer or general users' input into system's inner representation, then hand over them to different structures; when output something, they transform the inner representation into the outer representation that is easy to understand, and show them to the according users.

The second component is knowledge acquisition structure. This is the knowledge acquisition structure in the expert system; it is composed by a set of programs. Knowledge acquisition structure's basic task is to input knowledge into the knowledge base, and guarantee the consistence and integration of knowledge. In different systems, the function of system acquisition and its according implementation methods are different. In some systems, the knowledge engineer first acquires knowledge from expert, then inputs the knowledge into knowledge base through some according knowledge edit software; some other systems have learning ability themselves, and they acquire knowledge from fields expert directly, or summarize new knowledge through the operation practice of system.

The third component is knowledge base and its management. Knowledge base is the storage agency of knowledge, it is used to store the basic knowledge of fields, the experience knowledge of expert, and some related facts, etc. The knowledge in the knowledge base is from the knowledge acquisition structure, in the mean while, it provides the required knowledge for the reasoning machine. The knowledge base management system is in charge of the organizing, searching and maintenance of knowledge base. In expert systems, any departments must ask for the management system if they want to communicate with knowledge base. In this way, the knowledge base management system can implement the uniform management and usage for knowledge base.

The fourth component is reasoning machine. Reasoning machine is the "thinking" agency of expert system, which is the core part of the expert system. The reasoning machine's main task is to imitate the thinking process of field expert, control and operate the solving process of the desired problem. According to the known facts, using the knowledge in the knowledge base, it can reason with a certain reason method and control strategy, get the problem's solution or prove the correctness of a certain assuming.

The performance of the reasoning machine is relative to the knowledge representation and organization style, but has no relation to the knowledge's concrete content. This is helpful to guaranty the independence between reasoning machine and knowledge base, that is to say, if there are some modifications in the knowledge base, we need not to repair the reasoning machine. But a severe problem we must face is, if the searching strategy of reasoning machine absolutely has no relation to the field problem, system performance will decrease much, especially when the scale of the field problem is extremely large, the problem may become a disaster. To solve this problem, on one hand, expert system uses some inspiring knowledge; on the other hand, it guaranties the independence of reasoning machine and knowledge base, and uses meta knowledge to represent the inspiring knowledge.

The fifth component is database and its management system. Database is also called "blackboard" or "integrated database", it is used to store the initial facts and the results conducted by every step in the reasoning process. According to the content in database, the reasoning machine chooses proper knowledge from the knowledge base, arranges them, and then saves the conducted result into the database. From this process, we can find that database is a work space that can not lack in the reasoning machine, because it can record the detailed information in the reasoning process, it provides the basis for the interpreter structure to answer users' advisory. Database is managed by the database management system; this has no essential difference with the database management in general program design, but we must guaranty the consistence between data's representation style and knowledge' representation style.

The sixth component is interpreter structure. The interpreter structure is also composed by a set of programs, and it can track and record the reasoning process. When users ask for interpretation, it will process according to the requirement of the problem, at last, it gives the interpreter answer to users through man-machine interface using the agreed patterns. When constructing a real expert system, we must not only consider these components, but also consider other additional components according to the characteristics of the field problems. For instance, when constructing the decision making expert system, we must add decision model lib; when constructing the expert that has complicated computing work, we must add algorithm lib, and so on.

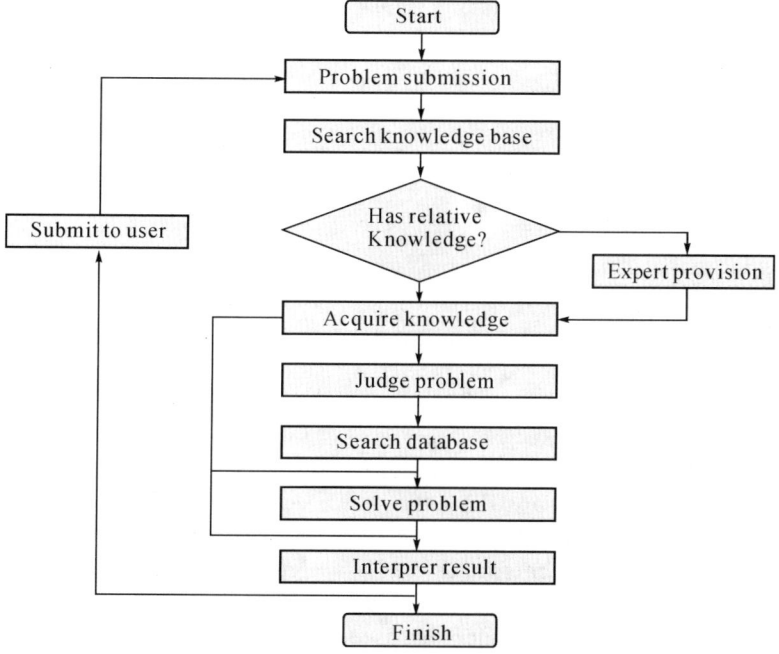

Fig. 2. 22　The workflow of ES communication method

In the last part of this session, we will describe the communicating method of expert system. Since knowledge base is the basis of expert system, in the communication of expert system, the main process is the operation to knowledge base controlled by reasoning machine. In the process of reasoning relied on knowledge, it is possible that expert must control in real time, to modify and complement the knowledge base. In the following part, we will use a simple instance to describe this process. The main workflow is shown in Fig.2.22.

At first, users submit the problem that he wants to solve; then the man–machine interface does the pretreatment work, so that reasoning machine can recognize the problem description. Under the control of reasoning machine, the expert system start searching the knowledge base, to require the desired knowledge K; if there is no available knowledge, the acquisition to expert provision is interrupted; otherwise, under the knowledge and reasoning rule, the reasoning machine judges the problem, then start searching data in the database. Under the available knowledge and acquired data, the reasoning machine solves the problem, gets the result R, then R is interpreted by the interpret machine. At last, the interpreted result is handed in to users through the man–machine interfaces.

In this process, the knowledge application of knowledge base is in all the phases, such as problem judgment, solving, and interpretation. The reasoning mechanism does the real operation using knowledge. Control to knowledge base when communicating is mainly implemented through the reasoning machine. At the same time, knowledge base can dynamically adjust the reasoning machine's content and mechanism, so as to achieve the goal of continuing learning.

2.7 Virtual Machine

2.7.1 Style Description

In some books, virtual machine style is also called interpreter; both virtual machine and interpreter style refer to the same thing. We think because Java is a language that uses interpreter to run the program, and Java has the characteristics of "Write once, run everywhere", and the interpreter is also called virtual machine, the virtual machine is equivalent to interpreter.

The core of system based on interpreter is the virtual machine. This type of machine often includes the pseudo code that is to be interpreted and the interpreter engine. Pseudo code is composed by the source code that must be interpreted and the middle code is generated by the interpreter engine analysis; the interpreter engine includes the syntax interpreter and the current state of the interpreter. So the interpreter has four compositions: an interpreter engine that finishes the interpreter work; data store field that includes the pseudo code; a data structure that records the current state of the interpreter engine; and a data structure that records the progress of the interpreted source code. The relationship between them is shown as Fig.2.23.

Some authors think layer system is a type of virtual machine, because every layer provides the interfaces to lower layer. The interpreter programs and rule-based systems share characteristics that have common essence, because they all provide semantic layer for some technology's top. The activation model of interpreter program is based on the interpreter program engines that read and execute command. In this mean, the interpreter engines activate every command.

Just similar to other architecture styles, the interpreter programs and rule engines can combine with other architecture style. For instance, interpreter programs can be activated when some certain rules or triggers are activated. An interpreter program, such as workflow engine, can control the system states that bring the rule to be triggered. The client and server components can be written using interpreter program style.

The virtual machine style has many real applications. An enterprise software developer often provides the application platforms based on virtual machine style, but not a single application. This method permits the max flexibility, because systems are customized by some certain program language or some user-defined operation rule, but not through the static parameter's configurations. This flexibility

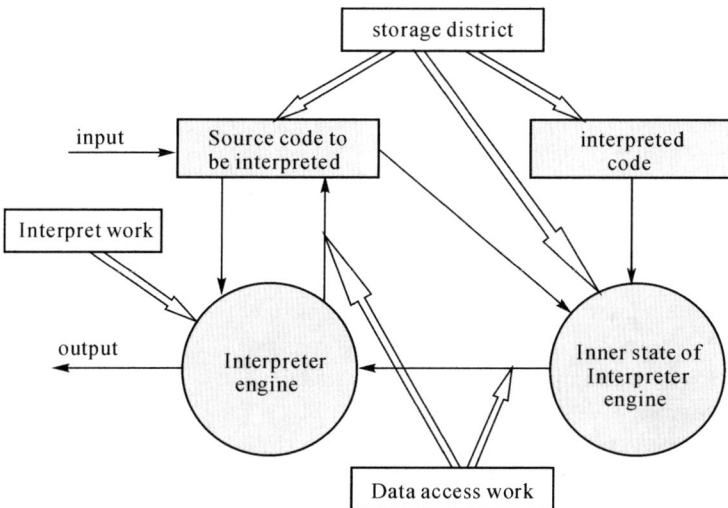

Fig. 2. 23 Interpreter style

also brings the cost problem; interpreter program systems are hard to design and test. You can not generate all the programs that are possible to be executed, so you can not test your interpreter in your programs fully. In some systems, only part of components are designed using interpreter program. For instance, a system can be configured or customized using workflow component, this is a type of virtual machine. Generally speaking, workflow language is not a universal language that has limited and simple grammar. But at the end, customers can customize the application's process rule and model the operation process and rule. Any enterprise application's developer must provide virtual machine as part of the whole software architecture.

2.7.2 Study Case

The interpreter style's applications in pattern matching and language compiler aspects are pretty mature in nowadays. We think it is boring and obscure to statically describe the interpreter style system in theory, so we plan to describe a Boolean expression interpreter, to analysis the running process of system based on interpreter.

Boolean expression evaluation is a common problem in science computation. The evaluation problem can be solved in many ways. In this part, we will take the syntax searching match as the theory basis of Boolean expression evaluation, to analysis and solve the expression evaluation problem from the syntax match perspective.

If the occurrence of a special syntax match problem is high enough, it is necessary to express the grammar of every instance as a language's sentence. Through this method, we can construct an interpreter. This interpreter can solve the syntax match problem through interpreting these sentences. The regular expression is the standard language to describe string. Compared with constructing a special algorithm for every pattern, it is better to use a general search algorithm to interpreter a regular expression, which defines the string set to be matched. The operation result of the regular expression's interpretation is the final result of the Boolean expression.

In this instance, we describe how the interpreter-based system defines a grammar for the simple language, how to represent a Boolean expression in this language, how to interpret these expressions, and how the Boolean expression is computed. If we use regular expression to describe this simple Boolean language, then the content of this instance can be summarized as how to define a Boolean expression for regular expression, how to represent a special Boolean regular expression, how to interpret this regular expression, and how to get the result of the Boolean expression.

If we use class in the object-oriented pattern to represent every grammar regular, then the right side of the rule's symbols is the instance variable of these grammar rule class, and the grammar rule is represented by six classes: one abstract class BooleanExpression and its five subclasses: AndExpression, OrExpression, NotExpression, VariableExpression and Constant. The variable defined in the subclasses represents the sub-expression. The abstract class and its subclass's UML class diagram are shown as Fig.2.24.

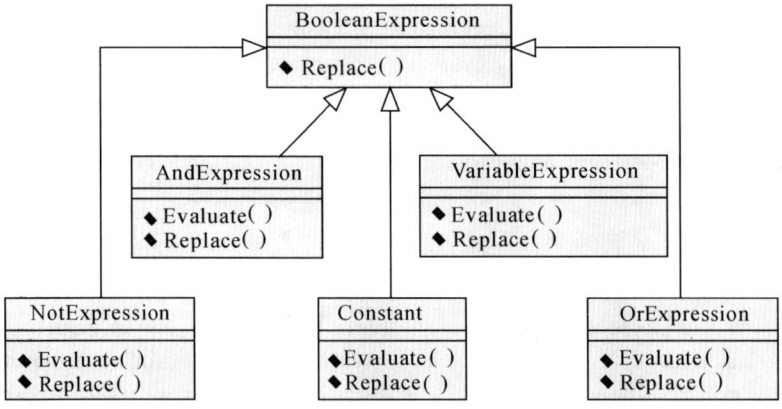

Fig. 2. 24   Boolean expression evaluation system

Every regular expression defined by this grammar is represented as a abstract grammar tree composed by instances of these classes, every node in this tree is an object instantiated by one of the five subclasses. These nodes are organized together similar to the binary tree's structure, forming the "interpret engine". For example, if we meet this expression:

(true and x) or (y and (not x))

We can define a grammar tree as shown in Fig.2.25 according to the above grammar.

If we define an evaluate operation for every subclasses of BooleanExpression,

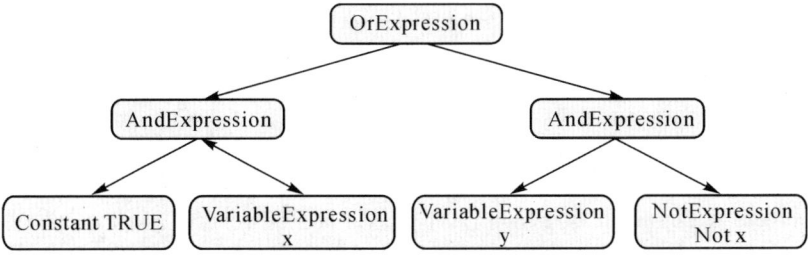

Fig. 2. 25   The instance of BooleanExpression abstract grammar tree

we can get an interpreter for these Boolean regular expressions. The interpreter treats the context of this expression as a parameter. The context includes the input Boolean expression and the information about the matched part of this Boolean expression. This context can be viewed as the "inner state of the interpreter engine". To match the following part of the Boolean expression so as to evaluate the value of this expression, every subclass of the BooleanExpression must implement the evaluate operation on the basis of the current context, these subclasses coordinate with each other, forming the "interpreter engine" of the interpreter model in this figure. For instance, the AndExpression will interpret and operate the "and" operators; the OrExpression will interpret and operate the "or" operators; the NotExpression will interpret and operate the "not" operators in the BooleanExpression; the VariableExpression and Constant will evaluate the variable and constant of the Boolean Expression.

It is obvious that the systems based on interpreter style have typical advantages and disadvantages:

(1) When the grammar rule is pretty simple, the interpreter will work well, but things will go to the other end when the grammar rule become especially complicated. The layers of the grammar will become large and hard to manage; the system must include many classes that represent the grammar rules. In this case, tools such as the grammar analysis program generator are a better choice. The grammar analysis program generator needs not to construct abstract grammar tree, nor to complete the interpretation of expression. It has advantages both in time and space.

The most efficient interpreter is not implemented by directly interpreting grammar analysis tree. It first transforms the grammar analysis tree into another form. For instance, regular expression generally can be transformed into state machine. Even in this case, the style of interpreter still can benefit much.

(2) The Boolean expression is easy to modify and extend grammar. Because interpreter style uses class to represent grammar rule, users can use inheritance to modify or extend grammar. The existed expressions can be extended by using incremental style, and the new expression can be defined as the variant of the old expression.

(3) It is easy to implement grammar. It is similar to define the class of every node in the abstract grammar tree, and these classes are easy to write directly.

Generally, they can be automatically generated by compiler or grammar analysis generator.

In this part, we will describe the roles in the Boolean expression system. Generally speaking, there are five roles in this type of system. The first one is BooleanExpression. This role declares an abstract evaluate operation, this interface is shared by all the nodes of the Boolean expression abstract grammar tree. The second role is TerminalExpression (such as VariableExpression and Constant). This type of role implements the evaluation operation in the BooleanExpression that are related to terminals, every terminal in the Boolean Expression needs an object instance of this class. The third role is NonterminalExpression (such as AndExpression, OrExpression and NotExpression). Every rule in the Boolean expression grammar needs an object instance of NonterminalExpression, and we must maintain object instance of Boolean Expression for every symbol in every rule in the Boolean expression grammar. We also need to implement the evaluate operation for every NonterminalExpression in the grammar. In the NonterminalExpression evaluate operation, we must call the evaluate operation for every symbol in the grammar. The fourth role is context (this is "the inner state of interpreter engine"). It includes the global information besides the interpreter. The fifth role is client. Client will constructs a special Boolean expression's abstract grammar tree in the Boolean expression's definition, and this abstract grammar tree is composed by the instance objects of TerminalExpression and NonterminalExpression. The client will also call the evaluate operation.

The collaboration relationship between these five roles can be simply described as follows:

At first, the client constructs a Boolean Expression, which is an abstract grammar tree which is composed by instances of TerminalExpression and NonterminalExpression. Then the client initiates the context and calls interpret operation. Then every NonterminalExpression defines the evaluating operation of the according expression, and all the evaluating operation of the expression forms the basis of recursive evaluation. At last, the evaluating operation of every node uses the context to store and access the states of interpreter system.

In this and the following part, we will introduce the implementation methods of Boolean expression evaluation system. When encountering the real implementation of Boolean expression, we have many details to deal with, and the process quality of these details directly influences the whole system's performance. These problems mainly incarnate in the following aspects:

The first problem is to construct the abstract grammar tree. The interpreter style does not specify how to construct an abstract grammar tree in detail, that is to say, the interpreter style does not involve syntax analysis. But when we are constructing an abstract grammar tree, we need to use a table-driven grammar analysis program to finish this task; we can also use the recursive decline grammar analysis program to construct the abstract grammar tree.

The second problem is how to define the evaluating operation. In fact, evaluating operation does not need to be defined and implemented in the expression's classes. If we need construct a new interpreter frequently, we can use the Visitor style in design pattern theory, put the evaluating operation in an independent "Visitor" object, this method may be better. For instance, a program design language has many operations on abstract grammar tree, such as type check, code optimization and code generation, etc. A proper way is to use a visitor, so as to avoid defining this operation in every class.

The third problem is the shared terminals. In some grammars, many terminals may occur in the same sentences (such as true and false in Boolean expression evaluating system). In this case, it is better to share the copy of that symbol. The terminal nodes usually do not store their positions in the grammar tree, in the process of evaluation, any context information they required is transferred by their parent nodes. So, the inner state and outer state in the terminal node are explicitly different. We can implement those using Flyweight design patterns.

In the implementation of Boolean expression evaluation system, we define two operations in the Boolean expression. The first operation is Evaluate, which evaluate the value of the specified Boolean expression in the context, and this context must provide "true" or "false" for every variable. The second operation is Replace, which replaces a variable with an expression so as to generate new Boolean expression. The Replace operation makes the system can not only finish the evaluation of Boolean expression, but also do the grammar analysis of the Boolean expression. Because of the manuscript length constraint, we will not describe the implementation details of each subclasses.

The interpreter style has an important characteristic: we can use many operations to "interpret" the same sentence. Among the three operations we defined in the BooleanExpression, the evaluate operation is the basic operation in the process of computing Boolean Expression. It interprets a Boolean expression and returns a simple result. But in the above system, we do not only have the evaluate operation, the replace and copy can also be treated as interpreter, and the only difference is the interpretation for the sentence.

2.8   Feedback Loop

2.8.1   Style Description

The so-called object control means make the controlled objects (or the controlled process), function or characteristics, reach the desired target. In this context, "target" means the performance characteristics which meet the specified rule, or in certain constraint, partly reach or approach the best one.

To design a control system successfully, we must know the controlled objects' properties and characteristics. At the same time, we must know the variation of these properties and characteristics with the modification of other factors such as environment. In the procedure of running, the controlled system can "recognize" or "master" the controlled object through measuring the characteristics of the controlled objects, and make control strategy according to the current characteristics of controlled objects that they have mastered, so that system's performance can reach the optimal condition or approach the optimal condition.

Control engineering is a specialized field that emphasizes methodology very much; hence, the control engineering methods are absolutely independent of other application fields. Although the problems they deal with are similar in essence, they need not to be engineering problem; they may also be in non-engineering's dynamic systems, such as biology, economics, sociology and informatics. The feedback loop style just borrows ideas from the kernel of process control system theory. It indrafts the control theory into computer software architecture, analysis and comprehends the functional components' interaction from the process control perspective, and applies them. To abstract the process control method from the pure control field, we will introduce the concept of dynamic system in the following part.

Dynamic system represents a functional unit that processes and transfers the signals (for instance, signals can be energy, materials, information, fund, or other forms). The causes are treated as system's input, and the effects in time are treated as system's output. Systems that only have one input and one output are called single variable system (such as measure organ, amplifier); systems that have multiple input and multiple output are called multiple variable system (such as distillation column, blast furnace); systems that have many layers are called hierarchical system. The dynamic system is fit for all these three systems.

Systems that are defined in this way have common characteristics. There are target's function, information process, closed loop control process, open loop control process, just as N. Wiener said, and the above concepts can all be summarized by the advanced concept which is called cybernetics. The aim of cybernetics is to recognize the common things of control process and information process in nature, engineering technology and sociology, and applies these analysis results to the integration of engineering system and improvement of nature system. Of course, this can also be applied in the construction of software architecture.

2.8.2 Study Case

The systems based on feedback loop architecture style can process the complicated adaptive problems; they are especially widely used in product line's automatic control software. Most of the MES also use the feedback loop style. In this section, we will give you a simple example to describe its basic characteristics.

Machine learning is an important search area in Artificial Intelligence; it is concerned with the development of algorithms and techniques that allow computers to "learn". At a general level, there are two types of learning: inductive and deductive. Inductive machine learning methods create computer programs by extracting rules and patterns out of massive data sets. It should be noted that a process employing pattern extraction should be categorized as data mining more accurately.

Fig.2.26 shows the basic model of machine learning. At first step, the training examples are input to the learning component, so that this component contains the basic information to be queried. At second step, the real data can be inputted to get result. After learning component's analysis and computation, the desired results are outputted. But at the same time, the learning component will check the results' invalidation, and then the check result will be fed back to learning component. Through this loop, the learning ability of learning component is improved, the knowledge in learning component is extended.

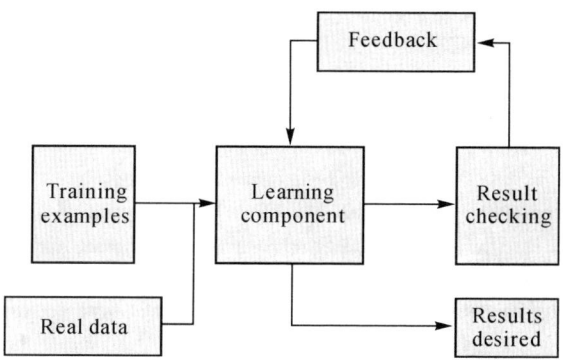

Fig. 2. 26   Machine learning model

2. 9   Comparison among Styles

Each architecture style has its own characteristics, advantages, disadvantages and applications. In this part, we will give a comparison among seven architecture styles from these four aspects.

The first is Pipes filters architecture style. Each functional component has a set of input and output; the filters are independent, and have no necessity to communicate with other filters; each filter reads data from its input interface, processes these data, and then outputs them to the output interface. The Pipes filters architecture style is easy to support reusability, easy to maintain and evaluate, supports special analysis and concurrent. But at the same time, this type of architecture style must process corporate data between two independent filters, and has poor interactivity. This type of style is used in communication fields and compiler systems.

The second style is object-oriented. In this type of style, data representation and operations to these data are encapsulated; objects of class are in charge of their integration. The methods' calls are considered to be connectors. For a certain object, only its interface is known to its outer environment. The advantages of OO style are the high modularization, code encapsulation, code sharing, easy maintenance, and good extendibility. The disadvantages of OO style are: callers must know the identification of called object's method, when the identification of an object is modified, it must notify all the objects that may call its method, which makes the system have high coupling. OO style is widely used as long as the systems are implemented by object-oriented programming languages such as Java and C#.

The third architecture style is event-driven architecture style. Systems based on this type of architecture style are composed by many subsystems or elements. The whole system has some certain goals, and works on the collaboration of message mechanism. Among those subsystems, there is one dominate subsystem which is in charge of the whole system's running. Each element has event collection mechanism and process mechanism. This type of style is easy to process the concurrent and multiple tasks, and has good extendibility. Subsystems can be composed to form more complicated management system; the customer code can be simplified. Just opposite to Pipes filters style, event-driven style supports good interactivity. But event-driven style has the following disadvantages: system's computing control ability is weak, hard to share data, and the logic between objects is complicated. Generally speaking, the integrated developing environment can be considered as event-driven.

The fourth architecture style is layer system. The whole system is decomposed by many layers. Each layer provides services for the upper layer, and accepts services from lower layer. This type of style supports graduate abstraction and software reusability, and has good extendibility. But because of the graduate call of methods, performance of the whole system is influenced. The typical layer system is network protocol.

The fifth architecture style is data sharing, which is also called repository style. Central data units are shared. It provides data access and store service for some modular. The whole system has a control unit. This type of architecture style has good extendibility of knowledge base, can solve special field problem, so this type of architecture style is usually used in expert system such as language process and pattern recognition.

The sixth is interpreter style. It has fixed structure, persuade code and interpreter engine. The interpreter engine includes its definition and its operation states. Systems based on this style can process the special field problems. The typical application is compiler.

The seventh is feedback loop style. The most typical characteristics of feedback loop are: the learning component, or the decision-maker component, can improve its ability through learning and information updating. The typical application is MES system.

From the comparison of these seven architecture styles, we can find a common quality attribute in all these architecture styles: Good extendibility. In fact, by the principle of software engineering, good software is always closed for change, and open for extend. Software that is hard to extend is certainly not good one, so an architecture style that can not support system's extendibility will not be popularized. Each style has its certain environment to use; it tends to get a good quality attribute at the cost of sacrificing other quality attributes. For instance, pipes filter style has bad interactivity, while event-driven style has good support to user interactivity; event-driven style is hard to share common data, while repository's most typical advantage is data sharing.

2.10 Integration of Heterogeneous Styles

After the detailed description of each architecture style, reader may have intuitive and academic knowledge about software architecture style. But all the introduced knowledge is introduced independently. As a matter of fact, all the architecture styles not only have strong relationships, but also are used together in most cases. For a practical system, you can not even judge it as A style, B style, or C style. Classifying it to any single architecture style has no abundant reason. This type of system can be called complicated system; the construction mode of this type of system is called the integration of heterogeneous patterns.

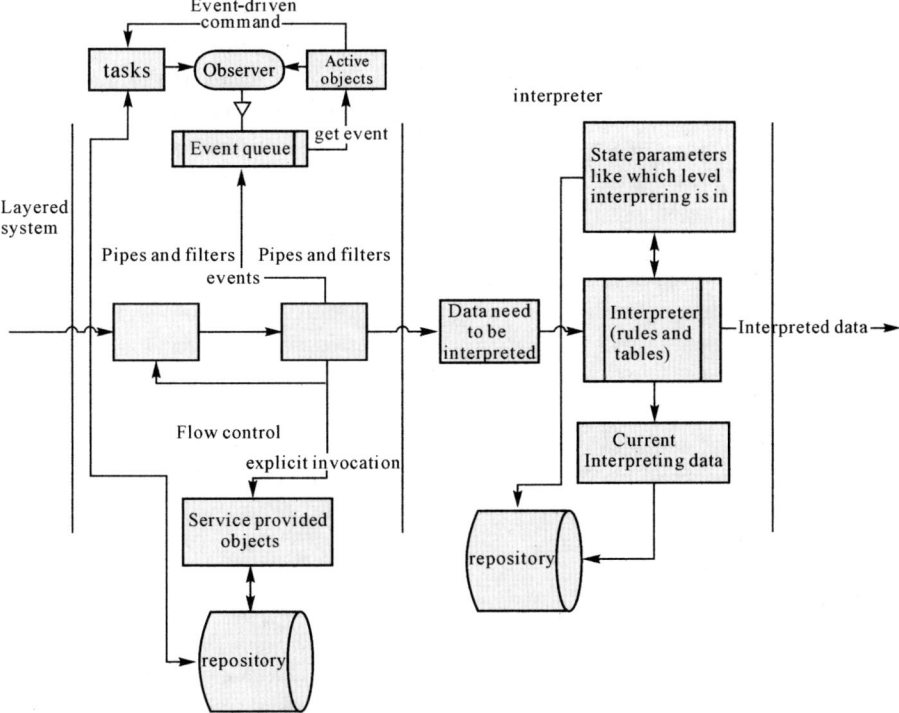

Fig. 2. 27   A heterogeneous system model

Fig. 2. 27 shows the architecture of a virtual system that integrates many architecture styles. The whole system can be treated as a layer system. In this case, it is divided into two layers: the first layer is the original data generation component, and the second layer is an interpreter.

In first layer, the main component is pipes and filters. Data in first filter can be sent to the second filter. When the second filter receives the data, it will generate corresponding messages, and then sends them to event queue component and service-provided objects component. While the event queue is not null, it will activate the corresponding objects to process the events, so as to finish the tasks. This part is a typical instance of event-driven architecture style.

When the service-provided component receives messages sent from the second filter, it will record the message in repository, which is another important component in the system. The repository component is just similar to the blackboard in the data sharing architecture style. In this repository, all the information, knowledge, and rules are recorded. When the "event-driven" part wants to finish some tasks, it may need to query useful information from the repository, then does correct action according to the rules. This part can be seen as a combination of data sharing and feedback loop. Because all the data are shared in the component repository, other components can access and retrieve data from it. Users can update the repository by recording new data into the repository, so the component also has the characteristics of feedback loop architecture style.

In the second layer, data from the first layer is interpreted. When interpreting data, component must know the context, the rule and the state of the interpreting machine, so there are state component, rule component and data component respectively. All the errors and bugs generated when interpreting are recorded in the repository. At last, the processed data are outputted.

From this example, we can see that a perfect system can be composed by a variety of architecture style, depending on the requirement of each component in the system, and the advantages of each architecture style. As we said earlier in this chapter, architecture styles are just some common patterns that are widely used in software engineering fields. They help developers to well understand the whole system and the quality attributes. But we can not subject ourselves to the concrete forms of each architecture style. The best system you have designed is not a system that contains the "so called" architecture style, but the one where you use the architecture style most properly, and the designed system which has the most required quality attributes.

2. 11   Summary

In this chapter, we first describe the fundamentals of software architecture style and patterns. We know that architecture styles are large scale patterns which have been used frequently, and achieve good quality attributes in some aspects. We also know that these architecture styles are classified in different aspects. For instance, a system not only can be classified into layer system if it is decomposed into several layers, but also can be classified into object-oriented style if data and operations are encapsulated into classes. At last, we declare that almost no system has "pure" architecture. That is to say, most large complicated systems are combinations of different architecture styles, each of which can reach its own quality attributes. So placing different style in their proper places will reach good system design quality attributes, this is just the benefit of using architecture style.

Software design has three levels. The lowest level is programming level; this is the most concrete level. In this level, we consider the structure of program such as loop and condition branch, etc. This level is relative to programming language. The second level is design patterns. In some components, we may use abstract factory pattern, or singleton pattern, etc. These patterns will help us to make the special component have better extendibility, or reach good quality attributes. This level is transparent to programming language. The highest level is software architecture. This level considers the organization of the whole system, which can make the whole system have high performance, good extendibility, or some special quality attributes according to their special requirement. After reading this chapter, readers have to know the abstraction level of architecture style and its usability.

We describe the characteristics of each style, and give plenty of examples to show the application of that style. At the end of this chapter, we compare these styles from four aspects: architecture style's characteristics, advantages, disadvantages and applications. We find these styles all have good extendibility. Besides, each style can reach its special quality attributes at the cost of sacrificing some other quality attributes. The best way to achieve the benefit of software architecture style is to use each of them in designed system's most proper places; this is the topic of integration of heterogeneous patterns, at this part, we give a virtual system that uses many architecture styles as illustrating example.

We do not list all architecture styles in this chapter. As a matter of fact, we are impossible to list all of them, because they describe systems from different perspectives and have special quality attributes, especially in some special domain application fields. In our opinion, readers should not put their main time in remembering the described architecture style; they should understand the relationship between qualities attributes and the corresponding architecture styles; they also should comprehend the reflection from activate model to architecture style. The design thoughts are most important for each of architecture style. Only when you know what should do to reach your requirement, such as high performance, good data sharing, good data encapsulation, and how to implement your ideas through using proper architecture style, the goal of this chapter is reached.

References

(Albin, 2003)   Albin, S. T. *The Art of Software Architecture: Design Methods and*

Techniques, John Wiley & Sons.2003.

(Giarratano, 2005)   Giarratano, J. C. & Riley, G. D. *Expert Systems Principles and Programming* 4th ed.: Course Technology.2005.

(Shaw, 1996)   Shaw, M. & Garlan, D. *Software Architecture: Perspectives on an Emerging Discipline*, Prentice Hall.1996.

3

Application and Analysis of Architectural Styles

3.1 Introduction to SMCSP

3.1.1 Program Background

In recent years, mobile e-commerce and e-government have an enormous market prospects. With mobile users' continual increase, business of data transmission via mobile equipment has multiplied, users have brought up higher requirement on how to obtain a more direct and convenient e-commerce/e-government information and services. Furthermore, the speedy development of mobile e-commerce causes further strong demand of mobile collaborative business (government); how to construct mobile collaborative commerce (government) platform has become a challenging issue.

In the past phase, the traditional collaborative technology has been introduced to the field of mobile computing. Such integration formed a mobile collaborative technique, which caused great concern of the universities, research institutions and corporations such as Microsoft, Oracle, IBM, Nokia, Motorola and so on. Mobile Cooperation/Collaboration concept originated from the contribution of Mark Weriser who presented the possibilities of wireless communications and interaction in the office environment using portable mobile equipments. The first industrial application, the Mobile CSCW (Computing Support Collaboration Work) system, is the MOST multimedia collaboration system developed by British Lancaster University in 1995. In 1998, two scholars of Cambridge University—P. Luff and C. Heath presented the necessity of mobility support as CSCW system researchers.

Microsoft, Oracle, IBM, Nokia, Motorola and other companies or research organizations focused on the enterprise application which are applying traditional CSCW to the mobile computing environment; research institutions such as CMU, Brunel, Cambridge mainly focus on audio and video collaborative process, collaboration data transmission in wireless network, and so on. In China, Tsinghua

University, Shanghai Jiaotong University are also in the stage concerning theoretical study and laboratory research without application system.

The core of mobile e-commerce application system is a platform supporting mobile collaboration services. The platform consists of mobile communications equipment and internet; it is an e-commerce system which can facilitate both mobile service providers and mobile equipment users. Mobile communications equipment and SMCSP, SMCSP and service agents provided by mobile services providers communicate based on TCP/IP protocol. After mobile users register to SMCSP, they can subscribe the needed service (the service must have been registered to SMCSP). In addition, the platform also processes some collaborative tasks.

Mobile collaboration is the use of mobile computing technology and traditional collaboration techniques to make a group of members to work together for a common goal and also maximum interest of groups. The main issues of mobile collaboration includes: support for mobile collaboration, dynamic configuration, service independency, support for multiple types of network protocols, system platform independency and extensibility and so on. Employing multiple mobile agents framework is one of the effective ways to solve these issues. The concept of mobile agent is brought up by General Magic Corp. in its commercial system in the early 1990s; it is a new generation of key technologies of distribution following CORBA, EJB.

Mobile agent is a procedure which can move independently from a host to another host in heterogeneous networks, and exchange resource with other agents. It actually combines agent technology and distributed computing technology. By mobile agent technology the service-request agent dynamically moves to the server for implementation, so that the agent depends less on the transmission of network and directly faces the server resources; thus the large amount of data transmission network is avoided and network bandwidth dependence is reduced. Mobile agent does not require unified scheduling; an agent created by the user can run asynchronously in different nodes, and transmit results to the users after tasks are completed. In order to complete a certain task, users can create a number of agents; those agents run in one or more nodes at the same time, which forms capacity of parallel computing.

MMAS(Multiple Mobile Agent System) faces many problems of which the most crucial one is collaboration between agents. Multiple agent collaboration is necessary because of resource and time constraints and it can make multiple agents correspond to solve the problem. The collaboration is a key conception distinguishing the agent systems between other related areas such as distributed computing, object-oriented technology and expert systems.

MMAS mainly aims to make knowledge, desire, intention, planning of multiple agents correspond to achieve mobile collaboration. Combining mobile agent technology with collaboration technology is an effective way to solve the issue of mobile collaboration.

SMCSP is a mobile collaboration application framework supporting third-parties service employing mobile collaboration technology. The main issues of SMCSP are:

- knowledge framework presentation of mobile collaboration users (members), tasks and actions
- mobile resource discovery mechanisms
- computing resource scheduling and computing movement mechanism
- mobile network instability handling mechanism
- remote control of collaboration users' state at mobile state
- multiple groups (users) real-time collaboration mechanism
- mobile network congestion and protocol optimization handling
- mobile security mechanisms
- common problems in mobile collaboration
- openness, system platform independency and application independency
- dynamic configuration

3.1.2   Technical Routes

Distributed structure based on multiple mobile agents

According to the functional requirements and mobile agent technology features, we established the MMAS distributed structure, as illustrated in Fig.3.1.

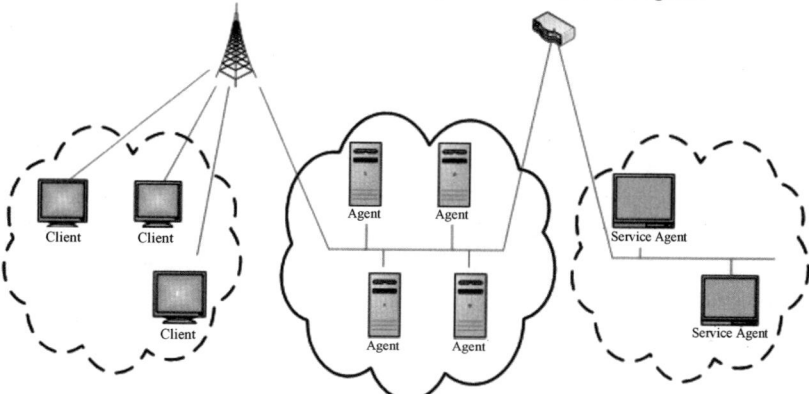

Fig. 3. 1   MMAS distributed structure

There are many service agencies collaborating with each others. When agents need collaboration services, such service agencies can offer to complete collaboration business.

Logical design based on layered model

The system employs a multiple mixture structure which combines layered model, knowledge base model and object-oriented model. We employ different layered strategies according to different application occasions. Each layer of the system is developed to solve a specified issue in SMCSP, which makes problems localized and simplified. It is to implement integration of the whole system by employing good reusability, extensibility of layered architecture. The whole system is divided into five layers, as illustrated in Fig.3.2.

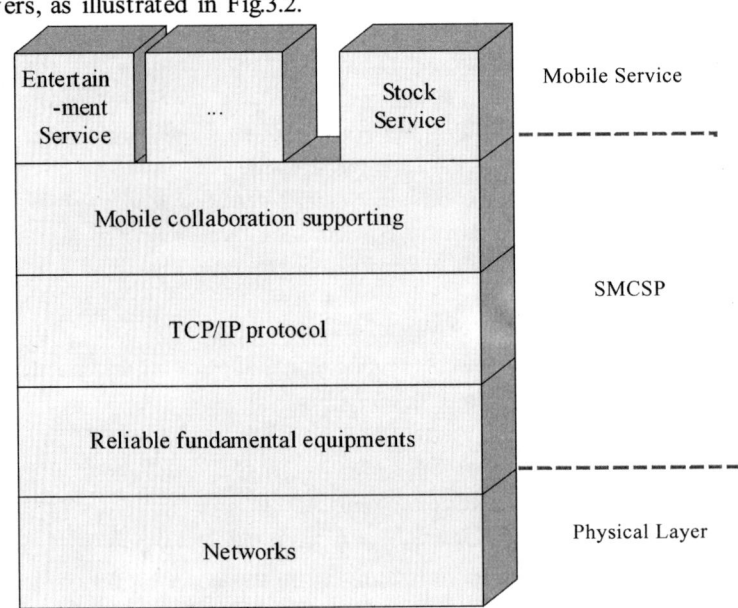

Fig. 3. 2   The layered structure of the system

With the support of SMCSP, application layer completes service collaboration via mobile net. The mobile collaboration layer is the core of the platform, which completes the discovery, scheduling, collaboration and movement of resource. Furthermore, reliable infrastructure provides effective security support for the platform; optimized TCP/IP protocol provides effective improvement mechanism to ease network congestion; application layer presents the application function of by mobile police, entertainment, stock and other concrete mobile applications.

SMCSP is a mobile collaboration application framework for third parties constructed by mobile collaboration technology. Hence, the platform needs to establish a knowledge presentation framework to describe collaboration members and mutual relationships. In order to develop such a platform, we need to master scheduling and movement technology, resource discovery technology, business collaboration technology and so on.

The pivotal issues of mobile collaboration framework includes dynamic multiple mixture structure, establishment of mobile collaboration knowledge framework and relative knowledge visible system. The mobile collaboration technology mainly includes movement mechanism and resource discovery mechanism and so on.

As supporting foundation of collaboration platform, security mechanism is achieved by design and realization of a special mobile encryption card. Based on the card, we analyze and realize a two-stage-handshake improved SSL protocol.

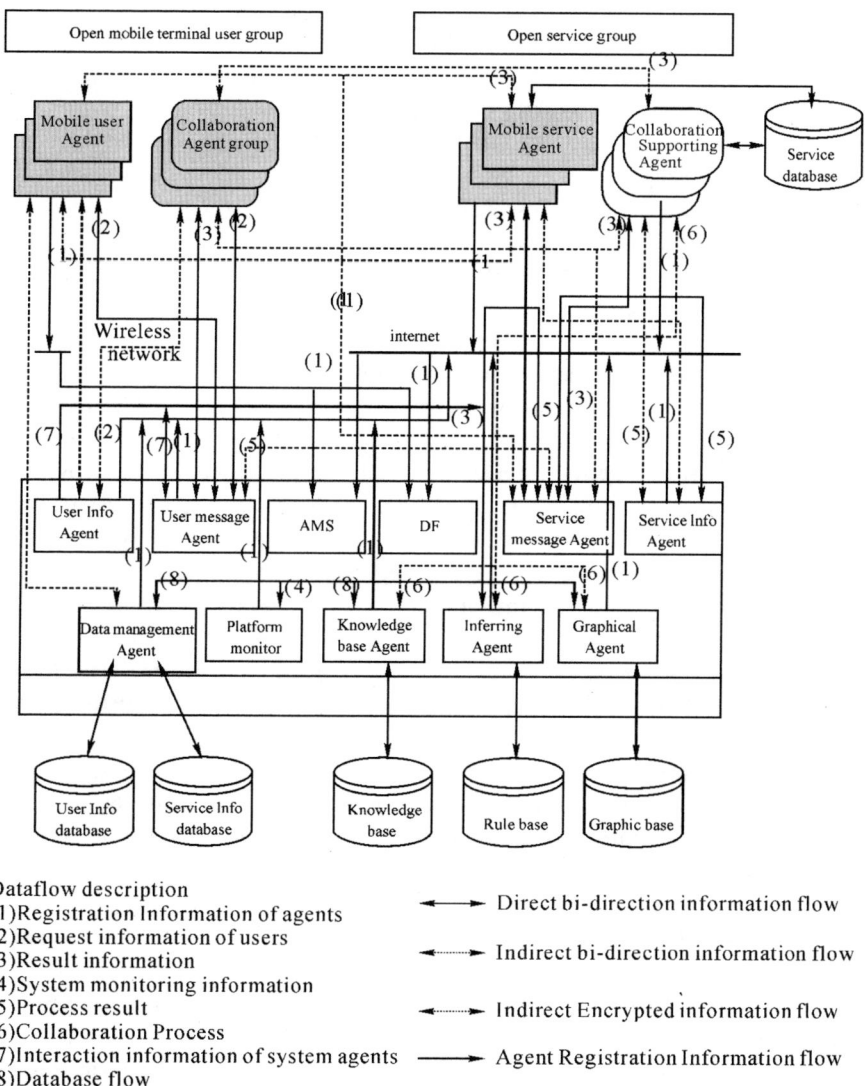

Dataflow description
(1)Registration Information of agents
(2)Request information of users
(3)Result information
(4)System monitoring information
(5)Process result
(6)Collaboration Process
(7)Interaction information of system agents
(8)Database flow

⟷ Direct bi-direction information flow

⟵⋯⋯▶ Indirect bi-direction information flow

⟵⋯⋯▶ Indirect Encrypted information flow

⟶ Agent Registration Information flow

Fig. 3. 3 The function design for platform at logic lever

3. 1. 3 Function Design

The Function Design for Platform at Logic Lever

The entire system consists of three parts—clients, media network, SMCSP.

SMCSP's main components are:

- **AMS (Agent Management System)**: AMS manages and monitors all the agents running state in the system. AMS manages the transition of agent runtime states such as registration, deregistration, monitoring, inquiring, running.

- **DF (Directory Facilitator)**: DF manages functions of all agents in the system, and handles registration, deregistration, inquiring of agent functions and the communication with the other agents.
- **Knowledge Management Agent**: manages all the original knowledge and field knowledge involved by the whole system. It handles maintenance, description, transition, exchange and limited updating of knowledge to support the adaptive system configuration.
- **Platform Monitoring Agent**: manages maintenance of agents running state to support movement of codes.
- **Inferring Agent**: offers relative inferring support during working process of collaboration groups, and enlarges inferring rules.
- **Graph Agent**: responsible for access to the pictures information required by the related services.
- **User Message Agent**: receives and analyzes the messages sent from users, then invokes function agents to solve the messages and returns relative result to users.
- **User Information Agent**: handles registration request, certification request from mobile equipment terminal users, and manages the list of user's services and the list of online users.
- **Service Message Agent**: waits for request messages sent for User Message Agent and service agent, and invokes service agent to respond the messages and returns results.
- **Service Information Agent**: handles requests from mobile service providers such as registration, service information modification and so on. It also manages basic information of services, and manages the list of registered services and online services at the platform.

The client mainly includes:

- **User Agent**: completes display and handles user response by embedding in the mobile nodes.
- **Communication Server**: handles communication with all agents and accomplishes the functions of AMS and DF.

Personalized service subscription module: is responsible for the maintenance of the list of the services subscribed by users.

Authentication Module: in order to improve the integrity of the application system, it provides authentication function aiming to the mobile nodes.

Encryption module: in order to improve the integrity of application systems, it provides the reliable transmission of confidential information between mobile nodes and the services terminal.

The functional design for platform application

With the support of relative libraries and subsystems, SMCSP has three major types of application functions:

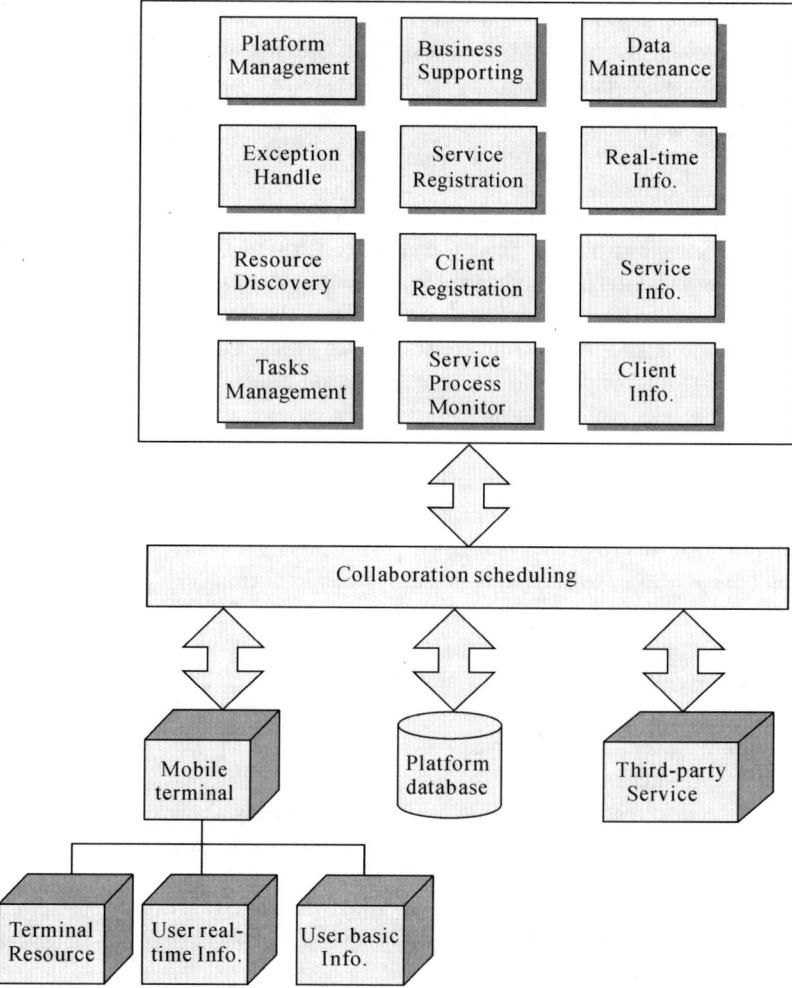

Fig. 3. 4   The function design for platform application

- Platform management

Exceptions handling: in the running process of platform, exceptions and unpredictable mistakes will affect the functions of entire platform. Facing exceptional mistakes or paralysis of partial functions, exceptions handling agent assures that the whole system continue to serve the users and the providers. Exceptions handling agent can provide a detailed report about exceptional mistakes, and may restore some functions to ensure the system robustness.

Critical resource discovery: In order to support various mobile services including mobile collaboration services, the platform needs to discover and support the third-party services. When mobile users concern and need some services, the platform can discover these services, and optimize quality and accessing speed of these services.

Task handling: analyzes and schedules various complex tasks. With the support of knowledge agent, inferring agent, and various mobile collaboration libraries including knowledge base, inferring base and visual model base, processing on complex tasks becomes more reasonable. Such reasonable processing also depends on optimized collaboration scheduling and movement strategy.

- Operation support

Services registration certification: manages the relative services at the platform. Only if a service provided by the service provider meets certain platform specifications and interface standards, can the service become part of the system. Services registration to the platform is necessary; the service could be provided to mobile users after the successful registration. In the circumstances when upgrading is needed, platform also handles the unregistration request of agents. Because of its openness, the system can also support recovery after service agents work exceptionally.

Customer registration certification: after mobile terminal client registers successfully and logs in, mobile users can use all the services registered to the platform, supported by the platform, owned by providers. The platform also handles unregistration request submitted by mobile clients.

Service flow monitoring: as service providers are different, the service agents vary at sizes and other characteristics greatly. In order to support services provided by all the providers, the platform monitors the service flow and ignores concrete function distinguishing. Such monitoring includes establishment of services information base and resources base

- Data Maintenance

Real-time information collection and storage: during the runtime, the platform monitors information flow, various collaboration task scheduling and analysis information flow, collaboration work information, various agent service information flow, requests information flow from all kinds of mobile terminal clients, services agent state information flow, experienced knowledge data flow, exception information and relative handling.

The monitoring for various information flows can facilitate the management of the platform and relevant optimization; the information will be collected, processed and stored as platform running log files.

Service information maintenance: platform can support various types of services, nonetheless, services provided by different providers have their own dependent features. Those dependent features make it more complicated to maintain services information.

In order to assure the service quality, the maintenance is critical for mobile collaboration.

Customer information storage: there are two main kinds of client information: (1) basic customer information includes customer card number, account, age and the list of subscribed services. (2) real-time customer information includes user online information, network linking state, location information and relevant collaboration information.

In conclusion, SMCSP is developed to serve mobile services providers and mobile users. All the function design concentrates its specified clients. The implementation of those functions cannot go on well without relevant information libraries and other needed libraries.

3. 2   System Realization

3. 2. 1   The Pattern Choice

About SMCSP, we have introduced the background, various designs based on different perspectives, also the key technologies. Now we focus on the concrete system realization. As we know, SMCSP works as a foundation services platform for both mobile clients and mobile services providers. Briefly speaking, mobile providers register their services to the platform, and then mobile clients can query and access the registered services via the platform. In fact, such mobile business can simply be implemented without the media platform. That means mobile providers can directly provide their services to mobile clients while mobile clients directly access the providers to obtain needed services. Employing client-server pattern is also adequate to solve above business application. Why do we use the client-server-provider model instead of client-server pattern? We will present the reasons during the following discussion.

Client/Server pattern

Client/Server pattern takes important part in information industry. Network Computing has experienced such evolution from the computing model based on host to client / server computing model.

After the 1980s, centralized structure has gradually been replaced by microcomputer network consisting of personal computers. Usage of personal computers and workstations changes the collaboration computing model. Distributed personal computing model emerges for such reasons. From one hand, the inherent defections of mainframes, such as lack of flexibility, makes it difficult to accommodate the sharp increase of information and to provide complete solution for enterprises. On the second hand, rapid development of microprocessor, its powerful processing capability and comparatively low price also promotes development of network. User can choose workstation, operation system and application program according to what they need.

Client/Server software architecture emerges for realization of resource share based on unequal resource. C/S architecture defines the linkage of workstations and server to realize the distribution of data and application programs to multiple computers. C/S model is a classical model in software architecture and a common example for teaching. The most architecture description languages will illustrate how to describe a C/S model as a basic example, which we will introduce in Chapter 4.

The structure of C/S architecture is shown roughly in Fig.3.5. The linkages represent that client submits the request and then server makes response and returns relevant results.

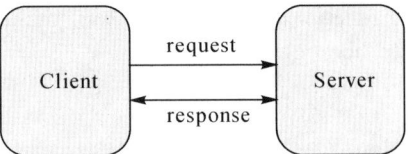

Fig. 3. 5   C/S model

In fact, the structure of C/S is more complicated than that shown in Fig.3.6. In general, three main parts in C/S architecture are database server, client application program and network.

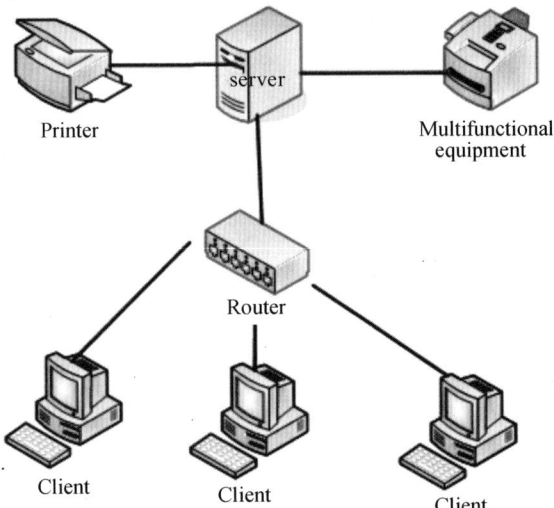

Fig. 3. 6   The architecture of C/S structure

The server manages resource of the system, whose main tasks are:
- to assure the security of database
- to control the concurrent access to database
- to ensure the consistency of data
- to make data duplication and recovery

The main tasks of client application program are:
- to provide GUI (Graphic User Interface) for users
- to submit user's requests to database server and receive message and response from database server
- to execute logic processing on data from database in fat client model

The data transmission is completed by network communication mechanism in fat client and thin server model in order to reduce the burden on the server. Hence, client executes logical processing and analyses of data; the data flow of such model is shown in Fig.3.7.

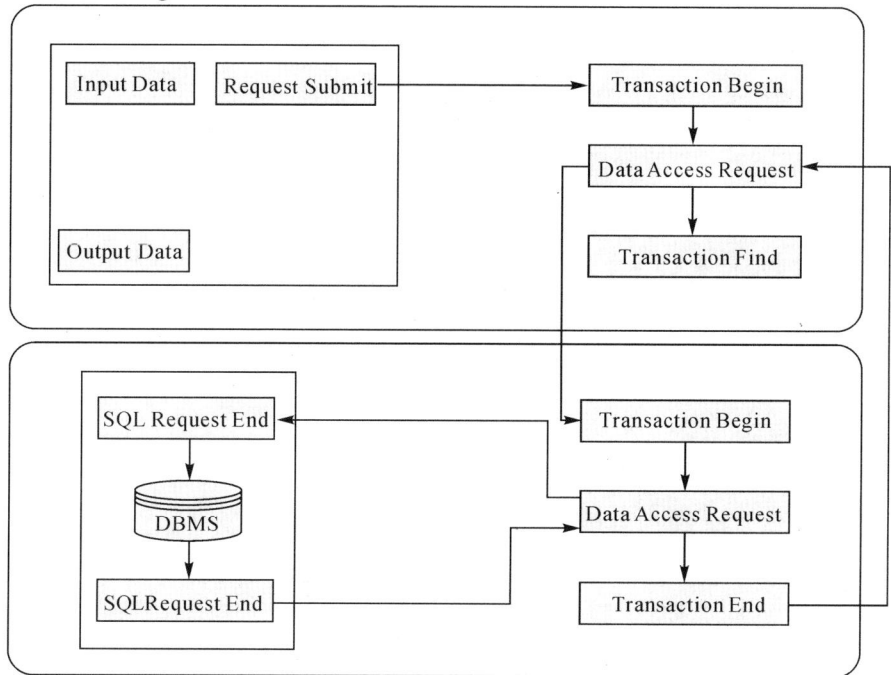

Fig. 3. 7   Handling process in C/S architecture

The advantages of C/S architecture are dominant. The most significant one is adaptability and flexibility brought by definite isolation of function components. In deed, C/S architecture owns powerful capability of data operation and transaction processing. The concept of C/S model is simple and intuitive for engineers to understand and utilize. However, C/S also has following defects:

• The develop expense is comparatively higher. C/S architecture of client hardware and software configuration sets higher requirements on client software and hardware configuration. Continuous upgrading of software and hardware definitely raises the cost of the system.

• The program design of clients is complicated. Program design of client accounts for a very large proportion of software development based on C/S model.

• Software maintenance and upgrading is more difficult. Clients need to be upgraded to assure synchronization with the server.

• It is not easy to take new technology, because we cannot change a software development environment casually.

Client/platform/provider pattern

In addition to those reasons (defects) mentioned above, there are some other reasons to support that C/S architecture is not suitable for such a mobile application.

• mobile communication defect

Compared with general networks, wireless network is more instable. Hence, the efficiency of direct communications of providers and mobile clients is low and dissatisfying. Customers cannot enjoy better services and are dissatisfied with mobile services providers because of the own defections of wireless network. Service providers definitely do not want to see such a situation. Adopting the mobile platform as an intermediate is effective to alleviate the existing problems of mobile communications.

- Services management and services integration

As we know, there are numerous mobile service providers in the mobile service markets. Each provider specifies its own service standards and interfaces. If a mobile client directly accesses the services provided by various mobile providers, the client needs all of service standards and interfaces specified by different providers.

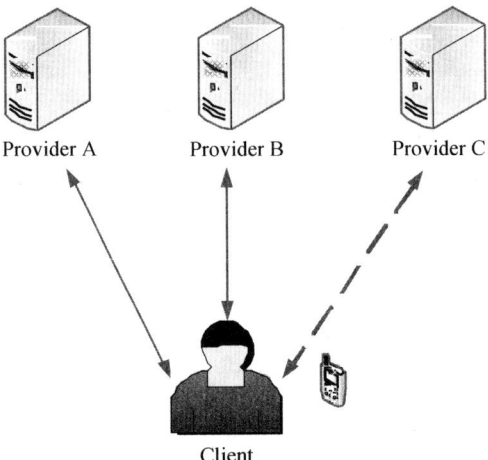

Fig. 3. 8   Provider and Client

As shown in Fig.3.8, a client already takes service from providers A and B, then the user needs services from C, then it has to reload interfaces specified by C. Otherwise, the C service will not be able to run in the client. What if the provider E or F comes?

Even if the number of service providers is limited, but the large amount of services also cause confusions. So, the above mechanism will cause high cost and be inefficient. In our design concept, the mobile platform provides relatively unified standards and interfaces to mobile clients and service providers. Based on this unified foundation, service providers register their services to the platform; then mobile clients will visit the platform to complete the service browse, service subscription and service access with the help of platform service integration. The measures greatly improve the integration efficiency of service and facilitate large amounts of mobile users.

- Mobile collaboration

In addition to the two reasons above, there is a key reason for employing Client/

Platform/Provider architecture. The platform realizes mobile collaboration, which we emphasized in introduction to background.

Mobile collaboration is the use of mobile computing technology and traditional collaboration techniques to make a group of members to work together for a common goal and also maximum interest of groups, which can not be realized by simple client-server architecture. We have introduced the research history of mobile collaboration, its significance in such a mobile application, and several relative issues in background introduction. In the following section, we will focus on how mobile collaboration is achieved.

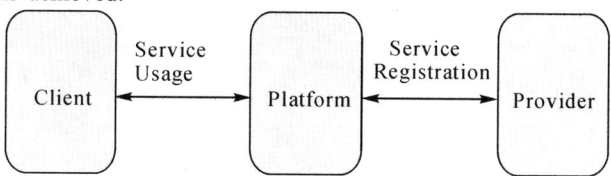

Fig. 3. 9   CPP model

The CPP architecture is roughly shown in Fig.3.9.

Client: Mobile client also provides the same function with representation layer (application user interfaces) and completes dialogue function between users and application. In addition to GUI, it completes the communication between client and the service platform. The client is responsible for submitting users' request and accepting the return massage from service platforms, subscribing services provided by platform according to user's need.

Platform: The platform is responsible for service integration and service management, and provides a unified interfaces and service standards. The platform manages service registration, information query on registered service, service subscriptions, service access and so on. The platform also maintains the relationships between service providers and their service, and the relationships between clients and their subscriptions.

Provider: Mobile service providers develop various mobile services and register their services to platform according to platform standard.

Simply speaking, the linkage between platform and mobile clients represents service usage, while the linkage between platform and service providers represents service registration. Of course, the actual deployment of mobile clients and providers is much more complicated. Fig.3.10 shows a simple network deployment situation.

After the introduction to roles of this application system, we focus on interaction mechanism and implementation of mobile collaboration, which are important realization mechanism to build the mobile platform.

3. 2. 2   Interaction Mechanism

The SMCSP system specifies own message class for communication. The detailed design MessageClass and MessageQueue are depicted as following:

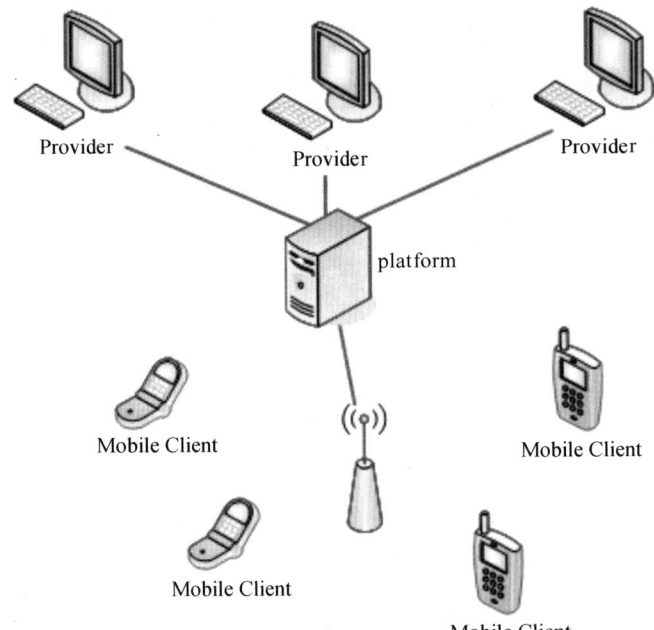

Fig. 3. 10   The architecture of CPP structure

- MessageClass: MessageClass defines the formatted message sent and received in this program.
  - Properties

No.	Variable	Type	Description	Comment
1	StrRecv	String	The original received string	null
2	Service	String	Service name	null
3	Sender	String	Message Sender	null
4	receiver	String	Message Receiver	null
5	content	String	Message Content	null
6	seperator	char	Seperator of message string	static public

  - Methods

No.	Methods	Parameter Type	Return Type	Description	Comment
1	MessageClass	Void	Void	Construction function. To analyze original message string.	public
2	getSender	Void	String	To get sender info. from analyzed message string.	public
3	getReceiver	Void	String	To get receiver info. from analyzed message string.	public
4	getAction	Void	String	To get service info. from analyzed message string.	public
5	getContent	Void	String	To get message content from analyzed message string.	public

- MessageQueue: MessageQueue class manages message queue in the program.
  - Properties

No.	Variable	Type	Description	Comment
1	vector	Vector	The vector for messages storage and access.	private

  - Methods

No.	Methods	Parameter Type	Return Type	Description	Comment
1	clearAll	void	void	To clear the message queue.	public
2	get	void	MessageClass	To get a message from the message queue.	public
3	put	MessageClass	void	To put a message into the message queue.	public
4	MessageQueue	void	void	To initialize a new vector.	public

The platform and client respectively define their own message listener class to realize communication, employing socket and multithreading mechanisms. Take platform as an example, the detailed design is depicted as follows:

- ClientListening: The class listens on clients.
  - Properties

No.	Variable	Type	Description	Comment
1	ss	ServerSocket	Message storage vector.	private
2	mf	MainFrame	Program mainframe.	null

  - Methods

No.	Methods	Parameter Type	Return Type	Description	Comment
1	ClientListening	ServerSocket ss, MainFrame mf	void	Construction function.	public
2	run	void	void	Listening function.	public

- Client: The class processes the messages sent from mobile clients.
  - Properties

No.	Variable	Type	Description	Comment
1	s	Socket	Message storage vector.	private
2	mf	MainFrame	Program mainframe.	null
3	mq	MessageQueue []	Message queue for management.	null
4	br	BufferedReader	Input message stream reader.	null
5	dos	DataOutputStream	Output message stream.	null

■ Methods

No.	Methods	Parameter Type	Return Type	Description	Comment
1	Client	ServerSocket ss, MainFrame mf	void	Construction function.	public
2	run	void	void	To transfer massage by realizing Runable interface.	public
3	registe	String name, String password	void	To handle user registration.	public
4	loginCheck	String name, String password	void	To check for login and to send services list.	public
5	chooseService	String username, String service	void	To handle users' service choices.	public

The run method codes are shown as follows. When a new client connects to the service platform, run method will call the functions of Mainframe to record visit information, and then build a new thread. The new thread will make a new instance of Client, which will handle the logic processing of information.

```
public void run() {
    while (true) {
        Socket s = null;
        try {
            s = ss.accept();
        }
        catch (IOException ex) {
        }
        String ip = s.getInetAddress().toString();
        mf.GetClientPanel().AddLine("Mobile client" + ip + "is connecting to the
server");
        mf.GetClient2Panel().AddLine("Mobile client" + ip + "is connecting to the
server");
        new Thread(new Client(s, mf)).start();
    }
```

3.2.3 Realization of Mobile Collaboration

People built abstract model and divided it into a number of modules to handle in order to solve more complex real problem. If the domain of a particular problem is very huge, complex and unpredictable, the only appropriate and reasonable approach to solve such problem is to develop lots of components with specified function. And each component is designed to solve a specific area of this problem. For this collaboration reliable service system, employing multi-agent technology to describe and analyze system is the best option.

The decomposition of mobile service system makes each agent take most appropriate pattern to solve specific problems. An agent has to collaborate with the other agents in the system to solve interdependent problems. How to assure high-efficient and dynamic information sharing and collaboration is the core issue of mobile collaboration. In order to achieve high-efficient and dynamic information sharing and collaboration, we adopt mobile agent technology to conduct effective information exchange.

Mobile agent is a procedure which can move independently from a host to another host in heterogeneous networks, and exchange resource with other agents. It actually combines agent technology and distributed computing technology. By mobile agent technology the service-request agent dynamically moves to the server for implementation, so that the agent depends less on the transmission of network and directly faces the server resources; thus the large amount of data transmission network is avoided and network bandwidth dependence is reduced. Mobile agent does not require unified scheduling; an agent created by the user can run asynchronously in different nodes, and transmit results to the users after tasks are completed. In order to complete a certain task, users can create a number of agents; those agents run in one or more nodes at the same time, which forms capacity of parallel computing.

In the process of collaboration, the agent completes its own job; the collaboration action must meet the following criteria: (1) Agents should mutually respond. (2) All agents should make commitment on its own decomposed job. (3) All agents should support the common action among each others to achieve the whole aim. (4) Each agent should be able to meet specific environmental constraints.

Mobile collaboration of this platform is reflected in three collaboration layers:

- Supporting collaboration

In this platform, multi-agent coordination can be communication and management over layers, can also be interactive communications among the inter-regional equipment or different services. Hence, we have established an ontology structure to describe the agent itself and its own attributes. The structure also specifies agent interactive communication, the constraint properties of non-communication action, the content and aim of actions.

- Members collaboration

Members collaboration refers to the collaborations between users.

We build an ontology structure to describe various mobile users, including users' location, mobile properties, personal information, activities and service records and other information, to support a variety of application services. Meanwhile, the ontology structure can also describe the interaction action. Hence, different terminal users can share knowledge, completed various complex interaction. This design approach is the best design based on mobile ontology and the mobile user's actual application. The mobile users autonomously collaborate to realize decomposition of services, service scheduling, interaction and so on.

- Organization collaboration

Organization collaboration refers to the division, distribution, sub-task coordination, collaboration rules management of collaboration tasks.

Typical Agent software architecture: Agent software architecture describes Agent functional modules and collaboration action. According to the characteristics of the Agent, software architecture should include following basic modules: (1) User interface for user to input information or output information to users. (2) Communication interface for communication with other software agent or application. (3) Perception module to process filtering and classification on input information. (4) Reasoning module to infer based on their own knowledge of Agent. (5) Decision module to do evaluation of the inferring results and decision-making. (6) Plan module to make action plan based on the decision-making. (7) Implementation module to act in accordance with the action plan. (8) Knowledge base to support reasoning, decision-making, planning and so on.

Mobile Agent Design Specification: OMG's MASIF specification standardizes agent management, agent movement, agent name, agent system name, agent system type and location syntax. Such a specification makes some basic recommendations to resolve interoperability between different agent systems of different manufacturers.

Interoperability is the basic characteristics of different agent systems' coordination. When an agent application runs at a node of the net, it can utilize data, processing capability and similar resources at other nodes.

Function summary

The main function modules are as follows:

- Interface agent or personal assistants

Its main task is to assist users to complete tedious and repetitive work. Agent will observe and monitor users how to perform some specific tasks. When such agent can identify the reaction of users in specific circumstances, it begins to replace or to help users to complete tasks. These agents have been personalized according to targeted users to adapt to the specific users' behavior. These issues are closely related with human-machine interface (HCI), user modeling and pattern matching.

- Task Agent

Task Agent is to help mankind to process complex decision-making and other knowledge management. The work principle of these agents is based on computer learning, planning, resource-constrained reasoning, knowledge expression in artificial intelligence.

- Information/Internet Agent

It supports users in distributed network or Internet to search information or intelligently manages network resources.

Now we describe the system functions according to the three aspects mentioned above:

SMCSP is the core of the whole design. Its function is to publish the service, which mobile service provider provides to the platform according to the standard of mobile computing visualization platform, to internet; then mobile users can choose and enjoy their favorite service expediently. Service providers only need to provide calculating subsystem with independent function in accordance with the requirements and standards of the platform. Hence, the service provider is not concerned about how users to access the services. In other words, the platform plays a role of intermediary between service users and providers.

We can divide the platform into two parts from the function aspect:

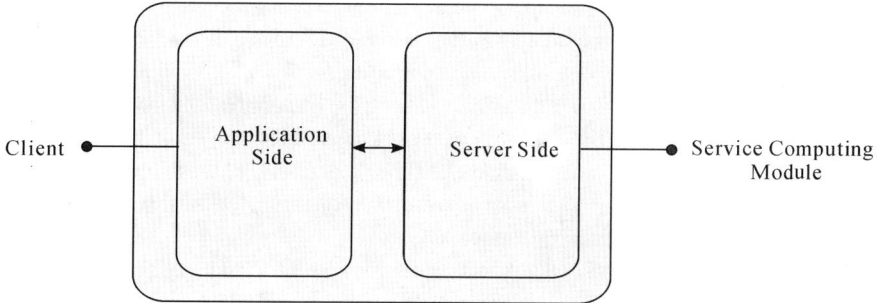

Fig. 3. 11 The interior modules of platform

- Application Side

It mainly manages users' information and interacts with users. Application side has four main modules; we will present the function analyses in details as follows.
  - User Management Module.
    - ◆ Mobile equipment users have to be registered as legitimate users before accessing the services. When a user requests to registration, the mobile equipment terminal submits the related information (such as user ID, personal information and so on), processes request of user management module, and then returns the registration result to the user (such as random user password.)
    - ◆ When a mobile user requests to deregistration, the module cancels all personal information about the user and updates the database. Finally the module returns the deregistration result to the user.
    - ◆ When a mobile user requests to login, the module checks the user's identity and returns the login result.
    - ◆ When a mobile user requests to update the list of personal services (for example, to delete the selected services or to add new services), the process approach is more complicated accordingly.

We have to know that there is also a personal service list in mobile terminal equipment. If the user wants to delete selected service, user can directly choose the service and make delete demand. The personal service list in mobile equipment will be updated while the service list in application side will be updated. If the user wants to add a service, the platform will send the system-registered service list to the user. The user picks up a service and submits the relevant request, then the service lists both in client and in application side will be updated.

There are some comments worth noting:

All the user request information is obtained through communication module A, meanwhile the return of the results is also completed through communications module A.

The registered service lists are consistent in application side and the service side. The maintenance of the online service list is completed by core controlling modules. If the registered list changes, the list of online services must also change, because the number of online services is less than that of registered services.

- Application Communication module A. It manages the communication between application side and mobile terminal equipment.
  - The module receives the request sent by mobile terminal equipment. The module will redirect the request message concerning user management to the user management module. The remaining requests are all service requests. The module will return request-failed information, if the service is temporarily unavailable.
  - The module will classify the available requests and manage the requests queue and then transfer the request to communication module B according to dynamic transfer scheduling rules.
    - The module receives the computing result of service from the communication module B and then returns the result to mobile terminal equipment. If the request is handled successfully, the module returns computing results, otherwise the module returns failing information.
- Application Communications module B. The module manages the communications between application side and server side.
  - The module receives the users' request sent from communication module A, and transfers the request to server side.
  - The module receives the service request results from server side and directly transfers the results to communication module A.

In a word, communication module B works as a transformation for requests and results.
- Core control module.
  - Core control module is responsible for collaboration of several other modules. The modules at application side will send normal signal to the core control module. When all the modules work normally, the core control module stays in monitor state. When exception emerges in a certain module, it is responsible for the exception handling.
  - The module receives updating message of the service list from core control module at server side.
- Database management module.
  - The module updates the database according to the requirements of the other modules. It also manages the access to the database.
  - The module manages the rule database. The rule database here makes inference about type of calculation according to the amonats of calculation tasks and service requests.
- Server Side

The server side mainly manages services and interacts with service computing module. Server side has five main modules; we will present the function analyses in details as follows.

- Service management module
  - When a service provider applies for registration of new services, the service computing module will offer such an application and then submit to the server relevant content (such as service content, communication atomic word, message format).
  - Service management module obtains requests such as service registration, service unregistration and service pause from the server communication module B.

    Service management module will handle such requests as following approaches: if the service management module receives service registration request, it returns the registration result (such as service number or communication port number); if the service management module receives service deregistration requests, it callbacks communication resources allocated to the service, returns the results and meanwhile notifies the core control module to deal with the deregistration; if the service management module receives service pause request, it only notifies the core control module to deal with such request.
  - The management module also monitors the real-time states of service computing modules. During the running of the system, the management module updates the online service list according the real-time state. If any exception occurs in service computing modules, the management module will notify the core control module to recover.
- Service communication module A .It manages the communication between application side and server side.
  - The module receives the request sent from application side. According to the online service list, it returns request failing message if the service is temporarily unavailable. The module will handle the rest requests according to computing rules and redirect them to server communication module B.
  - The module receives the service computing result from the server communication module B and then returns the result to mobile terminal equipment. If the request is handled successfully, the module returns computing results, otherwise the module returns failing information.
- Server communication module B. The module manages the communications between server side and service computing module.
  - The module receives the request sent from server communication module A, and transfers the request to server computing if the requested service is available.
  - The module receives the result from service computing module.
  - The module redirects the message from computing modules (such as

service registration, service deregistration and service pause) to the service management module.

In a word, communication module B works as a transformation for requests and results.

- Server core control module.
  - ◆ Server core control module is responsible for collaboration of several other modules. The modules at server side will send normal signal to the core control module. When all the modules work normally, the core control module stays in monitor state. When exception emerges in a certain module, it is responsible for the exception handling.
  - ◆ The module receives updating message of the service list from service management modules.
  - ◆ The module updates the registered services list and online services list. The module adds the newly-registered service into the registered service list and removes the unregistered service from the registered service list.
  - ◆ The module sends the updating message to the application core control module.
- Database management module.
  - ◆ The module updates the database according to the requirements of the other modules. It also manages the access to the database.
  - ◆ The module manages the rules database. The rule database here makes inference about type of calculation according to the amonats of calculation tasks and service requests.

The Whole framework

In order to support mobile equipments produced by different manufacturers and various services provided by providers, the SMCSP needs a unified standard for interoperability. Here we employ MASIF standards. We build the system on such basis; meanwhile we have to ensure the flexibility of the system. The platform employs the Java technology because of Java platform's independence, operating system's independence.

The core composing parts of the platform collaboration mechanism:

- **Computer Supporting Collaboration Work Environment:** The distributed computing environment, adopting computer technology, network and communication technologies, multimedia technology and human-machine interface technology, organizes the collaboration members to complete the certain task.
- **Collaboration Supporting Agent:** The agent coordinates the cooperation of mobile collaboration group consisting of mobile clients and other agents. The agent realizes the mobile clients collaboration, the arrangement of service decomposition, service scheduling, and interaction.
- **AMS (Agent Management System):** AMS manages and monitors all the agents' running states in the system. AMS manages the transition of agent runtime states, such as registration, unregistration, monitoring, inquiring,

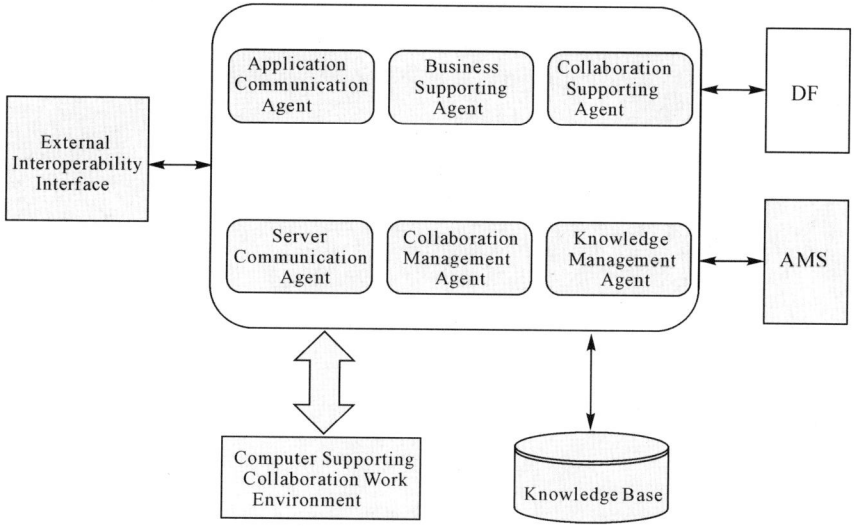

Fig. 3. 12 Multi-agent collaboration structures

running.

- **DF（Directory Facilitator）:** DF manages functions of all agents in the system, and handles registration, unregistration, inquiring of agent functions and the communication with the other agents.
- **ACC（Agent Communication Channel）:** Agent Communication Channel manages all the communication between the agents. It provides all kinds of transmission services needed by communication.
- **External Interoperability Interface:** We have mentioned that interoperability is the basic characteristics of different agent systems' coordination. When an agent application runs at a node of the net, it even can utilize data, processing capability and similar resources at other nodes.

Multi-agent system platform provides an operating system indecent platform for the entire application system. The platform is distributed on the networks, therefore there is not restriction on physical location of the agent in the system. Once a machine of the platform collapses, the running agent can immediately move to other machines to ensure service continuity and consistency. The system can adjust the machine load to remain the balance, efficiency and security of the system according to the system's real-time state.

3. 2. 4　Knowledge-based Design

After we introduce the collaboration realization of the platform, we present the knowledge-based design of the police service server. The knowledge-based design is closely related to expert system. As we know, both expert system and multi-agent system are hot issues in artificial intelligence (AI).

During the 20th century, a number of definitions of artificial intelligence were proposed. The earliest popular definition of AI is "making computers think like people". Fig.3.13 shows some areas of interest for AI. The area of expert systems is a very successful and approximate solution to the classic AI problem of programming intelligence.

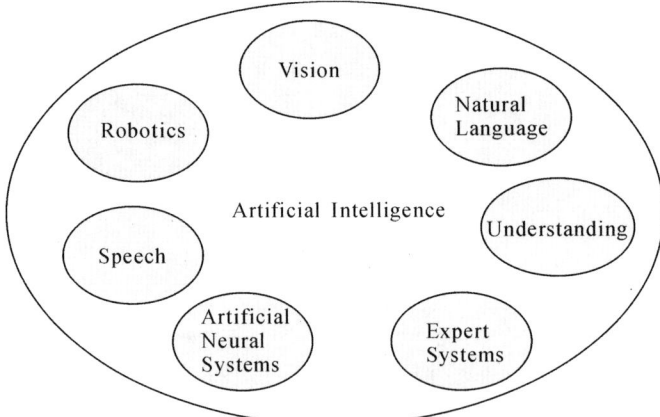

Fig. 3. 13   Research areas of AI

Expert systems have been combined with databases for human-like pattern recognition and automated decision systems to yield knowledge discovery through data mining and thus produce an intelligent database (Bramer, 1999). Professor Edward Feigenbaum has defined an expert system as "an intelligent computer program that uses knowledge and inference procedures to solve problems that are difficult enough to require significant human expertise for their solution".

There are a number of advantages of expert systems, such as increased availability, reduced cost, reduced danger, better performance, increased reliability, fast response and so on.

The design of the police service server is just a simple implementation of knowledge-based system. Through our introduction to this simple design, we may understand the design concept of knowledge-based system. In fact, the terms expert system, knowledge-based system, and knowledge-based expert system are often used synonymously. Most people use expert system simply because it's shorter, even though there may be no expertise in their expert system, only knowledge.

A knowledge-based system consists of the following components (Giarratano, 2005) which are shown in Fig.3.14:

- User interface: the mechanism by which the user and the knowledge-based system communicate.
- Explanation facility: explains the reasoning of the system to a user.
- Working memory: a global database of facts used by the rules.
- Inference engine: makes inferences by deciding which rules are satisfied by facts or objects, prioritizes the satisfied rules, and executes the rule with the highest priority.

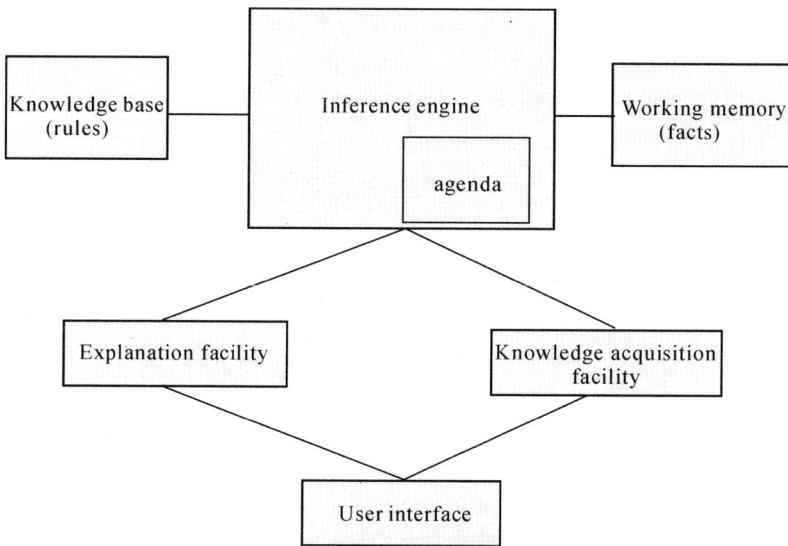

Fig. 3. 14   Knowledge-based system structure

- Agenda: a prioritized list of rules created by the inference engine, whose patterns are satisfied by facts or objects in working memory.
- Knowledge acquisition facility: an automatic way for the user to enter knowledge in the system rather than by having the knowledge engineer explicitly code the knowledge.

Our police service is still in the phase of concept. The service includes city map collection services, case information collection, and police collaboration control; and the server of the police service manages the distribution of police force. The server will maintain a list of spare staff and a tree of occupied polices. When the server receives the warning, it handles the police scheduling according to the relevant rules and current situation of the police force (the list and the tree). After the handling of the warning, the server will move the police staff from the occupied tree to the list. In such a simple implementation, the knowledge base is the rules for police force scheduling and the facts are the current situation of the police force.

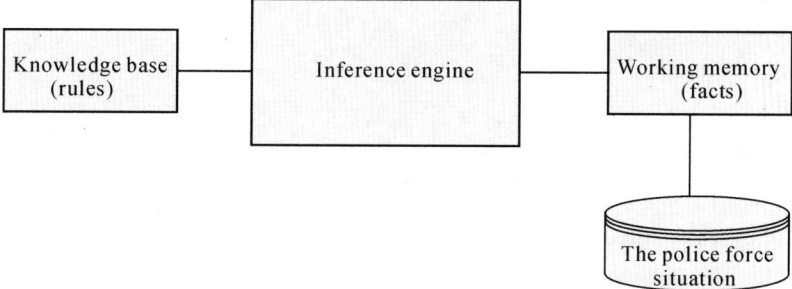

Fig. 3. 15   The inference mechanism of police service server

The following code shows the process after the warning handling.

```
private void handleFinish(String[] message, Socket socket) {
    //To record event information into the database of performance analysis
    DBA writetoperfdb = new DBA("update performancehistory set typepercentage =
typepercentage+1","update");
    Thread twritetoperfdb = new Thread(writetoperfdb);
    twritetoperfdb.start();
    try {
        twritetoperfdb.join();
        }
    catch (InterruptedException ex2) {
    }
    //To record the collaboration completed information into the database
    //To notify the client to leave from the collaboration group
    String userName = message[1];
    DBA missionComplete = new DBA ("update coproject set finished = 1 where
teamname=(select teamname from proj_member where name='"+userName + "'and
leader='1')", "update");
    Thread tmissionComplete = new Thread(missionComplete);
    tmissionComplete.start();
    try {
        tmissionComplete.join();
    }
    catch (InterruptedException ex) {
    }
    //To Notify the user end of the task.
    sendMessage("MissionComplete", socket, 5000);
    //To Move the police staff from the occupied tree to the list.
    DBA teamMem = new DBA("select teamname,name from proj_member where teamname=
(select teamname from proj_member where name='"+userName+"'and leader='
1')", "select");
    Thread tteamMem = new Thread(teamMem);
    tteamMem.start();
    try {
        tteamMem.join();
        ResultSet teamMemrs = (ResultSet) teamMem.returnrecords();
        String tn = new String();
        Vector membname=new Vector();
        int memb = 0;
        while (teamMemrs.next()) {
        tn = teamMemrs.getString("teamname");
        arena.freePoliceName.addElement(teamMemrs.getString("name"));
        memb++;
        }
        //To remove the node (police staff) from the occupied tree.
        for (int i = 0; i < arena.rootnode.getChildCount(); i++) {
            if (arena.rootnode.getChildAt(i).toString().equals(tn))
            {
                ((myTreeNode)arena.rootnode.getChildAt(i)).removeAllChildren();
```

```
        if((((myTreeNode)arena.rootnode.getChildAt(i)).getChildCount()==0)
      {
          ((myTreeNode) arena.rootnode).remove(i);
      }
    }
  }
  DefaultTreeModemodel=(DefaultTreeModel)arena.coEventTree.getModel();
  model.reload();
  arena.coEventTree.repaint();
// To add the node(police staff) in to the list.
  arena.freePoliceCounter = arena.freePoliceCounter + memb;
  arena.freePolice = new JCheckBox[arena.freePoliceCounter];
  String[] fpn = new String[arena.freePoliceName.capacity()];
  arena.freePoliceName.copyInto(fpn);
  arena.freePolicePanel.removeAll();
  arena.freePoliceScrollPane.repaint();
for (int j = 0; j < arena.freePoliceCounter; j++) {
  arena.freePolice[j] = new JCheckBox("");
  arena.freePolice[j].setText(fpn[j]);
  arena.freePolicePanel.add(arena.freePolice[j], null);
}
  arena.setVisible(true);
  }
  catch (Exception ex1) {
    ex1.printStackTrace();
  }
} //End handleFinish
}
```

3.3   Summary

This chapter concerns on the supporting mobile collaboration service platform (SMCSP); we employ such a mobile collaboration platform as a study case to present a further introduction to software architecture style. The mobile collaboration platform is a new application in the field of the mobile communication field; we introduce the program background, technology route and function design in details to present an explicit description concerning such an application.

We compare the C/S pattern with CPP pattern, and discuss the reason for our application to employ the CPP architecture. Furthermore, we present the communication mechanism and the module design for mobile collaboration. Eventually we make a simple introduction of knowledge-based system and the relevant application in our police service server. We hope that the content of this chapter could be a supplement to Chapter 2.

References

(Bramer, 1999)   Bramer, M. A., Ed. Knowledge Discovery and Data Mining: IEEE Press. 1999.
(Giarratano, 2005)   Giarratano, J. C. & Riley, G. D. Expert Systems Principles and Programming 4th ed.: Course Technology.2005.

4

Software Architecture Description

As the size and complexity of software systems increases, design problems go beyond the algorithms and data structures of the computation: designing and specifying the overall system structure emerges as a new kind of problem. Such change is inevitable in order to ensure software quality and to improve reliability, reusability and maintainability of software. The new concept of design focuses on the overall organization of software systems, processing the internal relationship between system components at a higher level, and understanding and analyzing the system behavior and characteristics from global perspective.

We have discussed why we need software architecture in Chapter 1; we have known what software architecture can bring to us: inchoate analysis and evaluation of system's quality, constraints to system's implementation, the reuse and the realization of software product line, facilitation for the communication among stakeholders and so on. All the advantages are just what we need to solve the difficulties in development of large and complex software.

Although we know the trend of software development and seize the potential last straw, there is an additional problem we have to face. How to describe a system with the concept of software architecture? In other words, how we make architectural description and ensure that it can contribute to the system development? In this chapter, we present the formal description of software, and focus on architectural description languages(ADL), the conception of which is based on formal methods. Among numerous ADLs, we choose to present a primer introduction to WRIGHT, an architectural description language development at Carnegie Mellon University. At the very first step, we should understand the necessity of formal language.

4.1 Formal Description of Software Architecture

4.1.1 Problems in Informal Description

Many developments of software systems start from architecture design, which is particularly necessary for large-scale systems. And good design for software architecture is often a key factor leading to software success.

The concept of object-oriented development (OOD) has gradually matured from being presented. The OOD can still be regarded as one of the mainstream development models. Obviously we have approaches to describe software architecture according to such concept. As we know, in software engineering, the famous Unified Modeling Language (UML) (Booch, 2005) is a non-proprietary specification language based on the concept of OOD for object modeling. The UML is an effort to create a standard, generic, graphical modeling language for software systems. As a general-purpose modeling language, UML includes a standardized graphical notation used to create an abstract model of a system, referred to as a UML model.

A software designer can describe the system architecture employing UML and kinds of models. What is the description like in UML? What kinds of models can be used to describe a system to be developed? Generally there are three prominent parts of a system's model:

Functional model showcases the functionality of the system from the user's Point of View, including Use Case Diagrams.

Object model showcases the structure and substructure of the system using objects, attributes, operations, and associations, including Class Diagrams.

Dynamic model showcases the internal behavior of the system, including Sequence Diagrams, Activity Diagrams and State Machine Diagrams.

UML is a common typical informal description approach. We will focus on the functional model of the three models as topic, namely the use case diagram and model; we discuss deficiencies of informal methods accordingly.

Before the discussion, let us go through some informal definitions: Actors, Scenarios and Use cases. An actor is something with behavior, such as a person (identified by role), computer system, or organization. A scenario is a specific sequence of actions and interactions between actors and the system; it is also called a use case instance. It is one particular story of using a system, or one path through the use case. Informally, a use case is a collection of related success and failure scenarios that describe an actor using a system to support a goal. (Larman, 2004)

The UML provides use case diagram notation to illustrate the names of use cases and actors, and the relationships between them, and system boundary optionally. (Larman, 2004) The relationships include Communicate Associations, Dependencies, Generalizations. (Alhir, 2003)

We do not introduce UML specifications in detais here, just present a simple use case diagram and a use case specification to illustrate our points of view.

In fact, with few exceptions current exploitation of software architecture and architectural style is informal. However, informal methods do not facilitate the communication and understanding of software. As shown in Fig. 4. 1, informal methods (e. g. UML) for analysis and design always make heavy use of natural language and a variety of graphical notations. The result is that depending on natural

use Case 1: play Monopoly Game

Scope: Monopoly application

Level: user goal

Primary Actor: Observer

Stakeholders and interests:

 - Observer:Wants to easily observe the output of the game simulation

Main success scenario:

 1. Observer requests new game initialization, enters number of players

 2. Observer starts play

 3. *System displays game trace for next player move(see domain rules, and "game trace" in glossary for trace details)*

 Repeat step 3 until a winner or Observer cancels

Extensions:

 *a. At any time, System fail
 (To support recovery, System logs after each completed move)

 1. Observer restart System

 2. System detects prior failure, reconstructs state, and prompts to continue

 3. Observer choose to continue(from last completed player turn)

Special Requirements:

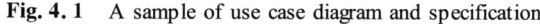

Fig. 4. 1   A sample of use case diagram and specification

language and informal graphical notations directly cause the difficulty of characterizing an explicit, independent architecture or architectural style. Such defect limits the extent to which software architecture can be exploited using current practices. Hence, we discuss deficiencies of non-formal approaches in describing system architecture as follows:

- Vagueness

Vagueness often occurs because a system specification is a very bulky document. Achieving a high level of precision consistently is an almost impossible task. (Pressman, 2006) Fundamentally speaking, vagueness is caused by ambiguity of natural languages. Meanwhile some graphic notations containing only a small amount of structural information will not completely eliminate the existence of ambiguity. Naturally, employing graphic notations are also limited by the expression capability of graphic symbols. In a word, informal methods cannot describe a system precisely.

- Barriers during communication caused by vagueness

Basically, the era of individual heroism has gone in the software industry. Nowadays, development of large software system requires collaboration of a whole team. Of course teamwork brings communication, which is an important part of team collaboration and a key factor affecting the result of development. As we mentioned before, informal approaches cause vagueness in architecture description. And such vagueness will make barriers during communication for certain.

- Infeasibility in System Validation

A system designer might hope that the architecture can be validated in the first design phase. Validation means to check out the consistency and completeness of a system, that is, whether the system as the description will work correctly. Likely an architect need to make sure the building in design can be turned into practice. In architecture, mathematics and physical mechanics can help architects to complete such validation. However, in software engineering, informal language for architecture description can not be used to validate a system. Even the natural languages and graphic notation are unambiguous, and express the designer's intention precisely, and also contain enough design information; less conducive to the machinery expression and computing, and the lack of the mathematical theory supporting analysis and computation make validation infeasible. Since we can not find out the contradictions-variances in sets of statements (Pressman, 2006), and incompleteness or the other defects, we are not able to ensure the quality of software products. And the system may encounter fatal errors eventually.

- Weakness in Architectural Behavior Description

In fact, architectural behavior description not only declares the functions of the system's modules and the communications between different modules, but also serves the validation. Hence, behavior description is very significant part of architectural description. Although informal methods, such as Sequence Diagrams, Activity Diagrams of UML, can describe the internal behavior of the system, the deficiencies still exist: (1) vagueness blocks the accurate expression of behavior design; (2) behavior can not be predicted according to computation; (3) the informal approaches are unable to express the dynamic behavior interaction in run-time. In that situation, we will suffer from inconsistency of interface communication protocols or even the deadlock problems. And those deficiencies in behavior description are also reasons for infeasibility in system validation.

The deficiencies of informal approaches do exist and are inevitable indeed. Nonetheless, can formal description help software architect to get rid of those deficiencies on earth?

4. 1. 2   Why Are Formal Methods Necessary

In this section, we try to answer the question raised at the final of the previous section. In computer science, formal methods refer to mathematically based techniques for the specification, development and verification of software and hardware systems. In other words, the formalism foundation is based on mathematical theories.

Formal methods can be applied at various points through the development process. Especially formal methods have the following advantages in architectural description:

- Formal methods may be used to give a description of the system to be developed, at whatever level(s) of details desired.

By providing a precise semantics for the system at the abstract level of architecture, a formal model of the system can provide the basis for rigorous, justifiable analysis of critical system properties. That is, applying general formal methods makes modeling and analyzing of architectures and architectural styles achievable. As we know, mathematic is the most accurate language. Unambiguous mathematic notation and operational rules will be of extinct vagueness. Software designers can precisely express their own concept and system requirements. In the development phase, to eliminate ambiguity, all development work will be in accordance with the design based on the mathematical theory. And all the developers will work or discuss with the guidance of formal methods, namely according to the only standards and interpret rules. Hence, the barriers during communication caused by vagueness will disappear.

- The formal methods have more advantages in architectural behavior description.

Compared with informal methods, the major advantages are as follows: (1) the methods are conducive to machinery expression and computation. (2) The methods provide formal and exact definitions to describe behaviors or behavior patterns, as well as behavior analysis and modeling rules. For example, process algebras provide algebraic laws which allow process (behavior pattern) descriptions to be manipulated and analyzed, and permit formal reasoning about equivalences between processes. (3) Such analysis and modeling of behavior is an important part of system validation.

- The formal methods make system validation feasible.

As we discussed above, the perfect supporting for behavior description contributes to system validation. Additionally, a formal model of the architecture can also be used as a basis for verification of an implementation. Because the constraints that must be met by a system are precisely defined, it is possible to determine whether a system conforms to an architecture and whether a given architecture conforms to a style. The constraints themselves can be validated for consistency.

With the theory of formal methods, proofs of correctness of such systems (validation) can be processed by automated means. Generally, automated techniques fall into two general categories:

- Automated theorem proving, in which a system attempts to produce a formal proof from scratch, given a description of the system, a set of logical axioms, and a set of inference rules.

- Model checking, in which a system verifies certain properties by means of an exhaustive search of all possible states that a system could enter during its execution.

Based on these features above, formal approach is especially important in high-integrity systems, for example where safety or security is important, to help ensure that errors are not introduced into the development process. Formal methods are particularly effective in early development at the requirements and specification levels, and can be used for a completely formal development of an implementation.

After thirty years of research and application, community has gained lots of significant achievements in the area of formal methods: the methods derived from initially the most simple method—the first-order predicate logic, evolve to several categories applied to different areas, including logic-based methods, the state machine, network, process algebra, algebra and other formal approaches. Of those categories, here are some famous formal methods,

- Petri Net

A Petri net (also known as a place/transition net or P/T net) is one of several mathematical representations of discretely distributed systems. As a modeling language, it graphically depicts the structure of a distributed system as a directed bipartite graph with annotations. As such, a Petri net has place nodes, transition nodes, and directed arcs connecting places with transitions. Petri nets were invented in 1962 by Carl Adam Petri in his PhD thesis. (Petri, 1962)

- Z Notation

The Z notation (universally pronounced zed, named after Zermelo-Fränkel set theory) is a formal specification language used for describing and modeling computing systems. It is targeted at the clear specification of computer programs and the formulation of proofs about the intended program behavior. It was originally proposed by Jean-Raymond Abrial in 1977 with the help of Steve Schuman and Bertrand Meyer. (Abrial, 1980)

Other methods also include Actor model (Hewitt, 1973), B-Method (Abrial, 1996), CSP (Hoare, 2004), VDM (Fitzgerald, 1973) and so on.

The formal methods can overcome some deficiencies in architectural description. Nonetheless, we have to admit that formal methods do have their own limitation, which is inevitable anyway. Although formal methods have their position in software engineering and relative fields, compared with object-oriented technology, formal methods still do not arouse the interest of software industry (except some certain fields). Generally, it is believed that the current problems of formal methods are mainly: (1) The diversity between specification and actual code is still great because program coding is mostly completed via manual way. (2) Limited by the characteristics of themselves, formal methods are difficult to be integrated into software development process smoothly.

The controversy concerning formal methods exists and will last, but formal methods have shown outstanding technical capability. As a kind of successful guidance, they are also necessary methods for describing software architecture. Note that formal methods are only mathematical theories and lack of expression of system structure for architectural description. Without topology information of software system, mathematic theory could only act as a tool. And such tools can be used in any fields and confuse our understanding. Hence, we need a tie to combine the concept of formal methods and software architecture. For such consideration, we have another approach to supporting architectural description and analysis through Architecture Description Languages (ADLs).

4. 2   Architectural Description Language

4. 2. 1   Introduction to ADL

As we mentioned at the last of the previous section, Architectural Description Language is a viable option for architectural description. That is, to support architecture-based development, formal modeling notations and analysis and development tools that operate on architectural specifications are needed. ADLs and their accompanying toolsets have been proposed as one feasible answer (Medvidovic, 2000). Hence, in this section, we present a shallow insight to the field of ADL.

Informally, an ADL is a computer language used to describe software and system architecture. This rough definition still emphasizes the purpose of ADL and lack of some necessary specifications. We positively hope to check up a dictionary to find out the precise definition for ADL. Unfortunately, there is still little consensus in the research community on what an ADL is, what aspects of an architecture should be modeled by an ADL, and what should be interchanged in an interchange language. (Medvidovic, 2000) Furthermore, the situation about little consensus has not improved in the recent years. Along with the increase and development of ADL family, such academic debates have got expanded gradually; to reach consensus on the definition has become increasingly difficult.

Based on our understanding, we recognize that an ADL is a kind of language for description; it can be employed to describe software architecture on specified abstract level. It usually has formal syntax and semantics, and strictly predefined notations for expression; or simple, understandable and intuitive and abstract expression. The former can provide designers with powerful analysis tools, model checkers, parsers, compilers, code synthesis tools, runtime support tools, and so on based on formalism; the latter provide those kinds of tools that aid visualization, understanding, and simple analyses of architectural descriptions employing graphical symbols. Most of ADLs can analyze and validate system description relying on formal methods; however, some ADLs only have syntax and semantic concerning structure, and complete formal description and analysis combining other ADLs. The latter kind is regarded as interchange languages, and we accept that such interchanges are also ADLs. Regreting that we have not proposed accurately and shortly on the ADL definition, we use a whole paragraph to make a relatively broad summary according to current ADL research.

Truly, a number of ADLs have been proposed for modeling architectures by various relative research institutions. Worth noting is that some kinds of ADLs are developed in order to describe systems within a particular domain while some kinds are as general-purpose architecture modeling languages. Generally speaking, developers want to present their own understanding to software architecture and specified design concept via each kind of ADL.

As we mentioned above an ADL focuses on the high-level (abstract level) structure of the overall application rather than the implementation details of any specific source module. Therefore, what kinds of description elements will such focus bring into an ADL? As a classical theory (Shaw, 1996), Shaw and Garland define their elements for ADL, including components, operators, patterns, closure and specification.

- Components (Shaw, 1996)

Computation modules that architecture consists of in abstract level. A module can be physically discrete software elements or compiling unit. A module can be a package with a logic independent function, even a more abstract concept peculiarly belonging to software architecture.

- Operators

Interconnection mechanisms of components. Operators can be regarded as functions for combining architecture elements into high-class components.

- Patterns

Compositions in which architecture elements are connected in particular way. Patterns are reusable compositions of elements. A design pattern (or architecture pattern) is a design template, which focuses on a specific issue, and will be actualized (instantiated) in a specific design. The template will present the constraints on elements election and elements interaction.

- Closure

Conditions in which composition can serve as a subsystem in development of larger systems. Closure is such a concept to facilitate hierarchy description.

- Specification

Not only of functionality, but also of performance, fault-tolerance, and so on.

In fact, there are various views related to ADLs' elements proposed by different scholars. Inspecting ADLs from the perspective of system description and analysis, it is not difficult to find something in common.

First, ADLs should support runtime system topology analysis employing some basic elements—components, connectors and configuration. As mentioned before, components are independent functions, or computation units. A component may be only a small procedure or the entire application. Components, as building blocks for software architecture and encapsulated entities, interact with external environment via interfaces. Connectors are building blocks used to establish the interactions between components and rule these modules participating to the interactions. Connectors, as main entities for modeling architecture, also have interfaces. Interfaces of connectors declaim the participants in specified interactions. Configurations specify topology information of components and connectors. Configurations also provide relative information for validation. In a word, configuration can present both design-time and runtime description for architect to analyze and validate, which is ADLs' unique contribution to software development. Furthermore, some ADLs can support system dynamic description, which means the system architecture can alter during run time, such as runtime component addition, runtime component removal, runtime reconfiguration and so on.

Worth noting is that the components, connectors and configurations are not necessary elements of an ADL, but such concept standing for computations, interactions and integrations is general-purpose.

Second, ADLs may support hierarchical description and style definition as extension mechanism. Hierarchical description allows architects to describe a specified system in different abstract levers. The architect can describe subsystem in order to reduce the description complexity, which means hierarchical description brings more flexibility. The configuration merely specifies the structure of a single system; its capability is limited. Architects may concern with an entire family of systems and their abstract commonality. Style (e.g. Pipe-filter style) description usually is about some constraints on system topology, components and connectors which could be employed; it could help architecture to model and analyze in higher-lever abstraction.

Third, ADLs can employ formal methods to describe system behavior and validate system. About this point, we have briefly discussed in Section 4.1.2 on necessity of formal methods, and we will propose a further discussion in details in next section.

We have always reviewed usage, description and analysis capability from the perspective of system architecture. However, if you design an ADL, what issues will you consider? First of all you have to identify your design purpose. The design of a language should reflect its intended purpose. As mentioned before, some kinds of ADLs are developed for a particular domain while some kinds are general-purpose architecture modeling languages.

The issues vary, and the solutions differ. If the primary purpose of a language is to support a domain-specific design activity, such ADL should satisfy the basic requirements of relative engineers, which means natural design vocabulary on specified domain is crucial. However, if the primary purpose of a language is to support formal analysis, then the design must most concern about minimality of features and semantic simplicity in the design process.

In order to simplify this issue, we present a brief insight to ACME, an architecture description language. We can acquaint with the design purpose from such an example. Perhaps we are still confused of those introductions concerning abstract conceptions and definitions. We need a simple example based on our own research for more intuitionistic and concrete knowledge. And we will present and discuss more design purposes and goals of various ADLs in Section 4.2.2.

ACME (Garlan, 1997) is designed to provide an interchange format for architectural development tolls and environments. The top-lever concern is to integrate a broad variety of separately-developed ADL tools by providing an intermediate form for exchanging architectural information. In addition to primary goal concerning interchange, the design also proposes some secondary goals: (1) to provide a representational scheme that will permit the development of new tools for analyzing and visualizing architectural structures; (2) to provide a foundation for developing new, possibly domain-specific, ADLs; (3) to serve as a vehicle for creating conventions and standards for architectural information; (4) to provide expressive descriptions that are easy for humans to read and write. (Garlan, 1997)

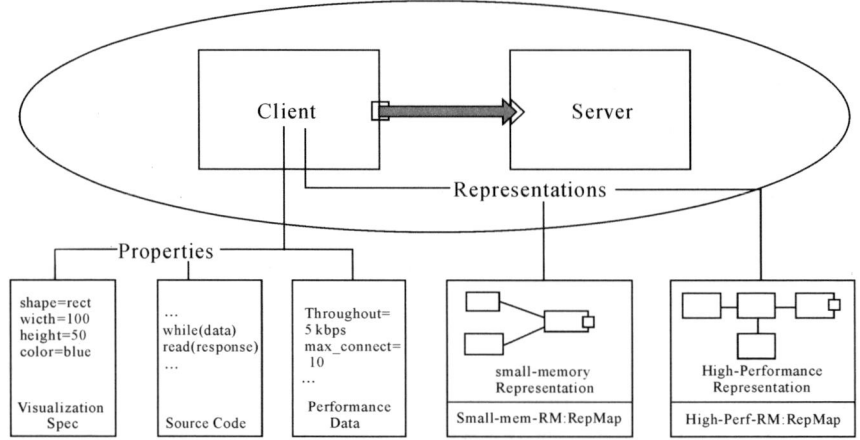

Fig. 4. 2   A simple Client-Server system

```
System simple_cs ={
    Component client ={
        Port send-request;
        Properties { Aesop-style : style-id = client-server;
                UniCon-style : style-id = cs;
                source-code:external = "CODE-LIB/client.c"}}
    Component server ={
        Port receive-request;
        Properties { idempotence : boolean = ture;
                max-concurrent-clients : integer = 1;
                source-code:external = "CODE-LIB/server.c"}}
    Connector rpc ={
        Roles {caller,callee}
        Properties { synchronous : boolean  =true
                max-roles : integer = 2;
                protocol : Wright = " "}}
    Attachments {
        client.send-request to rpc.caller;
        server.receive-request to rpc.callee}

}
```

Fig. 4. 3   Client-Server system described in ACME

A simple Client-Server system was shown in Fig. 4. 2, with several specific properties and two kinds of client representations. First we go through system specification in ACME depicted in Fig. 4. 3 omitting the properties and representations. The most basic elements of ACME are components, connectors and systems. Components are function units while connectors represent interaction; the client and the server are respectively abstracted as two components, and are connected via RPC connector. The ports of components and roles of connectors are interfaces, which indicate how to participate the interaction from perspectives of diverse participants (component or connector). Attachments describe link relationship of components and connectors, and support the configuration specification (*system*).

Furthermore, ACME supports hierarchical description by employing *representations*. Any components and connectors can be represented by one or more detailed, low-lever description. The architecture of client component in Fig. 4. 2, represented within two representations, varies according to specific requirements— small-memory and high-performance.

The above elements—components, connectors, ports, roles, system and *representations* are sufficient to describe a system architecture. Nonetheless, do not forget that ACME is an interchange language (Garlan, 1997). Each ADL typically has its own set of auxiliary information that determines such things as the run-time semantics of the system, detailed typing information, protocols of interaction, scheduling constraints and information about resource consumption. As an interchange language, ACME should own capability of containing the diverse auxiliary information. Hence ACME employs *properties* as its basic elements to accommodate such wide variety. Take the CS specification as example, properties of component client indicate the styles when it was described in specific targets ADLs-Aesop and UniCon. Likewise, the "protocol" property of the RPC connector is declared in WRIGHT. Note that properties are uninterpreted values to ACME. If we determine to make use of properties to do analysis, translation, and manipulation, we may need tool support of other languages.

4. 2. 2   Comparing among Typical ADLs

There are various kinds of ADLs developed in research domain of software architecture at present. We have mentioned the design purposes of those ADLs are distinct when we make a brief introduce of ADLs. Now we present a comparing among typical ADLs, e.g. WRIGHT, C2, Darwin, ACME, xADL, π-ADL, KDL. Of those above ADLs, we use KDL only as an example to illustrate the specific-domain-oriented design purpose; KDL is not mentioned in the following sections about comparison of basic description elements.

- Distinct Design Purposes
WRIGHT (Allen, 1997a)
WRIGHT is designed based on precise description of system architecture and abstract behavior, description of architectural styles, validation of systems' consistence and completeness. According to opinions of the WRIGHT's authors, an architectural description language should provide two things at least: (1) a precise semantics that resolves ambiguity and aids in the detection of inconsistencies; (2) a set of techniques that support reasoning about system properties. Another goal is to fit the architect's own vocabulary. WRIGHT aims to expose specified abstractions and provides means for the architect to use them in structuring the software system. In Section 4.3, we will introduce elements, syntax and semantics of

WRIGHT in details. We can see how it meets these goals by then.

• C2 (Taylor, 1996)

C2 supports component replacement and reuse in Graphic User Interface (GUI) development. Now, user interface accounts for a large fraction of software while reusability is very limited. C2 focuses on reuse of components, particularly the dynamic change of components in system runtime. Hence, goals of C2 include the ability to compose systems in which: components may be written in different programming languages; components may be running concurrently in a distributed, heterogeneous environment without shared address spaces; architectures may be changed at runtime; multiple users may be interacting with the system; multiple toolkits may be employed; multiple dialogs may be active and described in different formalisms, and multiple media types may be involved.

• Darwin

Darwin is a declarative language, it aims to provide general-propose notations for specifying the structure of systems which are composed of diverse components using diverse interaction mechanisms. It mainly focuses on specification of distributed software system. Recent research on maintenance of the software distribution system shows that employing distribution will help to simplify the complexity of software components. However, such advantage is insufficient to compensate an accompanying shortcoming of distribution systems—the complexity of the architecture greatly increased. Darwin is designed to solve this problem. In addition, Darwin also supports the specification of dynamic structures—system evolutions in runtime. The following figure shows how Darwin describes a client-server system.

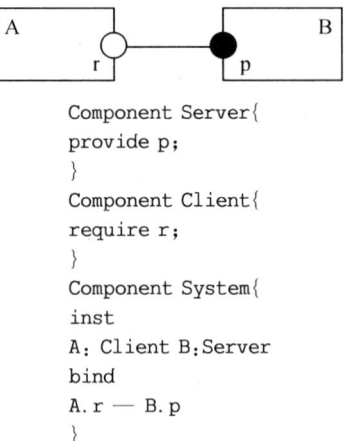

```
Component Server{
provide p;
}
Component Client{
require r;
}
Component System{
inst
A: Client B:Server
bind
A.r — B.p
}
```

Fig. 4. 4   Client-Server system described in Darwin

• ACME (Garlan, 1997)

ACME is designed as an interchange ADL. We have discussed the design purpose in previous introduction.

- xADL (Dashofy, 2005)

Many ADLs have borne during research over the past decade. This situation has led to a plethora of notations for representing software architecture, each focusing on different aspects of the systems being modeled. Meanwhile, reusability and extensibility is very limited. Adapting an existing notation to a new purpose is as difficult as redeveloping a new notation entirely. xADL is developed for better scalability for architect. It aims to provide rapid construction of new ADLs. Fig.4.5 shows an example description of connector.

```
<connector id="tvconn">
  <description>
  TV connector
  </description>
  <interface id="tvconn.in">
    <description>
    ChangeChannel Interface (in)
    </description>
    <direction>in</direction>
  <\interface>
  <interface id="tvconn.out">
    <description>
    ChangeChannel Interface (out)
    </description>
    <direction>out</direction>
  <\interface>
<\connector>
```

Fig. 4. 5   An example description of Connector in xADL

- π-ADL (Oquendo, 2004a)

π-ADL is designed to address specification of dynamic and mobile architectures. The dynamic architecture namely means the architecture can evolve at runtime. The mobile architectures are such architectures whose components can logically move during the execution of the system. π-ADL is a formal, well-founded, theoretical language based on the higher-order typed π-calculus. While most ADLs focus on describing software architectures from a structural viewpoint, π-ADL focuses on formally describing architectures encompassing both the structural and behavioral viewpoints. An example of component described in π-ADL is shown in Fig.4.6.

```
component SensorDef is abstraction() {
    type Key is Any. type Data is Any. type Entry is tuple[Key, Data].
    port incoming is { connection in is in(Entry) }.
    port outgoing is { connection toLink is out(Entry) }.
    behaviour is {
        process is function(d: Data) : Data { unobservable }.
        via incoming::in receive entry : Entry.
        project entry as key, data.
        via outgoing::toLink send tuple(key, process(data)).
        behaviour()
    }
}
```

Fig. 4. 6   π-ADL component specification

- KDL (He, 2005b)

KDL is an ontology-based E-commerce (EC) knowledge description language. It can be regarded as an ADL developed for a specific domain—EC. Along with flourish and development of EC, EC model has shown automated, intelligent and mobile trends. Traditional EC platforms base on HTML lack of semantic information, mix display information with data; it is difficult to achieve new requirements of EC. KDL is designed as a simple and efficient approach for precise definition and information interchange. In addition, this approach is based on RDF (S) and concept of ontology. Finally, we can realize how KDL describes a category via the example depicted in the following figure.

```
⟨dkl :DefinedClass rdf : ID = "CD"⟩
⟨rdfs :subClassOf rdf :resource = "Item"⟩
⟨rdfs :subClassOf⟩
⟨kdl :Restriction⟩
⟨kdl :onSlot rdf :resource = "hasStyle"⟩
⟨kdl :sufficient⟩
⟨rdf :resource = "MusicStyle"/ ⟩
⟨/ kdl :sufficient⟩
⟨/ kdl :sufficient⟩
⟨/ kdl :Restricition⟩
⟨/ rdfs :subClassOf⟩
⟨/ kdl :DefinedClass⟩
⟨CD rdf : ID = "MyCD"⟩
⟨hasStyle rdf :resource = "CountryMusic"/ ⟩
⟨/"CD"⟩
```

Fig. 4. 7   CD described in KDL

Majority of ADLs support runtime system analysis via some basic elements—components, connectors and configurations. Hence, our comparing is based on modeling for these building blocks. (Medvidovic, 2000)

- Modeling Components

All mentioned ADLs, such as WRIGHT, C2, Darwin, ACME, xADL, π-ADL, model components. Here we discuss the modeling support provided by ADLs for different aspects of components.

- Interfaces

All mentioned ADLs support specification of component interfaces. They differ in the terminology and the kinds of information they specify. For example, an interface point in ACME , WRIGHT or π-ADL is a port and, in xADL, just an interface. On the other hand, in C2, the entire interface is provided through a single port; individual interface elements are messages. Hence, a C2 component has exactly two communication ports, one each on its top and bottom sides; top ports are responsible for communication with superstratum components while bottom ports are with substrate components. WRIGHT allows several ports in a components; each port indicates an interaction with the other components via a connector.

ADLs typically distinguish between interface points that refer to provided and required functionality. For example, provided and required interface providing services is terms as output and input ports in Darwin.(Shown in Fig.4.8) WRIGHT,

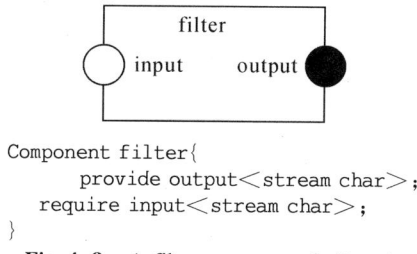

```
Component filter{
       provide output<stream char>;
     require input<stream char>;
}
```

Fig. 4. 8   A filter component in Darwin

xADL also support type definitions of interfaces. Particularly, WRIGHT specifies the protocol of interaction at each port in CSP.

♦ Types

All of the mentioned ADLs distinguish component types from instances. Especially, in ACME and xADL, components can be used as instances without type definition. In addition, several ADLs (ACME, Darwin, WRIGHT and π-ADL) make explicit use of parameterization of component interface signatures, which is similar to programming languages as Ada and C++.

• Modeling Connectors

ADLs model connectors in various forms and under various names. For example, ACME, C2, WRIGHT, xADL and π-ADL model connectors explicitly and refer to them as connectors. Darwin bindings representing connectors are modeled in-line, and cannot be named, subtyped, or reused.

♦ Interfaces

In general, only the ADLs that model connectors as first-class entities support explicit specification of connector interfaces. Most such ADLs model component and connector interfaces in the same manner, but refer to them differently. Connector interface points in ACME, WRIGHT are roles, in xADL still interfaces, in π-ADL ports. Likewise, WRIGHT, xADL also support type definitions of connector interfaces. WRIGHT specifies the protocol of interaction at each role in CSP as the same.

♦ Types

Only ADLs that model connectors as first-class entities distinguish connector types from instances. Hence, Darwin is definitely excluded. ACME, C2, WRIGHT, xADL, π-ADL base connector types on interaction protocols. Similarly, ACME and xADL support connectors used as instances without type definition.

ACME and π-ADL also provide parameterization facilities that enable flexible specification of connector signatures and of constraints on connector semantics. Similarly to its components, WRIGHT allows a connector to be parameterized by the specification of its behavior (glue) or the other parts.

• Behavioral Specifications

C2 supports specification of static component semantics via invariants and operation pre- and post-conditions. WRIGHT extends component and connector specifications with behavioral information, namely system behavior, in the language of CSP.

Darwin expresses models of interaction and composition properties of composite components in the π-calculus. Similarly, π-ADL describes system behavior via component and connector specifications in π-calculus.

As mentioned in Section 4.2.1, arbitrarily complex behavioral specifications are treated as uninterrupted annotations in ACME, and would be analyzed by supporting from the other ADLs; such mechanism employed in xADL is very similar. Hence, the behavioral specifications are in different approaches according to diverse ADLs supporting behavioral specifications independently (e.g., WRIGHT, π-ADL).

- Modeling Configurations
- Compositionality

Most ADLs support hierachical description of components, where the syntax for specifying hierarchy is similar to specifying configurations. Hierachical description is viewed as a subsystem configuration from intuitionistic perspective.

It is interesting to note that Darwin does not have explicit constructs for modeling architectures. Instead, it models architectures as composite components instead of the concept of configuration. ACME supports hierarchical description termed as representations; both any components and connectors can be represented. WRIGHT allows both composite components and connectors: The computation (glue) of a composite component (connector) is represented by an entire configuration.

In π-ADL, components and connectors can be composed to construct composite elements, more complex components or connectors. Furthermore, composite elements can be decomposed and recomposed in different ways or with different components in order to construct different compositions.

- Heterogeneity

Of those ADLs that support implementation of architectures, several are also tightly tied to a particular programming language. For example, Darwin only supports development with components implemented in C++. C2 currently supports development in C++, Ada, and Java, while xADL supports development in Java.

- Dynamism

Darwin, C2 and π-ADL support the dynamic description of configuration, which means the system can change at runtime.

Darwin specifies dynamic system architecture using lazy and direct dynamic instantiation. Note that in Fig.4.9, bindings are specified for the component type poller rather instances of this type as usual. The provided service newpoll is bound to service dyn poll. When invoking newpoll service, a new poller instance will be created and linked to component M. This is an example that Darwin allows runtime replication of components via direct dynamic instantiation. Furthermore, Darwin allows deletion and rebinding of components by interpreting Darwin scripts.

C2's architecture modification (sub) language (AML) specifies a set of operations for insertion, removal, and rewiring of elements in an architecture at

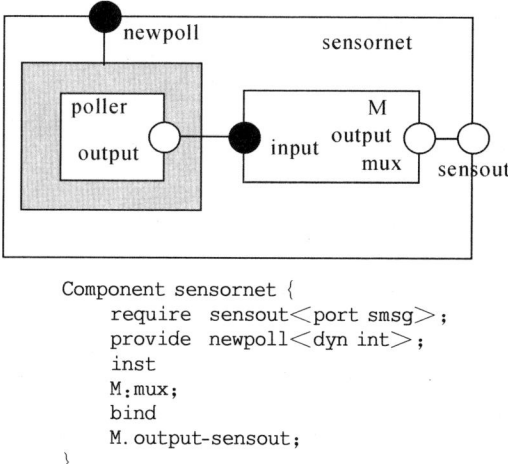

```
Component sensornet {
    require  sensout<port smsg>;
    provide  newpoll<dyn int>;
    inst
    M;mux;
    bind
    M.output-sensout;
}
```

Fig. 4. 9   Dynamic instantiation

runtime: addComponent, removeComponent, weld, and unweld. (Taylor, 1996)

π-ADL allows that behavior description creates instantiation of predefined component or connector type according to run-time parameters and certain condition. (Oquendo, 2004a) Hence a system architecture may depends on parameter or different environments. But this is not known at design time, it is only discovered at runtime. Particularly, π-ADL also supports description of mobile architecture.

After all most ADLs only support system description statically. The difficulty not only limits the creativity of architect, but also limits the use of ADL in software engineering. The designers of new ADL hope to meliorate such situation, so supporting of dynamism become a trend feature in area of designing ADL. For example, the designers of xADL plan to expand the xADL 2.0 schemas to include new modeling constructs, particularly those that will support the specification of distributed and dynamic architectures.

4. 2. 3   Describing Architectural Behaviors

Architect should describe the system architectural behaviors through certain approaches. The specification only concerning attachment of typed components and connectors without architect behaviors is not sufficient to describe a system, the designer's purpose either. We have to precisely specify the computation and interaction and so on which are combined to complete the function of the system, namely system behavior.

We have mentioned that the formal methods do have more advantages in architectural behavior description compared with informal approaches. Advantage of machinery expression and computation, formal and exact definitions without vagueness make formal approaches conspicuous. Among multitudinous formal methods, process algebras represent a diverse family of related approaches to formally modeling concurrent systems. Process algebras provide a tool for the high-level description of interactions, communications, and synchronizations between a collection of independent agents or processes (could be regarded as patterns of behaviors). The prominent contribution is that process algebras provide formal computation and transformation of processes, also foundation of system behavior validation.

Such diverse family includes CCS (Milner, 1980), CSP (Hoare, 2004), ACP (Bergstra, 1987), and some recent members as the π-calculus (Sangiorgi, 2001), the ambient calculus (Cardelli, 1998) , and so on. In this section, we mainly introduce CCS, CSP and π-calculus.

- CCS

The Calculus of Communicating Systems (CCS) is a process algebra as a model of concurrent system developed by Robin Milner. CCS is the pioneering work in the field of process algebra; some famous process algebras—both CSP employed by WRIGHT and π-calculus employed by Darwin and π-ADL are developed on the foundation established by CCS.

The basic elements of CSS are events and processes. Generally, capital letters donate processes and lowercase letters donate events. The events of CSS consist of two labeled sets $\Delta = \{a, b, c, \dots\}$ and $\overline{\Delta} = \{\overline{a}, \overline{b}, \overline{c}, \dots\}$. Δ is input event set while $\overline{\Delta}$ is output events set; Δ and $\overline{\Delta}$ need to satisfy the following conditions: $\overline{\Delta} = \{\overline{x} \mid x \in \Delta\}$. a and $\overline{a}$ is a pair of coordinated events; the communication of different processes only happens via a pair of coordinated events.

If P is a process and x is the first event P engages in, the rest after execution of x event can be described as Q; then the process P can be denoted as $x . Q$. Here, $x \in \overline{\Delta} \cup \Delta$, the notation "." is sequential operator. For example,

$P_1 = a . b .$ NIL (terminal process)

$P_2 = a . c . P_2$ (recursion process)

The process NIL is a special process which never engages in any events. NIL can be regarded as a terminal signature of a process. In the above example, P_1 is a process which engages in a and b sequentially, then finally terminates. P_2 is a recursion process which engages in a and c repeatedly, and never terminates. In CCS, description of complex problems can be simplified and expressed by composition of some processes.

- CSP

CSP is semantic basis of formal behavior description employed by WRIGHT. That is, WRIGHT supports behavioral description and validation via CSP. In brief, CSP provides a different model of behavior from the state-machine models. Rather than describing a machine as a collection of states composed into a graph of transitions, a behavior is described through an algebraic model of processes, in which complex behaviors are constructed from simpler ones via a small set of operators. Such approach of simplification is very similar to CCS, the relative foundation of CSP. In the study case of WRIGHT, we will introduce CSP syntax and those operations in details.

- π-calculus

The π-calculus is a process calculus originally developed by Robin Milner, Joachim Parrow and David Walker as a continuation of the body of work on the CCS (Calculus of Communicating Systems). The aim of the π-calculus is to be able to describe concurrent computations whose configuration may change during the computation. A brief introduction to π-calculus can be found in the Section 8.2.1.

4.3   Study Case: WRIGHT System

The WRIGHT architecture description language was proposed by Robert J. Allen in his dissertation for degree of doctor of philosophy, in 1997 (Allen, 1997b). In order to figure out the problems facing architecture designers that software systems become more complex, the author combined formal methods and purely structure-based ADLs to design the WRIGHT language. The author claimed that WRIGHT is designed to support description of architecture configurations and styles, analysis of properties of interest and application to practical problems on real systems.

How does WRIGHT achieve these requirements above, that is, to support such description and analysis? We explain the question from both perspectives and make further discussion in this section.

As a structure-based ADL, WRIGHT is based on the formal description of the abstract behavior of architecture components and connectors, which is its basic design concept. The component and the connector are significant elements of WRIGHT; hence we discuss these two elements particularly in details within the following section. Additionally considering completeness of description ability, WRIGHT also permits designer to describe and analyze system configuration and architecture style.

Meanwhile, as a formal approach WRIGHT uses a notation developed from CSP (Communication Sequential Processes) to describe the abstract behavior between architectural components. It defines independent connector types as interactions type and uses predicts to characterize architecture style. With the support of relevant formalisms, WRIGHT is able to provide static validations over consistency and completeness and deadlock free of a certain architecture specification, which is most valued for architecture designers to use a formal approach. All these above make WRIGHT distinguished from the other ADLs.

We all realize that although all of the ADLs are concerned with architectural design, each of them exactly provides certain distinctive capabilities according to specified design concept. As a conclusion, the remarkable capability of WRIGHT is its support for the specification and analysis of abstract interactions between architectural components.

For the further discussion, we propose our study case based on Knopflerfish, an open source implementation of OSGi framework to introduce the basic elements and relevant behavior description formalism of WRIGHT. OSGi (Open Service Gateway initiative) is presented by OSGi Alliance which was founded by Sun Microsystems, IBM, Ericsson and others in March 1999. The initial target of OSGi is to provide home service gateway for service provider in order to provide various services for home intelligent devices. Now OSGi has gradually become a transmission and remote management service platform for applications and services of various network devices including home devices, vehicles, mobile phones and so on. And framework, one part of OSGi specification, provides a Java technology-based lightweight (fully J2ME-compatible) container for dynamic software components.

Since we discuss only a small portion of OSGi framework in high-lever abstraction with few details, it is not necessary to deeply understand the specification and technique details of OSGi of the implement details of Knopflerfish.

In this chapter, we mainly introduce the basic elements of WRIGHT including description of components and connectors, descriptions of configuration and styles. We also introduce how WRIGHT develops CSP to describe formal behaviors of interaction. After that, we show some validation mechanisms provided by WRIGHT to check our OSGi framework description.

4. 3. 1   Description of Component and Connector

WRIGHT, as an architectural description language, is built around the basic architectural abstraction of components and connectors. Components and connectors are the most basic elements of architectural description. WRIGHT provides explicit notations for each element it uses. In this section we introduce how to use these notations to describe the basic architecture in an accurate way and show how WRIGHT formalizes the notions of components as computation and connector as pattern of interaction using our study case. We discuss component and connector from architecture aspect, deliberately deferring the details of formal behavior description of computation and interaction to simplify the introduction.

We use a portion model extracted from Knopflerfish as a simple example to continue the introduction to WRIGHT. We concentrate those modules related to services. We call this simplified system "Bundle Management System" (BM System for short). The service in OSGi is an object that provides some well-defined functionality which is defined by the object classes it implements. It is possessed by a bundle and run within a bundle. A bundle owns services that might be provided to other bundles and might uses services provided by the other bundles. Users of this system control Framework through user interface, then Framework is in charge of starting or stopping a bundle. If a bundle wants to make functionality of a certain service available to the other bundles after being started, it must register the service to the framework. The framework handles service registration to manage the dependencies between the bundle owning the service and the bundles using it.

This architecture is shown informally in Fig.4.10. Actually WRIGHT doesn't support formal description for visualizing diagram, so there won't be a formal figure described by WRIGHT. The two components are Bundle and Framework,

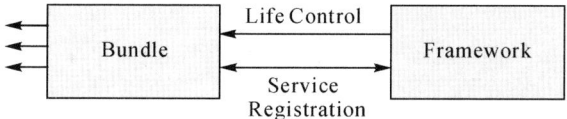

Fig. 4. 10 A model system extracted from Knopflerfish

which are related to services and the exact participants of service registration and unregistration. We only concern the operations of them related to services running. The Bundle initiates and sends the request about service registration or unregistration to Framework. And it might use services from other bundles or provide services to other bundles. The Framework controls life time of bundles obviously. Also it handles service registration according to the request and the limited condition and then sends response to Bundle. The life time of bundles is controlled via unidirectional connector. Requests and responses are transmitted between Bundle and Framework via the bidirectional connector.

- Components

As the definition made by the author, a component describes a localized, independent computation. Now forget the definition above because it is obviously abstract and increases difficulty to comprehension. Let's come back to look into different architecture styles to find out what a component is about. For example in a pipe-and-filter system, a component might be a filter which reads stream on input, does local incremental transformation to this input stream and outputs the transformed stream. In event-based system, components might be event announcer and event processor. In a layered system, component might be a layer which serves assigning distinct and special functions, hides lower layer and provides services to higher layer.

In WRIGHT, a component is divided into two important parts for description, the *interface* and the *computation*. An interface consists of several ports, each of which represents an interaction in which the component may participate. For example, in pipe-and-filter system, a filter component might have several ports for stream input or stream output. In event-based system, event announcer might have a port for announcing events to event processor.

The framework in Knopflerfish implementation is comprised by a series of classes, and implements lots of complex functions. Nonetheless, concerning the BM System presented in Fig.4.10, the Framework is simplified for the requirement of description aspect and discussion convenience. So it has only two ports (shown in Fig.4.11), one called Control to start and stop running of a certain bundle, one called Registration to receive request from the Bundle and send response back. All of these operations are accomplished through procedure calls. And descriptions of ports only indicate that Framework participates in interactions by procedure calls, but not indicate which component it interacts with. The words in brackets are only a supplementary explanation, but not parts of formal ports description.

Do not forget that there is another part of component description called

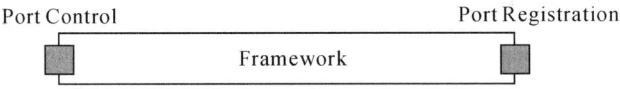

Fig. 4. 11   The illustrative framework component

computation. Computation describes the actual action of a component. Computation and port are not unrelated conceptions. The computation carries out the interactions described by the ports and makes the interactions as a meaningful coherent whole through statements in it. The computation of Framework involves starting and stopping a bundle by invoking function and managing service registration by providing invoked function. A sample description of the component Framework is depicted in Fig.4.12.

Component Framework
　　Port Control [invoke function (to *start or stop a bundle*)]
　　Port Registration [provide invoked function (to *receive request of service registration or unregistration, then send response*)]
　　Computation [*start or stop a bundle; get request from Registration, manage service registration, then send response by Registration*]

Fig. 4. 12   A component description

When we describe a component using WRIGHT, the port description indicates some aspect of the component's behavior and the entire behavior description is completed by computation specification. In addition, the description of a component above concerns about semantic structure of WRIGHT, so the behavioral description is still informal and will be formalized in following introduction. And for architecture designer and implementer, more useful information provided by port description is that it could tell us about the expectation of a component when it interacts with other components. From the Port Registration, we find out that Framework expects to obtain some request about services.

Although component is formally divided into two parts, the computation and the ports, that doesn't mean they are independent elements and could be described separately. To make a component description meaningful to system design, we must make sure the computation doesn't violate the interface. The component description must be consistent, which means that computation must obey the rules of interaction defined by port. WRIGHT provides such a mechanism to validate consistency by using formalism notation, which we will introduce in Section 4.3.4. Additionally the name of each port must be unique within a given component for distinction, so must the name of each connector role.

From the definition and description of components in WRIGHT, we recognize that a component completes its own independent computation through interactions with the system. Ports of the component describe how the component participates in interactions as a function module of the system and what the component expects in interactions. The description above does involve interactions, but it is actually around the computation of the component and isn't concerning interactions themselves. Hence WRIGHT employs a connector to describe an interaction itself, that is, to proclaim rules of an interaction.

- Connectors

We already know that a connector describes an interaction among several components. There are extremely distinguishing connectors according to different architecture styles. In a pipe-filter system, a connector is just a conduit for streams; in a layered system it represents communication protocols or interfaces between two neighboring layers; in an event-based system it is in charge of messages transmission. Coming down to actual implementation, we might realize connectors by an entire class, references between classes, or even a simple procedure call. And in our sample system, connectors between Bundle and Framework are procedure calls.

WRIGHT uses the conception of connectors to achieve two important purposes: First to extend the applicability of analysis, and second to increase the independent of components. For applicability of analysis, a connect type can represent a pattern of interaction, and the pattern can be used repeatedly in connector instances. WRIGHT reveals the commonality in a certain architecture by reusing the connect type. Although interactions between Buddle and Framework have different meanings, we can use the form of procedure calls to represent these interactions, evidently different procedure calls in implementation. Also we can use the form of procedure calls in other interactions of the system, such as service using and providing related to bundles. When we are developing a large and complicated system, adopting the interaction patterns simplifies management of change and the structuring of implementation.

Structuring the way in which a component interacts with the rest of the system does increase the independence of components. A connector provides an information hiding boundary that clarifies what expectations the component can have about its environment, which means a component specification can be used in multiple contexts. The Framework description doesn't concern about which component invokes its function through Port Registration or which component's functions it invokes. The component specification only concerns about its own functions which are open to the external, because the connector specifications describe how the components is combined with other components in the system.

After discussing the expressional meaning and author's design purposes of connectors, we introduce how to describe connectors. In WRIGHT, a connector is also divided into two important parts for description, a set of roles and the glue. It is clear that the roles and the glue serve the interaction description.

The roles indicate the expectation for any component participating in a certain interaction, as the ports of a component indicate the expectation of it when it interacts with other components. They are semantically same because they both involve the interaction expectation. Nonetheless they describe the expectation from different aspects; the ports observe the interaction from the aspect of components while the roles describe the expectation from the aspect of interactions themselves. For example, a pipe connector has two roles, the data source and the sink and an event broadcast connector has an event broadcaster and several event listeners.

The glue of a connector describes how the participants work together to create an interaction. That means glue establishes the rules for roles and coordinates the roles to accomplish an interaction according to the certain rules. For example, the glue of a pipe connector might specify that sink receives data delivered by source in the same order using first-in-first-out strategy. And the rules can vary for different design purposes; the sink of a pipe might receive data reversely using first-in-last-out strategy or the sink might get nothing because the glue of a pipe simply ignores the data delivered by source.

Procedure-call

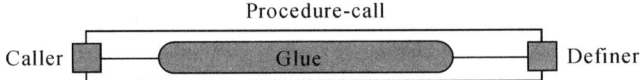

Caller   Definer

Fig. 4. 13   The illustration of a Procedure-call connector

In our sample system, a Procedure-call connector are shown in Fig. 4. 13. The connector has a caller and a definer, and its glue coordinates the Caller and the Definer to accomplish the procedure call, the actual interaction between the Bundle and the Framework.

Connector Procedure-call
    Role Caller [*invoke function*]
    Glue Definer [*provide invoked function*]
    Glue [*Caller invokes function of Definer; Definer returns the relevant results to Caller*]
        Fig. 4. 14   The semantic structure of a connector description

The description of a procedure-call connector is displayed in Fig. 4. 14. Each role specifies the behavior of a single participant in the interaction. The role Caller indicates that any component which participates in procedure-call and acts as a caller will invoke function while the role Definer indicates those component acts as a definer will provide invoked function. The Glue of the connector represents the full behavioral specification just like the computation of a component. As its description responsibility, the glue indicates that Caller initiates the invocation and then Definer returns the relevant results. Because the current behavior specification is temporarily informal, we aren't clear about the coordination of Caller's and Definer's behavior. We wonder whether Caller will just wait and do nothing until it gets return from Definer. This problem is caused by ambiguity of natural languages, and it will be fixed by employing CSP to describe the behaviors formally.

It is worth noting that the descriptions we introduce above represent types of components and connectors, because in a system there might be many components or connectors that are in the same type. A connector type is abstraction representing a certain kind of interaction; it can be used in different context of different components. That is, if components obey the behaviors specified by the roles, the connector can combine the components by the glue and ignore the actual computations of the components. A collection of components are combined by different connectors as roles so that the computations of components are coordinated by the glues to form a larger computation, that is, the system.

4.3.2   Description of Configuration

After presenting components and connectors, the most basic elements of architectural description in WRIGHT, we introduce how to describe a complete system architecture. Architecture designers need to draw a blueprint to describe the system architecture and behavior by link of component and connector instances of components and connectors. That blueprint is called a configuration. In this section, we introduce the elements of a configuration-instances and attachments, also hierarchical configuration. An example configuration of the BM System is depicted in Fig.4.15, but we omit that bundles provide services for each others to simplify the current description.

- Instances

The descriptions we introduce above actually represent types of components and connectors, because in a system there might be many components or connectors that are of the same type. That is, the type descriptions represent the properties and behaviors of certain types of components and connectors, rather than actual samples in use. For example, "Procedure-call" is a connector type; a certain system might use several instances of procedure-call. When we use it to describe the actual interaction of a given system, that type must be instantiated. We use the instances of different types to describe a system architecture just as we use object-instances of classes to program in object-oriented programming language. The name of each instance in a given system must be explicit and unique for distinction; otherwise the system architecture would be confused and ambiguous for system developers. As presented in Fig. 4. 15, instances specification follows type specification of components and connectors.

- Attachments

Suppose that we have all the necessary parts and screws to assemble a toy truck, we have to know how to attach specific parts to each others by screws. The blueprint should be instructional, so the configuration isn't complete without describing the attachments. The attachments indicate attaching relationship between a certain component with a certain connector. In other words, the attachments declare which component participates in which interaction, which is done by associating the component's port with the connector's role.

Attachments are declared in such form as "FrameworkA.Control as P1.Caller". It indicates that the component FrameworkA will play the role of Caller in interaction P1 defined by the Procedure-call connector. That is, FrameworkA will invoke function of P1's definer. The second attachment declaration "BundleA.Activator as P1.Definer" specifies that the BunndleA will provide the certain invoked function. Note that the attachment declarations about P2 indicate that BundleA plays the Callers while AFramework plays the Definer. The invoking relationships are just reversal in P1 and P2.

In addition, a port must be compatible to a role if the port is attached to the role. That doesn't mean the port behavior description must be exactly the same with the role behavior description, but that if a component wants to participate an interaction defined by a connector, the port of the component has to obey the rules specified by the role.

```
Configuration BundleManagement
    Component Framework
    ...
    Component Bundle
    ...
    Connector Procedure-call
    ...
    ...
    Instances
        FrameworkA: Framework
        BundleA: Bundle
        P1: Procedure-call
        P2: Procedure-call
    Attachments
        FrameworkA.Control as P1.Caller
        BundleA.Activator as P1.definer
        BundleA.Register as P1.caller
        FrameworkA.Registration as P1.definer
End BundleManagement
```

Fig. 4. 15   The sample configuration of BM system

- Hierarchy

Sometimes we might need to describe a given system in different abstract levers. We might divide the system into a number of subsystems for description in order to reduce the description complexity; and then integrate all the subsystem descriptions into an entire system description. That is, we need to describe a system with hierarchy support.

Fortunately, WRIGHT supports hierarchical descriptions. In WRIGHT, the computation of a component or the glue of a connector can be regarded as a subsystem and described just as a system configuration we mentioned above. In that case the component or the connector serves as abstraction boundary for a nested architectural system. Suppose now we use a nested architectural system description to describe the computation of a component. There must be one unattached port in the nested description at least because the computation should include specification about the interaction the component participates in. Meanwhile the component will define all of its ports outside computation—the nested description, so that unattached port is actually defined repeatedly. WRIGHT employs bindings to associate the outside port name and the inside name. And they are for roles when we use a nested architectural system description to describe the glue of a connector.

A hierarchical specification based on the BM System is shown in Fig.4.16. In fact, Framework has a collection of components with different functions and two of them are related to the BM System. The BundleControl is in charge of bundles survival control, while the ServiceManagement manages service registration. And the

nested description involves bindings specification to associate the certain ports that
represent the interaction with the outside component.

```
Configuration BundleManagement
      Component  Framework
          Port Control
          Port Registration
          Computation
              Configuration  BundleService
              Component BundleControl
                  . . .
              Component ServiceManagement
                  . . .

          . . .
          Instances
              BundleControlA : BundleService
               ServiceManagementA :ServiceManagement
          Attachments
              . . .
           End BundleService
           Bindings
                 BundleControlA. Control = Control
                 SeviceManagementA. Registration = Registration
           End  Bindings
      Component    Bundle
          . . .
      Connector Procedure—call
          . . .
      . . .
      Instances
          . . .
      Attachments
          . . .
End BundleManagement
```
Fig. 4. 16   Hierarchical specification of BM system

4. 3. 3   Description of Style

We have introduced the basic elements employed by WRIGHT, and how to employ
those elements to describe a complete system architecture in the system
configuration. As we know, the configuration merely specifies the structure of a
single system. However, as architects, we need to concern with a system in the
context of an entire family of systems. Software architecture styles represent the
relationships between components and components: the restriction of component
application and the composition and design rule relative to components.

Supporting description of style is one of main distinct characteristics of
WRIGHT. In this section, we briefly introduce the elements adopted to describe a
system architectural style, including interface types, parameterization and
constraints.

As we mentioned before, component and connector types represent the
conception of reuse to parts of system. However, we need certain conception of
reuse for interior of components and connectors to describe an architectural style.
That is, the properties of a style might concern about and constrain only part of a

component or a connector, such as ports and roles. For example, in the pipe-filter style, each component works as a filter for stream, so almost each of those components needs input and output ports for dataflow. Although the numbers or names of input and output ports differ according to certain filters (e.g. Usually the original source might only have output ports while the final sink might only have input ports.), the data input and output is a kind of commonality shared by all the filters (components) deliberately ignoring those distinguishing internal functions. In WRIGHT, we use interface types to describe such commonalities of components and connectors, namely patterns of ports and roles. Fig.4.17 shows how to define input and output ports within interface types.

Interface Type DataInput = [read data repeatedly, closing the port at or before end-of-data]
Interface Type DataOutput = [write data repeatedly, closing the port to signal end-of-data]

Fig. 4. 17   Interface types of ports

Obviously interface types most are used as the ports of a component, but also can be used as the roles of a connector. Take the roles of connector Procedure-call as example, we can realize that the definer should provide invoke function with return values as defined in Fig.4.18.

Interface Type ICaller = [invoke function, get return values]
Interface Type IDefiner = [provide invoked function which has return values]

Fig. 4. 18   Interface types of roles

How the architectural description can cover more situations and achieve flexibility is a significant question we face when describing families of systems rather than a single system. WRIGHT achieves such requirements by *parameterizing* the type descriptions. For example, in our BM system, a bundle as a component owns distinct services that might be provided to other bundles. However, Bundle components all have a port named Activator to receive starting demand, a port named Register to register services to Framework and numbers of ports related to service using and providing. Each bundle has three types of ports to participate interactions with external, but the computation performed by each bundle differs according to different services provided.

Component Bundle (S: **Computation**, n: 1···)
    Port Activator = IDefiner
    Port Register = ICaller
    Port Service1..n [invoke service functions or provide service functions]
    Computation = S

Fig. 4. 19   Parameterization in WRIGHT

As shown in Fig.4.19, we parameterize computation as above reason, so we can use this description to describe any bundle with any services. Note that we may not know how many bundles a certain bundle will interact with in service using and providing, hence we make the number of service ports to indicate that there may be more than one service ports in a bundle allowedly. In fact, WRIGHT permits any part of the description of a type to be replaced with a parameter. So the types of a port or role, a computation, the name of an interface, etc., are all parameterizable. Nonetheless, it is worth noting that all the parameters including the numbers must be determined when the type is instantiated. The determination of ports amount also demonstrates the static nature of a WRIGHT description. WRIGHT assumes that the set of components and the interaction do not change at run time. Although WRIGHT has the conception of parameterization, that doesn't mean WRIGHT is an ADL supporting dynamic architectural description.

Finally we introduce the constraints used in WRIGHT. If a system is in the pipe-filter style, one condition must be met at least—it must use only filter components and pipe connectors. A WRIGHT style description declares those properties any configuration of a style must obey with the constraints. The author of WRIGHT use first order predicate logic to express the constraints, which is intuitionistic. The constraints refer to the following sets and operators, and all the notations are predefined by the author (shown in Fig.4.20):

Components: the set of components in the configuration.
Connectors: the set of connectors in the configuration.
Attachments: the set of attachments in the configuration. Each attachment is represented as a pair of pairs ((comp, port), (conn, role)).
Name(e): the name of element e, where e is a component, connector, port, or role.
Type(e): the type of element e.
Ports(c): the set of ports on component c.
Computation(c): the computation of component c.
Roles(c): the set of roles of connector c.
Glue(c): the glue of connector c.

Fig. 4. 20   Constraints notations

Thus, we can use some of these notations to describe the pipe-filter style. Those constraints shown in Fig.4.21 mean that all the connectors must be pipes and all components in the system employ only DataInput and DataOutput ports. Employing first order predicate logic is intuitionistic and mathematical indeed, but the situation differs if we want to use first order predicate logic to express a particular or complicated constraint. Once we use a lot of predicates, correspondingly, the constraints become complicated, unreadable and difficult for analyzing.

Style Pipe-Filter
    Connector Pipe
        Role Source [deliver data repeatedly, signalling termination by close]
        Role Sink [read data repeatedly, closing at or before end of data]
        Glue Sink [will receive data in same order delivered by Source]
    Interface Type DataInput = [read data repeatedly, closing the port at or before end-of-data]
    Interface Type DataOutput = [write data repeatedly, closing the port to signal end-of-data]
    Constraints
      $\forall_c$:***Connectors . Type***(c) = ***Pipe*** $\lor$ $\forall_c$:***Componenets***,
    p:Port| $p \in$ Port(c) · Type(p)= DataInput $\lor$ Type(p)= DataOurput

Fig. 4. 21   Constraints in the Pipe-Filter style

4. 3. 4   CSP—Semantic Basis of Formal Behavior Description

CSP is short for Communicating Sequential Processes, established by Hoare in 1978. (Hoare, 2004) Actually, the original CSP presented in Hoare's 1978 paper was essentially a concurrent programming language. After the development and refinement by Hoare, Stephen Brookes, and A. W. Roscoe, CSP was transformed into its modern form. (Brookes, 1984)

Current CSP is a formal language for describing patterns of interaction in concurrent systems. It is a member of the family of mathematical theories of concurrency known as process algebras, or process calculi. The process algebras are a diverse family of related approaches to formally model concurrent systems. Process algebras provide a tool for the high-level description of interactions, communications, and synchronizations between a collection of independent agents or processes. As a member of process algebras, CSP provides algebraic laws which allow process descriptions to be manipulated and analyzed, and permit formal reasoning about equivalences between processes. CSP is practically applied in industry as a tool for specifying and verifying the concurrent aspects of a variety of different systems.

WRIGHT employs CSP as semantic basis to describe behavior formally. Basically, CSP can be regarded as a mathematical tool, which possesses its own large set of notations and complex operational rules. CSP provides a different model of behavior from the state-machine models. Rather than describing a machine as a collection of states composed into a graph of transitions, a behavior is described through an algebraic model of processes, in which complex behaviors are constructed from simpler ones via a small set of operations. These operations include sequencing (one behavior occurs after another), alternative (one of two behaviors will occur), and interaction (two behaviors are combined by synchronizing on shared events). We are unable to introduce CSP in detail because of restriction incurred by content of this section; we strongly suggest readers read relevant CSP books before reading following contents.

4. 3. 4. 1   Events and Processes

The fundamental elements of CSP are events and processes. What are events and processes on earth? This is a problem encountered by every CSP beginner.

An event is the basic unit of a CSP behavior specification. Suppose we are describing behavior of an arbitrary object such as clock or basketball or vending machine. To describe different patterns of behavior, first decide what kinds of event or action will be of interest. In the words, different events mean different actions. For example, the call event means that Caller invokes functions while the return event means Definer return relevant results to the Caller. Particularly note that each event name denotes an event class; there may be many occurrences of events in a single class, separate in time. Additionally, the exact timing of occurrences of events has been ignored deliberately. The set of names of events which are considered relevant for a particular description of an object is called its alphabet. The alphabet is a permanently predefined property of an object.

WRIGHT does concern how different components control interactions, which means that an initiated event and an observed event are different for different components, although they may refer to the same event. In an interaction, a component may initiate an event to accomplish its own job or to communicate with the other component, or to make a response according to an observed event which is initiated by the other component. Hence, the authors of WRIGHT add notation to CSP to distinguish events initiated from observed between initiating an event and observing an event. An event that is initiated by a process is written with an overbar within that process' definition while an event written without overbar represents that it is observed by that process. For example, the specification of the Registration port of the Bundle would use the event $\overline{call}$ to indicate that it initiates this event. On the other hand, the Activator port observes the event call initiated by Framework and returns relevant results, therefore no overbar appears. Additionally, WRIGHT regards signaled events as initiated events. The pipe mechanism signals end of data, so its event would be written $\overline{end\text{-}of\text{-}data}$.

Event can also carry data, which is one of important properties of events. If a process supplies data as output, the specification is written with an exclamation point. If a process receives data as input, the specification is written with a question mark. For example, the caller for a Procedure-call supplies data when it invokes functions with parameters: call!x; relatively the definer as an invoked function waits for input parameters: call?x. Output is usually signaled (e!x) and input is usually observed (e?x). However, note that this is not always the case.

In CSP, $\sqrt{}$ is a special event, which denotes the successful termination of the process. This special event is not a real event initiated or observed by any components, but just a symbol representing a successful end of the communication. We call that process engages in the successful termination because it's not necessary to distinguish whether $\sqrt{}$ is initiated or observed. Actually the CSP does not have overbar notation and do not distinguish the initiated and observed event, so in CSP the specification is usually as that process P engages in event E.

Now we have known basic conception about events, which is the first step to understand CSP. We can use events, the basic element of behavior to construct process. Process stands for the behavior pattern of an object, as it can be described in terms of the limited set of events selected as its alphabet.

Learning the following conventions in CSP before we introduce the specification of processes and operations of processes would be helpful: (Hoare, 2004)

- Words in lower-case letters denote distinct events.
- Words in upper-case letters denote specific defined processes, and the letters P, Q, R (occurring in laws) stand for arbitrary processes.
- The letters x, y, z are variables denoting events.
- The letters A, B, C stand for sets of events.
- The letters X, Y are variables denoting processes.
- The alphabet of process P is denoted αP.

We can regard a process as a special script for an object to follow. The script records the sequence and possibility of all the events rather than the time when an event is engaged in or the time length an event last for. In order to describe the sequence and possibility of all the events engaged in, processes are depicted by combining events and other, simpler processes.

Prefix is the simplest way of constructing a new process within the conception of sequencing. Let x be an event and let P be a process. Then $(x \rightarrow P)$ (pronounced " x then P") describes a process which first engages in the event x and then behaves exactly as described by P. The simplest process in CSP is STOP, the process which does nothing. The more formal definition is that the process with alphabet A which never actually engages in any of the events of A is called STOP_A. WRIGHT defines the success process with prefix. The success process $\S$, namely $\sqrt{} \rightarrow \text{STOP}$, which successfully terminates immediately. Note that the $\rightarrow$ operator always takes a process on the right and a single event on the left. Hence, if P and Q are process, it is syntactically incorrect to write $P \rightarrow Q$. Similarly, if x and y are events, the specification $x \rightarrow y$ is not allowed. Such a process could be correctly described $x \rightarrow (y \rightarrow \text{STOP})$. In addition, the brackets could be omitted in the case of linear sequences of events on the convention that $\rightarrow$ is right associative. So the above process could be written $x \rightarrow y \rightarrow \text{STOP}$ simply.

Employing only prefix is not possible to describe more meaningful behaviors. The only processes we can describe would be those that engage in a single string of events, of a fixed length, and then stop. How to describe the everlasting behavior of a process? In CSP, we can employ a recursive definition to achieve this. For example, consider the following process definition: $P = e \rightarrow P$. The process named P performs the event e and then acts as the process P. That is, this process only engages in the event e and never stops.

But we have to note that the recursive equation $X = X$ does not succeed in defining anything because everything is a solution to this equation. A process description which begins with a prefix is said to be guarded. If $F(X)$ is a guarded expression containing the process name X, and A is the alphabet of X, then the equation $X = F(X)$ has a unique solution with alphabet A. It is sometimes convenient to denote this solution by the expression $\mu X : A \cdot F(X)$. The alphabet A could be omitted usually.

By means of prefixing and recursion it is possible to describe objects with a single possible stream of behavior. However, some objects behave according to different events, which mean their behaviors are influenced by interaction with the environment. It is called choice. If x and y are distinct events $(x \rightarrow P \mid y \rightarrow Q)$ describes an object which initially engages in either of the events x or y. After the first event has occurred, the subsequent behavior of the object is described by P if the first event was x, or by Q if the first event was y. Since x and y are different events, the choice between P and Q is determined by the first event that actually occurs. The definition of choice can readily be extended to more than two alternatives, e.g.,

$$(x \to P \mid y \to Q \mid z \to R)$$

Need to add is that alphabet must be consistent in prefix and choice. For example, $\alpha(x \to P)$ must be equal to αP, that is, $x \in \alpha P$. And $\alpha(x \to P \mid y \to Q)$ must be equal to αP, that is, $\{x, y\} \subseteq \alpha P$ and $\alpha P = \alpha Q$.

State is added to a process definition through adding subscripts to the name of a process. P_i is a process with a single state variable, i. For example,

$$P_1 \text{ where } P_i = \overline{\text{count}!i} \to P_{i+1}$$

is a process that counts: $\overline{\text{count}!1}$, $\overline{\text{count}!2}$, $\overline{\text{count}!3}$, etc.

Sometimes, however, a process is needed to have different behavior depending on the value of its state variables. For example, we might want a circular counter that counts to three and then resets: 1, 2, 3, 1, 2, ... A state dependency is introduced with a conditional definition, written by adding a test on the state variables:

$$P_v = Q, \text{ when } P(V)$$

defines a process P over variables V only when the boolean expression $P(V)$ is true. Multiple alternatives are indicated by stacking them with a large curly-brace. For example:

$$P_1 \text{ where } P_i = \begin{cases} \overline{\text{count}!i} \to P_{i+1}, \text{ when } i < 3 \\ \overline{\text{count}!i} \to P_1, \text{ otherwise} \end{cases}$$

defines the circular counter.

Thus, we have introduced basic approaches for processes description, such as prefix, recursion, choice and state. Actually we have a general expression to describe all the processes with:

$$x : E \to F(X)$$

In the general expression, the letter x is a variable denoting events. And the letter E stands for a set of events. The set of events could be void (the process STOP); the set could contain only one event (the simplest process described with prefix) or several events (multiple alternatives). From all these expression introduced above: prefix, recursion..., it is not difficult for us to discover that the process description is very similar to grammars of formal languages. CSP is employed as semantic basis of formal behavior description for WRIGHT for CSP provides algebraic laws which allow process descriptions to be manipulated and analyzed and all the descriptions are formal. So learning and mastering some theory on formal languages and automata would help you to understand CSP more easily.

In the following section, we introduce the compound operations between processes, including *deterministic* choice, *non-deterministic* choice and *sequential composition*.

An important property of CSP for WRIGHT is its handling of choice. CSP provides two forms of choice. The deterministic choice, called general choice or external choice, is very close to choice we have introduced in expression of process. We use operator $\square$ to describe such a choice. It is called external choice because the behavior of the process is entirely determined by what the environment does. For example,

$$P \square Q$$

means that the environment can control which of P and Q will be selected, provided that this control is exercised on the very first action. If this action is not a possible first action of P, then Q will be selected; but if Q cannot engage initially in the action, P will be selected. Take another choice with observed events as example, the process

$$e \rightarrow P \sqcap f \rightarrow Q$$

is the process that will behave as the process P if it first observes the event e and will behave as the process Q if it first observes the event f. In other words, the choice is made according to what it observes. And the observation is the action of environment, external, so the choice is deterministic. Deterministic choice is typically made between observed events, and is usually described using the operator "$\square$". However, if the first action is possible for both P and Q, then the choice $P \square Q$ is non-deterministic. If the observed event e and f are the same event, the process does observe the event e but the event e cannot tell the process what to do next step. We call that situation as non-deterministic choice.

If P and Q are processes, the notation

$$P \sqcap Q$$

denotes a process which behaves either like P or like Q, where the selection between them is made arbitrarily, without the knowledge of control of the external environment. So, we call this non-deterministic or internal choice. Similarly, take a choice with initiated events as example for easily understanding, the process

$$\overline{e} \rightarrow P \sqcap \overline{f} \rightarrow Q$$

is the process that will either output $\overline{e}$ and then act as P or output $\overline{f}$ and then act as Q. That is, the process itself decides which to do, without consulting the environment. Thus, non-deterministic choice is typically made between initiated events.

It is difficult for CSP beginners to distinguish between the deterministic choice and the non-deterministic choice. The distinction is really confusing. The confusion is more clarified in WRIGHT because of initiated and observed events. The authors of WRIGHT regards that this distinction is the key to the description of certain critical properties of architectural interactions. These properties include the ability to characterize the dynamic behavior of inter-component communication, to specify which components are responsible for making decisions during interaction, and to detect mismatched assumptions that could cause a component to get "stuck" midway through its interaction with another component. Because of those reasons, we will discuss the differences between them in section concerning validating description from other aspects.

We have mentioned that if P and Q are processes, it is syntactically incorrect to write $P \rightarrow Q$. Actually, we use sequential composition to express sequencing of two or more different processes, using the operator ";". $P ; Q$ is the process that behaves as P until P terminates successfully and then behaves as Q. For example,

$$(e \rightarrow f \rightarrow \S) = e \rightarrow f \rightarrow g \rightarrow \S$$

If P never terminates successfully, neither does $(P ; Q)$. That is, if the process P does not terminate, then $P ; Q$ acts as P forever.

In order to make process more flexible, the choice and sequential composition operators can also be quantified over a set

$$\langle op \rangle > x : S \cdot P(x)$$

This operator constructs a new process based on a process expression and the set S, combining its parts by the operator $\langle op \rangle$. And its form is very similar to the general expression of process we have introduced before. For example,

$$\square i : \{1, 2, 3\} \cdot P_i = P_1 \square P_2 \square P_3$$

It is more complicated when the sequencing operator ';' is used. In such situation, we must take into account the fact that it is not symmetric($P ; Q \neq Q ; P$). The meaning of quantification over sequence is some unspecified sequencing of the processes:

$$(; x : S \cdot P(x)) = (\sqcap x : S \cdot P(x) ; (; y : S \backslash \{x\} \cdot P(y)))$$

Thus,

$$(; i : \{1, 2, 3\} \cdot P(x)) = (P_1 ; P_2 ; P_3) \sqcap (P_1 ; P_3 ; P_2)$$
$$\sqcap (P_2 ; P_1 ; P_3) \sqcap (P_2 ; P_3 ; P_1)$$
$$\sqcap (P_3 ; P_1 ; P_2) \sqcap (P_3 ; P_2 ; P_1)$$

Combine with the three compound operation between processes and replace the operator $\langle op \rangle$ by three forms accordingly:

$(\square x : S \cdot P(x))$ indicates an external choice between different $P(x)$;

$(\sqcap x : S \cdot P(x))$ indicates an internal choice between different $P(x)$;

$(; x : S \cdot P(x))$ indicates the execution of all of the different $P(x)$ in some order.

4.3.4.2 Example

Review the example on simple procedure-call connector we show in Section 4.3.1, which introduces basic concept of component and connectors.

In our sample system (BM system), a Procedure-call connector (shown in Fig.4. 13) has a Caller and a Definer, and its glue coordinates the Caller and the Definer to accomplish the procedure call, the actual interaction between the Bundle and the

Framework. The informal description is as follows:

Connector Procedure-call
   Role Caller [*invoke function*]
   Role Definer [*provide invoked function*]
   Glue [*Caller invokes function of Definer; Definer returns the relevant results to Caller*]

We all know that the above behavior specification is informal, which causes that we do not confirm the coordination of Caller's and Definer's behavior. We wonder whether Caller will just wait and do nothing until it gets return from Definer. Such problems are caused by ambiguity of natural languages; we hope to fix such problems and specify the behavior of architectural elements precisely. We can achieve these by employing CSP and all those notations we have mentioned.

Now we have the formal WRIGHT specification of this procedure-call interaction as follows:

Connector Procedure-call
   Role Caller= $\overline{call}$→return→Caller $\sqcap$ §
   Role Definer= call→$\overline{return}$→Definer $\square$ §
   GLUE= Caller.call→$\overline{Definer.call}$
         $\square$ Definer.return→$\overline{Caller.return}$→Glue
         $\square$ §

We ignore data for simplifing our discussion here. There are some elements in this specification worth noting. First, the two kind of different alternatives (choices) adopted by the Caller and Definer actually indicate their different roles. As we know, in a procedure call, the Caller decides whether to initiate a procedure call or not, and so it uses the non-deterministic choice operator to indicate that the choice is made by the Caller itself. The Definer, on the other hand, offers the option of a procedure call, so it uses deterministic choice. It is up to the other parties (in this case the Caller) to determine whether a call will occur or not, that is, the choice is made by external. When we introduce the deterministic choice, we always claim that the determination of the deterministic choice is dependent on environment. But the "environment" is an abstract and confusing conception. From the above illustration on different roles of the Caller and Definer, we might regard environment as other processes participating the interaction or the system where the interaction occurs.

Second, the Glue of a connector describes how the participants work together to create an interaction. Because the Glue mediates the interaction between multiple participants, its specification must indicate which role's event is indicated in any situation. This is done by prefixing each event by the name of a role. So Callercall indicates the Caller component executing the call, and Definercall indicates the Definer component being notified of the call. The meaning is similar for Definerreturn and Callerretrun. In practice, these events actually occur simultaneously in the software system, but for various technical reasons WRIGHT considers all events in different roles to be distinguishable events.

Third, the Glue indicates how the behavior of the roles corresponds to form a complete interaction. Each of the two main branches of the Glue process indicate how an event of one participant triggers another event in the other participant. Where a role represents the behavior of a component, the Glue represents the composition of different components. Thus, the Glue's use of initiated and observed events is complementary to that of the roles: If a role initiates an event, it is observed in the Glue. If a role is to observe an event, it must be initiated by the Glue.

Thus, "Role Caller= $\overline{\text{call}}$→return→Caller □ §" indicates that the Definer will observe a call event following its initiation by the Caller. "Role Definer= call→ $\overline{\text{return}}$→Definer□ §" indicates that the Caller will process a return following the signal by Definer.

This particular glue structure, where an event initiated by one role (thus, observed by the glue) is always echoed at another role, is quite common in connector interactions. In fact, it is so common that many architecture description languages do not permit any other form of glue. However, WRIGHT does not restrict the kinds of interaction patterns that can be described to just this simple class.

Why do we need two deterministic choices to describe the glue in our simple example? What if we adopt the specification as follows?

GLUE＝Caller.call→$\overline{\text{Define.call}}$→Definer.return→$\overline{\text{Caller.return}}$→Glue□ §

Do the two glues work in the same way? The answer is no. The second specification of Glue indicates that the event Definer.return is immediately after the event $\overline{\text{Definer.call}}$, and the process Glue can not engage any other events in this interval. But the first specification of Glue allows it to engage other events because it uses the choice operator. In practice, the first description is more flexible and robust compared with the second one, because it allows the process Glue to engage in events in more flexible way.

4.3.4.3 Parallel Composition and Configuration Behavior

We have known that behaviors are specified by combining events into certain patterns called processes. In practice, there is a process description for each element in a WRIGHT configuration for a system, such as for each port, role, computation and connector glue. Of these, the port and role specifications represent the interfaces to the components and connectors, while the computation and glue represent the overall, complete behavior of the components and connectors, respectively. How these distinct processes work together to define the behavior of the configuration? Could they help us to determine whether the configuration contains inconsistencies? Inconsistency means the system cannot operate correctly. Now we focus on these questions above.

Let's start with the simplest situation: two process work together. When two processes are brought together to evolve concurrently, the usual intention is that they will interact with each other. These interactions may be regarded as events that require simultaneous participation of both the processes involved. We call this kind of compositions as **interaction** when the alphabets of the processes are identical.

If P and Q are processes with the same alphabet, CSP uses the notation

$$P \parallel Q$$

to denote the process which behaves like the system composed of processes P and Q interacting in lock-step synchronization as described above.

For example: assumed that $\alpha P = \alpha Q$

$$(c \rightarrow P) \parallel (c \rightarrow Q) = (c \rightarrow (P \parallel Q))$$
$$(c \rightarrow P) \parallel (d \rightarrow Q) = \text{STOP if } c \neq d$$

The general formalization:

$$(x:A \rightarrow P(X)) \parallel (y:B \rightarrow Q(y)) = (z:(A \cap B) \rightarrow (P(z) \parallel Q(z))$$

Furthermore, the operator described in the previous section can be generalized to the case when its operands P and Q have different alphabets: $\alpha P \neq \alpha Q$.

When such processes are assembled to run concurrently, events that are in both their alphabets (as explained in the previous section) require simultaneous participation of both P and Q. However, events in the alphabet of P but not in the alphabet of Q are of no concern to Q, which is physically incapable of controlling or even of noticing them. Such events may occur independently of Q whenever P engages in them. Similarly, Q may engage alone in events which are in the alphabet of Q but not of P. Pay attention to that the rules are different from the identical alphabets, and we call it concurrency rather than interaction. Eventually the set of all events that are logically possible for the system is simply the union of the alphabets of the component processes

$$\alpha(P \parallel Q) = \alpha P \cup \alpha Q$$

Let $a \in (\alpha P - \alpha Q)$, $b \in (\alpha P - \alpha Q)$ and $\{c, d\} \subseteq (\alpha P \cap \alpha Q)$. The following laws show the way in which P engages alone in a, Q engages alone in b, but c and d require simultaneous participation of both P and Q.

$$(c \rightarrow P) \parallel (c \rightarrow Q) = (c \rightarrow (P \parallel Q))$$
$$(c \rightarrow P) \parallel (b \rightarrow Q) = \text{STOP if } c \neq d$$

These two laws are exactly the same with the former situation. Read the following laws and analyze the difference:

$$(a \rightarrow P) \parallel (c \rightarrow Q) = a \rightarrow (P \parallel (c \rightarrow Q))$$
$$(c \rightarrow P) \parallel (b \rightarrow Q) = b \rightarrow (Q \parallel (c \rightarrow P))$$

Given a general understanding of parallel composition, we introduce configuration behavior via a sample system. The system, shown in Fig.4.22, contains two components and a connector. The component A will engage in the event a some number of times and then decide to terminate. The component B is capable of executing the event sequence $< c, b>$ any number of times, or terminating. B will execute b whenever it observes c. The connector C is responsible for ensuring that whenever a occurs, c follows. Thus, for each a, the connector transmits $a\,c$, and this triggers $a\,b$ event in B. The overall effect should be that there will be exactly one b for each a. This models a kind of connector where one component triggers a particular behavior in another component; for example, the reaction from one component to the receipt of a message from another component.

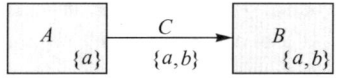

Fig. 4. 22　The ABC system

The processes for the components and the connector are described as follows:

$$A = \overline{a} \rightarrow A \, \S$$
$$C = a \rightarrow \overline{c} \rightarrow C \square \, \S$$
$$B = c \rightarrow \overline{b} \rightarrow B \square \, \S$$
$$\alpha A = \{a\} , \alpha B = \{b,c\} , \ \alpha C = \{a,c\}$$

According to the system structure and the three processes above we can make an actual WRIGHT configuration description formally.

```
Configuration ABC
    Component A-type
        Port Out=a̅→Out⌐⌐ §
        Computation=Out.a̅→Computation⌐⌐ §
    Component B-type
        Port In=c→In☐ §
        Computation=In.c→b̅→Computation☐ §
    Connector C-type
        Role Origin=a̅→Origin⌐⌐ §
        Role Target=c→Target⌐⌐ §
        Glue=Origin.a̅→Target.c→Glue☐ §
    Instances
        A:A-type
        B:B-type
        C:C-type
    Attachments
        A.Out as C.Origin
        B.In as C.Target
END ABC
```

Now, we come to the first question we have brought up before: How these distinct processes work together to define the behavior of the configuration? Basically, we combine the behavior specifications of each instance of an architectural element in the system via parallel composition. That is, there will be a process for each component instance and one for each connector instance. Then we have to face two new difficulties.

As we know, behavior specifications in the configuration are associated with a type, not an instance. But we need a process associated with each instance.

Meanwhile, the types' specifications are context-independent: How can the attachment declarations ensure that the right interactions take place? If we look at the way behaviors are specified in a component's Computation and a connector's Glue, none of the event names match up. The Glue will refer to an event with a role name, and the Computation will refer to it by a port name.

WRIGHT uses two different kinds of renaming functions to solve the two problems above. The first kind is called *labeling functions*, which add the names of the instances to each event name. Thus, an instance of the A-type named A would refer its events with name A: A. out.a. Relying on such approach, even multiple instances of a type will never cause confusion.

The second kind called *attachment functions* matches up the names of attached ports and role. Consider such an attachment declaration in:

A. Out as C. Origin.

In fact, A. out.a should be the same event as C. origin.a, although in different perspectives (described in process for different components) which makes that one is initiated and the other is observed. To achieve this, WRIGHT uses attachment functions to make sure that all of the events for the Out port in the A computation match up with the events from the Origin role of the C glue. The definition of attachment functions is as follows: (Allen, 1997b)

Definition For any names N, N', M, M', not necessarily distinct,

$$R_{(N',M')}^{(N,M)}(e) = \begin{cases} N'.\, M'.\, e' & \text{if } e = N.\, M.\, e' \\ e & \text{otherwise} \end{cases}$$

And WRIGHT defines a configuration behavior as follows:

Definition (Configuration Behavior) If a configuration declares component instances $Cp_1 : CpT_1 \ldots Cp_n : CpT_n$, where each component type CpT_i has computation process CpP_i, connector instances $Cn_1 : CnT_1 \ldots Cn_m : CnT_m$, where each connector type CnT_i has glue process CnP_i, and attachment declarations with attachment functions $R_1 \ldots R_k$, let $\bar{R} = R_1 \cdot \ldots \cdot R_k$. Then the behavior of the configuration is the CSP process

$$G \,\|\, (\,\| \, i : 1 . . n \cdot R_i : P_i)$$

In this definition, $Cp_n : CpT_n$ means Cp_n is an instance of the type CpT_n, the same as the notation is used in instances declaration. $\bar{R} = R_1 \cdot \ldots \cdot R_k$ indicates that the attachment functions are composed to form a single function. Recall that the definition of the attachment functions makes it a *total* function over events, but that only the relevant events (of the specific role on the connector) are changed by the definition. The requirement that all connector names be unique and all roles be attached to at most one port ensures that there will be no conflicts when composing attachment functions in a configuration.

An alternative explanation of expression above with human easily acceptable language is that configuration behavior is parallel composition of all computation processes of components and all glue processes of connectors. Generally speaking, computations (the actual jobs of components) and glues (the coordination for interactions) work together to represent the running of a system. In addition, we use renaming functions to avoid confusions and conflictions. Finally, we get the configuration behavior of the sample system as follows:

$$A = \overline{A.\ \text{Out}.a} \rightarrow A \, \S$$
$$\| \ C = A.\ \text{Out}.a \rightarrow \overline{B.\ \text{In}.c} \rightarrow C\Box \, \S$$
$$\| \ B = B.\ \text{In}.c \rightarrow \overline{B.\ b} \rightarrow B\Box \, \S$$

4.3.4.4   Validation

In fact, we most concern whether the configuration contains inconsistencies, that is, whether the system would work incorrectly. WRIGHT realizes validation for system by employing CSP as its semantic basis of formal behavior description.

First of all, we introduce the non-deterministic process model of CSP. Formally, a CSP process is modeled as a triple (A, F, D), where A is the process' alphabet, F is its failures, and D its divergences.

The failures of a process as such a relation (set of pairs):

$$\text{failures}(P) = \{(s, X) \mid s \in \text{traces}(P) \wedge X \in \text{refusals}(P/s)\}$$

Before understanding the conception of failures, we have to understand the conceptions of trace, traces and refusals. A trace of the behavior of a process is a finite sequence of symbols recording the events in which the process has engaged up to some moment in time. A trace will be denoted as a sequence of symbols, separated by commas and enclosed in angular brackets. And the complete set of all possible traces of a process P can be known in advance, and CSP defines a function $\text{traces}(P)$ to yield that set. The process $P = a \rightarrow P \square b \rightarrow P$, for example, can generate the traces $< >$, $<a>$, $<a, a>$, $<a, b>$, $<b, a>$, etc. And the entire set of traces is indicated by $\text{Traces}(P)$. $\text{Traces}(P) = \{< >, <a>, <a, a>, <a, b>, <b, a>, \cdots\}$ and it is a infinite set.

Now we focus on the definition of refusals. In general, let X be a set of events which are offered initially by the environment of a process P, which in this context we take to have the same alphabet as P. If it is possible for P to deadlock on its first step (that means any event in X can not be engaged in by process P for initiation.) when placed in this environment, we say that X is a refusal of P. The set of all such refusals of P is denoted refusals (P). In addition, we have an extensional definition that the refusals of the process P after trace s is denoted refusals(P/s). Note that each element of refusals is a set of events.

We review the definition after the relevant basic introduction: If (s, X) is a failure of P, this means that P can engage in the sequence of events recorded by s, and then refuse to do anything more, in spite of the fact that its environment is prepared to engage in any of the events of X. Generally speaking, failure describes those traces the process P can generate and how (what environment the process is placed in) the process P will deadlock after those traces.

A divergence of a process is defined as any trace of the process after which the process behaves chaotically. The set of all divergences is defined

$$\text{divergences}(P) = \{s \mid s \in \text{traces}(P) \wedge (P/s) \in \text{CHAOS}_{\alpha P}\}$$

The process CHAOS is termed divergent because it is the most unconstrained, unpredictable process: It can either refuse or accept any event at any time. The past behavior of the process is no help in predicting its future behavior, and it is defined as follows:

$$CHAOS_A = STOP \sqcap (\sqcap x : A \cdot x \rightarrow CHAOS_A)$$

As its definition, divergences record the traces a certain process can generate, and the process turns unpredictable after those traces. Hence, divergences are used to represent catastrophic situations or completely unpredictable programs (such as those containing infinite loops without any communication events). Obviously, we hope that our system configuration do not contain such divergent processes.

As a formal specification language, WRIGHT has value beyond enabling architects to write down an architectural description. Another important aspect of the language is its support for analysis and reasoning about the described system. And such analysis and reasoning, as analysis of consistency and completeness is based on the processes model, supporting by CSP.

Consistency and completeness are two criteria for an architectural description that under all of these analyses. Informally, consistency means that the description makes sense; that different parts of the description do not contradict each other. Completeness is the property that a description contains enough information to perform an analysis; that the description does not omit details necessary to show a certain fact or to make a guarantee. Thus, completeness is with respect to a particular analysis or property.

The WRIGHT tests concerning analysis of consistency and completeness are summarized in. In parentheses, we have indicated the containing language construct in configuration to which each test applies. And we discuss connector deadlock-free as emphasis.

- Port-Computation Consistency (component)
- Connector Deadlock-free (connector)
- Roles Deadlock-free (role)
- Single Initiator (connector)
- Initiator Commits (any process)
- Parameter Substitution (instance)
- Range Check (instance)
- Port-Role Compatibility (attachment)
- Style Constraints (configuration)
- Style Consistency (style)
- Attachment Completeness (configuration)

Fig. 4. 23   Summary of WRIGHT test

A connector describes an interaction between components, and proclaims rules of an interaction. As we know a connector specification contains description of roles and glue. The roles indicate the expectation for any component participating in a certain interaction while the glue establishes the rules for roles and coordinates the roles to accomplish an interaction accordingly. Thus, the connector description must ensure that the coordination of the glue is consistent with the expected behavior of the components, as indicated by the roles. Otherwise, the specified interaction will crash and the system will eventually collapse.

Suppose that the specification of procedure-call connector changes in our BM system. The Caller works as before but it must receive an initialization signal before it can deal with invoking. The new specification could be as follows:

Counector Procedure-call
> **Role** Caller= $\overline{\text{call}}$→returndCaller $\sqcap$ §
> **Role** Definer= initialize→call→$\overline{\text{return}}$→Definer$\square$ §
> **GLUE**= $\overline{\text{Caller.initialize}}$→Definer.initialize
> > $\square$Caller.call→Define.call
> > $\square$Definer.return→$\overline{\text{Caller.return}}$→Glue$\square$ §

The BM system will face fatal disaster if the specification changes: The Caller initiates the event call and wait for return; the Definer calling for the event initialize completely neglected call event. Thus, the Definer might simply ignore the Caller, leaving it stranded waiting for a return value. Such a crash is shown in Fig.4.24.

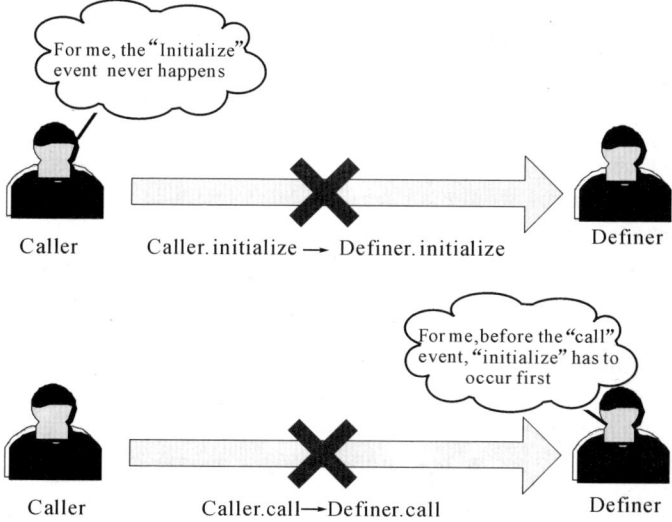

Fig. 4. 24   The deadlock between Caller and Definer

Such problem that participants in an interaction cannot agree on the next appropriate event can be detected as deadlock by employing CSP. A CSP process is said to deadlock when it may refuse to participate in (engage in) all events, but has not yet terminated successfully (by participating in the $\sqrt{}$ event). Obviously, we demand that all processes are *deadlock-free*. A process is *deadlock-free* means it can never get into a deadlock situation; WRIGHT has such a definition as follows: (Allen, 1997b)

Definition (Deadlock-Freedom) A process $P = (A, F, D)$ is deadlock-free if for every trace t such that $(t, A) \in F$, last $(t) = \sqrt{}$.

From such a definition, we can know that a deadlock-free process must always either be willing to continue its computation or eventually engage in *successful* termination($\S$: $\sqrt{}$ →STOP).

Now we can detect whether a connector is deadlock-free based on the definition above.

Test 1 (Connector Deadlock-free) If a connector has glue G and roles $R_1 \ldots R_n$ with processes $P_1 \ldots P_n$, then the process $G \parallel (\parallel i : 1 .. n \cdot R_i : P_i)$ must be deadlock-free.

As we know, the roles are used as stand-ins for the components (participations in an interaction). Thus, if the process (the parallel composition of roles and glue) will deadlock, the components and the connector will conflict in the interaction. Equivalently the system will face the inconsistency problems.

Another kind of inconsistency is also detectable as deadlock: if a role specification is internally inconsistent. In a complicated role specification, there may be errors that lead to a situation in which no event is possible for that participant, even if the Glue is willing to take any event. Thus we employ the following test to avoid that a role deadlocks itself.

Test 2 (Roles Deadlock-free) Each of the roles in a connector must be deadlock-free.

In addition, if the Glue deadlocks then the parallel composition of the Glue with its roles will deadlock, and therefore Test 2 is sufficient to check internal Glue consistency. That means we do not need an exact test to test whether the glue is deadlock-free.

The validation seems very complicated in computation for human-beings. Fortunately, a number of tools for analyzing and understanding systems described with CSP have been developed. The most well-known CSP is FDR2 (Failures-Divergence Refinement 2), which is a commercial product developed by Formal Systems Ltd. FDR is a model-checking tool for state machines, with foundations in the theory of concurrency based around CSP. (FDR, 2005) For example, FDR2 automates the test of whether one process refines another. A process P refines a process Q (written $Q \sqsupseteq P$) if the behaviors of P are consistent with (but possibly less general than) the behaviors of Q. And refinement is the key relationship employing in the test for port-computation consistency. Besides, FDR2 can also process the connector deadlock-free test we mentioned above. Other CSP tools include ARC (Parashkevov, 1996), Casper (Lowe, 1997) and so on.

4. 4   FEAL: An Infrastructure to Construct ADLs

4. 4. 1   Design Purpose

As we introduced before, there are many Architectural Description Languages (ADLs) designed for various domains and varied purposes. But most of them do not concern issues about reuse and extensibility, which lead to the unnecessary overhead to develop new ADLs or add new features to existent ADLs. Therefore, the corresponding tools have to be redesigned and implemented to follow ADL's changes. To address this problem, we develop Foundation of Extensible Architecture Language (FEAL). It solves the problem by providing an infrastructure to construct ADL's various notations. Through mapping ADL notations to FEAL-counterparts, extra ADL facilities can be added rapidly. Based on FEAL, a prototype system, which is an extensible visible architecture development tool, is created to support any FEAL-compatible ADLs. This costs much less effort in research of software architectural description and improves ADL's practical application.

Foundation of Extensible Architecture Language (FEAL) defines a set of descriptive abstractions, a referenced structure and a mapping mechanism. In this section, we address these issues in detail.

4.4.2 FEC

All ADLs define the notations which are used as the basic vocabulary for description. Some of them are unique, while others seem common or even identical in appearance. To unify the unique elements, their expression foundation should be finger out. For example, some ADLs provide information such as version and service ID that facilitates check of components assembly. Some ADLs support variables that can get value dynamically. Therefore, we abstract *Property* to meet these requirements. *Property* is a simple key-value pair, which can attach a formal expression to indicate the computation rules or constraints.

For the common ones, they essentially may be semantically different. The most famous example is component, which is defined in almost every mainstream ADL. Unfortunately, they may be related, but not always identical. Some components mean the computation unit existing only during runtime. Some indicate the binary reusable software package that can be imported in static design phase. Some components distinguish types and instances, while others not. In this concern, we need to clarify the intents of users rather than focus on the name itself. In FEAL, we define Entity, Type and Instance for describing the notations such as component. In this case, the real meaning of component is controlled by FEAL mapper.

According to the investigation of several popular ADLs, we define ten kinds of FEAL elements, named FEAL Element Categories (FEC). They are abstractions of architectural notations' meaning. We specify them as follows:

- **ViewModel**: a collection of elements which represents an architecture model. A ViewModel contains a series of other FEAL elements and the configuration of them. ViewModel can also have input parameters. The WRIGHT notation "Configuration" and the ACME term "Style" are suitable to be mapped into ViewModel.
- **Container**: Container is a vessel for other single FEC elements (including Container itself). Container set for a specific FEC is denoted as Container {FEC} in this article.
- **Entity**: Entity is an element that needs no type/instance support. This is

special useful in quick architecture modeling when type/instance concepts will trigger too much unnecessary footprint, such as the ones that is possible to be used only once.

- **Type**: Type is a special kind of Entity aiming to support reuse and consistent check. Upon it, we can define component type, connector type, port type, service type or whatever the like. Meanwhile, Type is also fit for the static design model whose elements will be referred in the runtime model. Besides that, several features of Type are different from normal Entity, such as type inheritance or export and import (Some ADLs support multiple description files with elements cross references which are similar to programming language). These special points yield special concerns. We assume that Type can only be singly inherited.
- **Instance**: Instance is a special kind of Entity that has to instantiate some Type elements.
- **PropertyType**: Some Type elements want to specify the properties to be filled in their instances. PropertyType is a set of properties which limit its instance's value. In PropertyType, you can define the base type, such as "integer", "double", "date" and "string", or mark the value as read only or optional. We assume that one PropertyType element cannot inherit another.
- **Property**: Property is a simple key-value pair keeping simple information records. The value can be a variable that can be calculated or constrained during runtime analysis through sub- SCRIPT element. Property can be instantiated from a PropertyType or exists independent. The reason for that no "PropertyInstance" exists is a design trade off in FEAL implementation.
- **Link**: Link indicates the relationship among other elements, especially the ones of Entity, Type and Instance. A collection of Link elements means a configuration where various elements are bound together. Noticeably, never mix up elements of Link and "connector" which should be categorized as an Entity, a Type or an Instance.
- **Script**: Some ADLs employ script to express behaviors, constraints or calculation rules. They are often coded in the format of process algebras, logic, or even self-defined grammar (Shown in Fig. 4.25). Script needs distinguishingly concerns in that they are different in parsing and have capability of execution. In our prototype system, all FEC elements can be recognized and visualized except Script which calls for grammar specific parser.
- **Comment**: A section of descriptive annotation assisting reading and learning.

```
script RestoreStandard
 in a: Account
 prv i: record (c:Customer; co:VIP)
 for i in match {c:Customer; co:VIP|co(c,a)} loop
   remove i. co;
   create standard(i.c, a);
 end loop
end script
```

Fig. 4.25   A script of Rapide

When developing a new ADL, the concepts and terms in its vocabulary are mapped into one of FEC.

4.4.3 FEAL Structure

FEAL does not want to cover every ADL. This will lead to excessive overhead counteracts what it brings about by putting too much uncertainty and complexity that force the users to drop it. FEAL only deals with FEAL compatible ADLs which means they have to follow the structure of FEAL. More concretely, ADL notations should be arranged as a tree and follow several rules. We present these rules by regular expressions as Fig.4.26 shows, which limits the legal sub-FEC for each kind of elements. These rules does not hurt FEAL's generality in that you can always find felicitous representation in expressing something.

Several rules should draw much attention. First, the FEAL_ROOT should contain only a container of ViewModel and optional properties prepared for meta information. In order to follow it, all definitions for Type, Instance and Entity elements need to be enclosed within elements of ViewModel. On the one hand, we expect to set scope to perform access and cross reference control for non-ViewModel elements. For realization of global Type, Instance or Entity definitions, you can define a ViewModel with global scope when implementing. On the other side, we hope that elements within a single ViewModel can be rendered in one view in the FEAL-based architecture modeling tool. Prohibition of global non-ViewModel elements helps reduce complexity.

```
FEAL_ROOT = C{P}?C{VM}
       VM = C{T}?C{I}?C{E}?C{P}?C{L}?C{C}?CO?ID
        T = C{T}?C{I}?C{E}?C{PT}?C{P}?C{L}?S?CO?ID REFID
        I = C{I}?C{E}?C{P}?C{L}?S?CO?ID REFID
        E = C{I}?C{E}?C{P}?C{L}?S?CO?ID REFID
        P = C{P}?S?CO?ID Value
       PT = C{PT}?C{P}?S?CO?ID
   C[FEC] = FEC *
    REFID = ID
       ID = ([a - z] | [A - Z] | [0 - 9]) +
    Value = String | Digital
Symbol:C:Container, VM:ViewModel, T:Type, I:Instance, E:Entity,
       P:Property, PT:Propertytype, L:Link, S:Script, CO:Comment
```

Fig. 4.26 FEAL structure

Another rule needing particular concerns is the one for Type. This is the principal difference between Type and other FEC that it explicitly considers the needs of sub-Type and PropertyType definition, the latter of which permits only sub-PropertyType elements. With the nested Type structure, you have a chance to express such as an interface type of a component type. Sometimes, a Type requires sub-PropertyType when it expects to prescribe its instances' properties.

Finally, look at the REFID equipped with Type, Instance and Entity, which means a valid id of existent ViewModel elements. This is prepared for the hierarchical structure. For example, in some ADLs a component or connector may expand its internal structures for inspecting or analysis. In this situation, the internal structure should be modeled in a separated ViewModel element as shown in Fig. 4. 27, which can be referred elsewhere when necessary. Another case of adopting is the fill of architectural style or pattern. It is different from hierarchical structure

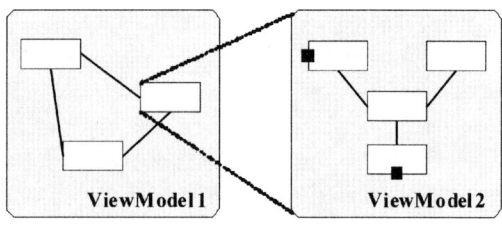

Fig. 4. 27   ViewModel reference indicating component's internal structure

requiring only a reference in that it needs parameters that can be handled by properties. Although REFID can also be expressed in Property element, it is used in several situations and hence we extract it from regular properties.

To employ FEAL in supporting existent ADLs which are not FEAL-compatible, you should first reorganize its structure. Our experiments show that this change will not hurt tested ADLs' expressive capability.

4. 4. 4   FEAL Mapper

The primary target of FEAL is to contribute in building an extensible architecture modeling system. When getting a FEAL-compatible ADL, the next step is to map ADL's terms into some FEC, which is achieved by FEAL Mapper.

FEAL Mapper has a series of map records which are listed in sequence, each of which access two issues. The first one is ADL-FEAL mapping. FEAL or FEAL-based architecture modeling tool do not understand the meaning of FEAL-compatible ADL. Hence, it is the ADL developer's responsibility to indicate that which term should be mapped to which FEC.

The second one is modeling tool related. FEAL mapper needs to tell FEAL-based ADP how to handle a specific ADL notation, such as how to shape it, how to fill the background color, how to decorate the line with certain end point styles, whether to attach one shape to certain location of another, and whether it can be edited.

FEAL Mapper offers the chance that a user can fine tune the appearance when FEAL-based ADP handles certain FEAL-compatible ADLs, which normally needs to change the source codes and rebuild the tool. It is easy to edit and change in that you can use any text editor to achieve this task.

4. 4. 5   Examples of FEAL Application

In this section, we give two examples to indicate how to use FEAL in ADL creation. The first one is modified WRIGHT through which we will show how to use FEAL Mapper to convert notation of WRIGHT to FEAL FECs. The second one is our ADL, mADL, in which we want to add a physical view to analyze its performance affected by physical elements.

- WRIGHT(Allen, 1997b)

In a conclusion, WRIGHT's primary notation includes:

Configuration, a wrapper of a system model, which contains all other definitions;

Component, a collection of Port and one Computation definition, where the former indicates a component's interface and the latter defines what a component does exactly with CSP script or nested sub-Configuration;

Connector, similar to Component, contains its several interfaces Role and Glue to describe all the roles' internal relationship;

Instances, declares the instances based on Component and Connector types defined before;

Attachments, binds all instances together;

Interface Type, a CSP definition which can be used as the type of Port or Role;

Bindings, available only when hierarchical description exists, indicates the communication relation between two layers;

Constraints, a formal description to indicate the valid situation of its enclosing element;

Style, a configuration template that has several parameters.

Here is the map table between WRIGHT notations and FEAL description:

Table 4. 1   Map from WRIGHT to FEAL

WRGITH Notations	FEAL	WRGITH Notations	FEAL
Configuration	ViewModel	Role (Defined by Interface Type)	Instance
Component	Type	Glue	Script
Connector	Type	Bindings	Container of Property
Port (Defined by CSP)	Entity with Script	Instances	Container of Instance
Port (Defined by Interface Type)	Instance	Attachments	Container of Link
Computation (Defined by CSP)	Script	Interface Type	Type with Script
Computation (Defined by hierarchical Configuration)	refer to another ViewModel	Constraints	Script
Role(Defined by CSP)	Entity with Script	Style	ViewModel with Property as parameters and Script as constraints

What should be noted is that we have to slightly modify the grammar of WRIGHT to make it FEAL-compatible before mapping. On the one hand, the structure such as hierarchical Configuration should be alternated by referred top-level Configuration to meet the need of ViewModel; on the other hand, several notations adopt different expressions in different situation, such as Computation, Port and Role, which requires special marks in the modified WRIGHT to indicate what it is exactly. From the table we can see that the slightly modified WRIGHT can be easily converted to FEAL representation without losing its expressive capability.

- mADL

mADL is the ADL written in XML aiming at modeling the mobile distributed applications which is used in our institute internally. We change it very frequently to allow explorative research. The great effort consumed in the development of its tool is a research to compel us to start the project FEAL. We give an example of modification of mADL's features.

Originally, mADL supports a runtime model comprised of several components and logic connectors through which the system is considered as a whole with no concerns about applications' physical devices and wireless network. When performance becomes the main aspect needing more attention, we want to add a physical view to estimate the overall latency by providing the computation or transfer speed of each individual physical elements. In this regard, we create several new tags for physical elements and put the performance parameters into Container of Property. Some properties depend on others, such as the transfer speed of a device is decided by the maximal value of the speed of network and itself. FEAL supports this point by Script-based Property. By FEAL and a FEAL-based ADP[1], we took just one day to finish the new edition of mADL and its mapper. Then we concentrated on the module responsible of performance calculation for another week. This task would be terrible if without FEAL in that we have take three or four weeks to redesign the data structure, complement the serialization and render modules and finally test the system.

4.5   Summary

In this chapter, we focus on software architectural description, the important part of software architecture. We have discussed the problems with informal description of software architecture; and illustrated the necessity of employing formal methods.

ADL is a hot issue in research of software architecture. Because it is difficult to make the precise definition of ADL, we briefly introduce design purposes and basic elements of some ADLs. And we present a comparison among some classic ADLs based on description capability; those ADLs include ACME, C2, Darwin, KDL, WRIGHT, xADL, π-ADL.

WRIGHT is a successful ADL in describing architectural behavior. We have introduced its syntax and semantics in detail, especially its semantic basis of formal behavior—CSP. Eventually we introduce our relevant work—FEAL; this work is still in process and we will adjust the syntax and semantics to achieve improvement in the future work.

---

[1] Architecture Development Platform, an integrated tool to provide general architecture modeling functions

References

(Abrial, 1980)   Abrial, J.-R., Schuman, S. A. & Meyer, B. *A Specification Language, in on the Construction of Programs*: Cambridge University Press.1980.

(Abrial, 1996)   Abrial, J.-R. *The B-Book: Assigning Programs to Meanings*: Cambridge University Press.1996.

(Alhir, 2003)   Alhir, S. S. *Learning Uml*: O'Reilly.2003.

(Allen, 1997a)   Allen, R. & Garlan, D. A Formal Basis for Architectural Connection, *ACM Transactions on Software Engineering and Methodology* 1997a(6): 213-249.

(Allen, 1997b)   Allen, R. J. *A Formal Approach to Software Architecture*. In: CMU SEI, p. 236. Carnegie Mellon University.1997b.

(Bergstra, 1987)   Bergstra, J. A. & Klop, J. W. Acp: A Universal Axiom System for Process Specification. *CWI Quarterly* 1987(15): 3-23.

(Booch, 2005)   Booch, G., Rumbaugh, J. & Jacobson, I. *Unified Modeling Language User Guide*, 2nd ed.: Addison-Wesley Professional.2005.

(Brookes, 1984)   Brookes, et al. A Theory of Communicating Sequential Processes. ACM.1984.

(Cardelli, 1998)   Cardelli, L. & Gordon, A. D. Mobile Ambients. *Proceedings of the First international Conference on Foundations of Software Science and Computation Structure*.1998:140-155.

(Dashofy, 2005)   Dashofy, E. M., Hoek, A. v. d. & Taylor, R. N. A Comprehensive Approach for the Development of Modular Software Architecture Description Languages. *ACM Transactions on Software Engineering and Methodology* 2005(14): 199-245.

(FDR, 2005)   FDR. *Failures-Divergence Refinement-Fdr2 User Manual*, 6th ed.: Formal Systems (Europe) Ltd.2005.

(Fitzgerald, 1973)   Fitzgerald, J. *Validated Designs for Object-Oriented Systems*: Springer Verlag.1973.

(Garlan, 1997)   Garlan, D., Monroe, R. & Wile, D. (1997). Acme: An Architecture Description Interchange Language. *Proceedings of the 7th Annual IBM Centre for Advanced Studies Conference (Cascon'97)*. Toronto, Ontario.

(He, 2005)   He, J., Qin, Z. & Jia, X. An Ontology-Based E-Commerce Knowledge Description Language. *Acta Electronica Sinica* 2005(33): 297-300.

(Hewitt, 1973)   Hewitt, C., Bishop, P. & Steiger, R. A Universal Modular Actor Formalism for Artificial Intelligence. IJCAI.1973.

(Hoare, 2004)   Hoare, C. A. R. *Communicating Sequential Processes*: Prentice-Hall International.2004.

(Larman, 2004)   Larman, C. *Applying Uml and Patterns: An Introduction to Object-Oriented Analysis and Design and Iterative Development*, 3rd ed.: Addison Wesley Professional.2004.

(Lowe, 1997)   Lowe, G. Casper: A Compiler for the Analysis of Security Protocols. 1997.

(Magee, 1995)   Magee, J., et al. Specifying Distributed Software Architectures. 1995.

(Medvidovic, 2000)   Medvidovic, N. & Taylor, R. N. A Classification and Comparison Framework for Software Architecture Description Languages. IEEE Transactions on Software Engineering 2000(26): 70-93.

(Milner, 1980)   Milner, R. A Calculus of Communicating Systems, Springer-Verlag. 1980.

(Oquendo, 2004)   Oquendo, F. Π-Adl : An Architecture Description Language Based on the Higher-Order Typed Π-Calculus for Specifying Dynamic and Mobile Software Architectures. ACM SIGSOFT Software Engineering Notes 2004(29): 1-14.

(Parashkevov, 1996)   Parashkevov, A. N. & Yantchev, J. Arc - a Tool for Efficient Refinement and Equivalence Checking for Csp. 1996.

(Petri, 1962)   Petri, C. A. Komunikation Mit Automaten. University of Bonn.1962.

(Pressman, 2006)   Pressman, R. S. Software Engineering: A Practitioner's Approach, 6th ed.: McGraw-Hill 2006.

(Sangiorgi, 2001)   Sangiorgi, D. & Walker, D. The Π-Calculus: A Theory of Mobile Processes: Cambrige University Press.2001.

(Shaw, 1996)   Shaw, M. & Garlan, D. Software Architecture: Perspectives on an Emerging Discipline 1ed.: Prentice Hall.1996.

(Taylor, 1996)   Taylor, R. N., et al. A Component- and Message-Based Architectural Style for Gui Software. IEEE Transactions on Software Engineering 1996(22): 17.

5

Design Strategies in Architecture Level

Design is an activity that gives tradeoff solutions to meet specified requirements. Design for software can be split into several processes with respect to various concentrations, among which architecture design is a crucial step, deciding whether the requirements can be met to a great extent.

In the Chapters 2 and 4, we have accessed the issues about architectural description. Through reading that you get the ideas about which elements are necessary to give complete information about architecture, as well as how to manipulate them to express the structures, relationships and behaviors. But, the question is how designers or architects start this description work. Design is always started from requirement specifications. Therefore, the key point is how to link some requirements to some architectural decision, such as creation of components and connectors with special features, adoption of architectural styles and patterns upon which the design will be built up, and establishment of communication protocols through which the whole system can be integrated.

The links between requirements and designs are design rules, accumulated and got agreement after couple of years' experience. Design rules in architectural level have got its concrete position since the importance of architecture drew the public's attention. Normally speaking, several designs, via different design rules, can be gained in different perspectives, which, thus, lead to a problem that how to choose the best one. In practice, this job is performed by architecture evaluation, accessed in Chapter 7 in detail. Evaluation is essentially a conference with stakeholders involved, including advising, discussing, debating, information tracking and analyzing, all of which are mainly based on participators' experience. Nevertheless, several regular metrics can be extracted to allow the semi-automatic or even automatic design. These metrics, the formal expression of rules of design and selection, can be put into a knowledge repository, achieving the expert system in software design. Design space is the intuitive tool to handle the metrics problems.

In this chapter, we will focus on design guidance through design space and rules, as well as the design processes along with them.

5. 1   From Reuse to Architecture Design

Currently, reuse is not a new concept for its popularity. Through tremendous amount of research on software production line, reusable software element, domain engineering and corresponding software development processes, software reuse has got its maturity. However, software reuse is not the silver bullet. Although it brings about the benefits such as reduction in cost and time-to-market as well as promotion in quality, it is, simply speaking, difficult to control and apply.

The reason for this difficulty is complicated, which combines concerns from various areas, such as economics and management. For example, building the reusable software element will cost more resource and effort, and the revenues for it always draw the managers' much attention. To apply reuse to practice, the development process needs refactoring which leads to the change of organizations. Whatever good or bad, changes like this often trigger arguments among the development team. I encountered the situation that I could not persuade my team members to feature several modules to enable its reuse because they insist that too much overhead which was absolutely unnecessary would be achieved. There are other issues about innovations and legality. For instance, a logistics service provider does not want adopt logistics software components for the third part, since it believe that keeping the kernel technology is far more important than the benefits brought about by reuse.

From this point, only a "good idea" is not enough to improve software reuse. What is needed is the technical solution. Maybe some of them are not so desirable at their initial stage, but at least it should seem a potential valuable nuisance. Object-Orientation is a feasible practical technology to allow reusable software elements wrap and assembly. Following it, a batch of tools, such as IDE and CASE, are released to improve experience of working with Object-Orientation. Through it, the early supporters of software reuse gain much, as well as others who kept watching and waiting gradually agrees with its power. Even if software reuse cannot be considered as elixir, rather only part of methods to fight against software crisis, when most software developers begin to depend on it, it becomes so trivial that no one can ignore it.

Even given the reusable software elements' (normally called components), the story is still too far to reach its end. Something has to be fixed to enable elements' assembly. It is obvious not to expect a part specified with "meter" can be installed in a machine made with the measurement "inch". I have to acknowledge that some elements have large and free range of use, such as the C++ STL library or part of JDK (Java Development Kit) library. The cost for this range is development efficiency and quality. With these "components", you still have to concern on issues about what the system's overall structure looks like during runtime and how they communicate with each other. They are essentially the "low level" reusable elements, laying the foundation for further development only.

However, some reusable elements are different. They can be put directly into an application container or something the like, and the whole system is finished. The reuse applied here yields the fixed software architecture. It is software architecture that guides the implementation of framework and defines the rules by following which components can run correctly. In this level of reuse, software architecture is the crucial issue that should be designed reused first. Otherwise, no concrete environment can be created, neither the components library and thus market. For example, the EJB components seem nonsense when no EJB application server is put into use. Software architecture depends on domain. The specific requirements, concepts and models provide the basic needs to drive the architecture design. For the GUI application, the framework that supports the architectural style "Hierarchical Layer" seems suitable. The "Model-View-Controller" tri-layers makes the views and models independent with each other, and thus protect extensibility and allow multiple views based on one model. An example is the JFace viewer, an Eclipse (www.eclipse.org) component that wraps the MVC pattern. It designates one SWT widget as view, a ContentProvider and LabelProvider as controllers, and any object as the model. In other areas, such as the reasoning system or signal filter and sample system, the architecture is another story.

We need a method to choose a suitable architecture for a specified domain. The design process concerns the dependent relationships and the structure of framework. Architectural styles and patterns cannot contribute to this task directly since its loss of formal foundation. We cannot define the concrete design rules with unclear describing methods. Alternatively, design space methodology shows its capability for categorizing architecture designs.

5.2　Architectural Design Space and Rules

Architectural design starts from a series of requirements specification on attributes and behaviors, and ends when a set of components, connectors, patterns, configurations is provided. A test can be made to check whether the requirements have been met by the instance of the set of architectural elements. If it is, the design can be considered as eligible.

Maybe you get familiar with a programming language, such as C or C++. Take function as an example. A function can be considered as a black box that gets some input via parameters and gives the result through return value [1]. By adjusting the input for each parameter, behavior of function may be different, although the variations are limited and controlled. The adjustability of function is decided by parameters only. Different configuration to them may generate distinct results in

---

[1] You may argue that some functions have no parameters or some return values through output parameters, but here we simplify this abstraction.

appearance. The typical example is the WIN32 API "CreateWindow", which has 11 parameters and controls the appearance, function and layout of created window. Several other examples similar to function are template of C++ or even the compiler's command.

Design can also be taken analogy to function, which generates the architectural alternatives available according to given inputs. One reason why multiple design results are returned is that not all the parameters are fixed, since some of them are unpredefined or leave a range. Another one is some of them are not independent. In reality, dimensions of a design space interact. Performance impacts extensibility. Availability impacts security. Synchronous event mechanism may bring the deadlock. Everything affects cost. And so forth. All in all, the term "design space" indicates all the possible results, and "dimension" to denote each kind of requirements, structures or configurations.

Before constructing a space, a codification or classification is needed, expressing the various values in a single dimension. Range of possible values is called "categories". For example, we can define the dimension "Principle in handling the situation of resource shortage", and two values of this dimension can be set as "Reject excessive requests to guarantee existent session's responses" and "Reduce the speed of response to allow requests as more as possible". A simple case of design space is shown in Fig.5.1.

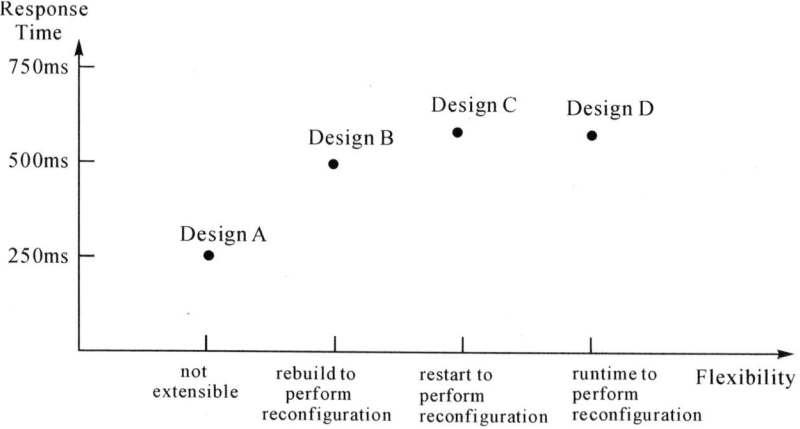

Fig. 5. 1   A design space example

5. 3   SADPBA

In this section, we provide our software architecture centered design process, called SADPBA (Software Analysis and Design Process Based on Architecture) (He, 2004a). This process uses the ideas of design space and has been applied in the ERP system and the mobile-based collaboration platform. In the following, we give the introduction to its overview, design space application and track relationships in them.

5.3.1 Overview

A process is a series of actions directed toward a specific aim. We define the term "action" as a tuple:

$$Action_i = \ <\ ID,\ SH_i,\ Res_i,\ Act_i,\ Cons_i>$$

where ID is the identifier of current action; SH_i is all the possible stimulation sequences, each of which abstracts the single input to the system; Res_i is all the responses to SH_i by $Action_i$; Act_i is all the semantical description of activities, erecting the rules from SH_i to $Action_i$; and $Cons_i$ is the constraints of $Action_i$, categoried by init, pre- and post-constraints.

A process is an ordered set of actions:

$$Process = \ \{Action_1,\ Action_2,\ ...,\ Action_n\}$$

SADPBA is a process formally defined with the terms above, and featured with its software architecture design action. SADPBA is an iterative process, each period of which finishes additional design work based on what are done in the previous one. SADPBA split the process into three actions: requirement analysis, software architecture design and system design, and thus design space used in this process follows this pattern, which is the topic of the next section. The overview of SADPBA is shown in Fig.5.2. Intuitively, through the analysis of SH, Res, Act and Cons of actions next to each other, designers can judge the correctness of transfer between design spaces.

5.3.2 Split Design Process with Design Space

In SADPBA, design space is extended and applied into three different problems through the whole design process. In other words, process is split by different design spaces for different concerns. More specifically, dimensions focusing on what the system can do according to function requirements are accumulated in the "Function Design Space", the ones on how components are organized may be put into the "Architecture Design Space", and those cover the detailed design within components or about algorithms are equipped in "System Design Space". More generally and formally, design space can be defined as:

$$DS = \{d_1, d_2, \cdots, d_n\}$$

where d_i is the dimension of the design space, holding the possible valid values called range. In a domain specific design process, we employ three spaces, meaning that design process go through three spaces and get projected between them sequentially, as showed in Fig.5.3.

This process performs the refinement from requirements to detail designs. Function design space concerns requirements, especially the functional ones.

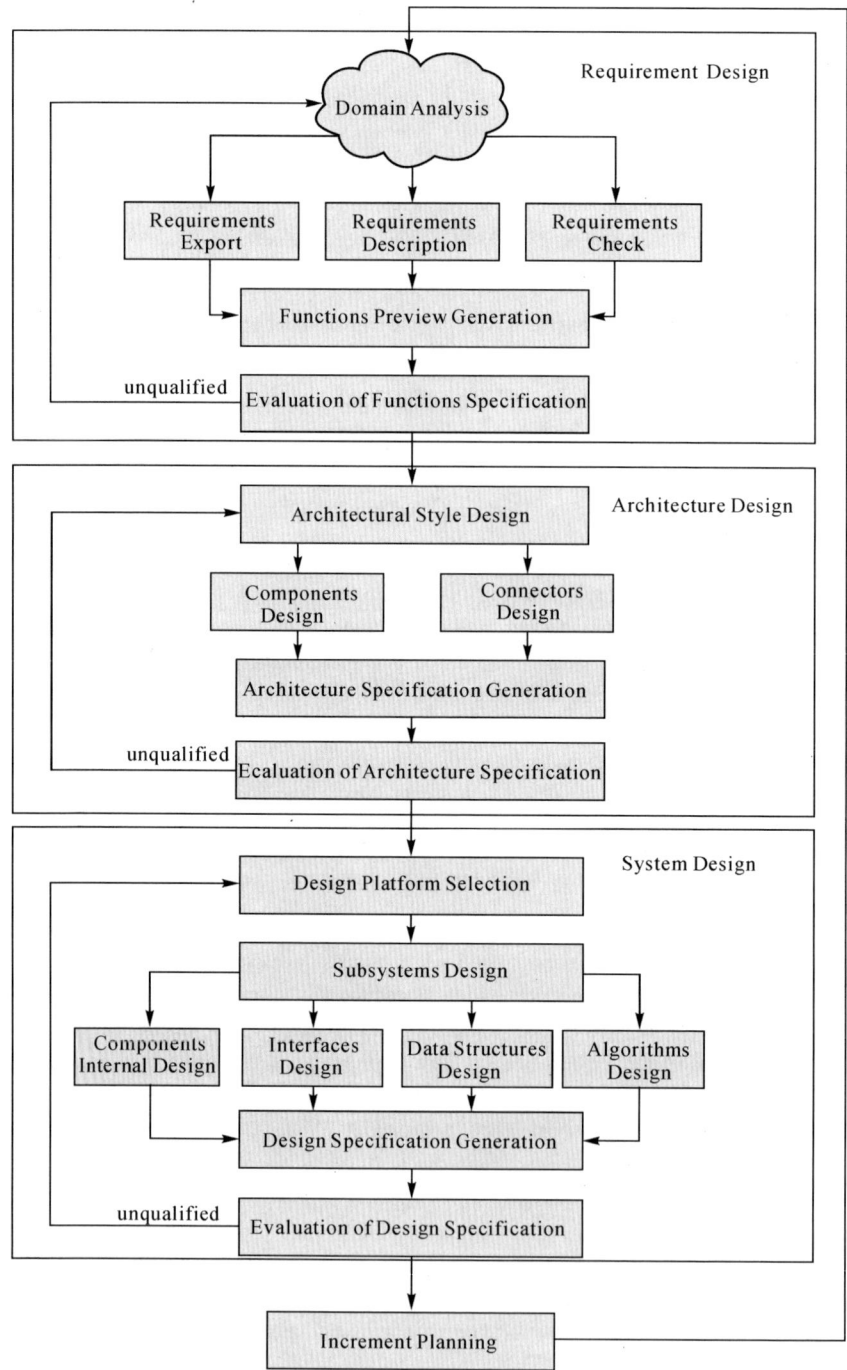

Fig. 5. 2　Overview of SADPBA

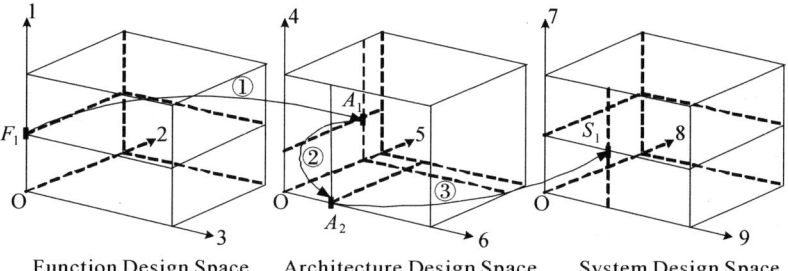

Function Design Space   Architecture Design Space   System Design Space

Fig. 5. 3   Design spaces and maps

Architecture design space can be dimensioned with architecture description mechanism accessed in the Chapter 4, such as components, connections, configurations as well as architectural styles and patterns. Besides that, system design concentrates on more detail, including the internal structures of components and connectors or critical algorithms. Although you may believe that the maps of design results between spaces are the job of human-being for their ambiguity and creative needs, which are normally handled by ideas and experience of designers, we can possibly find some fixed rules in them, if the process is limited in a single domain. Formally, we define the dependency as:

Given d_i and d_j DS and $d_i \neq d_j$, if the value of d_i is a function of d_j, we say that d_i depends on d_j, and expresses in the form of d_i dep d_j.

And define the map relationships as:

DS_1 and DS_2 are two design spaces (they may be the same one), if a rule exists, expressed as f, which makes any element $\alpha \in DS_1$ has a counterpart β in DS_2, we say that f is a map from DS_1 to DS_2. This relationship is expressed as $f =\!DS_1 \rightarrow DS_2$ and $f(\alpha) =\!\beta$.

For example, in the GUI system, if users want Undo/Redo support, this requirement is always met by a "command pattern" in architecture space (thus, we need components of command, command stack and command manager) and then gets further specification by taking what necessary command should do and whether extra features are required, all of which are the topics of system space. In the Fig.5. 3, the arrowed edges ①, and ③ reflect these maps. Map ② seems special since it is done in a single space, which means a pattern should be applied in the design of current space. For example, when adopting "command pattern" in a modeling system, a good decision following that is to link the commands and the objects involved in edit operations by reusable policies. After it is done, you can change the edit functions of a certain kind of object simply by adding or removing policies, or allow the edit of new object by assigning existent policies to them conveniently.

In this manner, it is possible to implement a "design machine" that is fed with requirements and give design results. This machine can also choose the best one, if we predefine an evaluation formula and assign weight to different dimensions. To achieve this point, we need gather the rules for mapping, normally in the way of comparing and summarizing the designs under design space specifications. Therefore, we own the capability of automatically judging whether a design is reasonable and potential pitfalls incurred by the hidden shortcomings.

5.3.3 Trace Mechanism in SADPBA

For a tool capable of automatic design, it is important to judge whether its output is good or not. A validation achieves this, which calls for the information about mapping between every design spaces. This is why we need to extract the "trace" relationship in SADPBA.

Trace means a bidirectional relationship between two elements in one or multiple design spaces, which defined by a certain rules. More formally,

> In design spaces, if element α can be tracked to the element β, we say that element α and β have traceable relationship, expressed as α Trace to β. (Since this relationship is bidirectional, given α Trace to β, β Trace to α holds definitely.)

> In SADPBA, we categorize three kinds of traceable relationships. They come from the completeness of design spaces used in SADPBA. The first one stands between DS_F and DS_A:

> Given DS_F is a Function Design Space and DS_A is an Architecture Design Space, and f is a rule of map between them. Only when any element $\alpha \in DS_F$ and all its dependencies can be mapped to the element in DS_A, DS_F is complete to DS_A.

Another one exists between DS_A and DS_S:

> Given DS_A is an Architecture Design Space and DS_S is an System Design Space, and f is a rule of map between them. Only when any element $\alpha \in DS_A$ and all its dependencies can be mapped to the element in DS_S, DS_A is complete to DS_S.

Purely from mathematics, completeness means every element in a domain of a map can find a counterpart in its range. In design space, completeness guarantees that given an input in one design space we can find a result in the next design space for sure. The whole design process of SADPBA thus behaves determinably, which is the foundation of automatic design capable tool.

SADPBA employs the sequence-based specification process. Each sequence indicates a use scenario. Through enumeration, permutation and combination of scenarios, SADPBA developers check and validate the design results and create deterministic traceable relationships.

- In the same space, elements that have dependency relationship have traceable relationship.
- When DS_F is complete to DF_A, the elements in DS_F and in DS_A have traceable relationship.
- When DS_A is complete to DS_S, the elements in DS_A and in DS_S have

traceable relationship.

5.3.4   Life Cycle Model of Software Architecture

Software architecture is critical to the success of large-scale of software system. Choosing unsuitable architecture will lead to a consequence of disaster which we take effort to avoid. Therefore, we create the concept of software architecture life cycle, based on which we establish formal reasoning system and principles. In a life cycle, software architecture comes through a process of creation, evolution and deconstruction.

The life cycle model of software architecture is the description of all phases software architecture will come through in all its life. This description is independent to the architecture specific to a certain project, guiding design of software architecture to follow the formal theory foundations and engineering principles.

A life cycle model of software architecture is composed of a few phases listed as below:

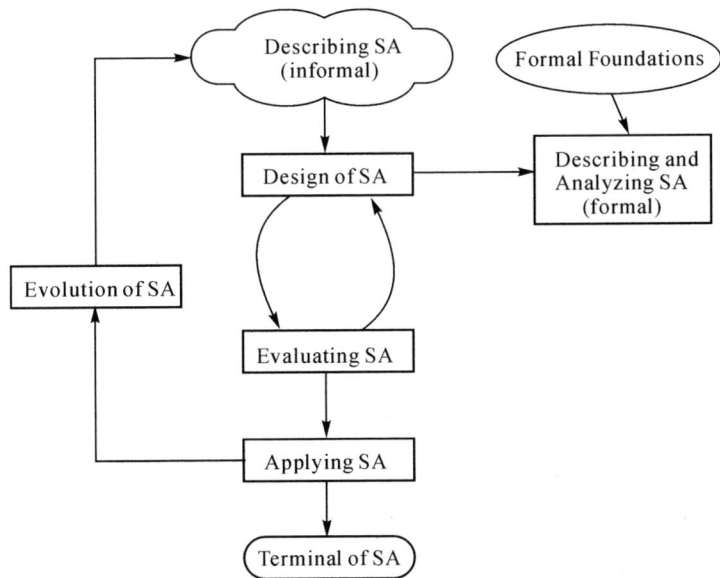

Fig. 5.4   Life cycle model of software architecture

- **Informally describing software architecture**

When the initial idea of architecture is generated, it is often not fully fledged. Designers share their mind about architecture with others in human language. For example, client/server architecture may be a good point to start the architecture design. Although native, this step is inevitable.

- **Formally describing and analyzing software architecture**

In this phase, architecture is refined with suitable formal theory, such as process algebra or Petri net. Precise definitions should be given to avoid the ambiguous semantics of architecture used in the specific project. In this way, with help of analysis tool, designers are able to validate the architecture to figure out the problems such as whether potential deadlocks exist, whether the system may enter a phase of chaos and so on. Through formally describing and analyzing, blindly choosing architecture will be avoided in most cases.

- **Evaluating software architecture**

Although formal analysis is powerful, it cannot deal with all the problems of architecture. In practice, evaluation is a critical step which involves stakeholders of the project and attempts to identify unsatisfied aspects of architecture. Extra model may be employed to check whether required quality attributes conform to the pre-specified conditions. It is this phase to determine whether current architecture can be applied.

- **Applying software architecture**

In this phase, the refined software architecture will be applied in the design of system, based on which an initial framework organizing architecture elements.

- **Evolution of software architecture**

Changes of requirements, techniques, environment, and deployment may lead to the change of architecture, which is called "evolution of software architecture". Architecture will be designed and validated thus to ensure its suitability in the new situation.

- **Terminal of software architecture**

If software architecture becomes so difficult to understand after a series of evolution or modification, thus cannot fulfill its blueprint responsibility, it should be dropped. The life of this software architecture is terminated and new one will emerge.

5.3.5   SADPBA in Practice

Based on the design space theory, SADPBA creates the architecture development tool to support query and move of dependency and traceable relationships in the design, assisting developers to check the validation of correctness, completeness and consistency of specifications about requirements, architecture and system details. Fig.5.5 illustrates the outline of this tool.

GUI		
Requirements Analysis and Management Tool	Architecture Design Tool	System Design Tool
Knowledge Repository		
Host Evironment		

Fig. 5. 5   Overview of SADPBA development tool

The functions provided by each part in the figure are listed as follows:

Knowledge Repository: Archiving and managing software requirements specifications, architecture documents, and dependency and traceable relationships.

Requirements Analysis and Management Tool: Help designers analyze and manage requirements, as well as generate requirements specification.

Architecture Design Tool: Help designers to design and describe software architecture, and create and maintain the traceable relationship between architecture description and requirements specification.

System Design Tool: Help designers convert architecture to the elements in implementation level, such as package, class and interface by Object-Oriented methodologies. Create and maintain the traceable relationship between design documents and architecture specification.

GUI: Integrate all the tools and offer the style consistent operating interface.

The kernel of this tool is its repository's structure. Even getting the general idea about design space, we also need solutions on the implementation repository, specifically for the three design spaces used in this tool. To handle them, we create three feature matrices. In the action of requirements analysis, we define the requirement feature matrix, each line of which contains the attributes for a single record of requirement, including priority, status, cost, degree of difficulty, steadiness and trace (illustrated in Table 5.1). In the action of architecture design, we define the architecture feature matrix, with the attributes category, semantics, heterogeneity, extensibility, constraints, non-function attributes and trace (illustrated in Table 5.2). In the action of system design, we use the system design feature matrix, with the lines that represent the design solution, expressed by the attributes category, name, function, concurrency, degree of difficulty, cost and trace (illustrated in Table 5.3).

Table 5. 1   Requirement Analysis Feature Matrix

features \ requirements	Priority	Status	Cost	Difficulty	Steadiness	Trace to	Trace from
Req1	2	Approved	2	Low	High	A_comp1	
Req2	1	Approved	4	Medium	Medium	A_comp3	
...	...	...	...	...	...	...	...
Req 74	3	Validate	4	High	Low	A_con4	

Table 5. 2   Architecture Design Feature Matrix

features \ elements of architecture	Cat.	Semantics	Extensibility	Heterogeneity	Constraints	Trace to	Trace from
Comp1	Prim	Windows	Low	Low		S_Comp1	
Conn1	Dcom	Internet	High	Low		S_Int2	R_Comp5
Comp2	Comp	Windows	Low	Medium		S_Comp1	R_Comp2
...	...	...	...	...	...	...	...
Config8	C/S	Three-tiers	High	High		S_Int21	R_Comp55

Table 5. 3   System Design Feature Matrix

features elements of architecture	Cat.	Constraints	Concurrency	Difficulty	Function	Trace to	Trace from
Comp1	Comp	Windows	Low	Low			A_Comp1
Alg1	FFT	Windows	High	Low			A_Comp1
Interf1	Prim	Internet	Medium	High			A_Config2
...	...	...	...	...	...	...	...
Comp30	Prim	Windows	High	Medium			A_Comp26

5. 4   Study Case: MEECS

In this section, we present the Mobile Embedded E-Commerce System (MEECS), by which we perform the explorative research on applying agent into mobile e-commerce. In the development of this system, we introduce and refine SADPBA discussed above. In the following content, we first give an introduction to this system and then explain how SADPBA was used.

5. 4. 1   Introduction to MEECS

E-commerce has been popular for about two decades. Carefully look around, and you can find that e-commerce exists everywhere. Today, you can buy almost whatever you want on the web site such as Amazon or e-Bay. This is the e-commerce in a narrow sense that is normally called "B2C" pattern. Besides that, there are also B2B, B2G, G2G and so on. In general, e-commerce is a combination of computer technologies, such as presentation, networking and data management, and commerce pattern, a fine-tuned set of activities, processes, principles and methods aiming to gain commercial benefits.

The mobile devices appear completely different compared to the ones seven or eight years ago. Their capabilities of computing and storage have exceeded that of a PC in 2000. Meanwhile, mobile devices have their own outstanding characters, such as you can bring and use them everywhere if you like or it accept multiple input modes including buttons, voice, and even context sensing. What follows these characters is the creative application and further the new commercial pattern. However, software system in the mobile environment is different, leading to the special concerns on their construction.

● Heterogeneity

A software system running on the mobile environment needs to handle the heterogeneity of devices and networking. For example, a message transferred from a mobile terminal may come through the GPRS network and then enter the backbone net comprised of fibers, which use complete different protocols and transfer techniques. Either, you cannot guarantee the devices involved in a system own the same architecture of hardware and software.

- Unstability

Different from the assumption from conventional software system that in most time the host environment keeps a healthy status, in the mobile environment, the unstable state is "normal". The networking may be cut off frequently, the power support may be off, and the devices participating in a system may be turned off at any time. When people are using mobile networked devices while moving around, the communication bandwidth changes dynamically. All of these forces that the software in the mobile environment cannot run in the long term online style but do everything when it is actually needed and gets ready for all kinds of potential errors.

- Asymmetry

The fixed nodes and mobile devices coexist in the system but have discrepant performance. This is the ultimate reason why mobile devices cannot play the role of server. In the design of system, much attention has to be paid to carefully avoid the excessive work load on the mobile devices.

- Limit Resource

Mobile devices, compared to the current desktop workstations or servers, behave weakly in computation speed, capacity of memory, power support and capability of display. This means why they cannot succeed with the all-in-one solution when facing the heterogeneity like the current fixed application servers.

Under these factors, current approaches for supporting distributed system lost their effects in the mobile environment, which is solved by MEECS. MEECS introduces the "agent" technology to avoid people's fulsome intervention into the problems mentioned above. An overview of MEECS is shown in Fig.5.6, separated into three parts.

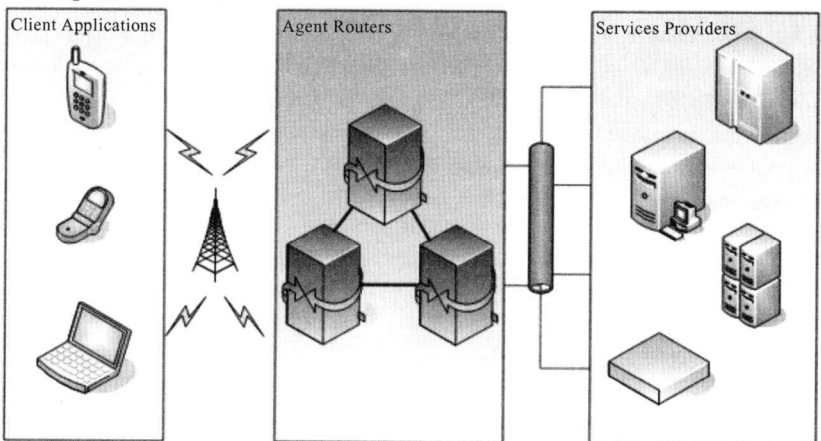

Fig. 5. 6   Overview of MEECS

The core of MEECS is the Agent Router, containing a collection of independent agents capable of finding the services they are responsible of, which are called "service agents". This kind of agents do not execute directly on the mobile devices, but stay on the platform that implements the agent router. The mobile users who want to use this router should download a "UI agent" (we implement it as a GUI MIDlet) and tell it what they need (such as a dynamic stock diagram). And then this UI agent forwards the request to the agents on the Agent Router, who actually knows the location of service providers. The selected service agent connects with the service and finally return the displayable result to the user.

Of course, all of above, the core technique, the overview and its work mechanism, are only our general idea about how to achieve this task. The detailed process, where we use SADPBA, will be depicted in the next section.

5.4.2   Applying SADPBA in MEECS

In this section, we briefly introduce the design process based on SADPBA, and describe how the decisions about architecture of MEECS are made by comprehensive consideration of requirements and other concerns such as techniques and research related. We start from the enumeration of primary requirements of our project.

Just like what most people are doing nowadays, we use the artifact "use cases" document to record our project's goals. First, we categorize three kinds of actors in this system, the client users who use the handheld mobile devices, the administrators of Agent Router, and the vendors who provide services.

5.4.2.1   Requirements Analysis

The goal of client users is very simple: they should see the result generated by the service through user interface and can send requests to find and choose some services. The heterogeneity of display in various devices should be taken into account, which triggers our another research project, the Language Facilitating Interface Representation under Limited Mobile Computing Environment (FIML) (Wang, 2003). Simply speaking, this is a markup language specifically for graphical display in different mobile devices. It is rather trivial to talk more about this language in this section. What you should know is that this language needs parsing and behaviors represented by it should be executed. Therefore, the use case diagram seems like what is shown in Fig.5.7.

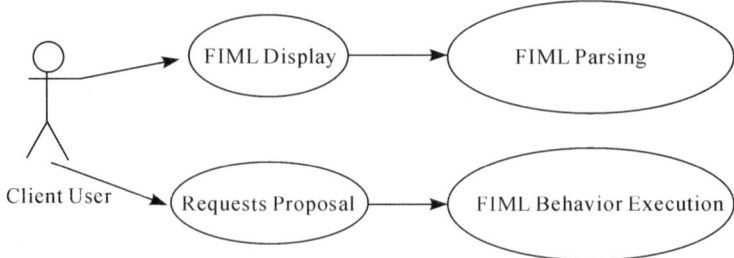

Fig. 5.7   Use case diagram of Client User

The tasks of administrators are to maintain the Agent Router's map records, each of which bind a client user to a service. For this, we introduce the idea of administrator agent, an independent component capable of performing administrators' duties, such as registering or unregistering a client user, finding the suitable service brokers and finally clearing the channel enabling communication between client user and service directly. Other than the functional requirements, the performance and availability concerns need to find their solution here. In the architecture design of this part, you can see that how these requirements are met.

The vendors have fewer responsibilities. For this system, they only need to implement their services by following a specification which guarantees that their services can be recognized and used by the agents. Since it is relative easy and not the key point of MEECS, we postpone its design until the late phase of system.

Generalizing the points above, we generate three associated packages of use cases (illustrated in Fig.5.8) as the start point to the architecture design phase.

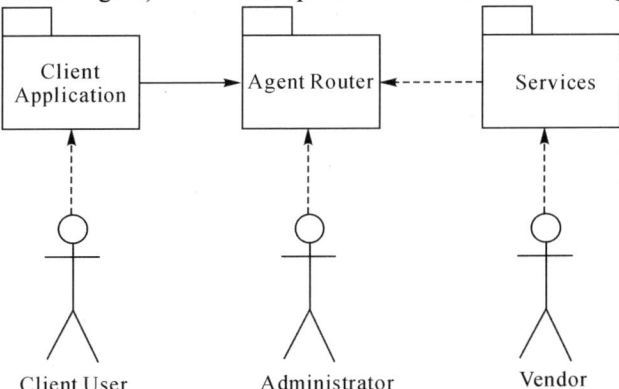

Fig. 5. 8   Packages of use cases

5. 4. 2. 2   Architecture Design

In the architecture design phase, we separate the whole system into three sub-ones. The client, which is called as "terminal component" in the architecture design, focuses on the representation functions. And the Agent Router is designed as Mobile Embedded E-Commerce Platform (MEECP).

- **Terminal**

The architecture of terminal is shown in Fig.5.9.

Terminal contains the components listed as following:

- **Facade:** Responsible of construct and display of user interface. More specifically, the controls, text field, text area, check box, group, button and image are generated and rendered by this component.
- **Command:** Parsing the behavior mark in the FIML interface, generating the command objects and then performing their execution.
- **Parser:** Parsing the mark of FIML and extracting the data embedded in them, preparing for further operations such as command execution or interface display.

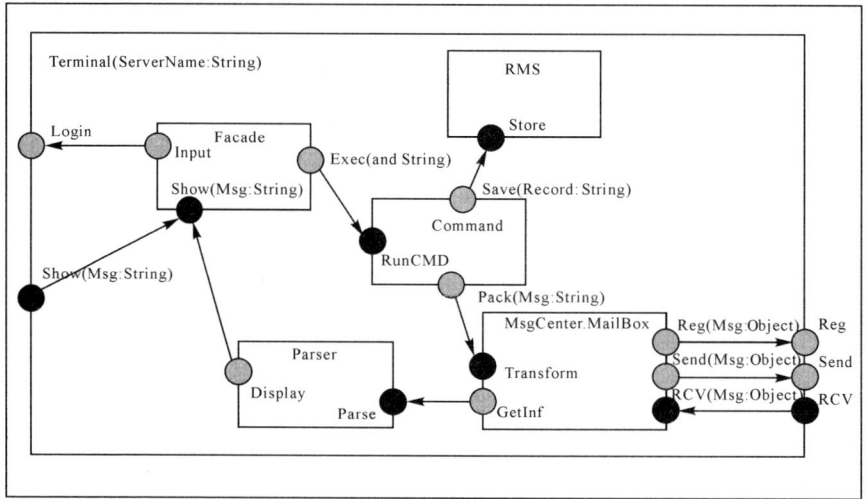

Fig. 5. 9   Architecture of MEECS terminal

- **RMS**: Archiving the data permanently in the mobile terminal, enabling the operations of records query, insert, delete and update. RMS (Record Management Storage) originally is the facility provided by J2ME for permanent record storage. We extend it to make convenient the operations of records designed in our own system.

- **MsgCenter**: The daemon component taking charge to the message communications related issues, including the bidirectional transform between message objects created by users and byte streams fitting for the transmissions on the network, as well as sending and receiving of messages. Under the mobile environment, network breaking off is the conventional problem. In this concern, MsgCenter is designed to work in the mail box style, or more canonical, the asynchronous transmission, allowing connection interrupt and resume. MsgCenter is the sole port that links the terminal distributed discretely in the net.

The architecture for client supports three main processes: the generation of flexible user interface, the execution of behavior and the messages handling.

The user interface is generated in the following steps. The FIML Parser component parses the control description in the markup language, and then extends the variables, replacing the configuration table, the system parameters and page parameters. The Facade component gets the parse result, a description of controls, and finally renders the display area.

Execution of behaviors starts from the interaction from users. Once people trigger some behavior, its description is fed into the Command component, which first replaces the parameters in the description and extracts the elements of that behavior. The command queue accepts the command and keeps it, until the command execution thread gets started and fetchs this command for execution.

In the process of behavior execution, if message should be sent to the MEECP, the MsgCenter component is activated. It maintains two queues, one for the received messages and another for the messages to be sent. To tackle this task, MEECP employs two threads respectively.

• **MEECP**

The MEECP component is responsible of service register, terminal register, handle of users' message and gives feedback. It has three ports: Reg, Send and Rcv. Reg is the port enabling terminal's register and unregister. Each terminal which expects gain some services in MEECS should record its identifier and properties first, the latter of which is the basis to automatically reason about which services should be bound to them if more than one can be found and seem satisfactory. Send and Rcv are the ports for message communications. The register of services is finished by message manipulation. MEECP has five top level components, Bus, Super Server Agent, Administrator Agent, Broker Agent and Function Agent, where Bus is composed of MsgCenter (similar to the one in Terminal), Agent Management System (AMS) and Directory Facility (DF). The architecture of MEECP is shown in Fig.5.10.

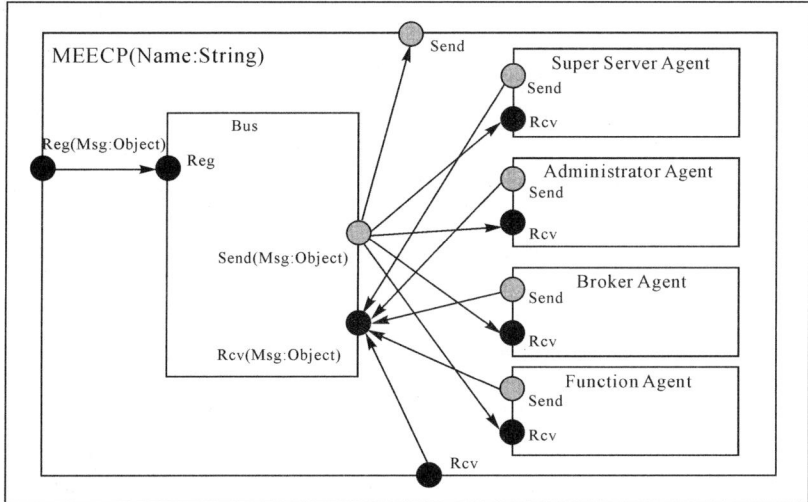

Fig. 5. 10   Architecture of MEECP

To solve the problem of task allocation and the efficiency of communications among agents, MEECP introduces the Agent Layered Management Architecture. The agents are separated into five layers according to their duties, as in Fig.5.11.

The Layer of Common Utility, supported by Agent Management System and Directory Function, facilitating the basic agent information keeping, including the identifier, status, time stamp and bound services. The messages coming from outside will be handled by this layer. Therefore, administrators of MEECP can impose policies by filtering out the messages needing to ignoance.

The Layer of Management control all the agents deployed on the platform. And

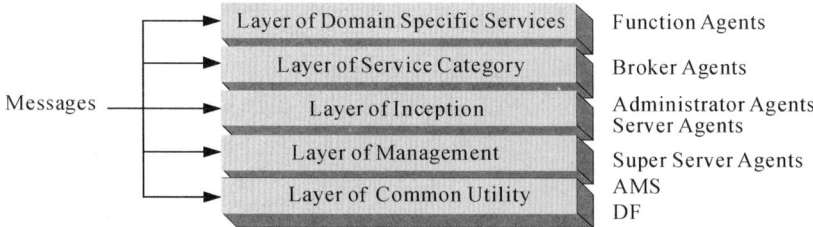

Fig. 5. 11   Agent layered management architecture

noticeably, it is itself also an agent, called Super Server Agent. In the perspective of functions, Super Server Agent does nothing about what the terminal wants, but is the start point of task allocation.

The Layer of Inception finishes the job of connecting one terminal to a carefully selected Function Agent, the proxy of actual services. In this layer, two kinds of agents, Administrator Agent and Server Agent cooperate to balance the load of numerous agents.

The Layer of Service Category is set for category of services. It is this layer that keeps the information of a set of related services registered and prepares to choose one for the terminal according to the guide tips attached by it in the form of properties.

The Layer of Domain Specific Services provides the final service proxy. After all steps of registering, the terminal and its bound services are linked by this kind of agents. Of course, one can realize the function in this agent so that there is no burden of service objects. However, doing this too much will extremely increase the load of MEECP and affects the response generation to normal requests from other terminals.

The reason of creating such a pyramid like agents layers is to reduce the opportunities that some agents can afford the load while others stay leisure. In this architecture, terminal register in fact is a process of fetching different agent. On the one hand, the terminal can be implemented in a simple way in that it needs to know the other side of communication must be an agent (no matter which kind of agent, they have the unified communication protocols and identical access interface). On the other hand, MEECP guides the terminal to where they should go, that is, Super Server Agent chooses one Server Agent, Server Agent choose one Administrator Agent, Administrator Agent chooses one Broker Agent, and at last Broker Agent chooses one Function Agent.

But why set five layers? Is all kinds of agents in the layer expect those of function only do the same job, that is, choose one agent in the next layer? This is not the case. Each kind of agents has duties of its own. Super Server Agent is created to allow the cluster of MEECP servers to compose a logic integrated whole, in which case several MEECP component instances can coexist and collaborate, wherever their physical location are. Similar for each MEECP server, agents are separated into multiple groups equipping with distinct administrative policies. And Broker Agent, as mentioned above, manages a collection of services that can fall in the same category, facilitating the implementation of match engines that attempt to follow terminals' requirements for service because different categories of services have different concepts and rules.

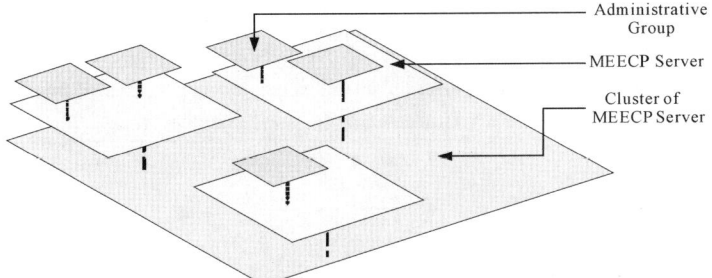

Fig. 5. 12   Reference model of MEECP

The Agent Management System (AMS) is a framework in which various agents can be created, disposed, located, transferred and communicated to. With the help of AMS, agents are able to enter an agent group, search services provided in it or even connect with agents in other group or server. What's more, AMS controls the activation of agents. AMS will allocate a thread from a thread pool to execute code embedded in the agent and collect the taken resource if an agent's reference count reduces to zero.

The Directory Function (DF) is a table maintaining the information about terminals, agents and services. Aside from the respective information of these three entities, DF records their bind relationship. For example, when a terminal finishes its register, the corresponding Super Server Agent, Server Agent, Administrator Agent, Broker Agent and Function Agent will be attached in the record. DF uses the transactions based on the database, to guarantee the atomicity and consistency.

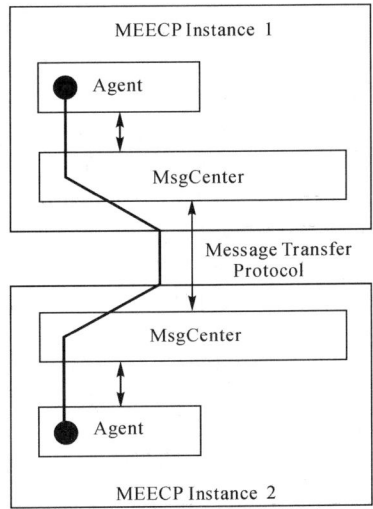

Fig. 5. 13   Model of message communications of agents crossing MEECP instances

5. 4. 2. 3 System Design

It is time to convert architecture to implementation-related models, where we use UML to sketch the system that will be coded in Java. Fig. 5. 14 is the package diagram of MEECS. And Fig. 5. 15 is the class enumeration diagram (relationships among classes are ignored here). Explaining every class is trivial and thus we do not want to rove in the detail of implementation with more broad statements. But we want to clarify the path from requirements to implementation.

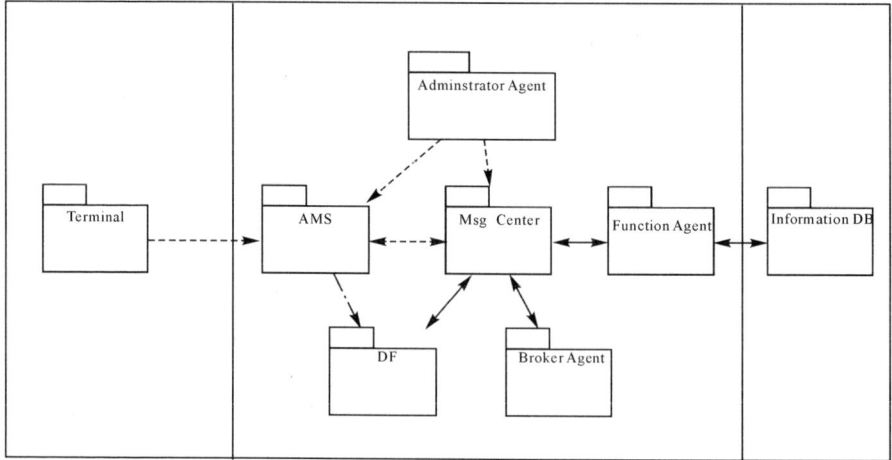

Fig. 5. 14   Package diagram of MEECS

In a domain, the consideration should be emphasized on extracting and describing the domain specific concepts during the requirements analysis. Those concepts related to the solution of problem require much more attention. The result of this phase is so called domain model, which although cannot solve the problem but provide an order-of-magnitude sense to aid developers to gain a deeper insight. In the case of MEECS, the concepts such as mobile client, agent, register information keeper, are identified to define the requirements. The requirement analysis is in fact an action that finding the constraints and conditions the entities in the domain model have to conform to. Note that the object model is neither a description of architecture nor class or objects in the Object-Oriented development, but only a simplification and visualization of concepts in the problem world.

The architecture design is the first step getting approach to the solution in the high level of the system. Although algorithms are so important to succeed, they only deal with the problems about computation, which is only a small part in the usable software. More broadly, requirements of quality attribute, performance, usability, availability, security and so on, have to be tackled by the cooperation of decomposed elements. In the architecture design, concepts are separated according to the requirements into elements and regulate their interaction. In MEECP, for example, in order to balance the load, we design the layered agents. Abstractly, this is a map from function design space to the architecture design one, which if gotten

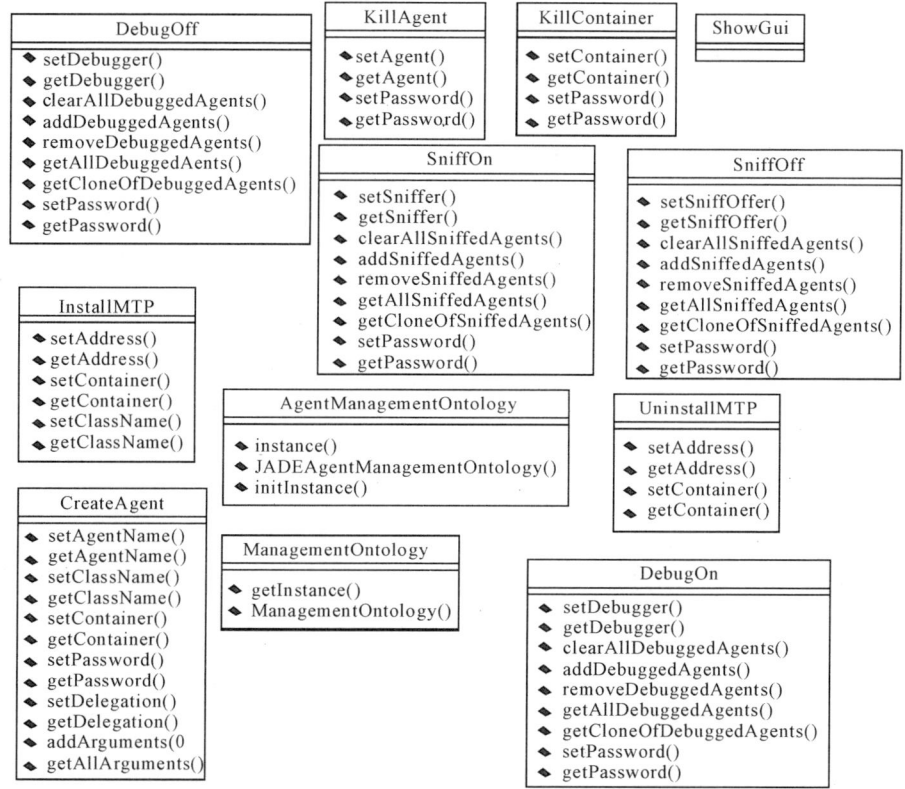

Fig. 5.15 Class diagram of administrator agent (relationships ignored)

verified again and again we can put in the rules of map created for this domain, and then contributes to the automatic design. Architecture design is programming language neutral in which only the overall sight of final system is generated. However it is a good guide to explore further which techniques should be used or which elements should be built or bought. In SADPBA several iterations occur during architecture design to refine the architecture incrementally.

Finally in the system design, we determine the techniques and convert the architecture into the model that is easily to be coded. Special tricks and features in the programming language are concerned. For instance, we use RMS provided by J2ME to achieve the permanent information storage. We convert ports in the architecture to the methods enclosed by Java interface. And we implement various agents into a tree of generalized hierarchical agent classes.

5.5 Summary

In this chapter, we introduce the design strategies in the architecture level. Actions of design are abstracted as design space. We extend the design space by splitting it into function design space, architecture design space and system design space, which is the core idea of SADPBA, an architecture-centered design process. We present the concepts and terms in SADPBA, and discuss the architecture life cycle model.

We develop MEECS, a system of mobile e-commerce, in the design phase of which we use SADPBA. In this case, three design phases are listed in more detail to illustrate how an element of one design space is mapped.

References

(He, 2003)   He, J., et al. A Component Based Distributed Software Architectural Description Environment. Mini-micro Systems 2003(24): 1637-1640.

(He, 2004a)   He, J., et al. Model of Software Analysis and Design Process Based on Architecture. Journal of Xi'an Jiaotong University 2004a(38): 591-594.

(He, 2004b)   He, J., et al. E-Commerce Oriented Knowledge Description Language. Journal of Chinese Information Processing 2004b(18): 37-42.

(He, 2005a)   He, J. & Qin, Z. Modeling and Checking the Behavior of Software Architecture. Journal of Computer Research and Development 2005(42): 2018 -2024.

(Jia, 2005)   Jia, X., et al. A Distributed Software Architecture Design Framework Based on Attributed Grammar. Journal of Zhejiang University Science 2005 (6A): 513-518.

(Wang, 2003)   Wang, Z. & He, J. An Effective Language Fiml Facilitating Interface Representation under Limited Mobile Environment. Proceedings fo the 7th International Conference for Young Compuer Scientists.2003.

6

Software Architecture IDE

6.1   What Can Software Architecture IDE do

6.1.1   A Comparison with Formalized Description Approach

In the previous chapter, formalized description approach is discussed to describe software architecture. However, researchers incline to draw much more support from software architecture integrated development environment (IDE), a development aid tool, for its powerful functions. Recently, more and more researchers begin to study tools' support in architecture that aids practitioners to create domain-specific architectural design. The shift from formalized description approach to software architecture IDE description is a necessary tendency during the growth of software architecture.

Compared with formalized description approach, IDE is skilled in many aspects. Firstly, the situation that architects have to remember a large number of notations, grammars, formulas and variables in formalized descriptions has gone for ever. With IDE, they would free themselves from these rough tasks and concentrate great attentions to architecture design. Secondly, as to a highly complex system, it is necessary to automatically manage resources with a reasonable mechanism. Formal approach cannot support this function directly. Generally, almost IDE provides file system to manage resources. In this case, researchers can develop and maintain system with serviceable documents, which would be a great increment of efficiency and a reduction of cost and work. Thirdly, IDE integrates a group of tools' to accomplish tasks automatically instead of working by hand. The formalized description can not rival IDE in this point. For example, IDE holds friendly user graphical interface and allows visible operations. In the meanwhile, diverse views and editors are used to inspect and modify system; almost all of the current IDEs support analysis tool whose function, at a minimum, covers from syntax check to semantics validation. It can help you keep a closely check on the system and detect errors at program running time; furthermore, some IDEs allow developers to define their own tests by themselves or add other tools to extend check function; IDE also can map a software design to codes with relative tools, like parser, compiler, code generator and so on. Obviously, the introduction of IDE will improve working efficiency many times and reduce time and cost as much as possible.

The above advantages are considered from the perspective of developers. What is more, IDE provides a much more transplant and comprehensive design to end users. The visual result is not only an ideal channel to communicate among stakeholders but a perfect platform to explore from multi-viewpoints. All in all, the emergence of IDE caters to the software architecture development.

6.1.2   Important Roles of Architecture IDE

Every surveyed ADL provides some tool support, with emphasizing on its concerned fields and directing attention to a particular technique. The limited supports of ADLs directly reflect the tool's functions. In this section, we want to give a view of what software architecture integrated development environment can do.

An integrated development environment is an all-in-one tool for writing, editing, compiling, and running computer program. Software architecture IDE focuses on software development from the perspective of system architecture on the basis of software architectural formalized description. It directs at accelerating development speed, increasing productive efficiency and assuring software quality.

The computer-aided software architecture development tool is well established for its flexible operations and mighty functions. It not only provides tools like graphical user interface, textual and graphical editor, but also equips system model analysis, implementation, and evaluation. Besides, IDE also supports system description, definition, design and extension. It allows developers to analyze and design the architecture at component level, which means that software architecture can significantly increase the opportunity for reusing at component level availably. In conclusion, IDE is a powerful tool whose crucial roles are elaborated as follows.

6.1.2.1   Aid Architectural Modeling

One of the most important functions of IDE is helping architects to model. IDE changes the current situation that singular software architecture description method exists. Developers not only get out of boring and obscure semantic rules but also, inconceivably, just click mouse and hit keyboard to accomplish the tasks which cost plenty of time and efforts before. As we mentioned in the front section, during the formalized description approach period, model is the process of decomposing system into components, connectors or any other elements, and describing their relationships and configures. On the contrary, IDE furnishes a series of tools to support model from stem to stern. Specially speaking, it provides designing tool, modeling tool, analyzing tool, validating tool, implementing tool and so on. Different IDE integrates various tools and stresses one or more of them according to practical situations, such as end users' demands, application domain, architectural description language, architectural style and so forth. In addition, IDE provides diverse kinds of views for stakeholders to explore models from flexible concerns. Developers can benefit much from those available tools during work.

6.1.2.2 Support Hierarchical Description

As it known to all, elements with simple architectural type can not express complicated system adequately. Fortunately, a complex or hierarchical architectural type designed for component and connector appears to address this problem. The hierarchy mechanism has been elaborated in previous chapters; in this section, we prefer to enumerate how IDE realizes this mechanism. We cite a simple example, its framework showed as the underside view, to provide a glimpse of hierarchical architecture.

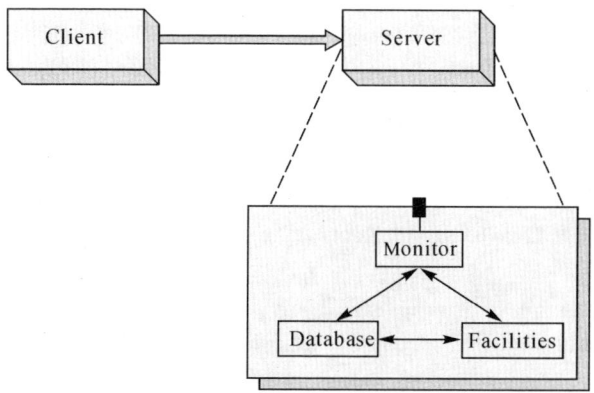

Fig. 6.1   A hierarchal component

This figure illustrates the use of hierarchy on a server-client system. At the top level, the whole system consists of two components, server and client. Server considered as an independent sub-architecture consists of three elements. In order to represent this relationship in IDE, sub-type and sub-architecture support is provided to realize hierarchy efficiently. In a concrete software development environment, you can define a complex type as a new architecture type. This new type attaches to a sub-architecture which is an independent-function entity. If you want to build a component with such type in IDE, you will do nothing more than evaluating component type with this complex type. Similar to components, connectors can also be served as high level abstract elements for a nested architectural subsystem.

6.1.2.3 Support Validation Test Mechanism

Almost all of current IDEs provide validation test mechanism. Architectural description language parsers and compilers are necessary components of IDE. Parsers analyze syntactic correctness, while compilers establish semantic correctness. Furthermore, many IDEs do not limit these basic testing mechanisms. Certain features of IDE can be characterized as intrusive: WRIGHT uses a model checker to analyze individual components and connectors attached to each other for inconsistency and deadlocks; C2 ensures style specific topological constraints and type conformance among architectural elements; SADL uses refinement maps to establish relative correctness of two architectures. In ArchStudio, Archlight not only checks system's consistency and completeness whose results would be showed in an issue panel but also supports part test by choosing your concerned elements. For instance, if you forget to connect an interface to an entity, it will report bug with warning message: Link endpoint should point to an interface.

Nowadays, IDE supports two various validating methods: proactive and reactive (Medvidovic, 2000). The former limits the available design decisions based on the current state of architectural design. For instance, IDE may provide tool that prevents selection of components whose interfaces do not match those current architecture or disallow invocation of analysis tools on incomplete architectures. The latter refers to the tools detecting existing errors. They may either inform the errors of architecture and allow to correct them later or force to remedy current problems before moving on. To take an example, in the MetaH's graphical editor, with Apply button depressed, any errors must be rectified before the architect may continue with the design.

6. 1. 2. 4   Provide Graphical and Textual User Environment

IDE is a visual tool for researchers to develop systems. Like other common development tools, it is a basic ability to supply a user-friendly graphical and convenient environment. We elaborate this point from four aspects.

Firstly, IDE supplies graphical user interface which includes many interface items such as toolbar, navigator view, outline view, workbench and so forth. Toolbar lists many common buttons; views usually display information as list or tree form. Secondly, aiming to release developers from a large number of boring grammars, IDE provides graphical editors which contain a series of graphical elements and correspond to an architectural object each. With visual operations like choosing graphical notations, editing their properties, building connections among them, you can depict the system. Take Darwin system for example, there is a toolbar containing several graphs which represent different kinds of architecture elements: a hollow rectangle denotes a component, a straight line means a link, a circle signifies an interface. Those graphs can be dragged in workbench to establish an architectural view. Designers can directly modify elements' features in attribute tables rather than editing source codes. There is no doubt that it improves efficiency greatly. Thirdly, in order to help developers record architectural configuration document which is an efficient assistant to understand system, IDE introduces a textual editor. Usually, IDE automatically generates these documents according to the graphical descriptions. When the model is changed, its textual depictions respond at once. This synchronous mechanism ensures system's consistency. On the other hand, editor can detect conflicts and confirm the grammar correctness. At last, IDE helps to store running states and testing information which are valuable data for analyzing or advancing system. Sometimes, a pane will be left to display errors or warnings. In a word, the integrated visual architectural design tool facilitates developers to capture, edit and update architectural information.

6.1.2.5   Support Multi-views

Software architecture involves so much complex information that it must be described by multi-views. Developers model diverse serviceable views to satisfy actual needs and long-term targets. IDE provides automated support for alternating between graphical view and textual view which are two common views. Aside from them, there are some particular ones for special demands. For example, Darwin system employs hierarchical system view which shows all the component types and their relationships in a tree structure, while ArchStudio supplies file management view to manage documents facility. C2 visualizes the execution behavior of a architecture by building an executable simulator and providing tools for viewing and filtering events generated by the simulator. Additionally, graphical view is an abstract conception which covers logical view, process view, physical view, development view and so on. These various views express the same architecture from different aspects. They are sub-system architectures from a particular perspective direct to emphasize the noteworthy information, and ignore the rest. Although there is only an active view at a time, fortunately you can choose others by alternating tags.

6.2   Prototype

Nowadays, more and more software architecture IDEs have emerged to cater to the flexible software architectures. Though these IDEs are applied to special ADLs with their own particulars, they share similar bases and frameworks. We draw out the essences from current software architectural IDEs and abstract a prototype. The prototype is just a general frame which cannot perform any actual functions. The prototype is provided to assist developers to understand principles and structures thoroughly and even build a brand-new one if necessary. In order to avoid a hollow illustration, we plan to introduce eXtensible Architecture Research System (XArch system) which is an experimental platform for system architecture studies. The XArch system realizes its particular function of extensibility with Foundation of Extensible Architecture Language (FEAL)-based ADLs. With this concrete instance, you can get a distinct acquaintance of this section.

From the viewpoint of software architecture IDEs' work mechanisms, the prototype is divided into three layers: user interface layer, model layer, and foundational layer. On the top is the user interface layer; the middle layer is so complex and significant that it has to include many modules; the bottom layer covers all support conditions. The Mapper document is related to both user interface layer and model layer. Its skeleton is diagramed as Fig.6.2.

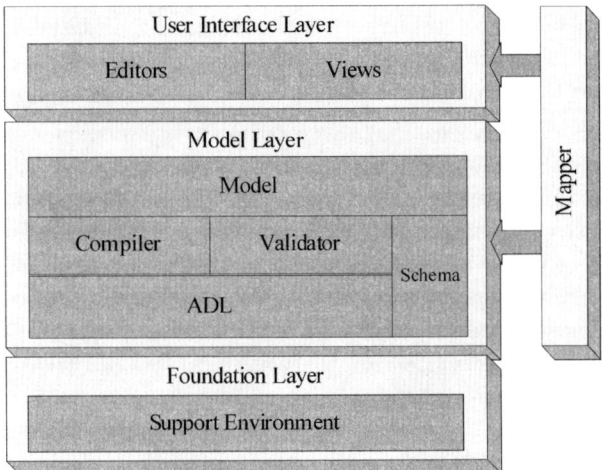

Fig. 6. 2   Framework of IDE prototype

6. 2. 1   User Interface Layer

User interface layer is the external level of the system which is the only one communicating channel between users and system. What users can touch directly is various visual panes in this layer. These panes fall into two major categories: editors and views. Both of them are visual components, but they hold their own distinguishing qualities. Editors allow users to open, edit, and save objects of the resources. They are document-centric, following an open—save—close lifecycle similar to file system-based tools such as Microsoft Word, but they are tightly integrated into the workbench. More than one instance with editor type can be exited at one time in a workbench window. Views allow users to browse resources in a hierarchical way; help to open editors; and display the objects' properties of active editors. Unlike editors, there can only be an instance with special view type in a workbench window. Once a view is modified, its corresponding model would be changed, and the new features will be reflected in other views simultaneously. Views and editors are tided up closely by focusing on the same objects. Views support editors by providing information about the content in the currently-selected editor; and results of modifications could be exhibited via views.

The workbench of XArch system which is a single application window allows to represent a number of different sorts of views but one editor at any time. The workbench is base on Rich Client Platform (RCP), which is designed to serve as an open tool platform. Its major advantage is giving users the chances to build or extend any client applications by themselves. That is to say, except for the existing editors, you can add new functions flexibly by a set of extensible interfaces. Fig.6.3 gives you a glance at views and editors. On the left workbench, outline view navigates you to the target document with a hierarchal structure. The property view on the right shows items' attributions. Any modifications that can be made in it such as editing a property value or changing the binding between two components are saved immediately. The bottom pane is a log view that records user's concerns and crucial system states.

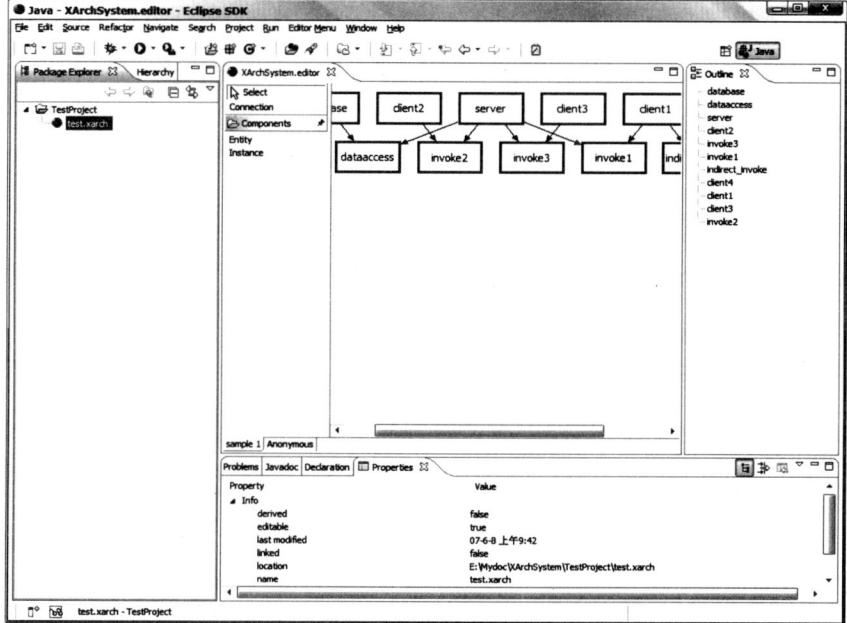

Fig. 6. 3 XArch system

The main area in the middle is an editor which is an interactive measure. You can draw objects and drag them to any places at will in the pane. It is typically used to browse or edit objects and the modifications made in it follow the open—save—close model. To satisfy stakeholders' different demands, it is effective to provide many views from diverse perspectives. The single pane supports containing different types of views in a tagged note. You may alternate views by choosing different tags, as you can choose logical graph or physical graph in this system.

6. 2. 2 Model Layer

Model layer is the kernel of the system, for it covers the most essential functions and assists to realize them. It aids IDE to address how to model system architecture. Before explaining its working mechanism, we give an account of several elements in the layer.

ADL document is the input of the system, which is a software architectural description. Some IDEs limit ADL types, so it is necessary to modify its grammars slightly to make compatible. You can refer to Section 4. 2 to get an explicit explanation of ADL. Unlike common compilers which translate source codes from a high level program language to a lower level language (e. g. assembly language or machine language), compiler here is an architecture analysis tool which converts a software architectural description language to an architectural model. The compiler is likely to perform many or all of the following operations: lexical analysis, parsing, semantic analysis, mapping, composition. Lexical analysis is a processing of a source document as input to produce, as output, a sequence of symbols called token list. Parsing, formally named syntax analysis, is the process of analyzing an input sequence in order to determine its grammatical structure with respect to a given formal grammar. Semantic analysis is a pass that adds semantical information to the parsing results and performs certain checks based on rules. Mapping is a converting process that mapping ADL notations to model's counterparts with particular regulations such as a Mapper document. Composition logically follows the mapping phase, in which the components or modules are generated. In such a case, it is relatively easy to form a system model. During the above phases, a simple check is preformed. It enforces constrains implicit in type information, component attributes, relationships among modules and so forth. Validator which is the major checking tool detects semantic errors to guarantee the latter processe' going smoothly. It supports explicit specification of criterions, and provides means for their checking and enforcement. Schema defines a series of rules to describe the document structures and data structures. It is a guard to judge whether the document or the data is valid or not. When the above conditions are ripe, modeling is assured. A system can be simplified and abstracted into several models. Different models may hold different kinds of views. In this case, stakeholders can focus attention to their concerns and inspect system from various perspectives. The system architecture can be modeled with a special structure like a tree or a graph. Which is the most proper structure depends on the practical circumstances and the concrete requirements. Mapper is a group of regulations which abstract ADL's elements and their attributers. It plays two roles, and each affects on a single layer. One is helping IDE to recognize ADL notations, that is to say, in the mapping phase. ADL notations will be decomposed and classified according to some specifications, and then endowed with abstract meanings which IDE can understand. Another role relates to the model visualizing, since it defines the rules about how to portray the model. Generally, it is a key factor in the prototype.

In XArch system, only ADLs written in the format of XML, definitely speaking, FEAL-compatible ones are accepted, which simplifies the work on language parsing. When a language does not confirm this rule exactly, it would be adjusted to follow FEAL's expected structure requirements. The system aims at not only describing architecture with multiple views, supporting conversion between ADL and model, but also offering analysis, validation and serialization of the architecture. The validation contains two requirements, for a XML document holds a set of strict formal criterions to satisfy any kinds of application needs. There are two kinds of criteria used for it. One is requested to obey XML grammar constraints, following which it is called a well-formed XML. Besides, in order to express the data information and satisfy requirements adequately, it is necessary to define structure rules, following which it is called validated XML document. The

XML schema is just the rules which are used to validate the XML document. The XML file must be confirmed to be a validating one before a further process.

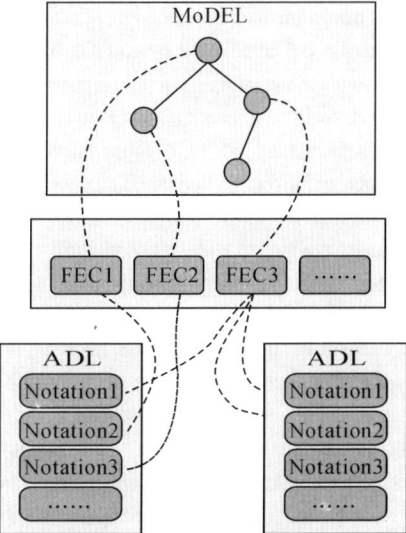

Fig. 6. 4   The relationship among ADL, FEAL and MODEL

Besides being used as a software architecture IDE, the XArch system also contributes to extension as a particular tool platform. This distinguishing feature incarnates two aspects. One is a new ADL can be defined or new features of ADL can be supported rapidly. The upper model contacts with an intermedium directly instead of ADLs. (Fig.6.4 shows the relationship among ADL, FEAL and MODEL.) ADLs' elements must be mapped into other forms, FEAL Element Categories (FEC). It is a category of elements defined in FEAL's description through abstraction of ADLs' notations. Almost all of the further operations are based on it. In this situation, if only the mapping from ADLs into FEC is valid, whichever ADL is not care. In this way, new ADLs and features can be suitable for use as usual. Another one is the XArch system provides a series of extensible visualization-editing interfaces. With this flexible function, you can display a new visual element facility by defining a new object rather than a hurry-scurry handling.

6. 2. 3   Foundational Layer

This layer likes a substantial cornerstone to support the system building. It collects hardware and software environment to sustain system running; at the same time, it manages all resources during runtime automatically. Generally speaking, a common PC is enough to run the system; operating system is able to provide enough software equipments; nevertheless, some IDEs may need more. To cite an instance, ArchStudio 4, an Eclipse plug-in, must run in Eclipse, a Java development environment.

6. 2. 4   IDE Design Tactics

Existing IDEs have put the greatest emphasis on visualization and analysis of architectures, however, some supports more powerful functions such as refinement, implementation, and dynamism. Our IDE prototype provides a framework and aids developers to realize an IDE with sufficient functions. IDE design is a brainstorm with researchers' great efforts which could be summarized into three tactics.

- IDE design is a target-oriented process that needs concentration on specific requirements. The IDE design process is a software development process in which the requirement acquirement phase is necessary and primary. Only with the exploration of practical demands, developers can have a clear and definite design. You should consider many matters from IDE itself to end-users. What problems can IDE address? What functions can it perform and how is it measured? What is its structure? Which kind of ADLs and architecture styles is suitable? Who will use it? The questions and any others act as a guide leading developers to a right design. Additionally, in view of future extensibility, it is a necessity to prepare enough extensible API for advancement. Once a new requirement specification appears, a strenuous functionality-based redesign would be avoided.

- To design an extensible IDE, it is necessary to category the aspects for generic and specific issues, upon which decisions about modules and layers are driven. The generic part is the fundamental for all IDEs like support environment, user interface and so on. Nevertheless, different IDE directs at different domains and solves distinct problems. In this case, IDE has its own unique parts. For example, Rapide's development environment allows visualization of an architecture's execution behavior by building an executable simulation of the architecture and providing tools for viewing and filtering events generated by the simulation. In particular, it uses simulator tool to build the simulation and its Animation Tools to animate its execution. SADL's assistant tool provides support for refining architectures across multiple levels of abstraction and specificity. It requires manual proofs of mappings of constructs between an abstract and a more concrete architectural style. After that, it automatically checks whether any two architectures described in the two styles adhere to the mapping. (Medvidovic, 2000)

- Our IDE prototype's usage. To extend a function, you need add notations or constructs to ADL definition that require FEAL's support. After that, ADL-specific functions should be implemented as plug-ins to be dynamically added into our IDE. At the same time, schemas and Mapper documents which act as a middle bridge should be modified to meet new concerns.

6.3 ArchStudio 4 System

6.3.1 Introduction

It is practically impossible to illustrate all of the popular software architecture IDEs. The sheer variety and the rapid evolution of them would require quite a book to discuss. So we have tried to emphasize a particular tool, ArchStudio 4, on behalf of others.

6.3.1.1 A Brief History of Software Architecture IDE

Revolutions of Integrated Development Environment have not been interrupted since the first IDE created for BASIC. For years and months, its definition has been shifted from initial doing simple development in front of console or terminal to current being a single program in which all development can be done. It is not a command-line tool anymore; it provides typically large numbers of features for system design, modification, compilation, deployment, validation, implementation and evaluation. Its development course could be fall into three successive phases.

The first phase is the period of repository-centric IDEs (Khare, 2001). In such stage, different tools would work upon a central, shared database representing the product-in-progress. The archetype of this generation was the Stoneman reference model for the Ada Program Support Environment. Interlisp can be seen as one instance of this approach with suite of tools operating on a shared parse tree. A versioned file system was another popular variant, notably Revision Control System (RCS). Continuing the ascent, the second generation of process-centric IDEs emerged in the 1980s which took relations between development processes and their associated workflows into account. Tools such as Marvel assisted developers by automating basic process steps and coordinating the work of tools "outside" the development path proper. In the extreme, IDE support tools maintained only those relations, as in the Chimera Linkbase. Nowadays, we see the current era as the advent of architecture-centric IDEs that control the evolution of software throughout its lifecycle using architecture descriptions as its primary unit of discourse. As an example, ArchStudio assumes the existence of versioned repositories and process automation in its foundation, and so focuses on the design, evaluation, implementation, and editing of software architectures. Supporting tool integration in this generation now requires an open, hypertext web representing the entire product, from architecture down to development artifacts. This architecture-centric approach represents a major new trend in software engineering.

6.3.1.2 What Is ArchStudio 4 and What It Can Do

ArchStudio 4 is an open-source architecture-oriented software architecture-integrated development environment created by the Institute for Software Research at the University of California, Irvine. It creates and manipulates architecture descriptions expressed in the xADL 2.0 architecture description language. xADL 2.0

is a XML-based ADL (Dashofy, 2005), which is defined in a suit of XML schemas. As such, xADL 2.0 architecture descriptions are simply XML documents that conform to the language defined in xADL 2.0 schemas. ArchStudio 4 is implemented as a set of Eclipse plug-ins and runs on Windows, Unix/Linux, MacOS, and other platforms that support Eclipse and Java. Founded with the core of its predecessor, a mature tool, it adds many exciting new features and performance enhancements. It distinguishes from previous tools with special features: extensibility, implementation, and engineering. ArchStudio 4's primary goal is extensibility for settling the "one-fit-all" problem, which we will interpret in detail later. In the terms of implementation, it successfully accomplishes its development by using itself. It treats the development process as an engineering not a common artifact for it takes development lifecycle, architecture style and any other software engineering concepts into account.

Generally speaking, its significant effects in architecture come through system modeling and meta-modeling. That is to say, it not only directs to modeling, visualizing, checking and implementing software architecture but also gives a great support for these functions' future extension.

- **Model**: As a software architecture development-aided tool, ArchStudio 4's primary function is the model which allows stakeholders to document or portray the design thought of the system. Model abstracts system into a framework at a high level that is similar to a blueprint. The design result, architecture model, is stored and manipulated in a XML format; it can be investigated from different viewpoints with diverse ways. Superior to other tools, ArchStudio 4 for specifying architectural type consistency, hierarchical modeling, product-line modeling and capturing architectural changes over time.
- **Visualize**: ArchStudio 4 provides different visualizations, like views and editors for contemplating models. In this case, stakeholders are able to pay close attentions to their concerns. Interacting views and editors to visualize architectural descriptions in textual or graphic manners, such as Archipelago, ArchEdit and Type Wright. In this way, it provides different perspectives for inspection and interaction with more chances of communication and understanding.
- **Check**: ArchStudio 4 supports to analyze and test architecture with a powerful tool, Schematron which allows complex architectural tests to be specified in about a dozen lines of code. It runs suites of tests on architecture to check it for consistency and correctness. The Archlight framework provides a way to automatically test architecture descriptions against many different criteria. Errors can be detected and displayed, and users can be navigated to the site of a problem in any editor with a few mouse clicks.
- **Implement**: It helps to tie architecture to implemented systems. Interestingly, ArchStudio is realized with its own architecture-centric thoughts and notations. ArchStudio's architecture is specified in a xADL 2.0 file, and this file is part of the ArchStudio implementation. Whenever

ArchStudio starts up on a machine, its architecture description is being parsed, and the information in that description is used to instantiate and connects the components and connectors in the architecture.

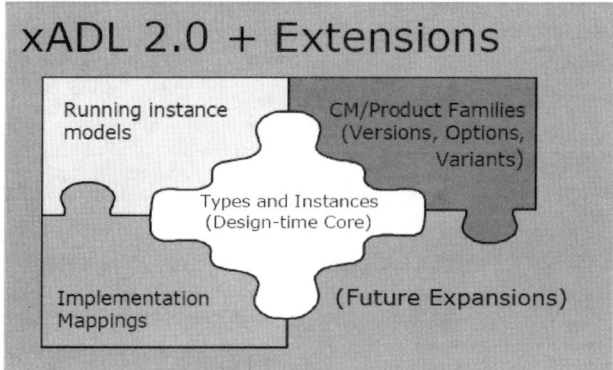

Fig. 6. 5   xADL 2.0 and extensions

Beyond that, it provides well-defined extensibility mechanisms attributed to the fact that it is based on xADL 2.0, which is as useful as an ADL by itself, and in particular, extensible to support applications and domains. xADL 2.0 is modular, rather than monolithic. Rather than defining syntax and semantics monolithically in a huge block, it decomposes modeling features into modules with XML schemas. Four modules relate to a common core, and the five parts make up the whole system (Fig. 6.5). For example, components and connectors can be broken up into modules which are defined in XML schemas. To date, modules have been developed for capturing traditional concerns like components and connectors along with more innovative concerns such as product-lines, implementation mappings, architectural states, and so on. Tools read schemas and automatically generate a data binding library that provides a foundation for other tools. Thus, users can extend the xADL language with new features and automatically generate libraries used for building tools that interact with those new features.(Fig.6.6)(Dashofy,2007) In a word, xADL 2.0 allows developers to define new semantics and rules by themselves to capture more data and meet new demands; if current tools and notations are not sufficient for a particular project, ArchStudio 4 and xADL allow integrating new ones to provide effective support to capture particular concerns.

- **Extensibly Model**: ArchStudio 4 has pursued extensible model when it came into being. It introduces xADL that is the first extensible architecture description language, extended by adding new XML schemas. With the addition of new schemas, it can be extended to support new specific concerns and modeling needs. New elements can be added to the core xADL 2.0 from time to time when developed and contributed.
- **Extensibly Visualize**: Visual editor has an extensible plug-in mechanism for adding editing support with new ADL elements.
- **Extensibly Check**: Users can write new tests in the Schematron constraint

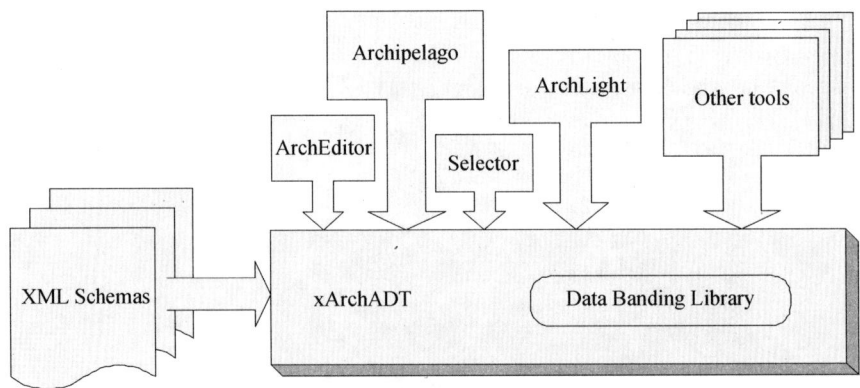

Fig. 6. 6   Tools of ArchStudio 4

language, and can integrate new analysis engines to check these properties. In keeping with ArchStudio 4's extensible nature, all tests are provided by Archlight plug-ins, and users can add their own tests through plug-in API. Archlight ships with the powerful Schematron XML constraint engine, adapted to integrate other engines seamlessly into the Archlight user interface. (Fig.6.7)

- **Extensibly implement:** Users can bind their architectures to the flexible Myx framework, or use their own. Myx is an architecture style in which ArchStudio 4 is build. The goal of the "Myx" architectural style is to serve as an architectural style that is good for building flexible, high performance tool-integrating environments. (Myx-whitepaper) It is a set of rules for composing the components and connectors of an application. It provides patterns of composition for synchronous and asynchronous interactions among components. It also provides rules for what kinds of assumed components may make about each other, ensuring a directed/layered ordering of dependencies among components. By adhering to these constraints, Myx applications receive certain benefits. Components remain relatively independent from one another, and it is easy to reuse components. Components only communicate through explicit interfaces, so it is easy to reconfig components in different context without recoding. Dynamic proxies and event pumps can be used to connect and disconnect components at run-time.

6. 3. 2   Installing ArchStudio 4

- Hardware requirements

No one can tell exactly how much hardware is enough. As is know to all, the configuration of hardware depends upon concrete practical requirements, such as the scale of programs you will run, the expected amount of running time and so on. As for ArchStudio 4, the general hardware configurations, like Pentium Ⅲ, 128MB RAM, are enough for performing.

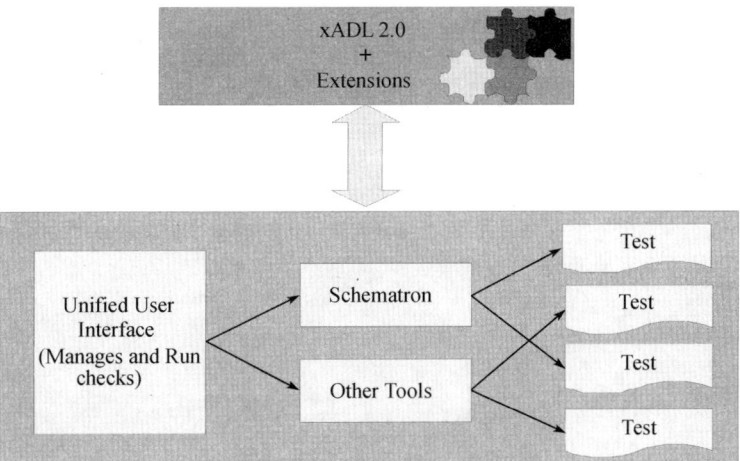

Fig. 6. 7   Extensible checking tools

- Software requirements

ArchStudio 4 is based on the Eclipse, a java open-source development platform. It can be run at any operation system that supports Eclipse, such as Windows 2000/XP, MacOS. Besides, the following three items are necessary, which are a JRE version 1.5 or better, Eclipse version 3.2.1 or better and ArchStudio 4 itself. You can download these tools by visiting their official websites, then set up them by guiding. You should assure the availability of them and the network. Once Eclipse runs, you can install ArchStudio 4 at once.

- Steps of installing ArchStudio 4

The installing process is easy with the guides. To set up ArchStudio 4, follow these steps:

♦ In the main perspective of Eclipse, click *Help* in the upper menu bar and choose *Software Updates*→ *Find and Install*···.

♦ Choose the option: *Search for new features to install* in the Install/Updates windows.

♦ In the Install dialog box, click *New Remote Site...*; then fill in the *Name* field with a name and fill in *URL field* with http://www.isr.uci.edu/projects/archstudio-update. Affirm this information and click *finish*.

♦ Once a license-queried dialog box is displayed, you must agree the rules for further steps. At last, click *finish* to accomplish the installation in the summary dialog.

At this time, wait for Eclipse downloading ArchStudio 4 and any other necessary features. A final confirmation dialog displayed asks you to confirm installation of the download. You will be asked to restart Eclipse and choose Yes to restart at once, or No to restart later. When it restarts, on the main menu bar, click *Window* in the upper menu and choose *Open perspective*→ *other*→ *ArchStudio*, finally, ensure your operations. At this moment, ArchSutdio 4 is installed completely and you can set about enjoying it. A screenshot of the ArchStudio 4 is showed in Fig.6.8.

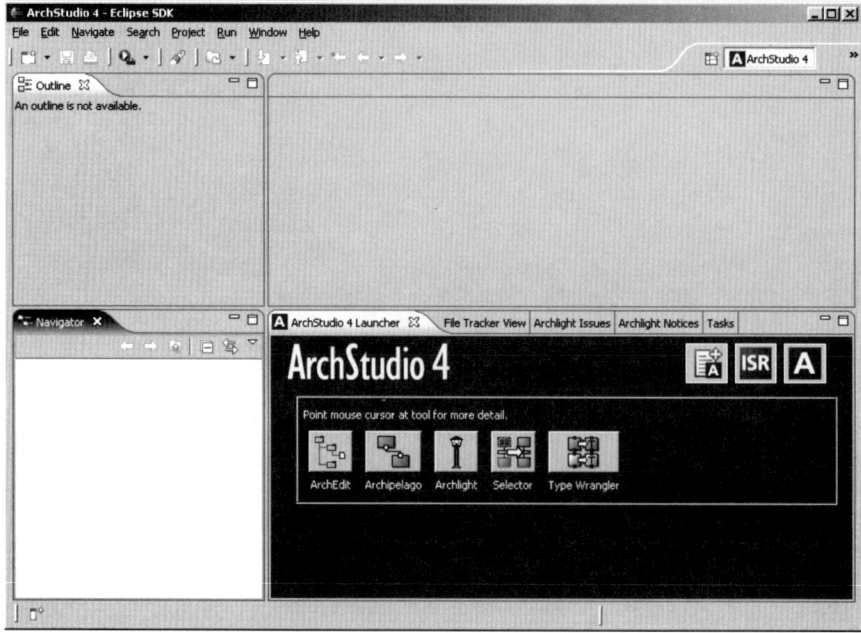

Fig. 6. 8   A screenshot of ArchStudio 4

6. 3. 3   ArchStudio 4 Overview

After installing, you can take a look at ArchStudio 4. Usually, we separate ArchStudio 4 into two parts according to its functions. The minor part covers projects, folders, and files which like a housekeeper to manage resources. The major one is the workbench of ArchStudio 4 on which all operations is performed. It is a single application window that at any given time contains several different types of pane. The paragraphs below will give an introduction of them.

6. 3. 3. 1   Projects, Folders and Files

In order to solve the problems of consistency among cross-platform systems, researchers make use of an abstraction mechanism above the native file system. Specifically, it uses projects at the highest level, and contains folders under the projects instead of using the hierarchy of directories and sub-directories, each of which contains files. Each project corresponds to a sub-directory of the root-directory and contains folders and files; normally each folder corresponds to a sub-directory of the project directory, but a folder can also be linked to a directory anywhere in the file system. All resources can be categorized into projects, folders or files. In fact, none of these three categories is specialized to Eclipse. The managing way has noting to do with Java, C++, or ADLs, and it is an effective method of storing value data.

Moreover, it is important to know the position where your files locate, for you may edit, cut, paste and move them manually, or make clear how much space they occupy in your disk. When you start a project, you will be asked for a workspace to locate the directory where it stores all project files, including ArchStudio 4 projects that contain xADL files; choose an independent document to save all resources.

6.3.3.2   The Workbench of ArchStudio 4

The workbench is the main window that appears when you start ArchStudio 4. It allows you to work with projects and navigates them. We can categorize the modules of the workbench into three kinds: views, editors, menus and toolbars. Now, we will give a detailed comment one by one.

Views

At a glance of the ArchStudio 4's interface, you may find four main panes occupy most of interface room. They represent different kinds of views with their own responsibilities. The main views contain navigator view, outline view and some special ArchStudio 4 views. For more details on view definition you can refer to the second section.

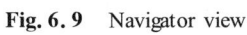

Fig. 6. 9   Navigator view

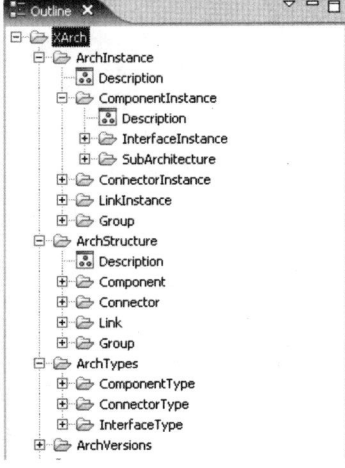

Fig. 6. 10   Outline view

• Navigator view

The pane at lower left is called navigator view; it displays the file system navigator which manages projects and files and represents all projects in a hierarchical way. The abstraction mechanism mentioned above is incarnated in it. With this view, you get a clear overview of resources and their relationships. You can fold or unfold files with addition and subtraction icons; you can also select or operate editing, inspecting or managing on them. Moreover, team operations are supported.

• Outline view

The outline view is on the upper left, showing the structure of a selected file in the navigator view with a tree structure. We can found the tree-based user interface of it to be cumbersome for hierarchical architectural compositions. The contents in this view are structural items of system architectures such as architectural types, components, connectors and links. You can design architecture with these off-the-shelf structures with ease without a sharp debate about a right abstract level.

- ArchStudio 4 views

The special views of ArchStudio 4 are on the lower right. In this area, ArchStudio 4 launcher is on a tagged panel with other five views: File Tracker View, Archlight Issues, Archlight Notices, Tasks, File Manager View. We can divide this pane into two parts: the tagged bar in the top and the display area below. The upper bar contains five tags with views' titles and the contents of the selected one would be showed in the display pane.

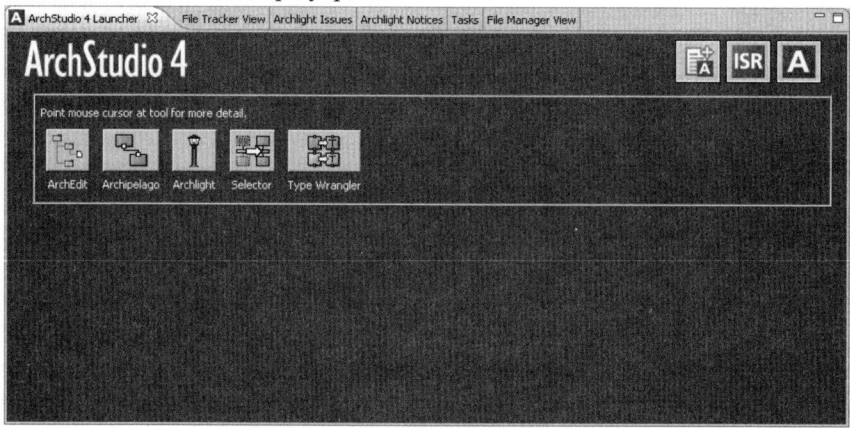

Fig. 6. 11   ArchStudio 4 views

- ArchStudio 4 Launcher

The simple duty of the launcher is to open documents and invoke tools. It doesn't know anything about editing, running, or checking; it only helps to navigate files to any required operations. Any tasks it can't handle will be delegated to editors. On the upper right, three shortcut buttons are located to facilitate users. The first one with a document icon is used to create a new architecture description file. The second one has a link to ISR website, and the last one is for visiting ArchSutdio 4 website. Under the logo of ArchStudio 4, there is a collection of several editor buttons including ArchEdit, Archipelago, Archlight, Selector and Type Wrangler. To open a file, you can drag it from the navigator view and drop it on the target editor, or click on an editor button and choose which you want to use from all resources listed in a dialog box.

- Archlight Issues

This view lists semantic and syntax errors detected by the validator. ArchStudio includes and adapts the Schematron XML validator for use as an architectural analysis engine. By right clicking the prompts, you can not only catch the detailed information of the errors but also track and think over them in more than one aspects. There are four kinds of tracking manners, namely, the selector dialog box, the type wrangler dialog box, ArchEdit view and Archipelago view. In this pane, the right column titled with Tool shows the checking tool, Schematron. It allows tests to be defined as compact constraints over the XML structure of xADL documents. It filters errors revealed in the middle column. The errors' information would not be disappeared until you correct them. If you test another file following closely a text, the latter mistakes will be listed behind the former ones. So it is unobvious to separate the new from the old.

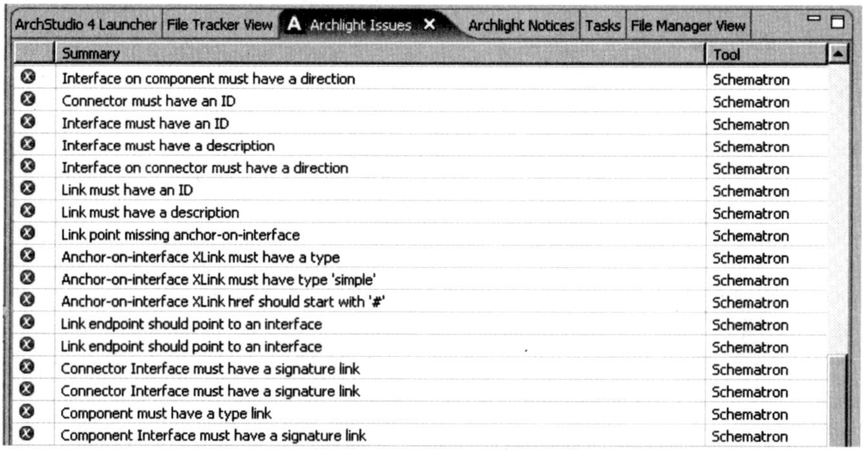

	Summary	Tool
✘	Interface on component must have a direction	Schematron
✘	Connector must have an ID	Schematron
✘	Interface must have an ID	Schematron
✘	Interface must have a description	Schematron
✘	Interface on connector must have a direction	Schematron
✘	Link must have an ID	Schematron
✘	Link must have a description	Schematron
✘	Link point missing anchor-on-interface	Schematron
✘	Anchor-on-interface XLink must have a type	Schematron
✘	Anchor-on-interface XLink must have type 'simple'	Schematron
✘	Anchor-on-interface XLink href should start with '#'	Schematron
✘	Link endpoint should point to an interface	Schematron
✘	Link endpoint should point to an interface	Schematron
✘	Connector Interface must have a signature link	Schematron
✘	Connector Interface must have a signature link	Schematron
✘	Component must have a type link	Schematron
✘	Component Interface must have a signature link	Schematron

ArchStudio 4 Launcher | File Tracker View | A Archlight Issues ✘ | Archlight Notices | Tasks | File Manager View

Fig. 6.12 Archlight issues

• Archlight Notices

It records the activities of Schematron from the moment when it starts. The information of initial state and Xalan version is always exhibited every start. Additionally, if a test is carried out, two pieces of news about the process will be added.

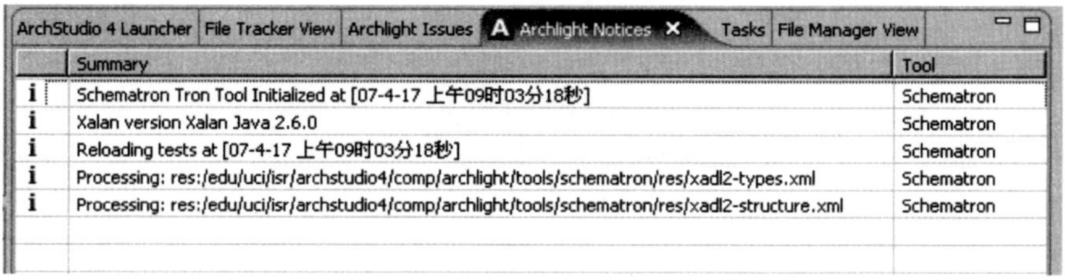

ArchStudio 4 Launcher | File Tracker View | Archlight Issues | A Archlight Notices ✘ | Tasks | File Manager View

	Summary	Tool
i	Schematron Tron Tool Initialized at [07-4-17 上午09时03分18秒]	Schematron
i	Xalan version Xalan Java 2.6.0	Schematron
i	Reloading tests at [07-4-17 上午09时03分18秒]	Schematron
i	Processing: res:/edu/uci/isr/archstudio4/comp/archlight/tools/schematron/res/xadl2-types.xml	Schematron
i	Processing: res:/edu/uci/isr/archstudio4/comp/archlight/tools/schematron/res/xadl2-structure.xml	Schematron

Fig. 6.13 Archlight notices

• Tasks

At the bottom of the window is a Tasks view. It is useful for keeping track of what needs to be done in a project. Tasks are added to this list automatically as ArchStudio 4 encounters errors in your code. You can also add tasks and set priority to the Task view by right clicking and selecting context menus. The view lists the task items with brief descriptions and used resources; it supports a relatively convenient way to keep a task list for projects.

ArchStudio 4 Launcher	File Tracker View	Archlight Issues	Archlight Notices	Tasks ✕	File Manager View		

60 items

✓	!	Description	Resource
		TODO Auto-generated method stub	DiagramActionBarContributor.java
		TODO To change the template for this generated file go to	Connection.java
		TODO To change the template for this generated file go to	ConnectionEditPolicy.java
		TODO To change the template for this generated file go to	ConnectionPart.java
		TODO To change the template for this generated file go to	CreateConnectionCommand.java
		TODO To change the template for this generated file go to	CreateNodeCommand.java
		TODO To change the template for this generated file go to	DeleteConnectionCommand.java
		TODO To change the template for this generated file go to	DeleteNodeCommand.java
		TODO To change the template for this generated file go to	Diagram.java
		TODO To change the template for this generated file go to	DiagramActionBarContributor.java
		TODO To change the template for this generated file go to	DiagramLayoutEditPolicy.java
		TODO To change the template for this generated file go to	DiagramPart.java
		TODO To change the template for this generated file go to	DiagramTemplateTransferDropTargetListener.j..
		TODO To change the template for this generated file go to	DiagramTreeEditPart.java
		TODO To change the template for this generated file go to	Element.java
		TODO To change the template for this generated file go to	ElementFactory.java
		TODO To change the template for this generated file go to	MoveNodeCommand.java

Fig. 6. 14   Tasks

Editors

ArchStudio 4 integrates a suit of editors operating on xADL documents much similar to a word processor operating on text documents. The major difference between them is that ArchStudio 4 furnishes synchronism which means that a change in any editor will be reflected in others instantly. ArchStudio 4 includes a plug-in-based framework for extending new editors. All aspects of the editor are constructed using the plug-in-based framework, allowing plug-in packages to be added to support new xADL schemas. We will elaborate on the effective editors supplied by ArchStudio 4.

- ArchEdit

ArchEdit is a syntax-driven editor to describe architectures in a tree format without coding. The contents of its user interface are generated automatically based on the underlying xADL schemas. It resembles a middle platform which allows architects to choose off-the-shelf architectural-level elements of the software system, and add them to their own concerns easily. The elements can be quickly constructed, combined with modeling features which are encapsulated in modules and conceal XML details; moreover, it is feasible to integrate new features as necessary. This helps developers release from designing right elements at the right level. ArchEdit dose not concern the semantics of the elements. It only generates behaviors and interfaces according to XML schemas, adapting to future extensions. Therefore, it will not be changed when new schemas are added or modified and can support new schemas automatically.

- Archipelago

Archipelago is a semantic editor to graph architectures by the box-and-arrow way like Rational Rose. However, the major difference is that, the graphical depiction in Archipelago is an integer with rich meanings rather than pictures simply pieced together. The ordinary rectangles play vital roles in the architecture, and the relationships among them must conform to some standards instead of linking any elements. The Fig.6.18 illustrates a simple system architecture in Archipelago.

This editor provides a click-and-point style to editing interface and primarily uses a context user interface rather than common toolbars or menus. Context menus are generally brought up by right clicking on the elements to be expected in the outline view. Double clicked in the tree structure view, the element will be displayed in the right editor pane which is a graphical editing canvas. Right clicking on the blank canvas could create new elements; right clicking on the elements could go over and edit their features. The graphical editing canvas supports arbitrary zooming and scrolling. Scrolling can be done with the scrollbars, and zooming can be done with the zoom dropdown box in the upper right corner of the canvas.

Additionally, almost all of the tools can be coordinated compatibly. Archipelago can work well in combination with ArchEdit or any other editors. On the one hand, Architecture descriptions created in Archipelago can be fine tuned by ArchEdit, or ArchEdit can be used to access schema elements not supported directly by Archipelago. On the other hand, all elements described by ArchEdit have relative objects in the Archipelago and refinements of those objects will be reflected in the ArchEdit at once.

- ArchLight

Archlight is a framework of components for integrating architecture analysis tools into ArchStudio 4. It provides a unified user interface for users to select and run tests that check various properties of architecture descriptions.

Several analysis tools in the Archlight framework provide users a unified suite of tests that can be run over architecture documents. These tests are presented hierarchically in a tree structure. Each test is a node in the tree. Due to the wide variety of architectures, architectural styles, and stages of development, not all documents will be expected to pass all tests. Therefore, Archlight gives the ability to choose any subset of tests to a given document.

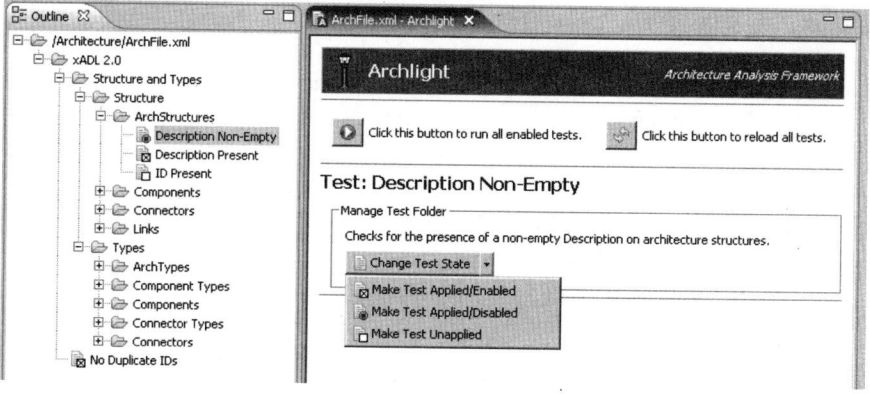

Fig. 6. 15   Archlight

There are three states of the tests.

- **Applied /Enable test:** This test is applied to the document. This means that the user expects that the document will pass this test. It will be run when all tests are run on the document.

- **Applied /Disable test**: This test is applied to the document. This means that the user expects that the document will pass this test. Unlike the first one, however, this test is temporarily disabled. It will be run unless no tests are run on the document, and issues that would be identified by the test will not be reported until the test is re-enabled.
- **Unapplied test**: This test is not applied to the document. This means that you do not expect that file document will pass this test. This test will not be run when all tests are run on the document, and issues that would be identified by the test will not be reported.

The suite of available tests is determined by the installed tools and the tests that reported they can run. Whether tests are applied, disabled, or unapplied is a property of each document. Each document stores a list of applied and disabled tests. If a document is encountered that references unavailable tests, those tests will be inserted into the tree as Unknown Tests. Unknown tests will not be run but they will remain associated with the document unless they are unapplied.

Each test has a unique identifier, called a UID. This is simply a string that identifies the test. In general, the user of Archlight will never see these UIDs which are created and managed by test developers. A test's UID generally will never change, even if the test's name, purpose, or location in the tree changes. Each analysis tool is expected to perform one or more tests. These tests are referred to by their UIDs. Each document stores a list of test UIDs and whether they are applied or disabled. If test UIDs are found in a document but no tool reports that it can perform a test with that UID, the tests will become Unknown Tests in the Archlight GUI.

- Selector

The full name of Selector is Product-Line Selector. At first, it is a necessity to introduce the conception of product lines. Software product resembles a part of a product line. A product line is a family of related software products that share significant portions of their architectures with specific points of variation. However, a single product line may contain products that are localized for specific regions or represent different feature sets for marketing purposes. The Product-Line Selector sculpts product lines down to smaller ones or single product by extracting any subsets of the whole architecture when you need to reduce the product lines to adapt new architectural descriptions.

The tool provides graphical user interface to bind the variables to values. And, you can click the button to perform the selection process. There are three kinds of performances: select, prune, version prune. Users can choose any one or more to satisfy needs. It is necessary to highlight the version prune. A version of the architectural model can be opened in ArchStudio for editing or for instantiation by providing a WebDAV URL to ArchStudio. An architectural model in ArchStudio consists of a single xADL 2.0 file. The current version of the architecture will be kept in the trunk directory, while versions will be kept in tags and branches

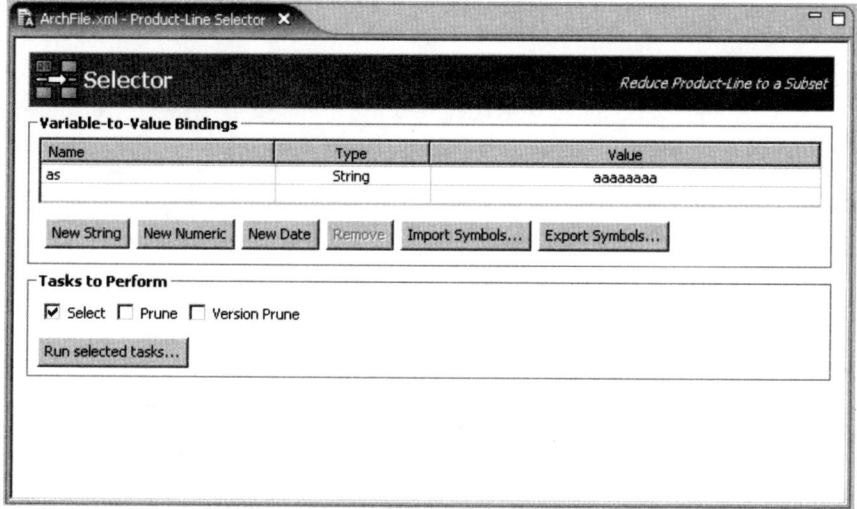

Fig. 6.16   Product-Line Selector

directories. It is important to point out that the workbench only shows the organization of directories for one architecture, but in reality the Subversion repository can contain any number of architectures for different systems. With the function of version prune, users can choose any version of the architecture (Nistor, 2005).

- Type Wrangler

Type Wrangler provides a view of architectural types that makes it easier to achieve type consistency. It not only assists users to add or remove interfaces and signatures which can be mapped or unmapped by clicking mouse, but also helps developers to judge whether components and connectors match their types properly or not.

Menus and toolbars

In addition to views, editors and other tools, several other features of the Workbench user interface are worthy to be mentioned: the main menu, the main toolbar, and the shortcut toolbar. Like the views and editors, the workbench's menu and toolbar can change depending on the tasks and features available in current windows.

The main menu appears at the top of the workbench, below the title bar. Users can invoke most actions from the main menu or its submenus. Below the main menu is the main toolbar, which contains buttons that provide convenient shortcuts for commonly-performed actions. These tool buttons don't display labels to indicate what they do unless you put the mouse pointer over them, showing a short text description to display as a hovering tool tip. In addition to the workbench menus and toolbars, some views or editors can also have their own specific menus. You can select any operations by clicking on the icon. This action lets you perform behaviors on the window. The menus and toolbars here provide a quick way to

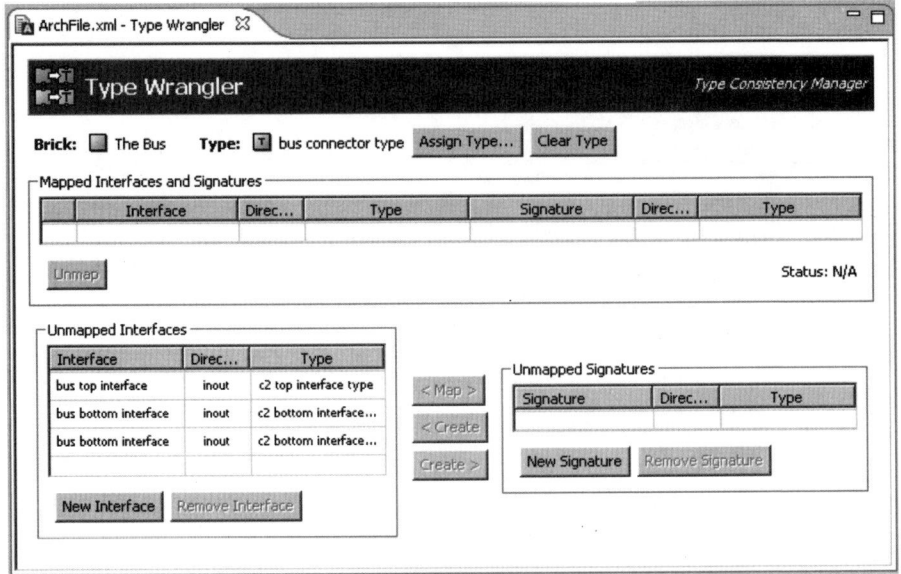

Fig. 6. 17   Type Wrangler

manage and operate projects.

6.3.4   Using ArchStudio 4

The content of this passage is guiding users how to use ArchStudio 4 effectively throughout a development process. Along the way, we will illustrate this issue with a simple application program which is a software system used to drive a television set. In order to achieve our purpose, we must abide by the underside essential steps. First of all, you should clarify practical requirements; then analyze system architecture; after that, model the system by creating architectural elements and constructing topology; finally, check this model. If it is necessary, you also can extend much more functions on the base of the old system. We define this system with the following basic requirements (see Fig.6.18).

- The system has two tuner programs: TV tuner and picture-in-picture tuner, both of which include a communication interface. All information and data are transported throught it.
- The system has a driven system which drives the infrared receiver detector used to pick up signals from the remote control.
- The above three sub-systems communicate with a middle system that allows the infrared receiver to send signals to two tuners for supporting the display of both channels simultaneously.

After acquiring application requirements distinctly, we set about analyzing system architecture. One of the most important tasks is choosing or defining a suited architecture style. Considering this mini-system just delivers and receives signals, C2 style is a judicious option which can satisfies those particular needs

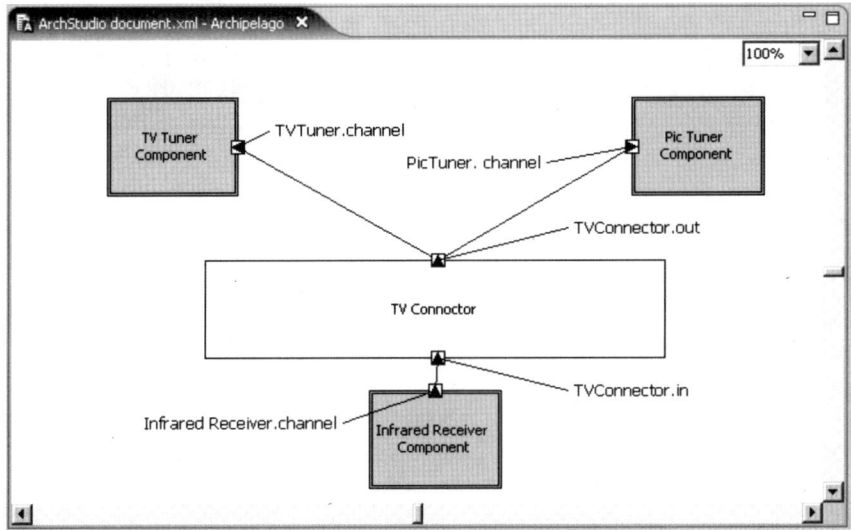

Fig. 6. 18   Architecture of TV system

perfectly. In C2 style, a set of principles govern whether system elements are composed legally or not; in this concern, system's behaviors could be confined. Specifically speaking, in this example, the system needs four kinds of elements: three component-type instance and a connector-type instance: TV Tuner component, Pic Tuner component, Infrared Receiver component and TV connector. Every element just has two semantically rich interfaces whose responsibility is delivering and receiving signals. Every component or connector has a clear top and bottom point which limits interaction manners. Followed with choosing style and any other analysis, the significant process is how to model with IDE. First of all, like building a C or Java project for a scientific management of documents, you also should create a new ArchStudio project, and then add a new file according to the prompts step by step. Name and store them in your disk where you can find all files created during programs running. The follow steps are designed to tutor you how to create a project.

• Click File and choose New in the main menu or right click in the Navigator view to bring up a context menu and select New Project.

• In the New Project dialog box, select a general project and name it, and then click Finish.

• Click File and choose New in the main menu or right click in the Navigator view to bring up a context menu and select ArchStudio Architecture Description.

• In the New Architecture Description dialog box, select a project you expect and name the file, at last, click Finish.

Now, you can start to model the system. Opening the new file with ArchEdit, you can see an empty fold named XArch without any sub-files. By righting click it you will find some ready-made notations which are designed according to the XML schemas; add them and further add sub-notations to enrich the architecture. In terms of design ArchTypes, we should take component type, connector type and interface type into consideration. An architectural type consists of a unique identifier and a textual description along with a set of signatures. Signatures are prescribed interfaces. Two components or connectors of the same type should have the same types of interfaces; the component or connector interface should have the same interface type as its signature. Furthermore, you may employ sub-architectures for component or connector in a high level to design large scale systems. In this TV system, there are three component instances which fall into two kinds of component type: Tuner Type and Infrared Receiver Type. And further, describe TV connector type as connector type. For interface type, it's ideal to separate Top Interface Type from Bottom Interface Type, because every element has a top and bottom side. With regard to modeling ArchStructures, many perspectives should be described. Two schemas about Structure & Types and Instances support the following features for its design (Dashofy, 2005).

- Components: every component has a unique identifier and a short textual description, along with a set of interfaces. It has its own component type which is defined later, and different components can share the same type.
- Connectors: Similar to components, connectors also have only a unique identifier, a textual description, and a set of interfaces and own type.
- Interfaces: In these schemas, interfaces have a unique identifier, a textual description, and a direction which implies the interface is provided or required.
- Links: In architecture notations, links connect interfaces and every link has two points to bind interfaces.
- Sub-architectures: Components and connectors can be intergraded into a complex entirety. Composite components and connectors have internal architectures, called sub-architectures.
- General Groups: Groups are simply collections of pointers to elements in the architecture description. In these schemas, a group has no semantics. Groups with specific meanings can be specified in extension schemas.

Take TV Tuner component for example, in order to simplify the model, we only consider the necessary attributes and omit the rests. The component model refers to the attributions such as ID, description, interface, type and so forth. Its type belongs to Tuner Type; its interface type is bottom type; its interface signature must be matched with the same signature of its component type. Aside from describing this information, an easily neglected thing is instancing its type: banding its type to the relevant type. You merely drag and drop the component to the target type or fill in its type details. With bindings, changing a kind of type is automatically propagated to all instances which are bound to it. Similar to TV Tuner component, other elements are designed in this way. These obscure definitions can be finished easily in ArchStudio 4, for it envelops ready-made functions such as adding type, adding instance. The only thing you just do is right-clicking mouse to put your design into practice. While, in the meantime, a more detailed descriptions and constrains should be attached to them. You can follow these steps.

• Add the first level nodes to the root, XArch. At a minimum, the ArchTypes and ArchStructure should be described.

• According to the analysis, three components (TV Tuner, Pic Tuner, and Infrared Receiver), a connector (TV connector) and three links (TV Tuner to TV connector, Pic Tuner to TV connector, Infrared Receiver to TV connector) should be considered during ArchStructure design. While, to design ArchTypes, two component types (Tuner Type and Infrared Receiver Type), a connector type (TV connector Type) and an interface type (channel Type) should be taken into account.

• Set the features of these elements and bind the relative links among them. The link only connects compatible direction interfaces, like in and out, but neither in and in nor out and out. Once you ascertain the topology of the system, the fold, RendingHints3, is created automatically with information of all hinted elements.

The last but not the least step is checking the model. Whether the architecture model is complete or not? Does the interface link the right interfaces? Do two elements have the same identifies? A group of uncertain factors should be assured. Fortunately, ArchStudio 4 supports a checking tool, Archlight. Open the document in Archlight and choose check sort; the validation process will give you a checking report. Then you can track and correct errors. Additionally, it supports modification of architecture at runtime by dynamically loading and linking new components or connectors into the architecture. Supposing an error pointed out in the Archlight Notice view likes the following Fig.6.19. How do you deal with it?

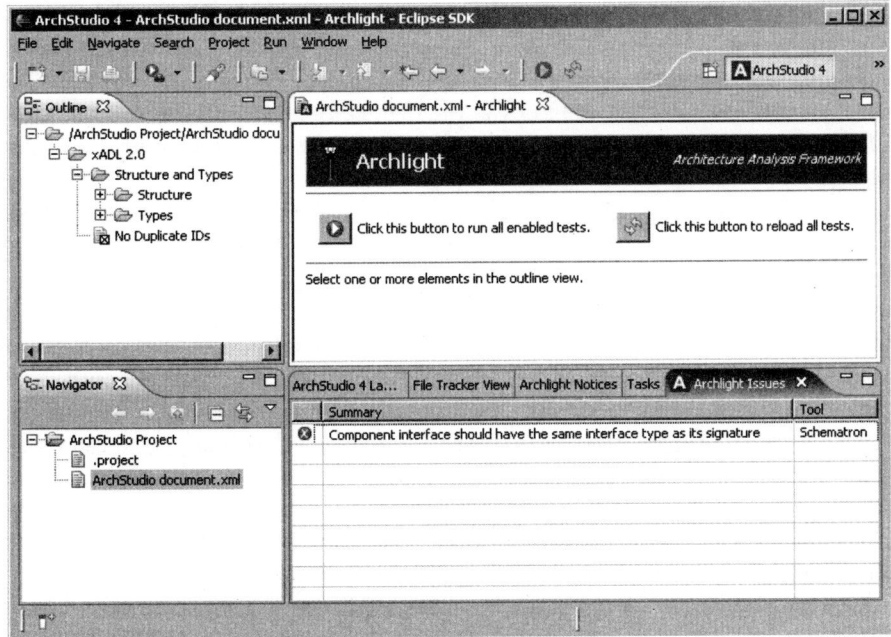

Fig. 6. 19   Checking in Archlight

First, you should get a more detailed prompt by right clicking the error. A message box is presented, which said the interface type of Interface TV Tuner Component on Component TV ArchStructure must be the same as the interface type of its signature. According to this, you can be aware of basis information. To further grasp error, you can focus on it through interface or component ways. Both of them give four manners to inspect error. Maybe a manner is not omnipotent or suitable. You can make full use of one or more ways. For example, if you choose Type Wright, a description with a red cross is presented.

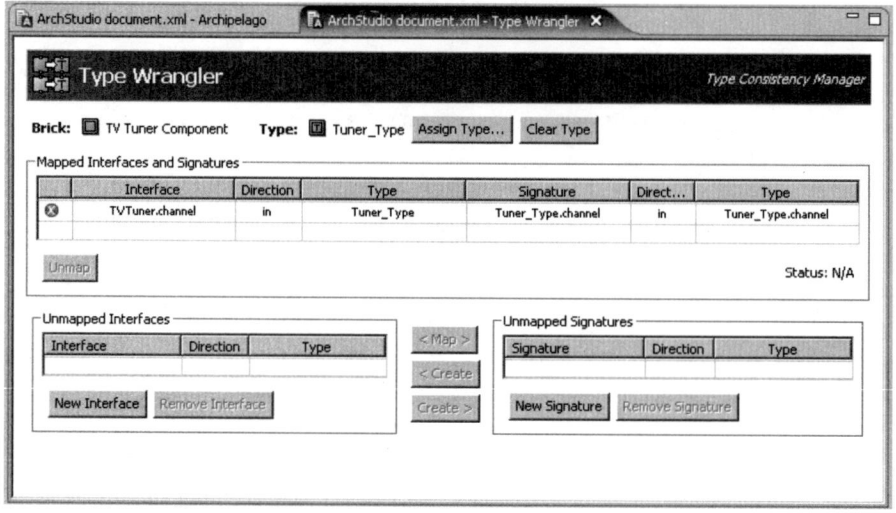

Fig. 6. 20   Checking in Type Wrangler

If you select ArchEdit, you will be led to the element with mistakes. At this time, you will modify the properties in the right editing pane. If you use Archlight, a dynamic image lays emphasis on the mistakes with a red mark. With this smart help, you can find faults visually and correct them quickly.

Once you carry out the validations, a fold named ArchAnalysis is created automatically which you can find in ArchEdit view. It collects all elements tests and particular descriptions. After validations, you can explore this artificiality with various views and editors. Open the document with Archipelago, a structure view is displayed. Open the document with Type Wrangler, all information of types is managed. Open the document with Selector, you can get any sub-architectures, even a single component or connector. At present, at a minimum, a simple software architecture development process is finished. However, if necessary, you can extend more functions.

6. 4   Summary

This chapter specifies one of the most useful issues during software architecture

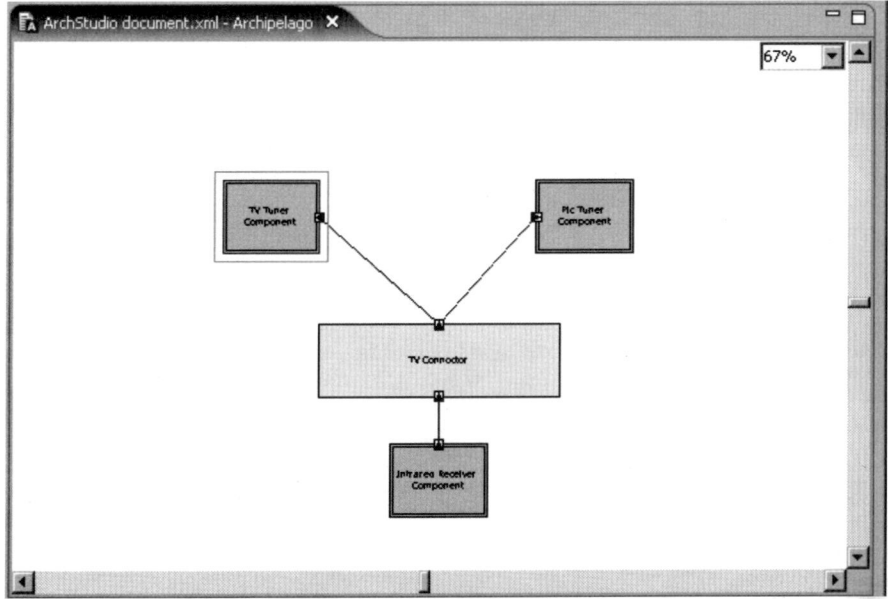

Fig. 6. 21   Checking in Archipelago

development—IDE which likes a bridge between design thought and system implementation. Before this software architecture assistant has appeared, in order to describe system architecture, practitioners had no choice but to resort to formal approaches. The work of remembering a great quantity of notations and grammars bother developers; in the meanwhile, the results in the form of formulas are deficient in visualization and explicitness. On the contrary, IDE smoothed away those confused problems. There is no doubt that it acts an essential role, which has been demonstrated by lots of facts. Suppose researchers developing a highly-complex software architecture only with pcn and paper, in particular, when requirement changes or new circumstance need to meet, the degree of work difficultly would rise at a geminate speed. We highlight its importance throughout this chapter. To provide a comprehensive introduction of IDE for readers, we start with its development history and end with a practical instance, ArchStudio 4.

At present, IDEs can fall into two categories: special and general. The first one takes greater part, the IDE of which kind meets a single ADL. Certainly, flexible requirement needs various solutions. Consequently, more and more IDEs have mushroomed for special purpose all over software domains. Though varied IDEs focus concerns on distinct domains, the functional framework is in common use; it is the real reason why we abstract the prototype of IDEs for the purpose of making a great convenience for IDE development. The latter kind is pursuing for universal IDEs. It directs at the tough question in the world of software architecture: can a single tool support the diverse array of issues, concerns, and stakeholders that occur in complex software systems? Fortunately, with the help of a foundational support platform, powerful extensible functions and some intermediary, this hypothetical tool is not a fantasy and some embryos have been emerged, for example, XArch system, ArchStudio. However, for current immature technology and approach, many challenges and obstacles may be encountered during its tortuous growth. Continuing the ascent, the architecture-oriented software development approach indicates that architecture-centric IDE is a necessary trend in the future.

References

(Dashofy, 2007)   Dashofy, E., et al. ArchStudio 4: Anarchitecture-Based Meta-Modeling Environment. *Companion to the proceedings of the 29th International Conference on Software Engineering*, Minneapolis, MN, US.2007: 67-68.

(Dashofy, 2005)   Dashofy, E. M., Hoek, A. v. d. & Taylor, R. N. A Comprehensive Approach for the Development of Modular Software Architecture Description Languages. *ACM Transactions on Software Engineering and Methodology* 2005(14): 199-245.

(Khare, 2001)   Khare, R., et al. Xadl: Enabling Architecture - Centric Tool Integration. *Proceedings of the 34th Annual Hawaii International Conference on Systems Sciences*, Hawaii, US.2001:9053-9062.

(Medvidovic, 2000)   Medvidovic, N. & Taylor, R. N. A Classification and Comparison Framework for Software Architecture Description Languages. *IEEE Transactions on Software Engineering* 2000(26): 70-93.

(Nistor, 2005)   Nistor, E. C., et al. Archevol: Versioning Architectural - Implementation Relationships. *Proceedings of the 12th international workshop on Software configuration management*, Lisbon, Portugal.2005:99-111.

7

Evaluating Software Architecture

If you are just a researcher to software, maybe it is enough when you finish describing architecture or communicate with other guys involved in software development. However, it is mandatory to figure out whether the architecture will lead a success. After all, nobody will reject to improve the chance of win before taking a bet, normally with a great fortune in terms of millions of dollars as well as company's reputation and future. Therefore, evaluation is necessary, appearing as a bridge between architecture and software engineering's ultimate goals.

Nevertheless, the solution is not so obvious and easy to handle, considering software's complexity and interweavement of a series of objectives, some of which stand against each other. You cannot sit at your workbench, input a list of requirement and architecture description to your lovely computer and get the nice answer. Completely automatic evaluation is still far away from us, which is the reason why architect becomes the leader of almost every development team and the top career in technique area. No generally suitable methods have been created. Evaluating methods focusing on universe, if any, must be so general that they lose actual effect in most projects or domains. Alternatively, a better idea to collect wisdom of former architects and conclude several principles or activities irrelevant to specific development and show creativity in applying them in your projects by enhancement or adjustment.

In this chapter, we provide an initial insight of software architecture evaluation. Here you can find the basis for evaluation, introduction to different evaluation processes and a comparison among them. But anyone who wants to use them should not copy them entirely, because the reuse elements are represented as thorough understanding to architecture which is covered by evaluation phases, activities and techniques.

7.1 What Is Software Architecture Evaluation

7.1.1 Quality Attribute

Before we describe evaluation itself, we must clarify its target to predicate software's quality. More precisely, the purpose of the evaluation is to analyze the software architecture to identify potential risks and verify that the quality requirements have been addressed in the design (Li, 1993).

So what is quality? When you buy a television, you will pay attention to whether there are flaws on its surface, whether it can response correctly and rapidly when you push a button, the extent to which its color makes you feel comfortable and the expected longevity. In general, three points should be noticed: Firstly, quality is a combination of features that affect your experience. It is important that functionality is only a non-dominant part of total quality. It is difficult to find a television in the shop's shelf that cannot show anything. Secondly, many features cannot be measured quantificationally, which means that it is almost impossible to create a calculation-based model in describing and comparing them. What's more, different people may give different opinions to the identical feature's appearance. Take the television's example again, some people prefer flamboyant color, while others believe that the color should be as closed as possible to the original video's capture. Finally, quality features have different priority with different things. A television has no obligation to keep working if you drop it on the floor, but that is not the case for mobile phones. For those important but conflicting features, manufacturers should take trade off among them.

In software engineering, quality attribute is referenced as the feature that can be used to illuminate software's features. In IEEE standard 1061 (IEEE, 1998), software quality is defined as "the degree to which software possesses a desired combination of attributes." Another standard ISO/IEC 9216 provides a quality model, too. Commonly, several quality attributes have been used and referenced frequently:

- **Modifiability** is the quality attribute about the cost of system change, measured in the range, workload and finance expense incurred by the change. It contains function extension, capacity extension (e.g. to increase the number of concurrent access), features deletion, data structures update (e.g. to add a field in database schema), communication protocol adjustment, cross-platform migration and so on. Much attention has been paid to the modification in post deployment phase, normally in source code level, build level (e.g. to use an alternative build option) and configuration level. Some people refer to it as "flexibility" or "maintainability". And some others believe that portability should be listed as a separate quality attribute.
- **Availability** is the quality attribute about how software reacts when errors,

exceptions or failures occur. Here we separate these three concepts as error is the situation that software stops its work for internal reason that can be recovered easily (e.g. a server may reject an access if maximal access number has been reached); exception means the input differs from the expected styles; and failure is the status that system cannot recover without losing anything (e.g. data, broken hardware). It is a common belief that software's availability can be measured in the probability of working in a good status. Here is the general formula that supports this measurement:

$$Availability = \frac{MeanTimeInWork}{MeanTimeInWork + MeanTimeToRepaire}$$

From this formula comes the terms such as "99.99% availability". But in the reality, this measurement is too vague for architects in making decisions of architecture design, because different errors, exceptions and failures need different recover solutions. Some people refer to it as "reliability".

- **Performance** is the quality attribute about reaction speed of a software system, or other metrics that are directly decided by it. This attribute is the crucial concern in military, control system and business information system. For example, we can define a requirement of performance as "the system must output the answer in 3 seconds if a specific event occurs" or "Sever must deal 1, 000 requests in a second". Performance has competing relationship with several other quality attributes, such as modifiability and security, which is the main source from which careful trade-off occurs. Some people refer to it as "efficiency".

- **Testability** is the quality attribute about the easiness degree to which system's defects can be detected by tests. A great architecture should take test into account. Considering the great amount of cost spent on test, special concern on test in architecture level will lead to considerable payoff. Currently, test guided by software architecture is the hot spot in architecture area. A common knowledge is trapped in the confusion between architecture evaluation and architecture test. In fact, evaluation is to deal with the problem of assessment and comparison among candidate architecture themselves, while architecture-based test tries to improve test effect with the help of architecture. A common testability measurement is the effect and efficiency of a test, such as "in 3 days finish the 65% execute paths of module A".

- **Usability** is the quality attribute about feeling, experience and efficiency of which users complete their tasks through operating the software. In a short word, it is the easiness degree to which users operate software. Beginners to architecture always disagree that this attribute is affected by architecture and insist that art designers and UI designers should be responsible for them. However, the facts tell us that many successful features of usability need the support of architecture, such as Undo-Redo and current popular Ajax.

- **Security** is the quality attribute about capability that software system defends unauthorized accesses or illegal operations. Attack is inevitable in any cases under any environment, drawing special attention among the stakeholders from system designers to end-users. During implementation, security-related codes often cross and interweave into components or connectors that need security guarantee, resulting in a challenge to architecture design.

The reason why we mention quality attributes is that software architecture is the foundation upon which they are realized. Although someone argues that a good architecture does not always result in a good realized artifacts meeting every expected quality attribute, taking into account the contribution of detailed design and implementation. I admit its correctness. However, a bad architecture must result in a bad system without any doubt. It is impossible to implement a secure program if you never prepare for it. Quality attribute is the fantastic idea that links software quality and its architecture because a batch of architectural tactics has been generalized and popularly employed. The fifth chapter of (Bass, 2003) provides a comprehensive reference about them.

7.1.2   Why Is Evaluation Necessary

Barry Boehm said "Marry your architecture in haste and you can repent in leisure". An awful architecture, as a matter of fact, pronounces project's calamity. Three concerns lays in this point.

• As we mentioned in the first chapter, software architecture description is the earliest artifact on which evaluation and analysis can be performed. To correct a problem in this phase costs orders of magnitudes less than during testing and deployment. After all, changing a notation in an architecture view is much easier to carry out than modifying source codes on a large scale, which, thus, requires additional cost that should have been avoided. With comprehensive architecture description, or even the partial one, we can simulate the system's runtime behaviors, discuss several design ideas and infer the potential effects if architecture applies to the final system. And all of these need only several additional days in the whole project's duration.

• Evaluation is the last chance that hidden requirements are discussed and complemented into the design. In short of communication perfectly and understanding of software project, a great many stakeholders do not know what they want exactly. In the requirement gathering phase, they may list several demands, the most crucial ones they believe in. But after evaluation, their opinions may entirely change, during which they start to be aware of some points they originally specified are not so important, while some other concerns begin to draw their attention. They are often surprised by the social power and get excited when they feel the positive improvement taken by their participating. And architects, during this activity, accept stakeholders' various ideas, some of which are not mentioned in the requirement specification, and take trade off by adjusting the initial architecture design (or comparing and choosing among several candidates). This is also the good opportunity for him or her to deepen the insight of the to-be-built system. Shortly, architecture evaluation clears the barriers among stakeholders, and empowers them with open communication channels. The direct result is the achievement of a commonly satisfactory system blueprint, which means a more than half success of a project.

- Architecture is the center of development process, deciding the team structure, work division, configuration repository, documentation organizations, management strategies and, of course, the development scheduling. An unsuitable architecture will draw a mass of mess when it must be modified to fit for the new concerns or those defects not uncovered in the early phase. The consequence of excessive cost spent on this alternation was accessed above. What's more, the whole team will face the terrible status that the project is out of control: More bugs are introduced after original bugs are fixed; demoded work breaks team structure which further disturbs lucid development; old plans and budgets are thrown away but the new ones cannot be created in time; all the guys, including customers, managers and programmers, expect vexedly for the end of this nightmare, but no one gets the exactly the idea of the due date. Impatience, inversely, beats everyone's morale and further guides them to the abyss. What great if architecture is analyzed before everything is happened!

Personally speaking, software architecture is destined to be evaluated, if it wants to be applied in practice. In fact, numerous architecture models are created specifically as the input of evaluation processes. Maybe experts who are concentrating on well-formed representation of architecture do not care about this very much. But is there someone who wants to pay a big fortune into a game only by guessing? Maybe in the gambling it is, but in business, people do that no more than suicide. All in all, we need architecture evaluation.

7.1.3 Scenario-based Evaluation Methods

From the discussion above we make clear that architecture evaluation is a process that judges whether an initial architecture description or a series of architecture description candidates represent the specified quality attributes (collected both in requirement gathering phase and evaluation phase). This is not an easy task because quality attributes are different from length or weight, which has unified measurement standards. Before evaluation is taken, we must define what the measurement of quality attribute exactly is which ensures it can represent the capability of software in meeting the requirements such as "We need an availability of 99.99%".

Less than a decade ago, two basis classes of evaluation methodologies, Measuring and Questioning, were defined in (Abowd, 1997) for architecture evaluation. Measuring employs quantitative metrics by defining precisely the numerical scale to the targets. Therefore, only those quality attributes which are easy mapped to quantitative metrics can become the input of this kind of techniques, for example, response time, throughout of a link in the network, etc. This class includes metrics, simulation, prototype and experience. Another methodology Questioning provides questions to check qualitative attributes, which expands its suitability to almost any given quality attribute. This class includes scenario, questionnaire and checklist. No doubt that we primarily evaluate architecture by Questioning techniques, which are commonly supplemented by Measuring.

Most notable architecture evaluation methods are scenario-based. Scenarios are a postulated set of uses or modifications of the system (Dobrica, 2002). Maybe you are familiar with "use case" in analyzing requirements and directing tests at least. But scenario is a superset of it, capable of covering any behaviors that can be imposed on the final system, ranging from pushing a button and getting expected answer within limit duration, to adding or deleting components to change system's behavior during execution. In architecture evaluation, we use scenarios to represent a concrete quality attribute. (Bass, 2003) provides a model to describe a scenario. Six elements are adopted to normalize various scenarios into a standard form, facilitating later evaluation processes:

- **Source of stimulus.** This is some entity (a human, a computer system, or any other actuator) that generates the stimulus.
- **Stimulus.** The stimulus is a condition that needs to be considered when it arrives at a system.
- **Environment.** The stimulus occurs within certain conditions. The system may be in an overload condition or may be running when the stimulus occurs, or some other conditions may be true.
- **Artifact.** Some artifact is stimulated. This may be the whole system or some pieces of it.
- **Response.** The response is the activity undertaken after the arrival of the stimulus.
- **Response measure.** When the response occurs, it should be measurable in some fashion so that the requirement can be tested.

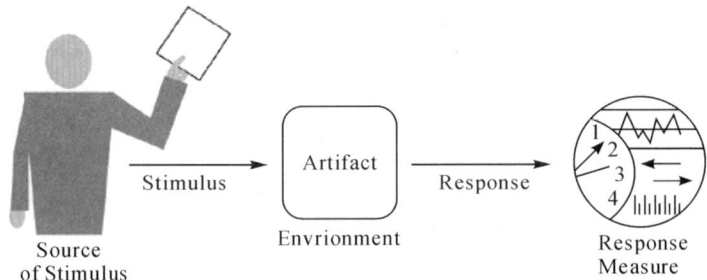

Fig. 7.1   Scenario representation model

But in practice, in the noisy and chaotic evaluation conference spot, it is unrealistic to force all participants to provide their ideas in this style, particularly in the case that most stakeholders do not have habit of limiting their vocabulary into the formal one, which is the hobby of computer scientists or programmers. They often open their mouths as soon as the idea comes out in their minds. But any proposition should be able to be converted into the form above potentially. This needs prolocutor, which is taken by architects in most time, to guide stakeholders' suggestion. The vague ones, such as "High security is required" should not be taken as scenario because it is too trivial to find architectural tactics corresponding to it.

An advantage of scenario is that it is system-specific, which means it is not limited by a domain, just like checklist techniques do. Scenario has sufficient freedom in expressing system's response to stimulus actuators. What's more scenario is capable of synchronizing multiple stakeholders' suggestions. It is possible for different stakeholders to interpret similar cases from their own perspectives, after which they are merged into a common scenario during a redundancy elimination process. Table 7.1 is an example of scenario list before future evaluation activities.

Several considered evaluation methods use scenario, including SAAM, SAEM, ATAM, ARID, etc. A systematic survey on scenario-based evaluation methods applied in practice can be found in (Kazman, 2000).

Table 7.1   Example of Scenario List

Scenario No.	Scenario Description
F1	Add a graphical editor to configure system.
F2	Change underlying database from the centralized one to the distributed one.
F3	Use CORBA to provide interface which can be used by other systems.
F4	Enable 1,000 requests in a second.
...	...

You may have the question that having scenarios, why clear quality attribute category is still necessary. That is, when we can describe such as "When a database server breaks down, the system has to recover in 5 minutes by using backup equipment", does the general term "availability" have any value? Sure it is, because the high-level classification is the basis for generalization countermeasures. Different detailed quality attributes share the common tactics, if they belong to the same one. Meanwhile, from general classification, we can figure out the main concerns, and try to solve the conflicts that have high priority. ATAM employs the Quality Attribute Utility Tree, by which the primary demands of the system are shown. Finally, not all the evaluation methods spread their power to each kind of quality attribute. Some of them focus on one or two attributes, but lose their effects on others.

Aside with scenario-based evaluation methods, several formalization-based ones have appeared for a long time and been referenced as the classic analysis strategies. Typical researches of these formal architecture models include Process Algebra (Allen, 1997a), CHAM (CHemical Abstraction Machine) (Inverardi, 2000), FSM (Zhang, 2001), LTS (Labeled Transition Systems) (Uchitel, 2003) and queuing theory

(Marco, 2004). The most benefits of this kind are preciseness and capability of automation. Through implementing a fixed algorithm, we can perform deadlock or performance checking. However, over consideration on completeness of formalization, these methods often require a great amount of source data, which incurs excessive overhead to a large-scale project in reality. Now, most of them still stay in the research lab while the rest are adopted in a very limited scope.

7. 2   SAAM

SAAM (Scenario-based Architecture Analysis Method, or called Software Architecture Analysis Method) is the first well-documented and carefully-designed analysis method for architecture analysis. It was created during 1993 and published in 1994 (Kazman, 1994). Later, it was improved in (Kazman, 1996b) and got more detailed description along with study cases in (Bass, 1998). Before that, there is a common case that sellers of a certain software product pronounce that their software contains remarkable properties that are superior to their competitors'. But they cannot evaluate it and thus prove it concretely.

SAAM is an intuitive method trying to measure the software's quality through scenarios, rather than the general and inaccurate quality attributes description. SAAM is simple, caring about only the relationship between scenarios and architecture structures, by taking not too many steps and specific techniques. Therefore, it is the ideal start point that beginners of architecture evaluation take. Initially, SAAM is designed to deal with modifiability of architecture. But after evolution and practice for several years, SAAM has shown its power in many other common quality attributes, and becomes the basis of some other evaluation methods, such as ATAM. It can detect the possible risks of evaluated architecture and take comparison among several architecture candidates with respect to meet predefined scenarios.

In addition, SAAM prepares a platform for many stakeholders discussing together, maybe for the first time since a project is set up. They have the chance to communicate with each other with what they care about, with human languages, and thus start to get the idea of what others care about as well as how these cares are processed in system's blueprint. During this process, one may find understanding deviations and incorrect design led by them.

7. 2. 1   General Steps of SAAM

Simply speaking, the general steps of SAAM seem rather naïve and intuitive. I find that many people, who have never touched architecture evaluation, when seeing the overview of SAAM for the first time, comment that "That's the one hidden in my mind", "Evaluation is as what it should be like that", or something the like. After all, most of them have learned how to test a system with use cases or the similar methods, and own adequate experience in evaluating existent designs. However, in the early 1990s, when the term "software architecture" had not been widely accepted and evaluation was in its initial stage, SAAM was undoubtedly a remarkable creation. In addition, the techniques used in it are carefully designed and tested through a batch of projects.

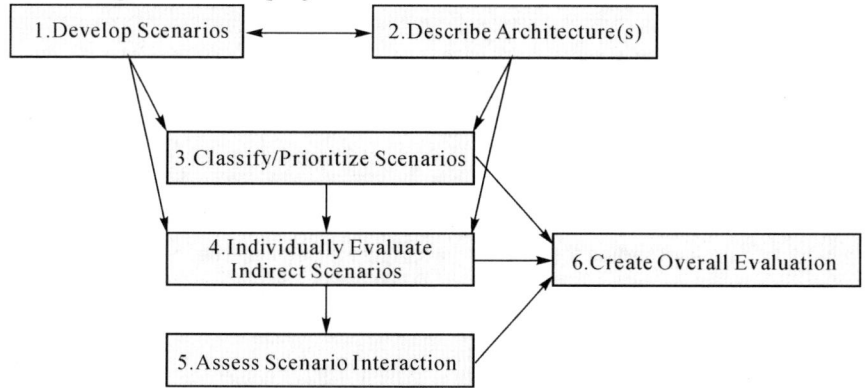

Fig. 7. 2   Activities and dependencies in a SAAM analysis

Compared to the relative fixed and inflexible algorithms, which are executed by machines, or pure formalized models, which are used by the people like machines, SAAM puts attention to improve stakeholders' communications and encourage active suggestions by making use of human's nature. That's the case with most evaluation methods look like. The steps tell the general phases of evaluation, what should be achieved in each phase, and the relations among these phases. The primary steps are shown in Fig.7.2(Clements 2003b, Fig.7.1).

Clearly, we can get the idea that what the input and output of SAAM are. To start the evaluation, a description of architecture should be provided. This description can be existed in any style, as long as it can be accepted and understood by evaluation participants. The degree of detail and concentrating of description depend on the targets and concerns of a specific evaluation, which, sometimes, calls for the renewal or supplement of architecture information. Multiple distinct architectures' descriptions can also be fed into the evaluation, in which case they can be compared and selected.

Aside from architecture description, another critical input is scenarios. The essential point of scenario-based evaluation is to check whether the current architectures can meet the expected quality requirements directly and if cannot, what modification should be taken. As mentioned before, it is almost impossible to describe quality attributes in accurate and measurable manners. To make them meaningful to evaluation, they have to be described in more concrete format. That is why scenarios are so necessary. Those scenarios can be some concerns extracted from the initial functionality requirements, but more of them come from the discussion or brainstorm of stakeholders, which may be crucial to stakeholders and brand new to architects or designers. After all, the architecture involving the evaluation has to firstly support all the functions documented in requirement specifications. In evaluation, the key is whether the architecture can meet the requirement functions with desired qualities, which are reflected by the interaction between various stakeholders and the software system.

The main output normally is given in the style of evaluation report, by which SAAM shows the defects that current design cannot reach the quality requirement, in the single architecture evaluation case; or indicates which candidate meets the scenarios best, in the multiple case. It also has the capability of figuring out the potential unsuitable design due to ugly decomposition or excessive complication. At last, SAAM provides the estimation of cost and range incurred by modification, avoiding the blind construction.

Besides that, SAAM will draw some great side effects. SAAM improves the stakeholders' understanding of current architecture, forces the better architecture documentation and clarifies system's most possible future evolution. Via stakeholder-wide presentation and discussion, the priority of business goals and potential scenarios can also be clarified.

In the following sections, the activities and techniques in every phase are accessed in detail. From them, you can see that how a complete evaluation is performed and how the benefits are generated.

7.2.2 Scenario Development

Scenario development is a process of discussion and brainstorming, participated by a variety of stakeholders. Each of them has his or her own perspectives and concerns, and provides scenarios based on them. For a modification, sponsors care about the introduced cost by it; programmers care about which modules are involved in it; customers care about the price after it; and end-users care about the benefits provided due to it. Relevant, or even inconsistent, scenarios may occur and be documented. But the most important point is to keep a criticism-free environment. Any generated scenarios should be recorded carefully and then listed to make convenience every stakeholders' later inspection. Sometimes, a pre-introduction or guide tutorial may be hold for those people who have little experience in evaluation in order to guarantee the "good" scenarios' generation, which means the ones reflecting the system's main use cases, potential modifications or updates, or other qualities the system's behaviors have to confirm to.

There may be several iterations during this phase. In collection of scenarios, participants may encounter the situation that some needed architecture information cannot be found in provided documents. And the complemented architecture description may, in turn, trigger more scenarios. Scenario development and architecture description are interrelated and drive each other.

7.2.3 Architecture Description

Architecture documents, most of which are prepared before evaluation, contain the information to be evaluated. For better evaluation, architecture description should be provided in a manner that every participant can accept, tells things such as components, connectors, modules, configurations, dependency, deployment and so on. Any form of description is allowed, such as human language, diagrams, data tables or formalized models, as long as it can highlight the architecture clearly and unambiguously. Sometimes, architecture description has to be complemented or renewed according to generated scenarios' requirement, which then introduces more scenarios. Passing scenario development and architecture description commonly takes two or more iterations.

7.2.4 Scenario Classification and Prioritization

In SAAM, scenarios are classified into two categories, the direct and indirect ones. Direct scenarios are those which can be supported by the current architecture without any modification. If the scenarios are similar to the original requirements that have been taken into account, they can be easily met. Architect can demonstrate this point by introducing a series of response behaviors under those scenarios. Normally, direct scenarios, although cannot help show architecture's defects, improve stakeholders' understanding to the architecture, and benefit evaluation under other scenarios.

Indirect scenarios cannot be directly supported by the current architecture. Achieving them result in some modifications, such as adding one or multiple components, removing an indirect layer, updating a module with a more suitable one, changing or enhancing interface, redesigning relations among elements, or everything in the between. Indirect scenarios are the most critical drivers for the subsequent activities. You can get the system's evolution in the future of great possibility, though maybe obscure sometimes, by taking various indirect scenarios into concerns comprehensively.

With architect's help, it is easy to categorize generated scenarios. Even so, the remainder may be too many to be carefully evaluated one by one. Therefore, scenarios need prioritization process to select the most critical ones, considering limited time and resource. CMU SEI recommends stakeholder-wide voting to decide which ones can be considered as "critical". Each person can get a fixed number of votes, through which they choose which scenarios in the list should be evaluated carefully. The number of votes allocated to each one is approximately 30% of the total number of generated scenarios. The voting strategy is that each one can vote 0 vote, all votes he or she owns, or every number in the between, to a single scenario, as long as that the number of total votes voted is not more than the ones owned. All scenarios, then, are sorted by the votes they received. How many scenarios are chosen is dependent on the situation. Sometimes, you can find a clear line in the ordered list. The scenarios above it receive most votes, while the ones below it get very few (shown in Fig. 7.3). In this case, you can keep the scenarios above the cutting line. In other cases, you can calculate the suitable number that can be accepted and finished within expected time allocated for evaluation. Assuming that, typically, one full day can finish 8 scenarios and you plan two days to perform individual scenario evaluation, then top 15−16 scenarios should be remained. Even though some scenarios should be dropped according to predefined filter rules, their providers can insist to add them to the remainder list, if most of other stakeholders agree with that, either.

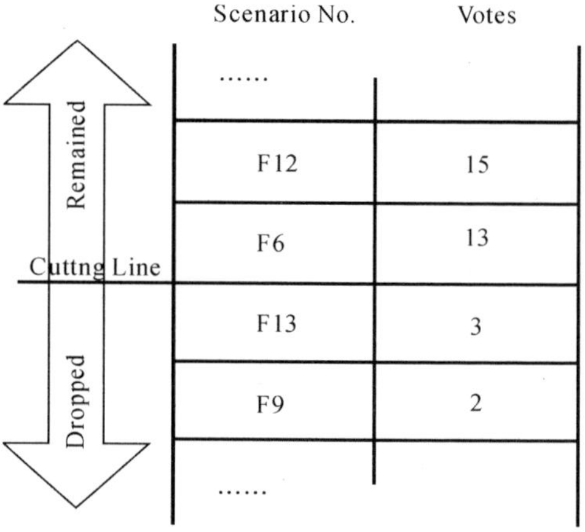

Scenario No.	Votes
......	
F12	15
F6	13
F13	3
F9	2
......	

(Arrow labeled "Remained" pointing up, "Dropped" pointing down, with "Cuttng Line" marking the boundary)

Fig. 7. 3   Choose critical scenarios

7. 2. 5   Individual Evaluation of Indirect Scenarios

The most important information cared by all stakeholders is how current architecture candidate is affected by indirect scenarios. What modification should be done? Is that feasible to accomplish within the project's expected cost, time and scope? If it is, how much work will be appended to do those things? Or, if not, is there some alternative solution? All these questions are accessed in this phase. For each architecture candidate, its appearance under each individual remained indirect scenario is estimated and evaluated. Here, the architecture's elements are mapped to the concrete quality attributes.

Indirect scenarios require modification for current architecture. In most cases, the architects are responsible of explaining the necessary changes. If they cannot precisely clarify the possible acts, the completeness of architecture description is suspicious. The detailed explanation should contain the range within which the modification is performed, the number of elements in this range and the estimated work amount. All of this information is summarized, commonly, in a style of table. Table 7.2 is an example.

This table gives the motivation of subsequent actions of modifications. Stakeholders, according to it, decide which ones are the most urgent and should be performed as quickly as possible, which ones should be delayed for a moment, and which ones should be ignored in the current project for their infeasibility of accomplishment. If a scenario needs too much modification, it is reasonable to believe that there are design defects, and thus an entire redesign at that location may be taken.

Table 7. 2   Table of Individual Scenario Evaluation in SAAM

Scenario No.	Scenario Description	Needed Modification	Number of Elements to be Modified	Estimated Work
F4	Allowing data exchange with other system	Data serialization module, Data exchange interface	2	12 work days
F8	Adding context-sensitive help	Context sensitive UI control, Help documents	2	30 work days
F9	Enabling multiple DBMS	Data Managing Abstract	1	3 work days
...	...	...	...	...

7. 2. 6   Assessment of Scenario Interaction

When different scenarios ask for modifications of the same architecture element, they are expressed as "interaction" to that element. Scenario interaction means the potential risks of original design. What have to be emphasized is that the "difference" of scenarios is the semantic distinctness, which can be decided by stakeholders. Before classification and prioritization, those scenarios which have something in common can be grouped or merged to avoid evaluation redundancy. The ones left reflect typical use, modification or other quality requirements with little overlapping. The case that scenarios different in semantics affect the same architecture element, such as a component, indicates something bad. High scenario interaction means the poor design of functions decomposition, except the case that some classic architecture pattern means to behave like that. Thus, scenario interaction may be the source of disaster, because it can lead a mess of change during the future evolution. Although not all the scenarios can be considered as malefactors, they should draw our great attention.

During identification of scenario interaction, however, be care of the fake cases. Sometimes, the architecture documents show that a single component taking part in the interaction. But in fact, its sub-components deal with "interactive" scenarios separately with perfect decomposition. At this time, you should return to Step 2 architecture description and check whether the granularity of documents reaches your need.

7. 2. 7   Creation of Overall Evaluation

This is the final step of SAAM, generating the final report. If only one single piece of architecture revolves in the evaluation, in this step all the evaluation results got in previous steps are inspected and summarized as evaluation report, based on which the following plan of modification will be determined.

If multiple architecture candidates take part in SAAM evaluation, a comparison can be performed. To do this, it is necessary to decide a weight of each critical scenario by considering its relations to business goals. In comparison, one architecture design may be good at a subset of scenarios, while another design is superior under others. By purely counting scenarios' number of a design appearing well, it is hard to decide which one is better in some time. As a matter of fact, scenarios, even though they are all the critical ones, have difference in their importance, which can be expressed with weight. Several strategies of deciding weight have been adopted for a long time. For example, stakeholders can hold a discussion or debate to agree on scenarios' relative importance. Or, if historical records are available, they will become remarkable reference materials.

Direct scenarios can also influence the overall evaluation result. Different candidates always have different number of direct scenarios. Supporting more direct scenarios indicates a better candidate, because those scenarios can be met without modification. Sometimes, importance of direct scenarios is mixed into this evaluation.

Finally, architect scores the appearance of each candidate under each critical scenario. Normally, a relative value strategy is used, such as "1, 0, -1" (or "2, 1, 0", "+, 0, - ", whatever). 1 means architecture behaves well under a scenario; -1 means it is unsatisfactory; and 0 means indifferent. You can choose a range of 5 or 10, if you need. With scenario weight and appearance value, an overall table can be made, as in Table 7.3. Then by combining it with individual scenario evaluation, scenario interaction evaluation and direct scenario support analysis, the best architecture design is selected as the basic of further development.

Table 7. 3   Example of Overall Evaluation in SAAM

Scenario No.	Weight	Candidate 1	Candidate 2
F4	8	1	-1
F5	8	1	-1
F8	5	1	0
F10	7	-1	1
F13	10	0	1
F14	6	0	1
...	...	...	...
Overall Evaluation		45	67

7.3   ATAM

In this section, we introduce another evaluation method, Architecture Trade-off Analysis Method(ATAM), which can be considered as the advancement of SAAM. From its name, it is clear that ATAM, besides exposing potential defects and risks hidden in evaluated architecture, leads to a better understanding and trade-off to multiple relative, or even inconsistent, quality requirements or targets. When most experts were working in trying to enhance SAAM with various concerns, just as

SAAMCS or ESAAMI did, inventors of SAAM turned their attention to the complicated relation among targets reflected by scenarios as well as their remarkable effect to the system construction.

ATAM is built on three areas: architectural styles, quality attribute analysis communities and SAAM. In this section, we will briefly give the general idea of the first two ones (SAAM has been discussed in the previous section in detail). Firstly, we retrospect the general steps with respect to history, then describe what should be done in several major steps and the adopted techniques in them.

ATAM, since its birth, came through continuous evolution and improvement, by combining wisdom of numerous architects, designers, software engineers and so on. You can find initial materials in (Kazman, 1998), (Bass, 1998) and (Kazman, 1999). And ATAM's further detailed introduction and study case can be found in (Bass, 2003) and (Clements, 2003b). In the ATAM page of CMU SEI, everyone can get the latest status of this method, including tutorials and support materials.

7.3.1 Initial ATAM

Most design is to deal with trade-off targets. Or, if there is no need to take trade-off, it is actually not necessary to perform "design". Instead, only fixed calculation according to requirements is required. This is well accepted. Lots of trade-offs are resulted from non-technical reasons. For example, to guarantee the scalability, more indirect intermediated layer will be added, leading to more coding and testing work, which, then, means more cost and possibly more time needed for the whole project. Or two stakeholders hold conflictive requirements blocking development process interceding. This job, more or less, involves social aspects.

The duty of architects is performing designs, by accumulating requirements and mapping them into structures and behavior specifications. Besides that, however, the more important responsibility is to take trade-off, both in technical and social perspectives. ATAM is just a handy tool to assist it. It has the principal differences, compared to other evaluation methods or technologies, that it explicitly considers the connections between multiple attributes, and permits principled reasoning about the trade-offs that inevitably result from such connections. To achieve this point, ATAM is divided into six steps allocated in four phases initially (Kazman, 1998), as Fig.7.4 shown.

This spiral model comes from (Boehm, 1986) where a similar spiral model of software development was described. It integrates evaluation into the whole design process. The six steps, "Collect Scenarios", "Collect Requirements, Constraints and Environment", "Describe Architectural Views", "Attribute Specific Analyses", "Identify Sensitivities" and "Identify trade-offs", construct an iteration. After finishing these steps, and if the evaluation's results indicate whether the current architecture is adequately closed to the expected quality requirements, more detailed design, or implementation, will follow. Otherwise, a plan of modification will be made to upgrade existent design, the product of which, then, will be put into another ATAM iteration again. Noticeably, these steps are not necessarily carried out one

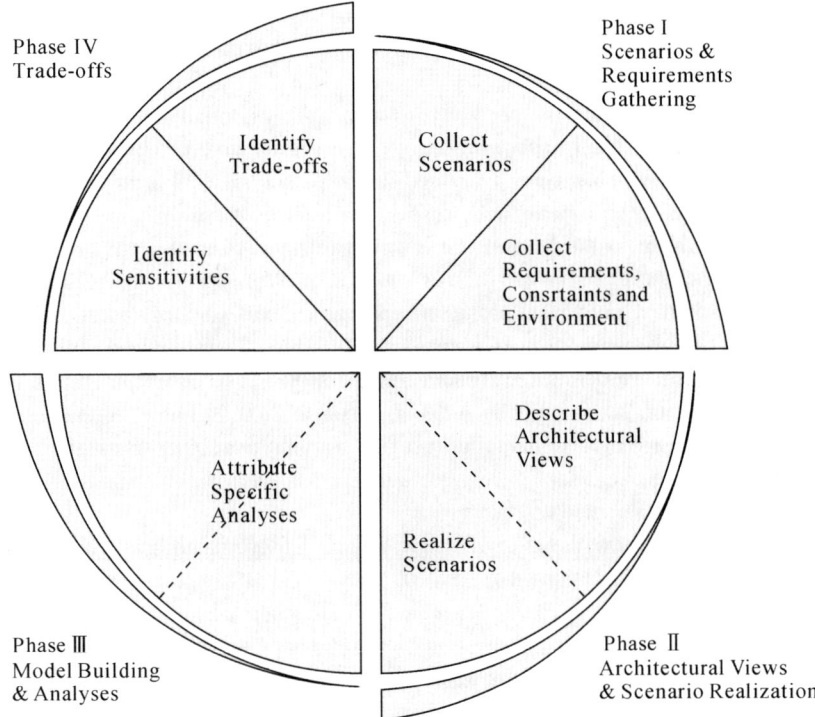

Realize Scenario is not mentioned in the following description because the original paper (Kazman, 1998) did this.

Fig. 7. 4   Steps of ATAM (1)

by one in a linear manner. Each of them can trigger the improvement of products of any other steps, as the figure shown that any part of the circle can touch each other in the center. For example, failures to identify trade-offs may lead to architectural views' renew. Or attribute specific analyses may collect more scenarios to keep various attributes' balance.

During one iteration, Phase I concentrates on the input of scenarios. The first step focuses on the "usage scenarios" only, and tries to improve participants' understanding of architecture. The basis of communication is constructed. The second step collects quality-related information, which is also expressed as scenarios. These scenarios, which can be considered as the quality requirements assumption, are the foundation of all following steps. After getting requirements, designing starts, with the constraints of requirements acquired in the first phase. Their architectures are documented and used to perform evaluation.

Then, the evaluation begins. Each quality attribute is analyzed in isolation firstly. At this point, scenario interactions are ignored. Separation in evaluation allows experts of individual quality attribute to take analyses with most attribute-specific technologies or models. For instance, Markov model is good at analysis of availability, while SPE (Smith, 2001) is handy in performance evaluation. The result of attribute-specific analysis is measured in modeled value, such as "a request can get its response in 500ms in the worst case" or "This system has availability of 99. 99% under assumed context".

The final job is to identify sensitivities and trade-offs. Before explaining them, the concept of "architectural element" has to be defined first. Architectural element means any component, property of component or property of relationships between the components that affects quality attributes. A sensitivity point is the modeled value that will change significantly under modification of architectural elements. For example, in the C/S-based system, the redundancy of server affects availability of the whole system. Adding a backup server may reduce average broken-down time per year by one order of magnitude. That is a sensitivity point. A trade-off point is the architectural element that is relevant to multiple sensitivities. That is, if one component, or property of component, or property of relationship is changed, several quality attributes will be varied greatly, better or worse. For instance, the server redundancy in C/S system is a trade-off point because its modification will lead to change of availability, cost, security and so on, some of which are conflictive. The trade-off points expose the issues that should be paid much attention by architects.

7.3.2 ATAM Improvement

Then in 1999, ATAM, after being applied in several practical projects, got upgrade and enhancement (Kazman, 1999). Steps of ATAM are changed by merging several original steps and complementing additional ones. (Shown in Fig.7.5) For example, "scenarios grouping and prioritization" is added, just as SAAM. Some steps are extracted and put as a step, such as "Architecture Presentation".

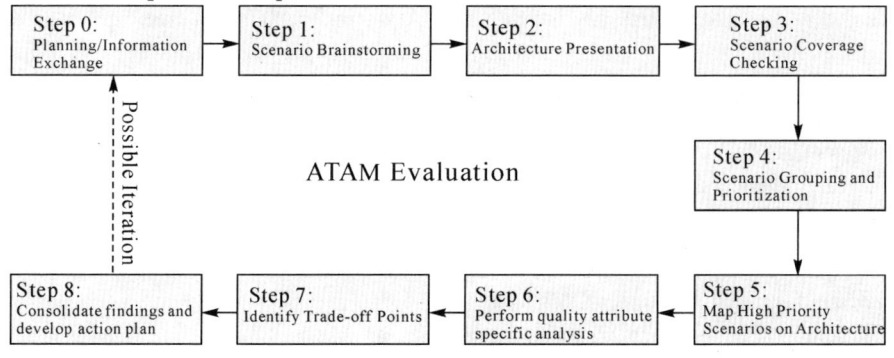

Fig. 7. 5 Steps of ATAM (2)

Two notable points about improved ATAM should draw our attention. The first one is the concern that how to know it is the suitable time to stop generating scenarios. From the figure above, we can see that Step 3 takes the scenario converge checking. For this point, CMU SEI has developed a set of quality attribute-specific questions, by which one can find that some useful scenarios are still missing and try to supplement them. You can get the question sets in CMU SEI's website.

Another point is the adoption of ABASs (Attribute-based Architectural Styles). ABAS is a kind of analysis-assistant tool to help stakeholders identify the quality attributes brought by architecture styles, such as performance, availability, security, testability, modifiability, and so on. Simply speaking, ABAS is architectural styles attached with attribute values to reflect quality information. A famous example of ABAS is the one for performance analysis for several concurrent processes. If a system uses a collection of processes, all of which compete for limit computation resource, therefore, it can be recognized as a performance ABAS. The questions associated with this ABAS should probe the parameters, such as processes' priority, synchronization location, queuing strategy and estimated execution time. But, it is not enough to own performance relevant information only. They will be fed into an analytic framework and facilitate analysis. For example, rate monotonic analysis is an effective performance analytic framework for real time system (Klein, 1993).

Comparing two versions of ATAM, a trend is exposed that more practical techniques and concerns are added into ATAM. The first version is built on spiral development model, releasing the flavor of theory. But in the second version, steps are rearranged to meet the needs of practical use. Besides that, some necessary assistant techniques are introduced, although some of them are not considered as the kernel ones in the perspective of evaluation. Shortly speaking, these changes try to provide answers to such questions as: How to help stakeholders to understand what to do and how to do in order to contribute evaluation? How to guide participants to get the precise and clear insight of architectures to be evaluated? How to generate scenarios that are positive to evaluation, avoid omitting something necessary, and select the most important ones from them? How to map scenario to architecture, thus identify sensitivities and trade-offs? And finally, how to perform concrete evaluation for specific quality attributes and generate evaluation report, which schedules the following activities? Just as what will be discussed later, these questions are the common problems for most evaluation methods. Through applied in numerous projects and improved by thousands of architects, designers and software engineers, ATAM adapts itself to pursuit the better and better evaluation results. In the next section, we will show what ATAM looks like currently and what new techniques are adopted.

7.3.3   General Process of ATAM

The complete process of ATAM currently contains four phases and nine main steps. Here, steps still do not mean that each of them has to be executed in a linear manner. In practice, evaluation leaders should make decisions to carry out which steps before to complement something, or jump to a step that should have been performed in several steps later. It depends on the situation. Steps indicate only the order of generation of intermediate evaluation products. Steps defined in the later always need products got in the former as inputs. Therefore, if evaluation team has own information that should be generated in a certain step or those information is useless for evaluation, that step can be omitted.

The general process of ATAM is shown in Fig.7.6. The work of Phase I and II are the kernel phases performing evaluation.

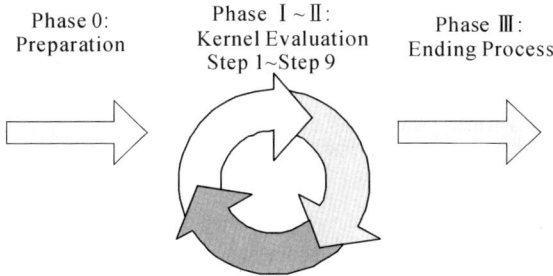

Phase 0:
Preparation

Phase I ~ II:
Kernel Evaluation
Step 1~Step 9

Phase III:
Ending Process

Fig. 7. 6   General process of ATAM

Phase 0 is a preparation process. Considering the scope, time and cost of ATAM evaluation, it is necessary to discuss or even sign up a strict contract about the issues such as evaluation schedule, cost plan, organization of participants, etc. People who expect evaluation should first figure out whether it is feasible to perform evaluation, who should get involved in, what the target of evaluation is, who should acquire the evaluation result, and what should be done after evaluation. In order to avoid interruption during kernel evaluation, every question above has to be carefully thought over and planned. After that, an evaluation team, if the organization expecting evaluation has no such a permanent team, should be created, which is responsible for the support work following up. Several roles are required in the team, including team leader, evaluation leader, scribe, timekeeper, questioner, observer and so on. For each role, it can be taken by the same guy. Normally, a meeting of evaluation team should be hold in Phase 0 to clarify responsibility and prepare for Phase I.

Phase III, in the contrary, is to end evaluation. There are two tasks that have to be done. The first one is producing the final report, documenting the process and information appeared in the kernel evaluation, and the conclusions based on them. Another one is taking a summary that facilitates evaluation improving. On the one side, you can question the evaluation team members or other participants which activities they feel good, which they feel ugly and why. Also, you can collect data during evaluation, such as consumed cost and earned benefits. Through data mining, maybe you can find some improvable points among various activities. On the other side, you can accumulate scenarios and their associated questions for the evaluation of the next similar project. In domain-specified development, this activity is effective for its powerful reusability.

In the kernel evaluation phases, nine steps, similar with the ones in the previous sections, are involved. They are, then, separated into four sub-phases, as the follow lists:

- **Presentation**

Step 1.   Present the ATAM: Present steps, activities, methods and techniques in ATAM.

Step 2.   Present the business drivers: Present business goals to identify main quality requirements.

Step 3.   Present the architecture: Explain how current architecture meets the business drivers.

- **Investigation and Analysis**

Step 4.   Identify the architectural approaches: Find which approaches are used to build architecture.

Step 5.   Generate the quality attribute utility tree: Get the prioritized scenarios reflecting system's utility in a tree style.

Step 6.   Analyze the architectural approaches: Analyze the architecture approaches that supports the critical scenarios shown in the utility tree, and identify risks, nonrisks, sensitivities and trade-offs.

- **Testing**

Step 7.   Brainstorm and prioritize scenarios: Generate more scenarios with more kinds of stakeholders.

Step 8.   Analyze the architectural approaches: Act the same as step 6, but use the critical scenarios selected from Step 7.

- **Reporting**

Step 9.   Present the results: Produce evaluation report.

In fact, the major Phase I and Phase II are two iterations through these steps, different in involved steps and scope of participants. Phase II requires more kinds of stakeholders to take part in scenario generation and analysis discussion. Phase I, however, tries to identify the primary quality attributes and lay the foundation for following evaluation by a few principles. Phase I only passes Step 1 to Step 6. Of course, it is not necessary to follow these two iterations by rote. Evaluation team should schedule how to iterate through these steps and who should take part in each iteration in reality.

Table 7. 4   Two Iterations in Kernel Evaluation

Sub-Phase	Evaluation Step	Major Phase I	Major Phase II
Presentation	1. Present the ATAM		
	2. Present the business drivers		
	3. Present the architecture		
Investigation & Analysis	4. Identify the architectural approaches		
	5. Generate the quality attribute utility tree		
	6. Analyze the architectural approaches		
Testing	7. Brainstorm and prioritize scenarios		
	8. Analyze the architectural approaches	N/A	
Reporting	9. Present the results		

You may find some unfamiliar concepts, such as "utility tree", "risk" or "nonrisk", or argue that Step 6 seems the same with Step 8. We will explain in more details in the later sections.

7.3.4 Presentation

This sub-phase targets to define which actions are beneficial and which not. It guides the participants to make effort in contributing design of system. Along with that, this sub-phase also provides the input products for the following steps.

Step 1. Present the ATAM

The first step answers the questions "what is ATAM?" and "what should we do during ATAM?" This is because, except evaluation team who is professional, other stakeholders may be the first time to participate evaluation. The evaluation leader is required to present ATAM's process to participants, and answer any relevant questions from them, during which the leader should focus on the steps, concepts, techniques used in such as scenario prioritization or construction of utility tree, input and output of evaluation and other relevant information.

Step 2. Present the Business Drivers

Then, the leader of project (project lead manager or someone the like) should explain the primary business drivers to every participant. After all, this information is necessary to scenario development and specific assessment. This presentation should contain the topics such as the main business targets, main functions documented in the requirement specifications, relevant constraints of technique, management, economics and politics, and important quality requirements by stakeholders. Be care of the "stakeholders" in this area. In different major phases, different range of stakeholders may be got involved, leading to the deviation of concerns possibly. This distinctness can be considered as a contraposition to expose the points that have not been taken into account.

Step 3. Present the Architecture

Lead architect present existent architecture, normally in the style of multiple architectural views. Most projects need decomposition view indicating static logic structures, component & connector view indicating runtime structures, allocation view indicating mapping between logic structures and physical entities and behavior view describing behavior expectation. But, under specific situation, architect has the privilege of deciding to use other views to focus one certain local area of the system. The additional views may explicitly provide architecture information against critical quality attributes. Degree of detail in architecture presentation affects the following analysis directly. Architecture is responsible of choosing a suitable level of detail, considering the needs of evaluation, whose expected effects have been set in the major phase of preparation. Of course, during evaluation, if necessary architecture information has never been accessed yet, stakeholders can query it to architects. An important task is to list the explicitly-used architectural approaches, which facilitates the next step.

7.3.5   Investigation and Analysis

Via this sub-phase, stakeholders start to map architecture to quality attributes. But unlike the versions of ATAM mentioned above, different and outstanding strategies are used. Instead of architectural elements, architectural approaches are captured and analyzed, and instead of brainstorming-like scenario generation, utility tree is adopted, where the prioritization of each scenario is measured with two-dimension estimation. During assessment, risks, non-risks, sensitivities and trade-offs are identified. The accomplishment of identification is not the end, but the start point of analyses.

Step 4.   Identify the Architectural Approaches

The reason of identifying architectural approaches is that these informations provide the rationale behind the construction of architecture. Simply speaking, an architectural approach means a design decision according to function or quality requirements.

It is a commonly held belief that architectural styles and patterns are good information carriers with respect to the reasons to make a specific design. Architectural patterns describe the abstract elements needed, their layout and relevant constraints. For each of them, quality benefits and defects can be concluded based on its thousands of times of usage, and therefore so does the rationale. ABAS[1], which has been mentioned in the second version of ATAM, is particularly useful. The attribute values associated with them expose the primary quality attribute targets, and also can be used to analyze whether those targets can be met.

But not all the architectural approaches can be expressed in the form of architectural styles or patterns. In this case, architects should explain with natural language why they make the design like what it looks like or why it behaves in the manner specified. Architects should be capable of telling any architectural approach they have used. Other participants can also capture approaches implicit for architects but important for evaluation.

Although clear explanations are necessary, no analyses on approaches should be taken. That is the task of Step 6.

Step 5.   Generate the Quality Attribute Utility Tree

In this step, the critical quality attribute targets are identified by the evaluation team and core project members, such as managers, customer representatives and lead architect. The primary goal of this step is to avoid a meaningless waste of time and cost spent on evaluation. If critical quality attribute targets cannot be determined and agreed on among participants, evaluation cannot gain the benefits that it should have. Quality Attribute Utility Tree is a powerful tool to reach this goal. You can

---

[1] ABAS is the abbreviation of Attribute Based Architecture Style. But the "style" here has different meaning from what we have defined in Chapter 2. It can be considered as "architectural pattern" of this book.

find a similar utility tree in (Boehm, 1976).

Quality Attribute Utility Tree (QAUT for short in the following) is a tree indicating the refinement of quality attributes. The root of QAUT is "utility", followed by sub-level of quality attributes, such as availability, modifiability or security typically. The next level is the categories of specific description of quality attributes, which decompose them into several topics. The fourth level, or the last level, is the concrete scenarios, which precisely define the quality requirements and allow the following analyses. Generally speaking, QAUT translates the system's expected utility to scenarios.

Each scenario is measured with a two-dimension metrics: (1) importance of this scenario to the success of system; (2) difficulty of development work to support this scenario estimated by architects. The used scale can be set as a range of 3 such as High (H), Medium (M) and Low (L), a range of 5, 10 or the like. After marked, scenarios are prioritized, the top of which are the critical quality attribute targets that participants want to acquire. Fig. 7.7 is a sample of QAUT. In fact, the scenarios generated in the real project are more complicated than the ones in this example.

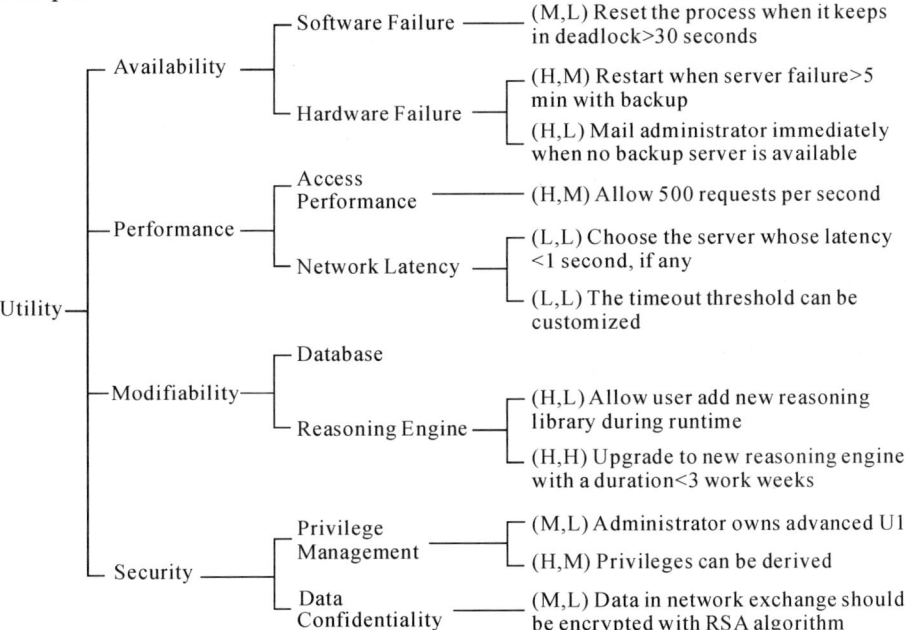

Fig. 7.7 A sample of quality attribute utility tree

QAUT finally generates a list prioritized scenarios, which should be considered in the later analyses in the order of (H, H), (H, M), (M, H) (L, L). This priority exposes clearly the various stakeholders' comprehensive concerns. Someone may believe that performance is the critical requirements, while some others insist that availability should be paid more attention. But until QAUT is built, every individual's thinking may be messy and deviated. QAUT guides and clarifies the quality requirements of system and their relative importance. Therefore, if time or cost for evaluation is not enough, scenarios with low priority will be omitted, because it is meaningless to analyze scenarios that are not important or rather easy to implement.

Step 6.   Analyze the Architectural Approaches

QAUT highlights the direction of evaluation. After that it is the time to analyze the mechanism by which architectural approaches deal with the scenarios of high priority. In this step, evaluation team, together with architects, identify risks, non-risks, sensitivities and trade-offs located in the approaches relevant to important scenarios.

Risks are the decisions that may be potential problematic under certain possible cases that have been made, while non-risks are the contrast. Maybe someone argues that risks need more attention, because they are the source of future problems. However, non-risks are equally important since they indicate which architecture approaches should be insisted. What's more, when context changes, non-risks may translate into risks. Hence, it is beneficial to list non-risk explicitly.

Sensitivity point is the modeled attribute value of system that can be affected greatly by some architectural elements. And trade-off point is the location of system which is related to several sensitivity points. Necessary information should have been prepared in Step 4 and Step 5. But if evaluation team feels there is something missing, they query it to architects.

To identify risks, non-risks, sensitivities and trade-offs, the whole participants will finish the following job:

- Identify the architectural approaches that try to support the important scenarios, and figure out how these approaches are instantiated in the current architecture.
- Analyze each approach, considering its notable good features and well-known problems. Judge whether they draw negative effects to the quality attributes. This is normally done by asking accumulated questions associated to those approaches.
- Based on those answers, identify the risks, non-risks, sensitivities and trade-offs. Record them in the documents respectively.

At the end of this step, the first major phase is over. If everything is successful, evaluation team will get the general idea behind the architecture, as well as good and bad points in it.

7.3.6   Testing

This phase aims at testing the analyses that have been done so far. More kinds of stakeholders will give proposals of system's quality requirements. Range of discussion is expanded. Therefore, additional problems and concerns may be touched to facilitate requirement supplement.

Step 7.   Brainstorm and prioritize scenarios

In Step 5, scenarios are expressed as QAUT, indicating what architecture looks like from core project decision makers. But in this step, larger community of evaluation is formed. The effective method to draw more scenarios in this case is brainstorming, just like what is taken during SAAM scenario development. Creative ideas and novel suggestions can be triggered under this environment. Characteristics of scenarios are concluded as three categories:

- Use Case Scenarios: Describe that how the system, whose architecture is being evaluated, behaves and responses under the end-users' certain manipulation.
- Growth Scenarios: Describe how the system, whose architecture is being evaluated, support rapid modification and evolution, such as adding components, porting to other platform or integrating with other systems.
- Exploratory Scenarios: Probe the extreme growth case of the system, whose architecture is being evaluated. If growth scenarios uncover expected and possible modification cases, exploratory scenarios provide evaluation participants a chance to see what will happen when great changes are required, such performance has to be increased by 5 times, or availability should be enhanced by one order of magnitude. According to this kind of scenarios, extra sensitivities and trade-offs may be exposed, based on which an evaluation test can be performed.

After brainstorming generation, scenarios are also prioritized by voting, same as ATAM. It is obvious that there are notable differences between scenarios generated in Step 5 and Step 7. Scenarios generation with QAUT is process of refinement, which appears as a top-down style. The evaluation team and core project dissension makers work on this to find the primary quality drivers for current architecture. However, scenarios generation by brainstorming need almost all stakeholders' contribution. This step starts with concrete scenario proposals. During test, scenarios generated in this step are compared to the result of QAUT. New scenarios may be the new leaves of existent branches of QAUT or missing completely before, which lead to new quality attributes. This matches the target of evaluation test.

Step 8.   Analyze the Architectural Approaches

This step uses the same methods and techniques as Step 6. The only distinctness is that stakeholders analyze architectural approaches against the ones produced in Step 7. If everything is OK, architects only explain the realization of scenarios by captured approaches. But if there are some scenarios that cannot be supported directly, evaluation team should record this in documents, helping constructing the plan of modification.

7.3.7   Present the Results

Step 9.   Analyze the Architectural Approaches

This is the final step of ATAM in one iteration. All information, including those collected by original architecture documents, generated by stakeholders and acquired through analyses, are presented in evaluation report. The most important ones, or the output of ATAM, contain documented architectural approaches (associated by guide questions), scenarios with priority, QAUT, critical quality requirements, risks, non-risks, sensitivities and trade-offs. All stakeholders hold discussion to handle current architecture's problems, specifically the risks and trade-offs.

7.4   Comparison among Evaluation Methods

Software engineering community has proposed a batch of methods to uncover the potential quality attributes, risks and defects from architecture. Besides SAAM and ATAM that we have depicted in detail, some other methods also draw attention from the public and get validation during applications, including SBAR (Bengtsson, 1998), ALPSM (Bengtsson, 1999), PASA (Williams, 2002a), and so on. Therefore, a systemized comparison should be taken in order to figure out their features and offer guide lines related to the judge which methods should be used under which context where which concerns are taken primarily.

7.4.1   Comparison Framework

Before taking the comparison, a framework should be created to normalize features of various evaluation methods without which we cannot give fair comments and assessment to them. That is, we must first find their common characters and activities, and then establish comparison metrics. As scenario-based evaluation methods, they are structurally similar and share analogical activities, phases and participants. These methods rarely use entirely-unprecedented structures, but are rather "variations on a theme". Upon this comparison framework, you will feel much easier in learning other methods not mentioned here, or the ones that have not reached their birth.

The evaluation taken by stakeholders is essentially held with the form of conference whose participants are all or part of stakeholders, decided by which method is applied. Generally, scenario-based evaluation methods work through four phases, as Fig.7.8 shown.

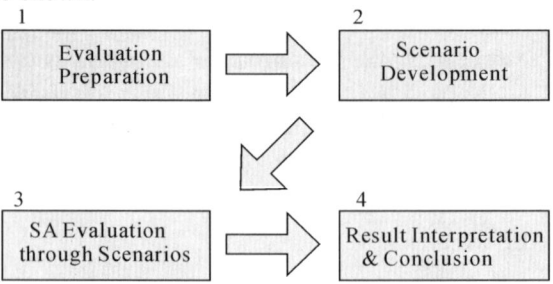

Fig. 7.8   General phases of scenario-based evaluation

Phase 1. Evaluation Preparation: Stakeholders need a frame of reference with which to communicate and thus lead to a great insight to the relationship between the system to be built and the problems to be solved, as well as understanding among each other, before any activity starts. Not every body involved in the next successive processes is familiar with system's general knowledge, nor do they make it clear that what should do during evaluation, and which ideas or proposals may be benefits to evaluation's result. So, a preparation phase is necessary, which should not be considered as secondary compared to other three phases. Although you might think you need not explicitly give the evaluation related information with which participants get warmed up, as activities go through one by one you will regret that decision after it is too late, because too much chaos and deviation are incurred and benefits shrink seriously. In this phase, three classes of information should be pronounced publicly. Firstly, the evaluation leader should explain exactly the evaluation method to be used and its activities, trying to set their expectations and answer questions they may have. This is a guide that avoids or, at least, reduces irrelevant or valueless discussion or other exceptions. Secondly, the system goals (or business motivations) should be presented, normally by project managers or representative customers. After all, participants need to know which goals mainly direct system's development and which quality attributes require special concentrations. Finally, architects should describe existent architecture and explain critical design decisions that meet system targets, which forces eligible architecture description or documents and at the same time improves design effort in the disguised form. When this phase ends, everybody will get a clear comprehension about system's synoptic structures and goals driving them. If it is not the case, there must be something wrong in the materials for preparation.

Phase 2. Scenario Development: The purpose of this phase is to generate as many valuable scenarios as possible and enable the next phase. Providing a pile of cases is relatively easy. The typical strategy is to encourage stakeholders sitting around the table take a brain storm, thus suggest anything that they want to say. But the open question is when to stop scenario generations and how to choose those which are most benefit to correct and improve current architecture design. Some methods keep generating until new scenarios always become overlapped with previous ones or do not affect architecture. Other ones use heuristic strategy which guides people to produce effective scenarios via, for example, providing preliminary question suit. Those methods which pay attention to single quality attribute usually define the metrics of relevance between scenarios and target attribute. Priority, as mentioned in the former section, is also the issue to be carefully concerned. Generally speaking, in a conference lasting 2 or 3 days, only no more than 20 scenarios are picked and evaluated, considering lengthy and complicated scenario evaluation phase, which means a prioritization mechanism is needed. CMU SEI recommends the "30% voting" skill, which means any participant hold a number of votes equal to 30% of the total number of generated scenarios. Votes of each individual can be allocated in any way that the person feels fit: all votes for one scenario, one vote for each scenario, giving up voting when no scenario is to his liking, or anything combined with them. Only scenarios that are "above the line" will be brought into the next phase.

Phase 3.   Software Architecture Evaluation through Scenarios: This is the core phase of scenario-based evaluation, creating the bridge between stakeholder's expectations or suspicions to system's skeleton and interaction manners. Here several questions have to be clarified for each scenario outputted by the previous phase, such as "does this scenario can be supported by current architecture directly?", "if architecture has to be modified to meet the new concerns, how much the cost associated with that scenario will be incurred by that modification?", and "What the influence led by the scenario is and how is it measured?" Architects and domain experts should illustrate the required change specified by scenarios according to estimation based on their experience and insight, and provide suggestions against objectives and risks related to the software architecture. Some cases deserve people's urgent attention, such as that the scenarios different in semantics affect the identical components or multiple scenarios stand against each other essentially. Architects are responsible of finding sensitive points and trade-off points, through which they perform fine-tuning on architecture to fit for multiple conflict targets. If multiple architecture candidates have been created in the design phase (this is the normal case), overall evaluation should be taken, during which they are compared by calculating the overall degree to which they support scenarios used in evaluation. In conclusion, this phase's input are scenarios filtered by the scenario development phase and software architecture description. The output is a raw evaluation result needing interpretation, such as a list with items indicating each individual scenario's influence to a specified architecture or the overall scores for involved architecture candidates.

Phase 4.   Result Interpretation and Conclusion: The tables or something the like which contain the information collected by the third phase do not mean the end of the whole evaluation. They are not so clear that we cannot gain all the possible benefits it should have brought. Evaluation should provide a series of clear final documents capable of guiding further design modification and implementation. Three categories of information can be extracted from the raw result. Firstly, you can choose which architecture candidate is the best one

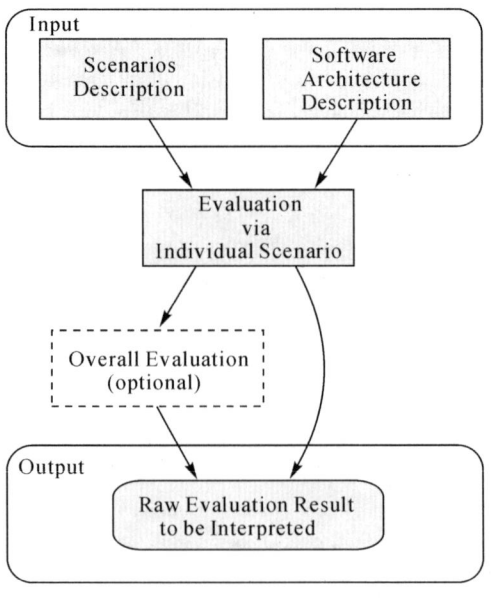

Fig. 7. 9   SA evaluation through scenarios

to become the fundamental model directing development, considering relative scores gotten from overall evaluation. We can guarantee that no architecture evaluates better than others in every area. An architecture may work better than others in some areas, while show its weakness in other areas. Evaluation can clearly reflect architecture's features, good or bad ones, via which project leaders can decide to adopt which one and abandon the others, or simply recreate one if all of them seem ineligible. Secondly, you can plan the modification plan by combining and organizing those clues documented during evaluation. Original architecture is created according to concerns from requirement specifications. They might appear not so fit with the respect to the issues introduced during evaluation, or stakeholders change their mind and want to fix architecture. Evaluation provides a chance that everybody's wisdom can affect the design, which is good at correcting the preconception of designers who build the blueprint based on, possible slant, understanding. Evaluation tells which part of architecture falls in defects needing repair and where exist risks needing attention and correction. Finally, you can accumulate practical skills and experience of evaluation, which help you take adjustment when you take part in the next evaluation for better effects. This, then, gradually develops the overall development atmosphere and promotes software development quality.

With these common evaluation activities, we can conclude the features that should be employed in the comparison framework. You can find other notable comparison frameworks in (Dobrica, 2002) or (Barbar, 2004).

Table 7. 5   Evaluation Methods Comparison Framework

Item	Element	Description
Context	Special Goal	What is the particular target of this method?
	Quality Attribute	Which quality attributes does this method cover primarily?
	SA Description	What kind of software architecture description is required?
	Involved Stakeholders	Which stakeholders should participate in this method?
Phases	Evaluation Preparation	What special concern should be taken by this method?.
	Scenario Development	What activities are adopted in scenario generation?
	Evaluation Techniques	What activities are used to accomplish the special goal of this method?
	Result Interpretation & Conclusion	Which conclusion can be concluded after the whole evaluation? Are there any additional benefits?
Application	Validation	Has this method been validated in the industrial cases? How about its effects?
	Support Tool	What is the support tool, if any?

In the next section, we will provide a brief overview and comparison among evaluation methods with the framework above, trying to guide the selection of these methods when evaluation is needed for your projects. Two phases, Evaluation Preparation and Result Interpretation & Conclusion are so trivial that they are not contained in the following overview, only get illustrated if they are rather noticeable in certain methods.

7. 4. 2   Overview and Comparison of Evaluation Methods

In this section, several common architecture evaluation methods will be accessed respectively by introducing and comparing their features, including SAAM, SAAMCS, ESAAMI, SAAMER, ATAM, SAEM, SBAR, ALPSM and PASA. Since in the preceding sections, SAAM, ATAM and SAEM have been described in detail, only outstanding features of them will be generally listed bellow.

7. 4. 2. 1   SAAM: Scenario-based Architecture Analysis Method

SAAM (Kazman, 1994; Kazman 1996b) is a method designed mainly to gear the extent to which architecture design meets the desired quality attributes in a very intuitive manner.

- **Special Goal:** SAAM tries to map desired quality attributes, which are represented by scenarios to the architecture description. In addition, SAAM provides a chance to take analysis of architecture's inherent dangerous spots and thus potential risks.
- **Quality Attribute:** SAAM was initially developed with respect to assessment of modifiability. But it can also be employed in evaluating other quality attributes, although ATAM is commonly used in these cases instead.
- **SA Description:** An architecture description that can be easily understood by various participant stakeholders should be used in SAAM, which at least shows the system's static composition of primary computation and data components and their relationships. Besides them, system's dynamic behaviors over time should be included in SAAM's needed description.
- **Involved Stakeholders:** All stakeholders should be present in this evaluation to guarantee the comprehensive concerns and harmonization.
- **Scenario Development:** Scenarios are generated during a discussion without debates. This phase may include several iterations, together with architecture presentation, to collect more scenarios that affect system's architecture. Scenario Development will end until no new scenario disturbs the design.
- **Evaluation Techniques:** SAAM divides generated scenarios into two categories: direct and indirect one, the latter of which is paid much attention since it will introduce modification of the original architecture. After prioritization and filtration, the resulted scenarios are evaluated in an individual manner by figuring out the architecture elements disturbed by them and the extent and cost of modification. Scenario interaction technique is employed to locate the implicit bad design of system decomposition or implicit risk spots. Finally, overall evaluation brings benefits of comparison and selection among multiple architecture candidates.

- **Validation**: SAAM is a mature method, experiencing many application cases.
- **Support Tool**: SAAM is supported by SAAMtool (Kazman, 1996a).

7.4.2.2   SAAMCS: SAAM for Complex Scenarios

The name of this method obviously exposes what it cares about most, that is, the complex scenarios. This method appeared in (Lassing, 1999). By inheriting most activities and techniques from SAAM, SAAMCS extends it with the method of finding which scenarios are complex and analyzing how architecture is stricken by them.

- **Special Goal**: The sole target of SAAMCS is to perform risk assessment of system modification.
- **Quality Attribute**: SAAMCS is an extension for handling specific problems, therefore its capability, unlike SAAM, is limited in modifiability, or "flexibility" in the words used by its author.
- **SA Description**: SAAMCS uses the final version of software architecture description to investigate the detailed information related with complex scenarios. Considering the relationship between a system and its external environment, system's architecture description falls into two categories: microarchitecture and macroarchitecture.
- **Involved Stakeholders**: Aside from that all stakeholders' involvement is recommended as SAAM, SAAMCS identifies the crucial role of scenario initiators, who are the people or organizational units that have great interest in the implementation of a certain scenario.
- **Scenario Development**: The feature of SAAMCS in this phase is the identification of "complex scenarios". To find them, SAAMCS defines a measurement instrument of complexity, including scenario initiator, architecture description and version conflicts. The eligible scenarios are categorized and listed, preparing for the next evaluation phase. A two-dimensional framework diagram is adopted to help locate complex scenarios. One dimension is sources of change, including "Functional Requirements", "Quality Requirements", "External Components" and "Technical Environment", while another one is scenario complexity, including "adaptations to the system with external effects, to the environment with effects to the system, to the macroarchitecture and to the microarchitecture, and the introduction of version conflicts."
- **Evaluation Techniques**: The inputs of SAAMCS are categorized scenarios, architecture description (micro- and macro-architecture) and measurement instrument of scenarios' impact. Evaluation is a process that measures the impact of these complex scenarios to the system design in a discrete and predefined values. The detailed measurement instrument is described in Table 7.6. The complete process of SAAMCS is illustrated in Fig.7.10.

Table 7.6   Measurement Instrument of Scenario Impact in SAAMCS

Measurement Items	Possible Values or Description
Scenario Impact	1. No affect 2. Affect one component 3. Affect several components 4. Affect software architecture
Number of Owners	The number of owners involved in the information system
Presence of Version Conflicts	1. No problem with different versions 2. The presence is undesirable but not prohibitive 3. Creates complications related to configuration management 4. Creates conflicts

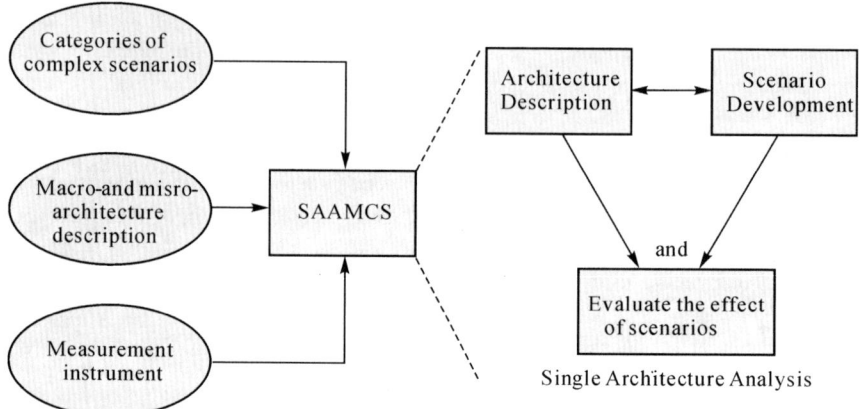

Fig. 7.10   Input and activities of SAAMCS

- **Validation:** SAAMCS has been validated in business information systems, still without getting tested in other areas.
- **Support Tool:** No available tools have been yet created to support this method.

7.4.2.3   ESAAMI: Extending SAAM by Integration in the Domain

SAAM does not concern the issue of evaluation reusability specially, thus that artifacts used in the evaluation, scenarios, hints, tactics and so on, cannot be used again with direct support of SAAM. ESAAMI, however, creates a framework for evaluation reuse within a domain, and builds architecture analysis templates and reuse knowledge base (Molter, 1999).

- **Special Goal:** ESAAMI integrates the reuse-based architecture evaluation processes tightly with the classic SAAM by accumulating the reusable evaluation materials and knowledge. The ultimate goal of introducing reusable evaluation is to reduce the evaluation cost and accelerate this process. What's more, reusable evaluation processes can be used as the attachment of reusable architecture.

In general, three concepts that interweave with each other become the barrier to understand this method: First, an evaluation method that can be reused with regard to a certain domain; second, a reusable architecture that provides the common basis for a variety of applications derived from this domain; and last, how to perform the analysis to guarantee an architecture's reusability. This is done by inspecting the factors such as architecture's abstract level, modifiability and whether it has been comprehensively and clearly documented. ESAAMI is an evaluation method that can be easily reused that requires the input of reusable architecture. The third item, however, does not concerned by ESAAMI just as mentioned in Quality Attribute section.

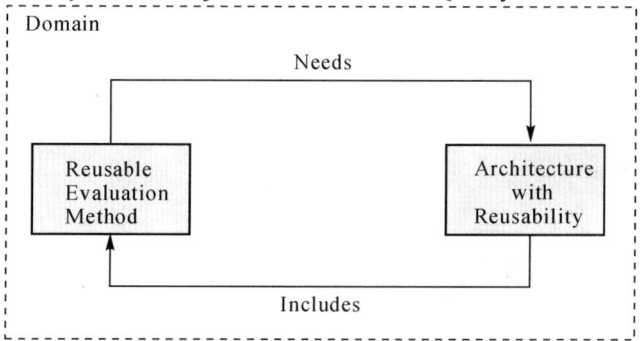

Fig. 7. 11   Core concepts in ESAAMI

- **Quality Attribute**: The quality attributes involved in ESAAMI are similar to SAAM. In fact, ESAAMI is itself reusable, but does not pay more attention to measuring or guaranteeing the reusability of an architecture. Architecture's reusability is an input or a preparation of this method, and might be evaluated, together with other quality attributes, by conventional SAAM. Some reusability-related scenarios, such as a series of changes that are possible within the range of a domain, can be employed to figure out the degree to which architecture owns.
- **SA Description**: For ESAAMI, a reusable skeleton architecture, which has to reflect the common basis of applications within a domain, is required. Authors of this method identify three kinds of software architecture description characteristics: The description has to provide information common enough to allow its reuse within the domain-specified area; has to be flexible enough to cope with various customizations; has to be documented detailed enough about architecture's properties to allow selection and reuse.
- **Involved Stakeholders**: Involved stakeholders of this method are similar to SAAM.
- **Scenario Development**: Authors of this method believe that it is necessary that the available knowledge is incorporated into the future analysis. Scenario is a typical example of this case. ESAAMI introduces the concept of "protoscenario", which transfers the information of common use or change cases of a domain. In fact, protoscenario is a scenario template indicating the

generic information about a certain use or change situation. Before performing the concrete analysis, protoscenarios have to be selected and refined with the specified concerns of system targets and application context. More scenarios can also be introduced just as what is done in the conventional SAAM. Similar to SAAM, scenarios in ESAAMI, whether generated by protoscenario refinement or proposed by stakeholders, will be classified according to classification hints, which are defined in the context of architecture. The whole scenario development process is shown in Fig.7.12.

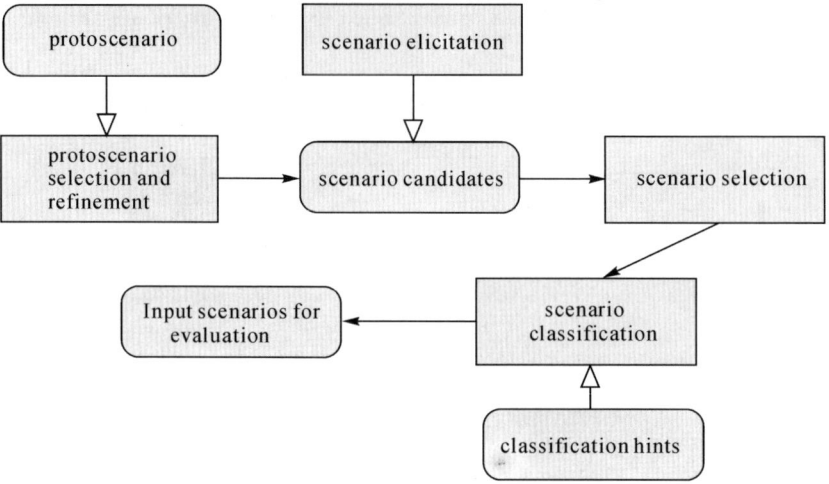

Fig. 7. 12   Scenario development process in ESAAMI

- **Evaluation Techniques**: The outstanding technique of ESAAMI is proposing "packages of analysis templates", which collect several products that can be reused over times. These products, focusing on the domain's commonalities on a high abstract level and ignoring those system-specified issues, are distributed in the various steps of ESAAMI. They are protoscenarios, evaluation protocols, proto-evaluations, architectural hints and weights for architecture comparison.
  Besides "protoscenarios" which have been accessed above, evaluation protocols and proto-evaluation provide a framework of how to deal with a scenario with a set of abstract architectural elements, which will also be extended and refined during the scenario evaluation process, just like what proto-scenarios are processed. And architectural hint is the additional architectural information which is bound to every scenario, facilitating the design guideline, a pattern, for example, which enables the specified scenario's requirements or helps to figure out which design characteristics are typical and which are risk-hidden. This information is the product of experience within the domain and can be applied again and again. Finally, weights are used to support the comparison among several architectural candidates. Typical uses of weight occur in the measurement of scenarios'

importance and scenario interactions. Weights are also reusable in many projects in the same application domain; therefore, the results of different evaluation have the chance to compare with each other. In conclusion, ESAAMI is the collection of almost all the potential reusable products resulted from SAAM. The evaluation process is shown in Fig.7.13.

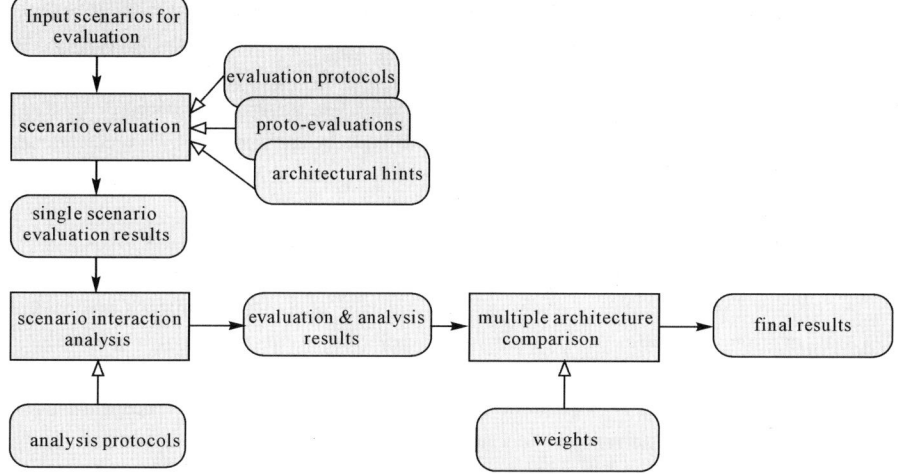

Fig. 7. 13   Evaluation process in ESAAMI

- **Validation**: Although ESAAMI has been published for quite a long time, and in the related articles, the detailed steps and general features are described clearly, but it seems that the authors have not yet finished this method and thus do not give any practical examples validating it.
- **Support Tool**: No available tools have been yet created to support this method.

7. 4. 2. 4   SAAMER:SAAM for Evolution and Reusability

SAAMER is another extension of SAAM, which was published in 1997 (Lung, 1997). Authors of this method believe that considerations of evaluation and reusability on the architecture level get high payoff more easily. They enhance the classic SAAM according to their experience accumulated during the work for Nortel's telecommunication system.

- **Special Goal**: SAAMER makes a series of optimization to SAAM in the perspectives of system's evolution and reusability. Through special categorization of scenarios, this method tries to capture the potential problems of them and evaluates their solutions.
- **Quality Attribute**: SAAMER concentrates on evolution and reusability primarily.
- **SA Description**: According to the authors, four kinds of architectural views are required to perform this method, that is, static view, map view, dynamic view and resource view. Static view provides system's elements topological

information while dynamic view reflects behavioral aspects. Map view, then, links the components to their corresponding functions and features, and resource view deals with resource utilization. They are, in fact, the needed architecture description in logic level, each of which is carried in some concrete artifacts. For example, the dynamic view can be implemented in the manner of state machine chart, operational diagram, casual diagram, messaging diagram or even Petri net. All of them give a concrete foundation for evaluation rationale. These views are not necessarily generated in a sequential order, but can be collected and complemented in several iterations.

- **Involved Stakeholders:** Aside from the stakeholders as SAAM recommends, domain experts play an important role during scenario development and evaluation of SAAMER.
- **Scenario Development:** An outstanding feature of SAAMER is its mechanism of scenario development stopping. Two techniques are created to complete this mission: Firstly, all the initially-generated scenarios are divided according to types of objectives, including objectives of stakeholders, architecture and quality. With the help of objective-oriented categorization and domain experts' experience, scenarios are clustered to make sure every objective is very covered. Secondly, SAAMER pays much attention to the balance among scenarios of different objectives. Therefore, SAAMER uses QFD (Quality Function Deployment) (Bot, 1996) to guarantee this point, which makes use of a cascade of relation metrics to figure out the relational strengths among three kinds of objectives, and thus get the priority of quality attributes. Imbalance factor is introduced by dividing a quality attribute's scenario coverage by its priority. A factor less than one means generated scenarios for a quality attribute is too rough compared to its priority, resulting in the creation of more scenarios.
- **Evaluation Techniques:** In SAAM, the change incurred by each scenario are counted to evaluate the needed effort. SAAMER extends changes information with their approximate estimation (low, medium, high) and relevant domain expert experiences. Another concern point of SAAMER is scenario interaction analysis. High level interaction means the terrible decomposition of components, except which is the nature of a specific architectural pattern. What's more, architectural styles and design violation are identified to serve the analysis, which are not included in SAAM, allowing overall consistent checking. Finally, three tabular representations are generated as the raw result of evaluation to be interpreted and concluded. They are an objective-based analysis result, a summary of scenario interaction and a summary based on quality. The evaluation framework is shown in Fig.7.14.
- **Validation:** SAAMER has been applied in the development of several telecommunication systems of Nortel.
- **Support Tool:** No available tools have been yet created to support this method.

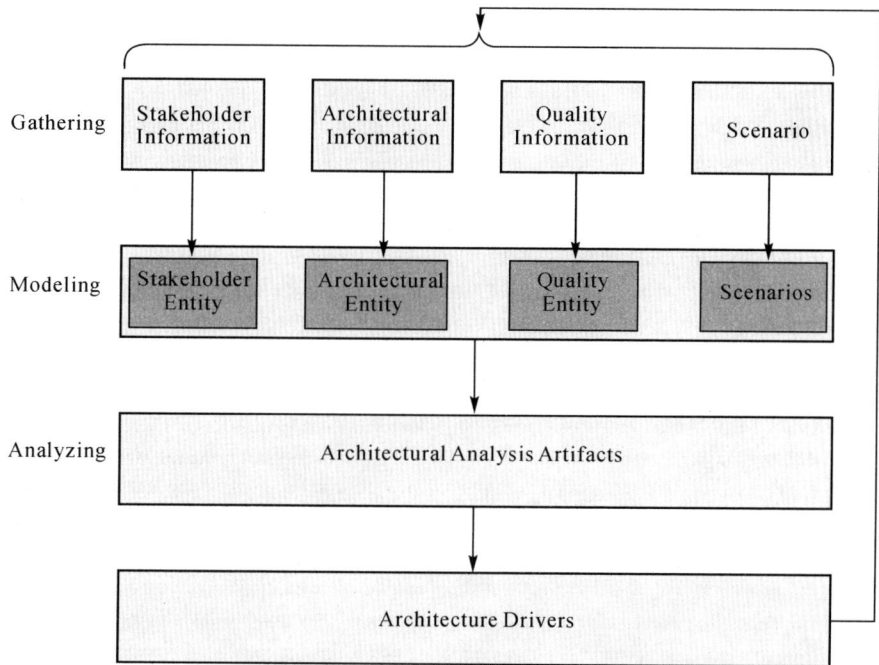

Fig. 7. 14   SAAMER framework [2]

7. 4. 2. 5   ATAM: Architecture Trade-off Analysis Method

ATAM is a powerful evaluation model which is suitable, unlike many other evaluation methods, for dealing with the competition of multiple quality attributes. Although SAAM can be deployed in evaluating quality attributes other than modifiability, currently missions of this like normally adopt ATAM. ATAM was released in (Kazman, 1998) and improved in (Kazman, 1999).

- **Special Goal:** ATAM's objective is to provide a principal way of understanding a software architecture's capability with respect to multiple competing quality attributes. (Barbacci, 1998). Besides the influence incurred by scenarios and potential problems hidden in the architecture, the links of several quality goals will be exposed and analyzed.
- **Quality Attribute:** ATAM is a process that tells us how to identify the trade-off points of architecture, rather than lean especially to any quality attribute, but focuses on the competing relation among multiple quality attributes. However, in the initial article about this method, availability, performance, modifiability and security were involved.
- **SA Description:** An architecture description that can be easily understood by various participant stakeholders should be used in SAAM, which at least

---

[2] The scenario in the figure means identical to "use case" for keeping consistent with term used in (Lung, 1997), rather than what we're declared in the start of this chapter.

shows the system's static composition of primary computation and data components and their relationships. Besides them, system's dynamic behaviors over time should be included in SAAM's needed description.

- **Involved Stakeholders:** This method is divided into two phases, in the first of which only architects and project managers are needed to participate, while in the second, all stakeholders' involvement is recommended to guarantee everyone's concerns can be taken into account.

- **Scenario Development:** Just as SAAM, ATAM encourages a brain storm and thus generating scenarios as more as possible. After that, through prioritization, only several most important ones are kept for later analysis. The principal difference exists in constructing a complete set of scenarios, for which CMU SEI develops a collection of assistant questions for each common quality attribute. Scenarios fall in three categories: the use scenarios, probing the typical use cases of target system; the growth scenarios, representing the potential changes; and the exploratory scenarios, inspecting the system's behaviors and status during "high stress".

- **Evaluation Techniques:** Aside from the skills used in generating scenarios, ATAM has three other outstanding features. The first one is the application of ABAS (Attribute-Based Architectural Styles). ABAS is a kind of architectural style that provides heuristic design guide information against quality attributes. The second one is utility tree. ATAM explicitly adopts sight to the system from two distinct perspectives, the designers' and other stakeholders'. By utility tree, the architects or project managers express that how they understand target system and what the final system looks like. What's more, through the comparison between scenarios in utility tree and in the list generated by other stakeholders, we can discover easily whether the original understanding is deviated or misses something important. The third one is the identification of sensitivity points and trade-off points. Sensitivity can be used to identify the significant changes of system's appearance by the change to some architecture elements, such as response time, available proportion, etc. Trade-off point, then, is the architecture element that contains multiple competing sensitivity points. They are the core of this method, helping people solve the problem of interweaving of various quality attributes.

- **Validation:** ATAM has been applied in many projects, such as Battlefield Control System, Remote Temperature Sensor System and so on. However, this method still stands in the evolution phase. Enhancement to it never stops.

- **Support Tool:** Some ATAM support tools have been published to reduce the heavy manual and facilitate the communication of stakeholders distributed in different locations of the world. For example, ACE (ATAM Collaborative Environment) (Maheshwari, 2005) is a Web-based common platform enabling stakeholders take part in ATAM without having to be physically co-located. Another tool that is under development is "ArchE" (Bachmann, 2003), where ATAM assistant is integrated into the architecture design environment.

7. 4. 2. 6   SBAR: Scenario-based Architecture Reengineering

SBAR is a framework of evaluating detailed architecture by introducing an iteration process of quality assessment and architecture transformation (Bengtsson, 1998).

- **Special Goal:** SBAR targets to drive the architecture redesign with respect to quality attributes. This method wants to make sure that system's architecture fulfill the desired non-functional properties.
- **Quality Attribute:** SBAR deals with multiple quality attributes. In fact, just like ATAM, SBAR does not create new methods against each specific attribute, but adopts the typical ones published previously, for example, for real-time, high performance and reusable system.
- **SA Description:** SBAR needs the initial architecture descriptions which are created according to the functionality requirements. Considering that this method is designed to facilitate system's reengineering, a detailed architecture should be fed for the subsequent evaluation processes.
- **Involved Stakeholders:** This method focuses on reengineering of architecture, resulting in that the designers have to take part in this evaluation.
- **Scenario Development:** SBAR does not mention how to develop needed scenarios in detail and unique techniques. However, it requires a representative set of scenarios concretizing each quality attribute needing concerns, both explicit and implicit ones, and thus facilitating reengineering processes. A weakness point of this method is that "a representative set of scenarios" has no clear definition, leading to that you cannot tell when to stop generating scenarios exactly.
- **Evaluation Techniques:** SBAR provides a framework in an iteration fashion, as Fig. 7. 15 shown. With new requirement specification, a functionality-based architecture redesign is performed, which, then, together with the architecture are fed as the input of evaluation processes. Two parts of evaluation, quality assessment and architecture transformation construct a loop, during which each necessary quality attribute is accessed and guaranteed to be supported. In the quality assessment part, four kinds of methods: scenario-based evaluation, simulation, mathematical modeling and experience reasoning, are used normally according to evaluation context, in which, of course, scenario-based method dominates. In the architecture transformation part, five methods are adopted. They are "Impose architectural style", "Impose architectural pattern", "Apply design pattern", "Convert quality requirements to functionality" and "Distributed requirements". This loop will end until most significant scenarios for each quality attribute are satisfied.
- **Validation:** SBAR has been applied in a measurement system for detailed

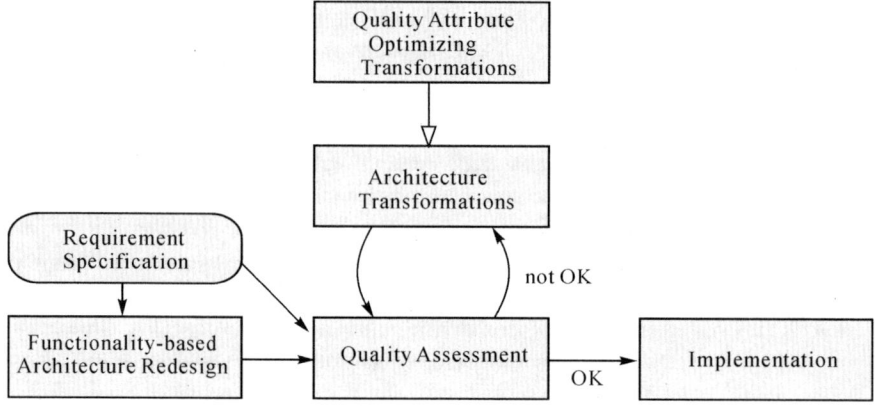

Fig. 7. 15   SBAR evaluation processes

architecture reengineering.

- **Support Tool:** There is no available support tool explicitly for this method, partially because it just describes evaluation framework, and will get contextually varied.

7. 4. 2. 7   ALPSM: Architecture Level Prediction of Software Maintenance

ALPSM is a distinct evaluation method for its predominant result, the estimation of maintenance effort needed in the system built according to the architecture, rather than figuring out the potential defects or trade-off points of architecture design which is generated by many other evaluation methods (Bengtsson, 1999).

- **Special Goal:** ALPSM provides the estimated maintenance effort needed in a series of change scenarios. Size of changes is used as the predicator to reach this point.
- **Quality Attribute:** ALPSM is not a method to check whether a single or multiple quality attributes are fulfilled by architecture, or the degree to which these attributes are satisfied. Therefore, its concerns do not meet this comparison framework very well. However, we can take the maintainability inspection indirectly by getting the needed maintenance effort.
- **SA Description:** ALPSM requires the final version of detailed architecture description.
- **Involved Stakeholders:** Only architects, designers, domain experts and maintenance members are needed to participate in this method.
- **Scenario Development:** In this method, only change scenarios should be generated for the subsequent analysis. The scenario development here is the job of architects or domain experts, who have much experience in predicting the possible changes to the system. These scenarios are distributed evenly in several categories of maintenance tasks, such as hardware changes, safety regulation changes, etc. Scenarios are also prioritized in this method, all of which are weighed by the relative probability of them resulting in a maintenance task during a particular time interval. The more frequent a

scenario is possible to occur, the higher its weight values. The possibility can be extracted from system's historical maintenance records from similar application or previous release, if any; otherwise, the architects or domain experts are responsible of estimating scenarios' weights.

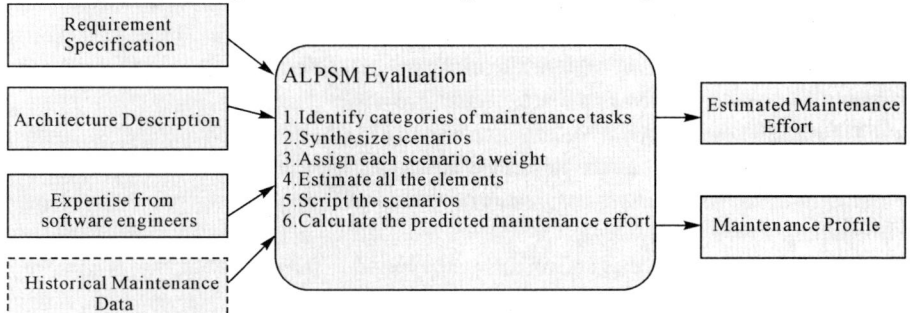

Fig. 7. 16   ALPSM evaluation method

- **Evaluation Techniques:** The process of this method is straightforward: Its input contains requirement specification, architecture description, expertise from software engineers and historical maintenance data, if any. Next, six steps, shown in Fig.7.16, are performed one by one, by which participants get the estimate information. Two points should draw our attention. One is that all the maintenance tasks are categorized in the first step, aiming at expressing the maintenance requirement more clearly and hence helping participants get a better understanding of the system. Another one is the measurement of maintenance effort. The size of all components in the system is determined by one of the three measurement methods: estimation technique of choice, adaption of an object-oriented metric "SIZE2" (Chidamber, 1991), or historical components' size data, if historical data can be found. The effort incurred by a specified scenario is calculated by determining the components that are affected by this scenario and the extent to which it is modified. And the total estimated effort of maintenance is predicted by the sum of the product of the effort incurred by each scenario and its probability weight, as shown in Fig.7.17.

$$M_{\text{total}} = \sum_{n=1}^{k_s} \left(P(S_n) \cdot \sum_{m=1}^{k_c} V(S_n, C_m) \right)$$

$P(S_n)$ the probability weight of scenario n
$V(S_n, C_m)$ the affected volume of component m in scenario n
k_s number of scenario s
k_c number of components in architecture

Fig. 7. 17   Formula for prediction of total maintenance effort

- **Validation:** ALPSM has been applied in a haemo dialysis system.
- **Support Tool:** No available tool has been released to support this method explicitly.

7. 4. 2. 8   SAEM: Software Architecture Evaluation Model

SAEM is an evaluation model which is based on quality model standards and quality assessment processes (IEEE, 1998; IEEE, 1989a; IEEE, 1989b). It was published in (Duenas, 1998). Compared to a concrete evaluation method, SAEM should be taken to a reference understanding of software quality assessment. In other words, concepts and models in quality evaluation are identified and described in such a general way that it can cover most specific evaluation methods.

- **Special Goal:** SAEM creates the foundation of software quality issues and evaluation processes. It describes what software quality is and the general strategies to analyses of the categories and degrees to which systems' architecture fulfill.
- **Quality Attribute:** The quality attributes referred in SAEM is different from those which we have been familiar with, due to their higher level abstraction. They are divided into "internal" and "external" ones. External qualities reflect the characters which can be seen from users' perspectives, while the internal ones express the characters relevant to developers' views. The external ones are specified by both users and developers and the internals ones are only decided by developers. The concept "user" and "developer" here have more general meanings, with respect to which every software development process can be split into several phases and each of them generates a product. The people creating products are developer and the people using products are user. For example, the final version architecture itself is an intermediate product whose users may be the programmers that implement it. Metric specifications for these quality attributes, internal or external ones, are benefit to their measurement and evaluation.
- **SA Description:** Following categorization of quality attributes, software architecture is also separated to internal views and external views. SAEM recommend a software architecture description attached with evaluation assistant questions or inspection techniques (such as software architecture model walkthrough), which provides the chance to detect the elements that support the desired quality attributes. Architecture Description Language (ADL) with formalization model is a good case facilitating this.
- **Involved Stakeholders:** SAEM does not regulate who should take part in the evaluation process explicitly, but only mentions that system experts are responsible of evaluating architecture.
- **Scenario Development:** SAEM does not focus on the effect of scenario. Scenario-based method should be one of several evaluation techniques, including checklists or questionnaires.
- **Evaluation Techniques:** SAEM is a general evaluating model, containing the phases: quality attributes specification, quality measurement and analysis and result interpretations. This model involves users and developers with respect to software's external and internal characteristics. System experts should link the quality attributes to architecture elements with the help of expert's

knowledge and company accumulated data.

- **Validation**: SAEM has never been validated in any practical application. But you may find its ideas in some more concrete evaluation methods.
- **Support Tool**: There is no support tool available for SAEM.

7.4.2.9 PASA: Performance Assessment of Software Architecture

"Software's performance cannot be retrofitted. It must be designed into software from the beginning. The make it run, make it run right, make it run fast' are dangerous." (Williams, 2002a). This is the basic motivation of PASA, a method coming from Williams and Smith's work presented in the report (Williams, 2002b). PASA is performed through 9 steps, as shown in Fig. 7.18. We provide a brief introduction to each of them.

Step 1: Process Overview: This is a presentation that introduces the general steps of PASA, motivation of assessment, and the whole process' outcome. It helps improve participants' familiarity with what they should do, which actions are suitable and benefit to the assessment, and thus avoid doing something nonsensical.

Step 2: Architecture Overview: As the basis for the subsequent activities, architects have to describe current architecture designs and explain those critical structure or behavior specifications that the assessment needs.

Step 3: Identification of Critical Use Cases: Try to find the external visible use cases that reflect the important system behaviors, especially those tightly relevant to responsibility and scalability.

Step 4: Selection of Key Performance Scenarios: From the critical use cases generated in the previous step, the important performance-related scenarios are identified.

Step 5: Identification of Performance Objectives: Each scenario involved in assessment should be measurable; therefore, assessment participants have to define the performance objectives against each key performance scenario.

Step 6: Architecture Clarification and Discussion: It is the time to inspect the architecture elements in more deep detail that influence the realization of the scenarios above. This is achieved by participants' further discussion about system's architecture, through which the potential problem areas will be exposed.

Step 7: Architecture Analysis: Against each key performance scenario, analysis of architecture is conducted to figure out that whether current design can support the corresponding performance objectives.

Step 8: Identification of Alternatives: If some problems exist (in fact, in most cases it is), original architecture should be fine-tuned in local area by alternating structures which are capacity to meet the objectives. Sometimes, the whole architecture style is replaced to repair its performance problems.

Step 9: Presentation of Results: This is the final presentation of assessment's conclusion, including the found problems, plan of architecture modification, estimated work and cost on modification.

You can find that PASA is a typical variation of common evaluation activities mentioned before, and armed with some unique features focusing performance.

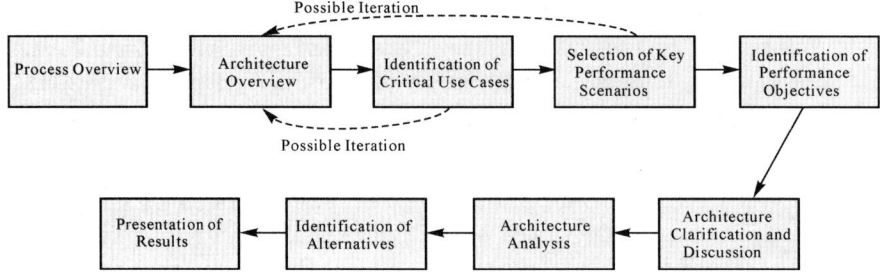

Fig. 7. 18   PASA evaluation process

- **Special Goal**: PASA aims to evaluate the performance capability of architecture candidates and deal with trade-off issues between performance concerns and other quality attributes, such as modifiability and reliability.
- **Quality Attribute**: Performance is the center of this method's target quality attributes. The authors believe that a system's performance is tightly related to its architecture, rather than coding issues. In PASA, all other quality attributes, which interact with performance, are also taken into account.
- **SA Description**: PASA needs very detailed architecture description to allow its execution. But according to authors' experience, there will be very little architecture information, if any, which has been documented. Even though architecture documents are available, they are also too informal to express their meaning or too old to reflect system's current state. Therefore, in order to overcome this problem, several techniques are used to recover architecture information, including deduction from developer interviews, source code, and other artifacts. Scenario development for the use of system is also a fantastic way to extract architecture information. Therefore, the second to fourth steps will be performed in an iterative way to guarantee architecture information's gradual clarification.
- **Involved Stakeholders**: Architects, project managers, developers and performance experts are required in this method. Other stakeholders' involvement will improve the effect of trade-off analysis between performance and other quality attributes.
- **Scenario Development**: Key performance scenarios are identified from those critical use cases, which are collected from requirement documents or other materials. If there is no enough information available to generate use cases, such as assessment for legacy system, assessment team should work together with development team to identify those use cases. Two kinds of scenarios should be kept, one of which is executed frequently and reflects users' perception of performance, and another of which is executed not so frequently but will incur severe influence to the system if it is bad in performance, e.g. crash recovery. All the scenarios, each of which is attached by one or several performance objectives, are documented in augmented UML sequence diagram.

- **Evaluation Techniques**: PASA adopts techniques based on architecture pattern to perform architecture analysis. Deviations from typical patterns or styles are identified and evaluated to show its effects to system's performance. If there is any negative effect or the deviated patterns to match any anti-patterns (Smith, 2000), architecture fine-tuning or refactoring (Brown, 1998) are performed to fix the problems. Some performance modeling strategies includes (Lüthi, 1997) and (Majumdar, 1991).
- **Validation**: PASA has been applied in several projects, including Web-based system, real time system and financial system. These cases are listed in (Smith, 2001).
- **Support Tool**: There is no support tool available for PASA.

7.4.2.10   ARID: Active Reviews for Intermediate Designs

Most methods mentioned above perform evaluation on the whole architecture. However, sometimes we may need a review on the early design or partition of the entire system, where some design strategies or decisions should be reviewed under the case that not all the architecture information is available. This kind of evaluating object is called intermediate design, which requires a different method to check its suitability. ARID is such a method by combing the best of Active Design Reviews (ADR) (Parnas, 1985) and scenario-based evaluation method, such as SAAM or ATAM.

"Active Design Reviews" features the review style that tries to improve effect by assigning reviewers the active review tasks that are carefully structured in order to eliminate the chance that reviews behave slackly on their duties. This is achieved, for example, by avoiding the questions that expect the "yes/no" answers. The target of ADR is to guarantee the actual consideration and understanding of the reviewed designs. ADR mainly depends on individually debriefing the reviews, which is not so effective in encouraging group buy-in.

The ATAM, however, will collect all kinds of stakeholders to carry out evaluation, and adopt evaluation techniques such as utility trees or analysis of architectural approaches. This is facilitated to evaluate the entire architecture, not to the preliminary designs, which may be short of detailed information. Besides that, complex evaluation techniques are also not necessary for intermediate designs.

ARID, created by CMU SEI, is the hybrid of ADR and scenario-based evaluation methods, providing useful techniques for preliminary designs (Clements, 2000). It contains 6 steps within 2 phases as shown in Table 7.7. They are self-explained, but the techniques used are something tricky and will be introduced in below.

- **Special Goal**: ARID is a lightweight review method for insuring the quality-detailed design in software with active driven techniques to avoid reviewers' carelessly-considered participating.
- **Quality Attribute**: Due to target not to architecture evaluation, but only checking the suitability of preliminary design, ARID does not focus on specific quality attributes. As a matter of fact, it is more like a test that the users of this design decide whether it can be used.

Table 7. 7   Phases and Steps in ARID

Phases	Steps
Phase 1: Pre-meeting	Step 1: Identify reviewers
	Step 2: Prepare design presentation
	Step 3: Prepare seed scenarios
	Step 4: Prepare for the review meeting
Phase 2: Review-meeting	Step 5: Present ARID method
	Step 6: Present design
	Step 7: Brainstorm and prioritize scenarios
	Step 8: Perform review
	Step 9: Present conclusions

- **SA Description**: No detailed information documents are required. This method can be performed in the early design phase when complete documents have not been finished, or to be part of software in the case that other parts' design information is unavailable. When certain architecture information is urgently needed, architect has the duty to take reasonable assumptions.
- **Involved Stakeholders**: ARID combines the concept "reviews" of ADR with "stakeholders" used in scenario-based methods, and divides them into three classes. The first one is lead designer who is the spokesperson presenting the design and following the review result. The second one is reviews, including various people who have the vested interests in the project. Among them, software engineers, the users of this design, are the direct benefit-gainers, and thus the most important participants. The third one is review team, where three roles should be filled. A facilitator helps preparing and running the review; a scribe is responsible of capturing reviews' input and result; and one or more questioners will facilitate eliciting and craft scenarios. Optionally, there is an additional role, process observer, who can record the encountered difficulties and provide suggestions for improving method.
- **Scenario Development**: Scenario development is split into two steps existing in each phase. In the pre-meeting phase, seed scenarios are generated to allow reviews' insight about what scenarios are suitable. In the review-meeting phase, a brainstorm on scenario generating is taken, in which various scenarios about how to "use" the design are proposed. All of them, including the seed scenarios, are put into the "candidate scenario pool", waiting for the prioritization process, which is usually based on voting. The most critical scenarios are identified to put as the standard of this review.
- **Evaluation Techniques**: ARID insists the ground rule that it inspects the

use of a design, not the rationale behind it, or other possible alternatives. This rule reflects in detail techniques among the review. For example, when the lead designer presents the overview of design, he or she has to concentrate on how to use that design and what services it provides. In the review step, for each scenario, the reviews simulate using that design, even in an extensive way by craft code (or pseudo code) to finish the task they concern, during which designers are not allowed to give any hints or help. But reviewers can ask designers to explain something they care. Another technique that features ARID is its activeness. To guarantee the high-fidelity review result, reviewers are forced to finish their job, such as reading design documents or making suggestions, with effort. Any questions that can be answered perfunctorily, for instance, with simple "yes" or "no", are banned, all of which are replaced with exercises that reviews have to take carefully. For example, the question "Are there any exceptions defined for every program?" is substituted by "Write down the exceptions that can occur in every program." The question "Are the program sufficient?" is replaced with "Write down the pseudo code that uses this design to complete a certain program task."

- **Validation**: ARID has been applied in a pilot control system. You can find this study case in (Clements, 2000) or (Clements, 2003b).
- **Support Tool**: There is no support tool available for ARID.

7.4.2.11   CBAM: Cost-Benefit Analysis Method

CBAM introduces cost-benefit into the consideration of decision making during architecture design. During architecture evaluation, sponsors or organizations have adequate reasons to expand their economic gains and avoid risks as much as they can. Other evaluation methods, some pay attention to a single quality attribute, e.g. PASA; some focus on trade-off among various quality targets, e.g. ATAM; and some lean to evaluation knowledge's reusability, e.g. ESAAMI. But most of them take the assumption that the stakeholders only care about software's quality without any cost limitation. Even so, this concern is ignored in evaluation methods' abstract description, and only appears in an informal manner when evaluation is applied. CBAM correct this problem by taking into account the finite resource (Asundi, 2001; Kazman, 2001a; Kazman, 2001b).

- **Special Goal**: The CBAM helps system's stakeholders get the information of cost and, possibly more important, benefit which are resulted from the architecture decisions, and thus guide them to choose a certain architectural alternative under finite resource concerns. From Fig. 7.19 we can find that business goal drives the architecture decisions, which incur cost and achieve some quality attributes, such as P, A, S, M (representing Performance, Availability, Security and Modifiability). They in turn lead to economic implications for the benefits. CBAM's ultimate goal is to identify these cost and benefits, and maximizes their difference.
- **Quality Attribute**: CBAM attaches the cost and benefits analysis information to the corresponding quality attributes. In this way, stakeholders

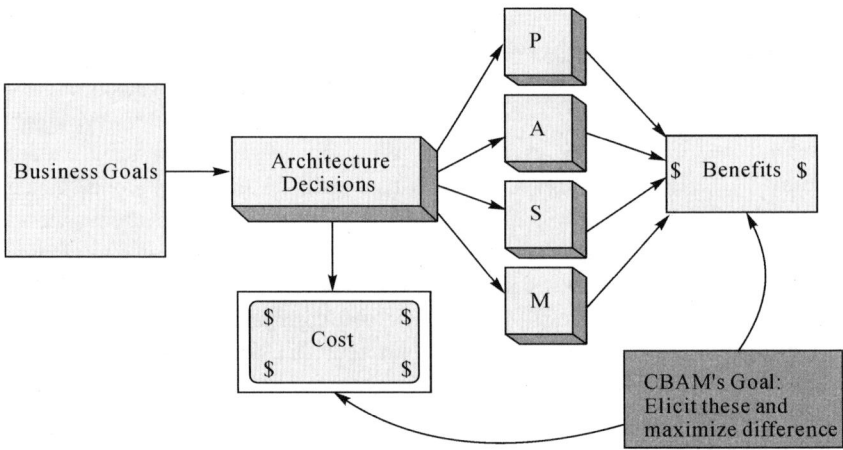

Fig. 7. 19   Context of CBAM

have the chance to make the decision that put most resource to the best
architecture strategy that increases benefits.

- **SA Description:** Only the architecture strategies which are clear enough for
  performing cost and benefit analysis are required.
- **Involved Stakeholders:** All the key stakeholders should take part in this
  evaluation. It is feasible that project managers decide which stakeholders are
  the key ones and necessary to be present.
- **Scenario Development:** Scenarios are generated just as ATAM to provide
  the concrete representation of quality attributes.
- **Evaluation Techniques:** Two phases are employed in this method. The first
  one is "Triage Phase", which means various architecture strategies are
  estimated cursorily. For example, architecture strategies' influence on quality
  attributes is rated with a five-point scale (++, +, 0, -, --) and their costs are
  estimated with three-point scale (High, Medium, Low). Those strategies with
  comprehensively high benefits and low cost are kept. Of course, some
  strategies, due to law or the standards, have to be reserved either, although
  they seem not so "good". The second one is "Detailed Examination Phase",
  where a more precise and quantitative model is used for estimating each
  architecture strategy's "Return on Investment" (ROI). Each quality
  attribute's importance is weighted as "QAScore", which has to fulfill the
  rule:

$$\sum_{j} \text{QAScore}_j = 100 \ \wedge \ \forall \ \text{QAScore}_j \geqslant 0$$

Architecture strategies' influence is also quantified as "ContriScore" with a
value during +1 to -1. Therefore, for each architecture strategy AS_i against
each quality attribute QA_j, its benefit value is:

$$\text{Benefit}(AS_i) = \sum_{j} \text{ContriScore}_{i,j} \times \text{QAScore}_j$$

The QAScore and ContriScore can be gained through voting. And then, each architecture strategy's cost is estimated by some methods, which is not limited by CBAM. Therefore, the return value of architecture strategies is calculated:

$$\text{Return}(AS_i) = \frac{\text{Benefit}(AS_i)}{\text{Cost}(AS_i)}$$

Finally, different strategies are ranked as their mean return value, together with some other concerns. This is under the assumptions that the distribution of return values is symmetric among the mean value. For more precise estimation, a more complex probability-based evaluation model and a Portfolio Theory Framework have also been developed.

- **Validation**: CBAM has been applied in NASA's Earth Observing System Data Information System (EOSDIS) Core System (ECS) which is still under development.
- **Support Tool**: There is no support tool published for CBAM.

7. 5 Summary

In this chapter, we inspect one of the most important activities based on architecture information—architecture evaluation. After all, if we have no handy tool like this, we cannot identify our architecture's suitability for quality requirements, especially when formalized methods cannot be applied in real projects well. Therefore, developers have to hold tests after accomplishment of part of codes, which will incur high, or even infeasible, cost and time-to-market. The reason why architecture evaluation takes effect is that software's quality is primarily determined by architecture. Never be doubt about this point, which has been demonstrated by thousands of development. The difficulty is, however, to find the bridge linking quality and architecture. Even that, evaluation is neither solving an equation or model purely, nor following a set of fixed steps. Most techniques are to encourage people to make use of the comprehensive ideas from them. Although we describe certain evaluation methods' steps, they are actually still reference to allow easy understanding. Practitioners should vary them according to what they want and what they need.

Before evaluation, software quality has to be defined and measured first. In this chapter, it is decomposed to several quality attributes, which further can be described in the format of scenarios. Scenarios, which can be defined precisely, avoid the ambiguous quality description. It is scenario that opens the gate to evaluation, because nobody is capable of assessing something that cannot be expressed and measured clearly. In short, scenario is the bridge we expect.

Most architecture evaluation methods are designed based on scenarios. We introduce two most famous evaluation methods, SAAM and ATAM, in detail. SAAM is an intrinsic method that searches affected architectural elements against scenarios, while ATAM, on the basis of SAAM, focuses on identifying potential risks, non-risks, sensitivities and trade-offs.

SAAM and ATAM expose the impression of common features of most scenario-based evaluation methods. They get the input of scenarios and architecture description, evaluate and judge whether current architecture (or several architecture candidates) is capable of meeting desired quality requirements. Potential defects and risks are identified, which then become the motivation of modification. Finally, raw evaluation results are collected and prepared for the following use, such as hints of future development or historical data accumulated for reuse.

From various varied editions of SAAM to the new CBAM, they follow the similar process as mentioned above. But each of them owns its unique concerns. SAAM is simple and particularly effective to evaluation system's modifiability, hence suitable for small and evolution-required system. ATAM is far more complicated, and it combines lots of information and identifies the places needing urgent attentions against desired quality attributes and clarifies why architecture looks like what it is before evaluation. Therefore, ATAM is good at large projects, particularly for those involving many undetermined factors. Some methods focus on one single quality attribute. If you care about maintainability, you may choose ALPSM. If you want to analyze performance, PASA should be your assistant. For cost concerns, then, CBAM is the best choice. Via reading the brief introduction to eleven methods and learning their features, you can find which one is what you want under specific needs, even though you do not know how it is performed exactly. For doing that, you should read reference materials specifically on them.

We emphasize again that do not use those evaluation methods by rote. Some of them are still in research. Some others have been verified, but may be ineffective in different environment. Reality is flexible, thus it needs flexible solution. Just remember the principles, think about why evaluation is so useful (we wrote them above). Maybe sometimes you will create some brand-new methods that earn numerous benefits in your job.

References

(Abowd, 1997)   Abowd, G., et al. Recommended Best Industrial Practice for Software Architecture Evaluation, Techincal Report, CMU/SEI-96-TR-025, 1997.

(Allen, 1997)   Allen, R. & Garlan, D. A Formal Basis for Architectural Connection. ACM Transactions on Software Engineering and Methodology 1997 (6): 213-249.

(Asundi, 2001)   Asundi, J., Kazman, R. & Klein, M. Using Economic Considerations to Choose among Architecture Design Alternatives, Techincal Report, CMU/SEI-2001-TR-035, 2001.

(Babar, 2004)   Babar, M. A. & Gorton, I. Comparison of Scenario-Based Software Architecture Evaluation Methods. In: Software Engineering Conference, 2004.

11th Asia-Pacific, pp. 600-607.2004.

(Bachmann, 2003)   Bachmann, F., Bass, L. & Klein, M. Preliminary Design of Arche: A Software Architecture Design Assistant, Techincal Report, CMU/ SEI-2003-TR-021, 2003.

(Barbacci, 1998)   Barbacci, M., et al. Steps in an Architecture Tradeoff Analysis Mehtod: Quality Attribute Models and Analysis, Techincal Report, CMU/ SEI-97-TR-029, 1998.

(Bass, 1998)   Bass, L., Clements, P. & Kazman, R. Software Architecture in Practice, 1st ed.: Addison Wesley/Pearson 1998d.

(Bass, 2003)   Bass, L., Clements, P. & Kazman, R. Software Architecture in Practice, 2nd ed.: Addison Wesley/Pearson 2003.

(Bengtsson, 1998)   Bengtsson, P. & Bosch, J. Scenario-Based Software Architecture Reengineering. Proceedings Fifth International Conference on Software Reuse, Victoria, BC, Canada.1998:308-317.

(Bengtsson, 1999)   Bengtsson, P. & Bosch, J. Architecture Level Prediction of Software Maintenance. Proceedings of the Third European Conference on Software Maintenance and Reengineering, Amsterdam, Netherlands. 1999: 139-147.

(Boehm, 1976)   Boehm, B., Brown, J. & Lipow, M. Quantitative Evaluation of Software Quality. Proceedings of the 2nd international conference on software engineering, San Francisco, California, United States.1976:592-605.

(Boehm, 1986)   Boehm, B. A Spiral Model of Software Development and Enhancement. ACM SIGSOFT Software Engineering Notes 1986(11): 14-24.

(Bot, 1996)   Bot, S., Lung, C. H. & Farrell, M. A Stakeholder-Centric Software Architecture Analysis. Approach Joint proceedings of the second international software architecture workshop (ISAW-2), San Francisco, California, United States.1996:152-154.

(Brown, 1998)   Brown, W., et al. Antipatterns: Refactoring Software, Architectures, and Projects in Crisis. New York: John Wiley & Sons.1998.

(Chidamber, 1991)   Chidamber, S. R. & Kemerer, C. F. Towards a Metrics Suite for Object Oriented Design. Conference proceedings on Object-oriented programming systems, languages, and applications. Phoenix, Arizona, United States.1991:197-211.

(Clements, 2000)   Clements, P. Active Reviews for Intermediate Designs, Techincal Report, CMU/SEI-2000-TN-009 2000.

(Clements, 2003)   Clements, P., Kazman, R. & Klein, M. Evaluating Software Architectures: Methods and Case Studies. Pearson Education.2003.

(Dobrica, 2002)   Dobrica, L. & Niemela, E. A Survey on Software Architecture Analysis Methods. Software Engineering, IEEE Transactions on 2002 (28): 638-653.

(Duenas, 1998)   Duenas, J. C., de Oliveira, W. L. & de la Puente, J. A. A Software Architecture Evaluation Model. In: Development and Evolution of Software Architectures for Product Families. Second International ESPIRIT ARES

Workshop. Proceedings (van der Linden, F., ed., pp. 148-157. Springer-Verlag, Las Palmas de Gran Canaria, Spain.1998.

(IEEE, 1989a)   IEEE. *IEEE Standard Dictionary of Measures to Produce Reliable Software*.1989a.

(IEEE, 1989b)   IEEE. *IEEE Guide for the Use of IEEE Standard Dictionary of Measures to Produce Reliable Software*.1989b.

(IEEE, 1998)   IEEE. *IEEE Standard for a Software Quality Metrics Methodology*. 1998.

(Inverardi, 2000)   Inverardi, P., Wolf, A. L. & Yankelevich, D. Static Checking of System Behaviors Using Derived Component Assumptions. *ACM Transactions on Software Engineering and Methodology* 2000(9): 239-272.

(Kazman, 1994)   Kazman, R., et al. Saam: A Method for Analyzing the Properties of Software Architectures. *Proceedings of 16th International Conference on Software Engineering*, Sorrento, Italy.1994:81-90.

(Kazman, 1996a)   Kazman, R. Tool Support for Architecture Analysis and Design. In: *Joint proceedings of the second international software architecture workshop (ISAW-2) and international workshop on multiple perspectives in software development (Viewpoints '96) on SIGSOFT '96 workshops* pp. 94-97. ACM Press San Francisco, California, United States 1996a.

(Kazman, 1996b)   Kazman, R., et al. Scenario-Based Analysis of Software Architecture. *Software, IEEE* 1996b(13): 47-55.

(Kazman, 1998)   Kazman, R., et al. The Architecture Tradeoff Analysis Method. *Proceedings Fourth IEEE International Conference on Engineering of Complex Computer Systems*. ICECCS '98, Monterey, CA, USA.1998:68-78.

(Kazman, 1999)   Kazman, R., et al. Experience with Performing Architecture Tradeoff Analysis. *Proceedings of the 1999 International Conference on Software Engineering*. Acm.1999.

(Kazman, 2000)   Kazman, R., Carrière, S. J. & Woods, S. G. Toward a Discipline of Scenario-Based Architectural Engineering. *Annals Of Software Engineering* 2000(9): 5-33.

(Kazman, 2001a)   Kazman, R., Asundi, J. & Klein, M. Making Architecture Design Decisions: An Economic Approach, *Techincal Report*, CMU/SEI-2001-TR-035, 2001a.

(Kazman, 2001b)   Kazman, R., Asundi, J. & Klein, M. Quantifying the Costs and Benefits of Architectural Decisions.2001b:297-306.

(Klein, 1993)   Klein, M., et al. *A Practitioner's Handbook for Real-Time Analysis*. Norwell, MA, USA: Kluwer Academic Publishers.1993.

(Lüthi, 1997)   Lüthi, J., et al. Performance Bounds for Distributed Systems with Workload Variabilities and Uncertainties. *Parallel Computing* 1997 (22): 1789-1806.

(Lassing, 1999)   Lassing, N., Rijsenbrij, D. & Viliet, H. On Software Architecture Analysis of Flexibility, Complexity of Changes: Size Isn't Everything. *Proceeding of the Second Nordic Software Architecture Workshop (NOSA'99)*.

1999:1103-1581.

(Li, 1993) Li, W. & Henry, S. Object-Oriented Metrics That Predict Maintainability. *Journal of Systems and Software* 1993(23): 111-122.

(Lung, 1997) Lung, C. H., et al. An Approach to Software Architecture Analysis for Evolution and Reusability In: *Proceedings of the 1997 conference of the Centre for Advanced Studies on Collaborative research*, CASCON '97, pp. 15-26. IBM Press, Toronto, Ontario, Canada.1997.

(Maheshwari, 2005) Maheshwari, P. & Teoh, A. Supporting Atam with a Collaborative Web-Based Software Architecture Evaluation Tool. *Science of Computer Programming* 2005(57): 109-128.

(Majumdar, 1991) Majumdar, S., et al. Performance Bounds for Concurrent Software with Rendezvous. *Performance Evaluation* 1991(13): 207-236.

(Marco, 2004) Marco, A. D. & Inverardi, P. Compositional Generation of Software Architecture Performance Qn Models. *Proceedings. on the Fourth Working IEEE/IFIP Conference on Software Architecture* (WICSA 2004), Oslo, Norway.2004:37-46.

(Molter, 1999) Molter, G. Integrating Saam in Domain-Centric and Reuse-Based Development Processes. In: *Proceedings of the 2nd Nordic Workshop on Software Architecture*, Ronneby, Sweden.1999.

(Parnas, 1985) Parnas, D. L. & Weiss, D. M. Active Design Reviews: Principles and Practice. *Proceedings of the 8th international conference on Software engineering* Longdon, England.1985:132-136.

(Smith, 2000) Smith, C. U. & Williams, L. G. Software Performance Antipatterns. *Proceedings of WOSP2000: Second International Workshop on Software and Performance*, Ottawa, Ont., Canada.2000:127-136.

(Smith, 2001) Smith, C. U. & Williams, L. G. *Performance Solutions: A Practical Guide to Creating Responsive, Scalable Software*: Addison-Wesley.2001.

(Uchitel, 2003) Uchitel, S., Kramer, J. & Magee, J. Behaviour Model Elaboration Using Partial Labelled Transition Systems. *Proceedings of the 9th European software engineering conference held jointly with 11th ACM SIGSOFT international symposium on Foundations of software engineering* Helsinki, Finland.2003:19-27.

(Williams, 2002a) Williams, L. G. & Smith, C. U. Pasa: An Architectural Approach to Fixing Software Performance Problems. In: *Proc. of Int. Conference of the Computer Measurement Group*, Reno, USA.2002a.

(Williams, 2002b) Williams, L. G. & Smith, C. U. Pasa: A Method for the Performance Assessment of Software Architecture. In: *Proc. of the 3rd Workshop on Software Performance*, Rome, Italy.2002b.

(Zhang, 2001) Zhang, B., Ding, K. & Li, J. An Xml-Message Based Architecture Description Language and Architectural Mismatch Checking. *Proceedings of the 25th International Computer Software and Applications Conference on Invigorating Software Development* (COMPSAC 2001), Beijing, China.2001: 561-566.

8

Flexible Software Architecture

So far, we assume that every software system contains architecture information, representing the high level structures, behaviors and other issues related to them. When a system has been built, it is a common belief that its architecture will keep stable or only very small parts of it will get modified. However, current software does not stay so tame. Under various factors, they have to response with the changes in the architecture level, and in the perspective of marketing, which should not beget too much overhead.

In this concern, the term "Flexible Software Architecture" (FSA) emerges to indicate a kind of architecture that enables changes during runtime under context's mutation and further a series of methods to analyze and validate the change cases. FSA embraces, rather than resists, the requirements expecting changes such as addition and removal of components and reconfigurations of software elements. Two aspects of issues are involved in architecture's flexibility. The first one is architecture's dynamism, which means an architecture allowing occurrences of changes; another one is the stimuli that trigger the change of architecture, such as environment awareness or users' instructions.

Performing design in the architecture level is difficult and complex where you have to take trade-off among the interdependent or conflict requirements. Performing design of flexible architecture is even harder, which forces you to consider software as a piece of sponge, rather than a rigid wood cube. In this way, you may want to avoid the risks incurred by flexibility or hate to deal with the similar decision-making to the change again and again. In this chapter, we discuss FSA, including its motivations and existent solutions and experiences. We will show how architecture researchers handle this problem with different ideas and skills. After understanding them, people will know that the flexibility is absolutely not changes out of control, but actions under monitoring and validation.

8.1   What Is Flexibility for

Software development is a business. Although requirement collecting, designing, programming, testing, maintenance or the like seems everything development should do, all of them do not concern the ultimate target of why these actions have to be done. In most cases, commercial benefit is the target. Today, more and more economic activities rely on software system in achieving their business goals. However, this environment is capricious, which must be reflected in the support software, otherwise software will lose its compatibility and meaning of existence.

Much effort has been paid to dealing with this issue. Extensibility currently becomes one of the most important quality attributes in software development area, although concentrating on it too much will draw overhead in performance. Developers of operating systems may hope they can be easily migrated to various hardware platforms; developers of applications may hope they should be easy to add some new features or language supports with less effort; developers of service provider server may hope those services can be customized to fit for customers' needs. Those are all the examples of changes, more precisely, in the level of program construction. Some design patterns focus on them, such as Factory, Mediator, or Visitor. In this case, you can follow the original design, and add, delete or modify some elements, rebuild, test and finally release a new edition that satisfies your needs.

But this is not flexibility in that the changes are achieved by programmers. Software can change until it is first shut down and then keep sleep during modification, just like a person who takes the surgery operation. What we want is the change that software achieves by itself, similar to the process of skin's becoming darker under insolation. In this kind of change, designers and programmers prepare something necessary and start the software, which can handle some change requirements automatically.

Maybe you believe that a good preference setting will work well in this case. Indeed, a comprehensive setting gives the user freedom to fine tune the application. The large scale systems such as Microsoft Visual Studio or Eclipse have hundreds of setting items. Essentially, they are a batch of switches of features, whose changes only affect appearance of build-in functions. But from Chapter 7, we should aware that software systems' quality attributes are decided by their runtime architecture. In some situations, we need to change architecture to improve performance, availability or add components bringing about new functions. Although by changes of program construction, architecture can be changed, sometimes it is intolerable. In large distributed continuous running systems, like telephone switching systems, banking systems, mobile systems, the offline status is undesirable for their high availability, where FSA is very useful.

There is another benefit of FSA prior to the traditional architecture. That is the separation of codes for business and for architecture adaptation. The adaptation part of FSA is common to many applications which means it can be abstracted and implemented as a utility. The style of mixture of business and architecture adaptation cannot be understood and analyzed easily. Practice tells us excessive "if else" statements, in more cases, incur the consequence of chaos. In the contrary, the separated adaptation part makes changes and validation easier, while facilitating reuse.

At last, a side effect of FSA is it explicitly keeps the architecture information which maintains the synchronization with the real global perspectives on the whole system. This is a common realization of FSA, which on the one hand avoids trouble of synchronizing manually or extracting architecture from source codes (a normal process before extending a legacy system); on the other hand makes the runtime change convenient because a sequence of complex actions contributing to changes has the foundation to coordinate.

Here are two examples of applying FSA. The mobile middleware encounters the conflict among heterogeneity and limit computation and storage resource. To enable as more services as possible, mobile middleware has to access different networking and gets service descriptor by different protocols. The desktop middleware handles this by installing every possibly used components, which mobile device cannot afford. FSA allows to dynamically load and activate the necessary components that are necessary under a specific context while removing the ones temporarily useless. That is not easy because the running applications may depend on the components to be removed. An invasive removal will make the whole runtime crush. FSA should avoid this case by validation before changing the architecture.

The other example is a shared file system. This system makes use of several interconnected computers, and distributes files among them. Its architecture is flexible to dynamically adjust the amount of occupancy in each computer, concerning their free space and access pattern. The location of administrator component and file fragments varies during its running to provide the most rapid response to the users who frequently access the file. When some involved computers are shut down, the system carries the fragments on them to the available ones. In this case, the shared file system has to record the physical location and status of its architectural elements.

Looking around, you may find there have been lots of systems capable of self-adaptive, self-healing or plug-ins loading. They may be developed under a strict validation in various ad-hoc methods to pretend potential risks that could lead to errors of disasters, or even constructed directly employing only simple tests or guesses. We often imagine the future of software, which is an entity alive and able to response under changed context by self protecting, generating and at last evolving. But current methods and technologies still stay in an initial state. They need refinement and improvement. FSA is an ideal start point to change this situation and even realize the dream.

8.2   Dynamic Software Architecture

So what is dynamic software architecture exactly? If we simplify the term "software architecture" to the collection of runtime components, connectors and their relationships, we can change each of them, or any of their combinations. They are not exiguous in current software area, especially in the distributed systems which can be configured. Some researchers prefer the term "dynamic configuration" to indicate the runtime change capability of the field above. (Cuesta, 2001) separates the dynamism into three levels by analyzing their implicit distinction. The first level is called "interactive dynamism", requiring the dynamic communication of data in a fixed structure; the second level, "structural dynamism", allows the modification of structures, usually expressed as the creation and removal of component and connector instances, which seems prevalent in most current researches and real projects; the third level, named "architectural dynamism" is able to describe the change of architecture's infrastructure upon which all the instance elements are defined, such as component or connector types. Cuesta insists that only the third [1] level deserves the term "dynamic architecture".

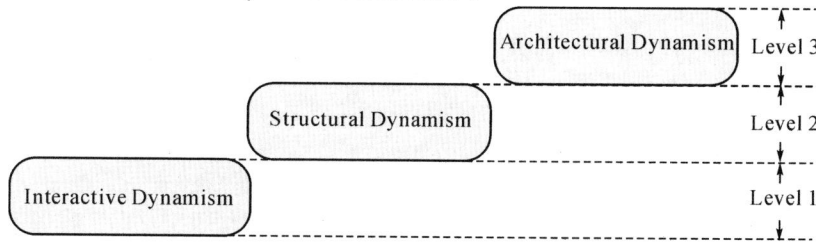

Fig. 8. 1   Dynamism of three levels

(Bradbury, 2004) gives a more general definition: " dynamic software architectures modify their architecture and enact the modifications during the system's execution". If elements in the architecture can be modified during runtime guided the predefined rules, it is considered as dynamic architecture. However, he extrudes the actions of initialization, selection and assessment of the changes without the assistance of external users, and defines the term " self-managing software architecture".

We tend to define dynamic architecture as "the architecture capable of performing changes in some elements of it under control and validation during runtime". We believe any elements' runtime changes should be categorized into the range of dynamic architecture. And at the same time, the arbitrary changes are meaningless because correctness cannot be guaranteed. During the change, validation by some methods, such as formal checking, is absolutely necessary for dynamic architecture. After all, we do not want software to execute to the state of chaos.

Dynamic software architecture is not a framework, a set of primitives or a theory with which we can model or identify roles in it. Just like design patterns, it is actually a general idea to drive the design if dynamism is identified as a required function. To achieve dynamism of different levels under different other conditions and constraints, the solutions are different. That is why there are lots of models and description infrastructures that have been published so far. We categorize mainstream trend of research as perspectives, and introduce the notable examples delegating them. Three perspectives are identified. They are the behavior perspective, which describes the behaviors leading to dynamism with process algebra; the reflection perspective, which models the meta-information explicitly upon reflection theory; and the coordination perspective, which focuses on the separation of computing and coordination part and handle interactions with coordination primitives. For each of them, we start from the general idea of a perspective, then introduce the classic formal method of it, and finally depict an ADL or model based on that. Although they overlap to some extent, such as that reflection in fact borrows the mind of coordination, and behavior-centered description may use the paradigm introduced by reflection and coordination, they have their own features and benefits.

There is still another kind of perspective that models dynamism with graph-base approach. It is a rather natural way to specify system's reconfiguration by setting rules of graph rewriting. However, it is inherently weak in describing behaviors. And they will become hard to manipulate and inspect when system's structure gets complicated, which pays off its benefit of intuition. Even this, it has been adopted in numerous projects since its simplicity. For the same reason, we do not want to spend a lot of time to introduce them. Readers who are interested in it can read materials about CHAM approach (Wermelinger, 1998), Hirsh et al. approach (Hirsch, 1998), CommUnity approach (Wermelinger, 2001), Taentzer et al. approach (Taentzer, 1998) and Métayer approach (Métayer, 1998).

8.2.1   π-ADL: A Behavior Perspective

Generally, architecture can be split into two parts of descriptions: structures-related and behavior-related. In dynamic software architecture, the focus has been placed on the behaviors that change its structures during runtime. Thereby, the key point is to find formal methods describing those behaviors, facilitating describing and validating. Parts of those formal foundations are identified as "process algebra", which has an intrinsic modular nature which makes it particularly useful for the description of composition structures, especially in the runtime viewpoint. In it, behaviors that execute in a sequential style are abstracted as a process. Thus communications of behaviors are simplified as composition of processes.

In the static architecture period, it was a common methodology to extend or modify a kind of process algebra to fit for the needs of architecture description. WRIGHT, which was mentioned in Chapter 4, is a case, which borrows the idea of CSP. Dynamic WRIGHT (Allen, 1998) is a progressive attempt to port WRIGHT to dynamic architecture. However, CSP itself does not support dynamic behavior. To complement this, Dynamic WRIGHT introduces special operations for control and an abstract entity named "configuror", which are responsible of altering configuration of the system during execution. They are essentially static, or at most able to describe parallel systems that communicate with each other.

For dynamic architecture, "process" should be able to perform operations on its host, normally a component or a connector, which includes changing their states of lives (add, activate, deactivate, remove, and so on), resetting their relationships with others (bind, unbind and so on) or evolving the internal structures of them. One of the most popular formal languages currently is π-calculus (Sangiorgi, 2001), a process algebra that is designed to model mobile system, which naturally own dynamic software architecture.

π-calculus separates mobility into two categories: the first one is link mobility, meaning that the changes of link relationships in the abstract space of processes. In π-calculus, links themselves can be transferred during other links, which may trigger an arbitrary change of system's configuration. For example, when a mobile phone that has created a connection with a fixed server moves around, which dynamically changes this reference, other mobile terminals can acquire this reference during runtime in the form of return result of such as an update method, and thus they can also correctly connect with that server at any time. π-calculus abstracts this kind of mobility as two basic entities, (link) names and processes, where processes can interact through links that share the identical names. Names are allowed to be sent or received during interaction. By getting a name, a process can interact with other processes that it is completely unaware of. This can be easily used for modeling share, a critical abstraction discussed more by coordination perspective as explained in the Section 8.2.3.

Another kind of mobility is the movement of process itself in the abstract space. It is an abstraction of code mobility that some components leave their birth place and get executed in some other hosts, helped by networking or the like. In this way, a device, such as a mobile phone, a laptop computer or an embedded device, can gain new functionalities. A kind of high level mobility, termed as "mobile agent" (Fuggetta, 1998), is a typical case where a whole computational component is moved among a networking and executes according to instructions or its internal states affected by environment on an arbitrary remote site. π-calculus examines a sub-theory based on process passing, called "Higher-Order π-calculus" (calculus based on name passing mentioned in the first kind of mobility is termed as "First-Order calculus").

π-calculus does not explicitly model locations. You cannot find any entity in π-calculus that is designed to be mapped to location information. This, however, should be concerned as a freedom rather than a drawback. Through name passing and process passing, one can easily refine it with the right additional notations in the right abstract level to meet one's particular needs, which maybe, for instance, require exchange of links, exchange of processes and any combination of them. Similarly, the link in π-calculus is also a general term that can be construed very broadly. For instance one can reify link as a physical network link in a distributed system, a logical channel for data transferring among components or a reference to use an object. Also, names of links can be naturally adopted as location identifiers when they are critical for design.

This book will not introduce the detailed syntax and semantics of π-calculus. For this target, we recommend (Sangiorgi, 2001) or (Parrow, 2001). But we will simply list its basic syntax for enlightening. The ν processes and the summations are given in the following grammar.

$$P::=M\,|\,P\,|\,P'\,|\,vzP\,|\,!\;P$$
$$M::=0\,|\,\pi.\;P\,|\,M+M'$$

More particularly, the grammar indicates notation system of π-calculus:

- 0 is inaction, a process doing nothing, which is often used as the end of expression.
- π is prefix representing actions which will be mentioned in detail later. When a prefix is finished, the subsequent process proceeds continuously.
- $+$ (Summation Operator) means selection. If two processes P and P' connected with this operator, only one of them will be exercised, leaving another one lost.
- $|$ (Parallel Composition Operator) indicates independent execution in parallel. $P\,|\,P'$ means these two processes perform their capabilities respectively, with possible communication by shared names.
- ν (Restriction Operator) limits the scope of name. vzP indicates that the name z is restricted locally in the process P, which cannot communicate with its environment through z, but can use z within P.
- ! (Replication Operator) is a short term equivalent to an infinite processes connected by parallel composition operator, which means a process can be executed repeatedly.

Processes evolve by performing actions, which are expressed via prefixes, termed as π, falling into four categories:

$$\pi::=\overline{x}y\,|\,x(z)\,|\,\tau\,|\,[\mathbf{boolean}]\pi$$

- $\overline{x}y$(Output Prefix) means "via the name x send the name y"
- $x(z)$ (Input Prefix) means "via the name x receive the name z"
- τ (Unobservable Prefix) represents a invisible action to its subsequent process. For example, $\tau.\;P$ will evolve to P without any interaction with environment.
- $[\mathbf{boolean}]\pi$ (Conditional Prefix) performs the prefix denoted as π when the boolean expression holds, which normally contains two kinds. The first one is match condition, in the form of $[x = y]$; while the second one is mismatch condition, in the form of $[x \neq y]$.

Take the mobile phone mentioned earlier in this section for example. There is a fixed server S, an intermediate mobile phone A and another phone B that connects to S through A, as drawn in Fig.8.2. It can be expressed as:

$$\overline{b}a.\;A\,|\,b(c).\;(\overline{c}d+c(e)).\;B$$

where on the one side A sends the link a through B to the outside while on the other side B gets a link through b and either sends d or gets e via that link. (We assume that d is a link accessing some data from B and e is a link accessing some data from S, both of which are not illustrated in the figure). By combining them, a is essentially acquired by B via which B and S can interact with each other. The result system is expressed as:

$$A \mid (\bar{a}d + a(e)). B$$

π-calculus also introduces concept of type. An assignment of a type to a name can be written in the form of $a : T$, where a is a name, termed "name of the assignment", and T is a type, termed "type of the assignment". Three kinds of types are introduced by π-calculus, that is, value type, link type and behavior type. Value types can be assigned to the value objects that can be exchanged via links. Link types can be assigned to the links through which communications are taken. One link type can be defined as the value types

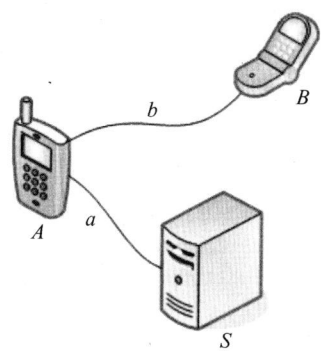

Fig. 8.2 π-Calculus example

permitted to be exchanged in the link. And finally, behavior types can be assigned to processes. Behavior types are the basis of Higher-Order π-calculus. Links, value objects and processes can be unified as names, based on which a type environment is defined: a finite set of assignments of types to names, where all the names of assignments are distinct.

Higher-Order π-calculus is an extension of typed π-calculus by involving process passing. The objects transmitted in interactions can be a typed process. To achieve this, the Higher-Order output prefix form is:

$$\bar{a}\langle P : T \rangle. Q$$

which means "via the name a send the process P and then continue execution as Q". And the Higher-Order input prefix form is:

$$a(X : T). Q$$

which means "via the name a receive the process X and then continue execution as Q". In both prefixes, the type parameter T may be omitted if they are not important. After the receive action, Q may employ the process represented by X, and a replace will occur. Follow the example above, if the server S wants A to send data to B by transmitting a mobile agent, while A can do something else in parallel. The interaction can be expressed as:

$$\bar{a}\langle \bar{b}e. 0 \rangle. S \mid a(X). (X \mid b(u)). A$$

In this interaction, S sends an agent capable of sending e via b. In parallel, A receives this agent by shared name a and this agent is activated in parallel with the job of A itself $(b(u))$. Finally, it can be transferred to:

$$S \mid (\bar{b}e \mid b(u)). A$$

Several ADLs adopts π-calculus as their formalism foundation, including DARWIN (Magee, 1995), π-space (Chaudet, 2001), Con Moto (Gruhn, 2004; Clemens, 2006) and π-ADL (Oquendo, 2004a). Among them, π-ADL is a typical refinement of Higher-Order π-calculus, especially for those requiring dynamism and mobility. In this concern, we give a more detailed introduction to it.

π-ADL, or called ArchWare ADL, models the system with a runtime viewpoint, which is comprised of components, connectors as well as behavior, any of which may evolve over time. Components and connectors are both represented as a set of external ports and internal behaviors, but different in architectural roles: components are the abstraction of software elements performing certain computation or maintaining the access of data; and connectors' role is communication channel between architectural elements. Ports are described as a set of connections attached by communication protocols. Connection is the minimal unit via which a certain kind of object can be transmitted. Three modes of connection can be set: output (objects can only be sent), input (objects can only be received) and input-output (bidirectional exchange of data is allowed). One port can contain an arbitrary number of connections. It can be viewed as the counterpart of notation "link" in π-calculus. π-ADL does not allow a direct connection between two components. In order to take communication, components have to put a connector between them. The model established by π-ADL is shown in Fig.8.3.

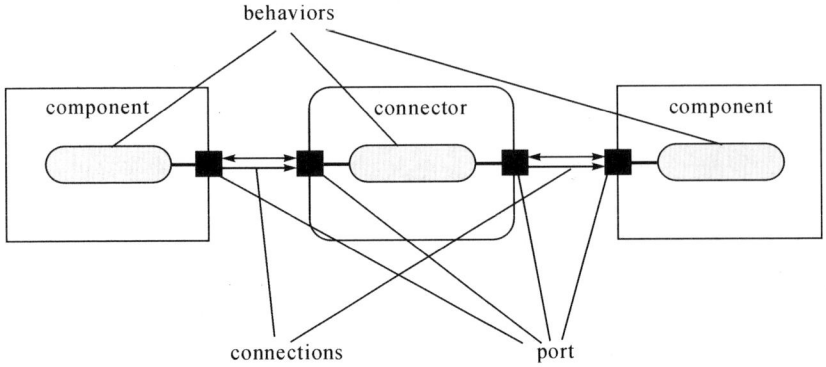

Fig. 8. 3   Architecture model established by π-ADL

Components and connectors can exhibit their internal structures by composition mechanism. Noticeably, composing is a kind of behavior that is able to execute during runtime, thus allowing the dynamic creation of new components. The composite components or connectors hold external ports as well as internal architectural elements that may be attached with ports too. Therefore, just as the name in π-calculus, some ports may be set as restricted, indicating that those ports can only be used internally but not as the interface to outside environment. More particularly, the architectures of a system are also composite elements. An architecture can contain a sub-architecture. In π-ADL, architectures, components and connectors are formally specified in terms of typed abstractions over behaviors.

The formal system of π-ADL is defined in layer style:

- Base Layer (π-ADL$_B$): This layer defines the fundamental language constructs for describing typed behaviors. More particularly, it defines void data type, connection, abstraction, and finally the basic behavior type Behavior.
- First-Order Layer (π-ADL$_{FO}$): This layer extends π-ADL$_B$ by defining concrete base types (Natural, Integer, String, Any, ...), constructed types constructors (tuple, view, location, ...) and collection types constructors

(sequence, set and bag). Connection mobility is also given birth here.
- Higher-Order Layer (π-ADL$_{HO}$): This layer extends π-ADL$_{FO}$ with full first-class constructs definitions including behavior mobility (process mobility of Higher-Order π-calculus).

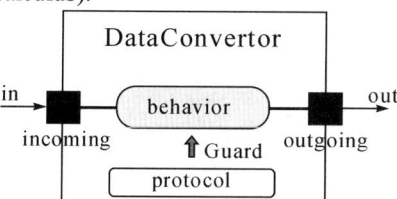

Fig. 8. 4   Structure of DataConvertor

In Fig.8.5, we specify a single component DataConverter that converts input arbitrary data to student information in π-ADL, which is illustrated in Fig.8.4. It first defines five value types, three of which are alias of base value types and two of which are constructed by tuple. After that two ports are specified. The port *incoming* is responsible of accepting entries of student information through shared input connection *in*. The port *outgoing* is used to send separated information via *out*. The behavior segment describes what DataConverter will do: it accepts the value object of type StudentInfo, converts it by projection operation into three fields (*id, name* and *info*), and finally sends a simplified object containing only student's *id* and *name*. The protocol enforces that before receiving the next entry, this component has to send the simplified entry first. For complete description of π-ADL syntax, one can read (Oquendo, 2003).

```
component DataConverter is abstraction() {
    type ID is Natural. type Name is String. type Info is Any.
    type StudentInfoEntry is tuple[ID, Name, Info].
    type SimpleStudentInfoEntry is tuple[ID, Name].
    port incoming is{connection in is in(Entry)}.
    port outgoing is{connection out is out(SimpleStudentInfoEntry)}.
    behavior is{
        via incoming::in receive entry:StudentInfoEntry.
        project entry as id, name, info.
        via outgoing::out send tuple(id, name)
    }
}assuming{
    protocol is{(    via incoming::in receive any. true * .
                     via outgoing::out send any) * }
}
```

Fig. 8. 5   A sample specification of a component in π-ADL

π-ADL allows to compose several components and connectors. The key word compose is equivalent to the parallel composition operator (|) in π-calculus. All the components and connectors involved in the composition execute in parallel and interact via shared connections. Normally, the connections with the same name are identical. But for decoupling reasons, there is no need to define the global accessible connections before assembling the whole system. Thereby, π-ADL introduces connection unification statement to handle this issue. Additionally, in the behavior specification of π-ADL composition can be adopted, which enables the dynamic creation of components, connectors and the connection unification relationships among them. The code segment of Fig.8.6 shows this. If the value x is greater than 1, a Client component, a Server component and a Channel connector are created, following which their configuration is established. If this behavior is executed for many times, a collection of instances of those architectural elements may be created and activated. Similarly, π-ADL also contains a construct decompose to dispose the sub-system.

Just as the First-Order and High-Order π-calculus, π-ADL allows transmission of connections and behaviors, facilitating modeling mobile systems. For this, π-ADL employs the behavior type Behavior and connection type, represented as "connection_mode[type]", where connection_mode can be in, out, and inout, and type specifies the allowable types whose instances can be transmitted.

```
behavior is {

    if x > 1
    then compose{ c is Client() and s is Server() and a ch is Channel()}
    where {
         c::outClient unifies ch::inChannel
    and      s::inServer unifies ch::outChannel
    }
    else
         done

}
```

Fig. 8. 6   Dynamic creation of a sub-C/S system

π-ADL is a well formed language capable of specifying static, conventional dynamic and mobile software architectures. Besides its formal basis, it also provides a graphical notation defined as a UML profile, improving the convenience of its applying in practice. Meanwhile, it is an executable language that can be used for simulation during design phase. Another more elaborate ADL, called ArchWare C&C ADL, has been proposed beyond π-ADL (Cimpan, 2005), which focuses on the defining of dynamic software architecture with component, connector and style.

8. 2. 2   MARMOL: A Reflection Perspective

One intuitive solution to the dynamic architecture is to implement architecture reflection. Reflection means the capability of a system to reason and act upon itself (Maes, 1987). Just like seeing yourself in the mirror and combing your hair, a system employing reflection contains an explicit model representing the system itself, which allows users' access or modification. A change to the model will finally reflected to the system itself in which what will be done depends on what the model represents. And the converse case holds too.

Formally, reflection model is a layer-based model, in which each upper layer serves as a "meta-system" to the base one, called "base-system". For each meta-base system pair, the meta-system describes how the system perceives or modifies itself, while the base-system describes the normal operations and structures. A system is said to be reflective when it acts as its own meta-system. In reflection model, two operations are defined. An operation that shifts up from the base to meta-level is named "reification"; conversely, the operation shifting down from the meta to base-level which means the modification in the meta-level is achieved in the base-system is called "reflection". In some publications, the meta-and base-level should be identified relatively because reflection model does not limit the number of reflective layers. However, in the practice use, less than three layers of reflection are employed.

In the object-oriented programming area, reflection has emerged for several years. A platform such as Java or Net archives the information including class definitions, method signatures, field definitions and their interrelationships, and binds them with the executive code. Therefore, any objects are self-explanative. That endows programmers the power of identifying and manipulating those objects instantiating from unknown types. Besides, programmers can program dynamically. It is possible by programming reflection to generate new code for types or methods during runtime, which is a foundation of program self-generating. The open source java framework Hibernate (http://www. hibernate. org) and Spring (http://www. springframework.org) employ reflection and thus achieve the success of improving agile development. Here is a segment of code using reflection, shown in Fig.8.7. This program analyzes the class definition whose name is specified by the program's first argument. All the methods defined in that class are dumped and their signatures are printed on the output console.

```
import java.lang.reflect.*;
public class MethodsDumper {
    public static void main(String args[]) {
        try {
            Class c = Class.forName(args[0]);
            Method m[] = c.getDeclaredMethods();
            for (int i = 0; i < m.length; i++)
                System.out.println(m[i].toString());
        } catch(Throwable e) {
            System.err.println(e);
        }
    }
}
```

Fig. 8. 7 Java code segment using reflection

Nevertheless, object-oriented programming reflection only maintains the information in the code level. Those for architecture are not embodied explicitly. Especially, this kind of reflection essentially depends on the process of compilation, which involves no runtime architecture-related issues at all. Architectural reflection, however, improves this point by keeping the runtime architecture when system is in execution. The architectural reflective system knows what its structures looks like, the active component and connector instances or even the infrastructure including various types. What's more, unlike the code level reflection, architectural reflection is given birth to be modified. Self-healing (Schmerl, 2002), self-adaptive (Oreizy, 1999) and self-organizing systems (Georgiadis, 2002) will reason architecture candidates and choose the best one according to situation and selection strategies.

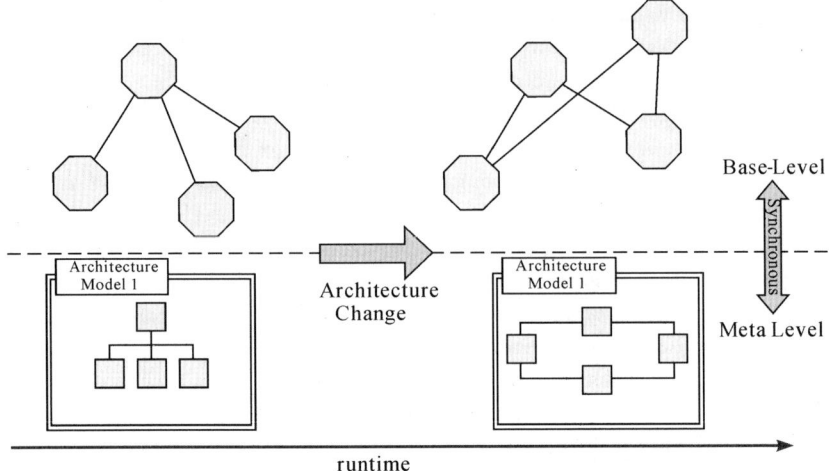

Fig. 8. 8   Architecture change under architectural reflection

Fig.8.8 illustrates an example of change based on architectural reffection. The system is separated into two parts: the meta-level and the base-level. The meta-level maintains the runtime architecture model during execution, and the base-level is the part that implements the functions or provides services to users, where the implicit architecture is held. In the architecture model, the squares mean the component nodes used fore representing and validating, each of which corresponds to the real one in the base-level, the component instances, which are shown in octagon. The difference between component instances in reality and nodes in model means that the architecture model ignores those architecture-unrelated details. At some time the change occurs, wherever the source comes, leading to the layout transference of structures. Before and after the change, the structures in the both levels have to keep synchronous.

MARMOL (Meta ARchitectural MOdeL) (Cuesta, 2001) is the first formal model trying to formalize the intuition of combining reflection and software architecture. The main idea of MARMOL is to introduce multiple levels of description in architectural specification and represent the software architecture with the concepts from reflection. Notably, MARMOL is neither a model for a specific problem or project, nor an architectural style or pattern, but for architecture specification. In MARMOL, primitives for describing dynamic software architecture are defined. In MARMOL, the following assumptions hold:

- The number of meta-levels is unlimited. The architecture described by MARMOL is composed at least of a meta- and base-system. But MARMOL allows a multiple layers style systems, in which each adjacent two layers form the meta-base pair. The total layers can be infinite.
- The relationship between any meta-base pair can be arbitrary. MARMOL does not suppose anything about it. This assumption means that the interpretation or conversion mechanisms of. a meta-base pair are the irrespective issues of MARMOL. They should be defined in the sub-models used in a single layer. In the extreme case, the meta- and base-system in a pair can be unrelated with each other at all.
- Each component in the base-level (relatively) has exactly one associated "meta-space", which logically hold all the meta-information about this component. Meta-space is composed of meta-components, meta-level components and their combination. Meta-component maintains a direct reflection with a base-component, which is termed the "referent" or "avatar" of it; meta-level components are the ones responsible handling the meta-information which are placed in the meta-level. A directional causal connection exists between the meta-space and its base-component, termed "reification" from the base to meta, and "reflection" from meta to base.
- Architectural component types can be reified as "meta-components", an idea similar to the Class class in Java. Expressing dynamism can benefit from this point.

Obviously, MARMOL is a perspective focusing on the dynamism brought in by reflection. It can be used collaboratively with other ADLs, which, for example, facilitates the description of one single layer as a composite component. However, MARMOL does not depend on any particular description methods. In this way, MARMOL makes possible for an ADL to deal with dynamic concerns using just the languages constructs designed for static structures or interactions. It concentrates on reflection and its effects to a certain concrete software architecture, and formalizes the relationships in the model. MARMOL will not inspect the internal structures within a layer. This is an entirely different issues that are not in MARMOL's goals.

MARMOL comes from the abstraction of current existent systems employing implicit reflection, that is, they use reflection without awareness of it. Those mechanisms allow dynamic capabilities, such as external control, changeable components or changeable connectors, hire the meta-model more or less.

Based and extended on MARMOL, a dynamic ADL, Pilar (Cuesta, 2001; 2005) has been proposed and refined to describe reflective dynamic software, representing a specialized edition of MARMOL. Within Pilar, there is really just one kind of element in the top level: component, a basic software unit composed of a set of interfaces or sub-components. Four parts are defined as a component's specification, interfaces, configurations, reifications and constraints, where the first ones are common among various ADLs, but the third part defines the reflective structure. The last part, constraints, different from the notations only identical in appearance defined in other architecture models or languages, provides the rules comprising dynamism. The Pilar model contains a reflective tower, just as MARMOL, where the elements that are controlled by reflection are said to stand in the base-level, and the elements which controls stays in the meta-level. A base-level components is known as an avatar. The relationship between an avatar and one of its corresponding meta-components is named as a "reification link", through which the operations reification (shifts up) and reflection (shifts down) can be performed. Of course, a meta-component can repeat another reification link with a meta-meta-component in the upper layer which allows an infinite number of meta-levels. An illustrative figure of two-tier reflection is shown in Fig.8.9. There are four base-components, three of which are linked with their meta-counterparts in the meta-level. It is the meta-components that control the dynamism of components in the base-level.

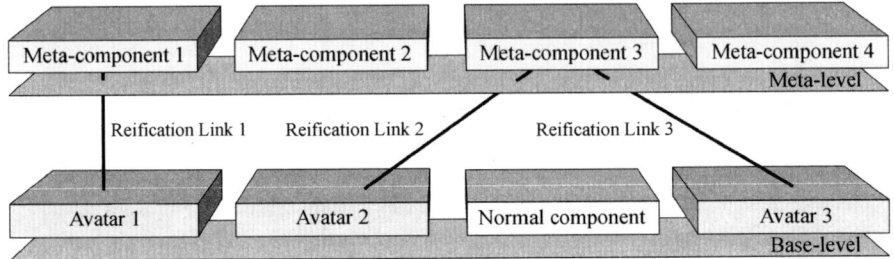

Fig. 8. 9   Reflection model of Pilar

There are two notations common in other ADLs are unified with meta-level abstraction in Pilar. The first one is type-instance relationship, a feature facilitating the reuse of architectural elements. In Pilar, types can be considered as meta-component managing their own instances through reification links, which is termed "reified types". Another one is the connector. In Pilar, only connections are concerned by reification. They are handled in the way same to the components owning reified types, but only different in their constraints. In this way, they can acquire a complex behavior, recovering all the power of original connectors. In other words, Pilar has meta-level connectors.

We borrow an example from (Cuesta, 2005) to illustrate the representation mechanism of Pilar, shown in Fig.8.10. This specification defines three components, related by reification links. The syntax used here is specified in Fig.8.11. First of all, a component called "Multiplier" is defined, with two ports A and B. From the constraints, its behavior is self-explanative: it reads any value got by A and sends the doubled value through B. Here the question mark (?) means input while exclamation mark (!) refers to output. The key word \rep indicates the behavior is repeated each time when A receives something, analogous to the replication construct in the π-calculus.

```
\component  Multiplier (
    (port  A | port  B)
    \constraint  (\rep(A? (x); B! (2x)))
)
\component Logger (
    (port  C)
    \constraint(\rep(\when avatar.A? (z)
                (C! (z))))
)
\component LoggedMultiplier (
    \config (mul: Multiplier)
    \reify (mul: Logger)
)
```

Fig. 8. 10   A partial example of Pilar

```
\component  name [<parameters>] (
    {[\interface]
        (interface definitions)}
    [\config (
        {instances declarations} |
        [\bind  (
            {binding declarations})]
        )]
    {\reify   explicit reification}
    [\constraint (
        {dynamic constraint})]
)
```

Fig. 8. 11   Pilar syntax

The second component is Logger, tending to log something when conditions hold. It defines a monitor with the guard key word, as well as access to its reified base-component through the keyword avatar. When Logger's avatar detects an input from port A, it performs the log actions that send the input from port C; otherwise the avatar will be affected by Logger. To enable the log behavior, the avatar should guarantee a port named A defined.

Then the component LoggedMultiplier is defined in a composite form. A component instance mul of type Multiplier is declared. What's more, it is reified to the meta-component Logger. Hence, the behaviors defined in the Logger can be reflected to this instance. The integrated effect of mul is that when it receives a value from port A it outputs the doubled value through port B and sends the copy of that value by port C as log.

Obviously this specification is not complete because it needs other components to link with port A, B and C. And it clearly illustrates the reflective structures depicted above. However this case does not involve the dynamism, a topic of following. Pilar provides several primitives by which architecture can be modified during runtime. Here is brief table that lists the operations related to dynamic architecture. These operands enable the creation, deletion of components and reification links, through which it is possible to dynamically alter the structures and behaviors of components in a certain level of reflective tower. Because the infinity of reflective tower, the structure of a system, the component, and even the component type may be modified during runtime.

Table 8.1   Dynamism Related Operands in Pilar

Operand	Description
\ new $(c:T)$	Creation of a new entity c of type T
\ del c	Deletion of any entity c
\ alias p as q	Scope extrusion of port p, possibly renamed
\ hide p	Hiding of port p
avatar	Reference to the avatar to the current meta-component
self	Reference to the meta-component itself
\ reify $R(c:m)$	Creation of reification link between the avatar c to a meta-entity m
\ findr $R(c:m)$	Search for a reification link between c and m
\ nullr R	Judge whether the R is not a reification link

With them we create a complete sample specification of a database access control system in Pilar. In Fig.8.10 is the specification:

```
\component DB (
    (port data)
)
\component Server (
    (port data_source)
)
\component DataChannel (
    (port input | port output)
    \constraint (\reify R(avatar: CommonLink(avatar. input | avatar. output);
output? (W);\del R;\reify S (avatar:CachedLink(avatar. input | avatar. output))
)
\component CommonLink (
    (port input | port output)
    \constraint (\rep (avatar. input? (X); avatar. output! (X))
)
\component CachedLink (
    (port input | port output)
    \config (ca: Cache | comm1: CommonLink (c. input | comm1. output) | comm2:
CommonLink(comm2. input | c. output))
)
\component Cache (
    (port input | port output)
    \constraint {ignore here}
)
\component System (
    \config (d:DB | s:Server | c:DataChannel(d. data | s. data_source))
)
```

Fig. 8.12   A Specification of Database Access Control System

To make the change process more clear, we visualize it in the Fig.8.13. Most of the specification is self-explanative except the components DataChannel,

CommonLink and CachedLink. Therefore we simplify those reified types in the format of italic rather than to place them in the meta-level in order to avoid the mess. Another simplification is that we draw all the meta-components actually staying in the different meta-levels in a single level. At last, the solid lines mean conventional bind relationships while the dash-curved lines indicate reification links.

Initially we define the system with three linked components: d (DB instance), s (Server instance) and c (DataChannel instance). From the constraint of DataChannel c is reified to the meta-component CommonLink, which simply forwards what is received from the input port through the output port, detailed in the constraint of CommonLink. When a signal "W" is detected by c, which means a warning generated from s in the case such as access overload (we omit the specification of generation of W), the previous reification of c to CommonLink is destroyed, and a new one to CachedLink is established, during which a component ca, instance of Cache, is created and linked to two additional CommonLink instances comm1 and comm2. You can see that this is not a simply creation, deletion or replacement of components but a combined modification to the architecture. The final result is a cache is introduced and improves the server's performance.

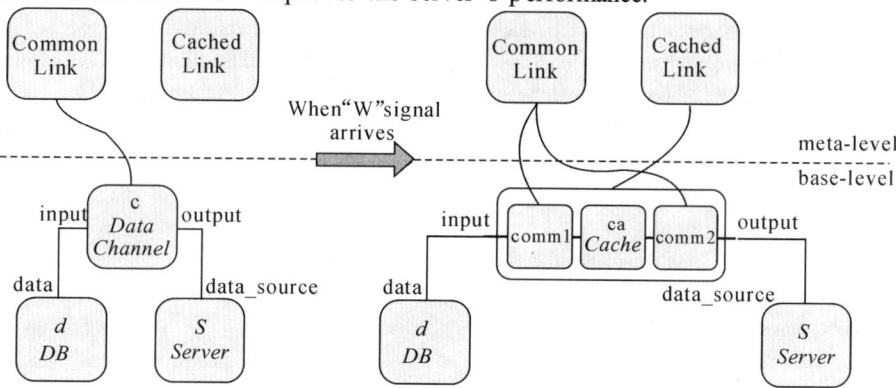

Fig. 8. 13   The change process of database access control system

Authors of Pilar believe that "dynamism based on the meta-level" is a very useful concept to improve the insight of dynamic software architecture, which can be used to unify other methods of dynamic facilities. The primitives of Pilar come from π-calculus, which changes only in the express form, rather than the ad-hoc criteria. What's more, as an extended MARMOL, it is feasible to employ other formal description, such as CCS or μ-calculus. This guarantees its power of validation and analysis.

8. 2. 3   LIME: A Coordination Perspective

With the evolution of distributed and parallel systems, the Coordination Model (CM) was developed to handle the massive parallel system. It provides a framework which enhances modularity, reuse of existent components, portability and language interoperability. Coordination Theory has been generically defined as "the management of dependencies between activities" (Malone, 1994) or "the process of building programs by gluing together active pieces" in the programming area (Gelemter, 1992). Lots of Coordination Languages (CL) have been proposed which are different in their special concerns and features.

So what is the relationship between CM and dynamic software architecture? Massive parallel systems are normally distributed among logic nodes, such as threads, processes, processors or hosts. Their interactions, behaviors are natively dynamic because any part in the system does not own the capability of overseeing the global status of system before execution. They cannot stop some nodes' crash or new components' joining. Besides, the communications involve code mobility that enables the separation between the location of some components' execution and of their initial generation. The needs of dynamic software architecture mostly are derived from the requirements of flourish of distributed system. CM adopts an outstanding perspective to abstract the problem. Any branch of CM has something in common. That is, they consider the system as the combination of two distinct activities: the actual computing part, in which several processes do the computing with resource, and the coordination part that manages the communications and collaboration among computing processes. This provides a paradigm to simplify the development of distributed and parallel systems with separation. Some notorious survey about CM in computer science includes (Andreoli, 1996), LNCS Series 1061, 1292, 1594, 1906 and 2315 (Coordination Models and Languages). A comprehensive discuss of CM and CL is beyond the scope of this book, but we will briefly introduce Linda, a classic fundamental CM, and then LIME, an extended Linda to fit for mobile environment.

Linda (Ahuja, 1986; Carriero, 1989) is historically the first CL applied in computer science, which provides a rather simple mechanism to allow the separation of computing and coordination parts. In Linda context, a process expecting to communicating with others can send the data (especially an active process can be considered as a kind of data, and thus is feasible to be sent) to an abstract shared "tuple space". Any processes within the range of a single system can read from or write to the global tuple space through which communications are performed. In order to make it feasible, each process has a unique identifier. Therefore any process involving the communication is unnecessary to be alive at the same time or stay in the fixed place, which is termed as a feature of Linda: decoupling of time and space. Each tuple is a list of typed parameters, such as < "hello", 0.3, 12> , that holds the data being communicated. Each item in a tuple is either an "actual" or a "formal". Actuals are concrete values, such as strings or integers; formals seem similar to wildcards or templates that can match a series actuals, facilitating the operations that will be mentioned below. All in all, the tuple space is a multiset of tuples capable of being accessed concurrently. Model of Linda is shown in Fig.8.14. For the beginner, there is no need to concern how the global tuple space is realized because it is an ad-hoc solution. This is why we draw the tuple space with dashed line.

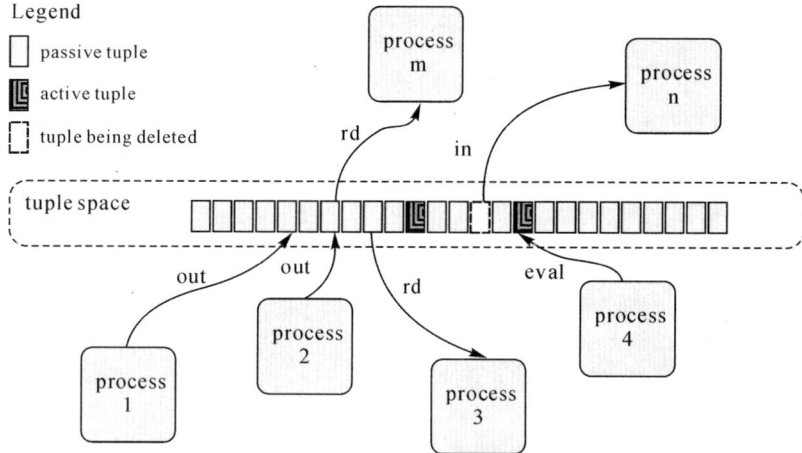

Fig. 8. 14　Linda model and operations

Linda defines a set of simple coordination primitives. In particular, out(t) is an operation to put a passive tuple t to the tuple space. in(t) retrieves a passive tuple t and removes t from tuple space. rd(t) gets a copy of t from tuple space, but leave the shared edition unaffected. eval(p) puts an active tuple p, in other word a process, in the tuple space, which then starts to execute and will turn into a passive tuple after finishing. Both in(t) and rd(t) can use formals to allow associative pattern matching. More particularly the parameter t is a tuple schema that can match multiple tuples at the same time. For instance, a template tuple < "abc", ? integer, ? double>　will match any tuple that contains three fields, the first of which is a string "abc", the second is an integer and the last is a decimal, such as < "abc", 1, 3.24>　and < "abc", 12, 4.5> . If the match fails, these two operations blocks until some eligible tuples are put in by some other processes. Conversely, out (t) and eval (p) are non-blocking operations. But they cannot accept the parameters containing formals. Several additional operations are added when Linda get evolved. For example, rdp(t) and inp(t) are non-blocking variants of rd(t) and in (t) respectively. They will return FALSE when they cannot find the desired tuples. All these operations are atomic.

Linda is language-neutral; therefore it is possible to implement Linda in the form of programming library. Fig.8.15 gives an implementation of Dining Philosophers in C-Linda (Papadopoulos, 1998).

This problem gets a number (such as 5 in the solution) of philosophers to sit around a table. In front of each of them, there are a plate of food and two forks placed in his left and right side respectively. To eat, one person has to pick up two forks next to him and eat. Without any control, it is possible that everyone picks up one fork on the same side and waits for another one, that is, deadlock occurs. In the solution above, Linda uses "ticket" to avoid the deadlock. For NUM people, only (NUM 1) tickets are put into the tuple space which makes sure that there must be at least one person who can finish the "eat" action. Therefore, deadlock never happens. Meanwhile, the maximal concurrent number of "eat" is achieved.

```
#define NUM 5                              int main()
void philosopher(int i)                    {
{                                              int i;
    while(true)                                for(i = 0; i < NUM; i++)
    {                                          {
        think();                                   out("fork", i);
        in("ticket");                              eval(philosopher(i));
        in("fork", i);                             if(i < NUM  1)
        in("fork", (i+1) % NUM);                       out("ticket");
        eat();                                 }
        out("fork", i);                        return 0;
        out("fork", (i+1) % NUM);          }
        out("ticket");
    }
}
```

Fig. 8. 15　Linda solution of dining philosopher

We can replace the process in the Dining Philosophers program to control a dynamic architecture. For instance, we implement the function "eat" to activate component, while "think" to deactivate it. Hence, we can control the lives of components that are related to each other regulated by the fork rule. Additional, through changing the value of NUM, we are able to control the number of components that can be activated. Of course this is only a simplified illustrative example, but designers may realize more complicated interaction mechanism with Linda primitives.

During the evolvement of two decades, various variants of Linda have been proposed. Bauhaus Linda (Carriero, 1994) unifies tuples and tuple spaces, tuples and tuple templates, active and passive tuples. In Bauhaus Linda, the original single flat tuple space is replaced with unordered multiset, therefore operations have to specify the target sub-set. Law-Governed Linda (Minsky, 1994) maintains a controller for each process where a set of communication related laws are applied, which verify requests of primitive operations and ban their executions if they do not adhere to some laws. LAURA (Tolksdorf, 1994) is a Linda-based approach to help communications and contract-making in agent-oriented distributed systems. More particularly, agents can send or receive messages with "forms" which can contain descriptions such as service-offer, and service-request. And a collection of primitives to handle forms are created. Sonia (Banville, 1996) is an adaptation of Linda in information systems, which changes the original primitives to more intuitive names such as "post", "pick" and "peek". Additional primitives and grammars for domain use are also introduced into it. Opus (Chapman, 1997) is a super coordination language based on High Performance Fortran (HPF). It aims to handle the problem of concurrent execution of several data parallel components. In this concern it creates a ShareD Abstraction (SDA), an ADT that behaves like tuple space, but provides methods to manipulate its state. Reo (Arbab, 2004) introduces the concept of mobile channel into coordination and takes connectors as coordinator. LightTS (Picco, 2005) constructs a context awareness suitable Linda style model to build the core of LIME (detailed later).

There are also coordination models of non-Linda style where the system evolves by means of observing state changes in processes, or termed "process oriented coordination", rather than exchanging data by an abstract global repository. They possibly realize coordination by broadcasting changed state or send events to the subscriber processes. For instance, Proteus Configuration Language (Sommerville, 1996) and Durra (Barbacci, 1993) can be categorized as this kind. But since our concentration is on LIME, we will not discuss it further.

LIME (Picco, 1999; Picco, 2000; Murphy, 2006) is the abbreviation of "Linda in a Mobile Environment". It is the derived Linda supporting development of mobile applications physically, logically or a combination of them. In LIME, the global tuple space featuring Linda is refined to handle the problems in the context of mobile computation, where the separation of mobile units has to be concerned. Tuple space is no longer a logical one piece but location awareness. Besides, more functionalities and verification methods are introduced into LIME.

We return the problem of Linda's implementation, which needs a global accessible space that is persistent and capable of decoupling the time and space. In a fixed distributed system, where all the nodes' locations and connections are relatively stable, it is possible to run the tuple space equivalent component in one or a cluster of hosts. However, in the mobile environment, where components tend to move arbitrarily in the system or crossing the system edge, you cannot use any of them to hold the tuple space since hosts cannot always remain accessible to all other components. What's more, issues such as power exhaustion, slowing down or even cutting off of the network connection and heterogeneity make it rather difficult, if not impossible, to establish a Linda-like framework. More concerns should be taken into account in the architecture level by adding assistant elements into the basic model.

The core idea of LIME is to break up the Linda tuple space into a set of sub spaces, each of which is attached to one mobile agent permanently and exclusively, referred to an "interface tuple space" (ITS). Each ITS contains tuples that a mobile agent is willing to make available to others. And there are some rules for transient sharing of individual tuple spaces according to connectivity. All the agents able to connect to each other form a LIME "group", within which contents of all individual ITS are merged and thus transparently shared. Therefore, a logical tuple space available to all mobile agents in a group is established. Noticeably, the number of ITSs owned by one agent is unlimited. They are distinguished by symbolic names, which is also the mark enabling share since in a group only ITSs named identically can be shared transparently. For example, an agent named "agent1" has two ITSs, S1 and S2, and another agent "agent2" contains S1 and S2. When they are connected, two ITS named S1 are merged, and thus two agents can access tuples stored in S1 by each other. But agent1 cannot assess content of S3 while agent2 cannot touch that of S3. Both S2 and S3 are accessible only in their own agent, or until new agents with ITSs of these two names join in. In short, LIME only concerns connectivity of ITS, whose names is the determining factor of transparent share. Each host may contain several mobile agents. And each agent may contain several ITSs. LIME abstracts the distinctness introduced by the hierarchy levels. But it is easy to implement an agent level or host level tuple space with LIME.

The joining of a group by a mobile agent and the subsequent merging of its local context with a group context is referred to "engagement", which is an atomic operation. When a mobile agent leaves the group, operation "disengagement" is performed, thus the local context of ITSs of agents to be removed is deleted from the group context, which can be perceived by other agents in the group transparently.

LIME is capable of describing both physical and logical mobility. Physical mobility means a host in the system moves within system range while keeping its connectivity with other hosts; logical mobility means the reconfiguration of the systems in which some components unbind the original connections and create new ones. Logical mobility may occur with physical mobility when a component, including code or resource, physically moves to another host during runtime. In LIME, the transiently shared ITSs belonging to multiple agents collocated on a host define a "host-level tuple space". Similarly, the transiently shared ITSs belonging to multiple connected hosts with host-level tuple space form "federated tuple space". Therefore, in a federated tuple space, the accessible tuples may exist in any agents running on any hosts (local or a certain remote one) in a group. When physical mobility is required, the system can be modeled as several federated tuple spaces crossing over physically distributed hosts. In the case of components physical migration, there is no need to employ federated tuple space but to use only a fixed host-level tuple space. If mobility is unnecessary, the model can be further simplified just as original Linda. In this perspective, LIME is flexible to suit for every mobility case. The effect of mobility manipulation, however, is not directly affected by LIME, but a production of levels of units that establish tuple spaces. This choice that sets the nature of mobility aside keeps LIME as general as possible.

LIME hides very much for its users. If communication is expected, one side can just throw a tuple in the space and the other side peeks or picks its interested ones asynchronously. But excessive transparence is not always positive. Consider the following case. When agent1 in the host1 puts a tuple in the federated tuple space, and then gets removed for some reasons, is this tuple accessible to any other agents? Obviously it depends on where the tuple actually locates. Also, performance and efficiency considerations may need fine-grained control of the tuple location. For example, you may hope there should be sole tuple that locates where it is accessed most frequently; or you estimate a great chance of disconnection and thus create multiple copies of a single tuple among several hosts. Location-related primitives are provided by LIME by adding location parameters to the operations manipulating transiently-shared tuple space. All tuples themselves also maintain two fields that represent the tuple's current location and destination locations respectively. The current location indicates which agent should hold this tuple when all other agents cannot be connected. The destination location means the target agent where this tuple will eventually stay. LIME employs and extends three Linda primitives: out, in and rd, but drops eval.

The out operation in LIME is written as out$[\lambda](t)$, where λ is the location parameter to specify destination agent. Its execution can be viewed as two steps: firstly, the tuple t is sent to ITS of the agent, named ω, which invokes this primitive, equivalent to out(t), and the destination location is set as λ. The second step depends on the connectivity of agent λ. If it is reachable, tuple t will immediately be transferred to λ; if it is not the case, tuple t will reside on ω until λ joins this group. During this process, the current location of tuple t is always the agent name it currently resides on. If a tuple's two location parameters are different, it is termed "misplaced" tuple, which will wait to change this state. If some tuples on ω are identified as misplaced targeting to λ, and then λ joins in, those tuples migrate from ω to λ during the process of engagement. This is shown in Fig.8.16.

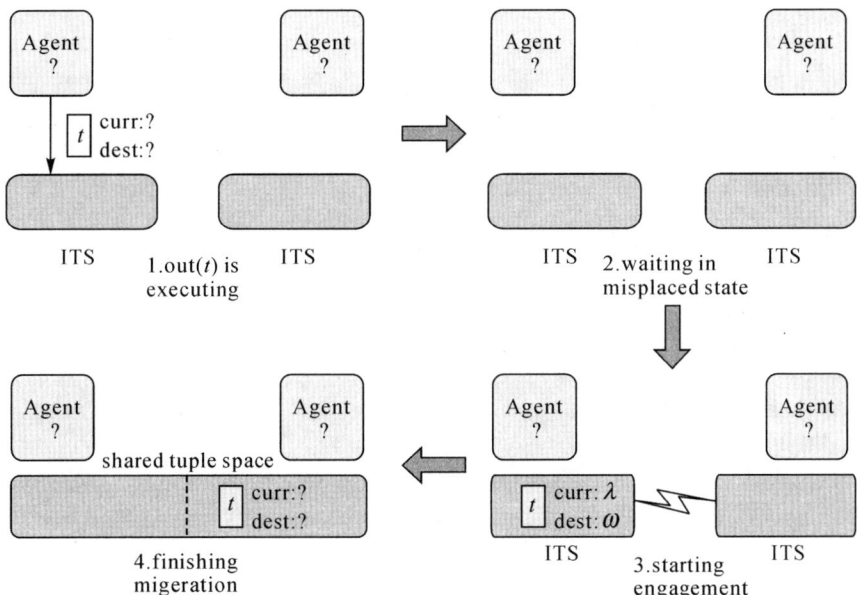

Fig. 8. 16   The process of out$[\lambda](t)$ when λ cannot be connected initially

Primitives in and rd also get extended by location parameters, in the form of in $[\omega,\lambda](p)$ and rd$[\omega,\lambda](p)$, which enable programmer to refer to a projection of the current context defined by the value of location parameters. The first parameter normally is used to specify the search scope within federated tuple space; and the second one is to identify whether it is misplaced or not. Further more, the parameters can be a name of an agent or a host.

LIME also provides the function of reaction extending Linda's event model, enabling some codes execution when some tuples' states are changed. A reaction will be fired when a tuple in the specified scope of tuple space, which matches a predefined pattern, changes its state. The complete form of reaction is $R[\omega, \lambda](s, p, m)$ where ω and λ are the location parameters with the semantics mentioned above. s is the code segment to be executed when conditions are met. s should not be the potential blocking code that will put system into a suspend state. p is the tuple pattern to specify the tuples that will fire reactions. And m is termed "reaction mode" defining the automatic actions after execution of s. Two modes are set for LIME: ONCE and ONCEPERTUPLE. When a reaction is registered as ONCE, it is allowed to execute only once. After its execution, it is automatically deregistered and then removed from current system. And a reaction registered as ONCEPERTUPLE mode is allowed to execute exactly once for each matched tuple, so that the number of execution is a function of system runtime.

Reaction is a powerful construct for designers to build their system. However, it incurs a problem of realization about its atomicity. If reaction code can be executed in a single atomic manner, it is named "strong reaction" which is an ideal model for dynamic architecture. However, it is often impractical in the mobile system which contains too many distributed nodes that bear low quality communications. In this case, implementing atomicity among distributed ITSs will bring about tremendous negative impact to performance. Therefore, LIME allows another kind of reaction, termed "weak reaction", in which detection of tuple state changes and code execution does not have to proceed atomically, and code execution takes place on the host of the agent that registers that reaction.

LIME is an outstanding model to handle physical and logical mobility that introduces dynamism by coordination perspective. Its basic model Linda greatly simplifies development of distributed systems by separating the computing part and coordination part, that is, decoupling time and space. LIME extends Linda by adding the context awareness of tuple space, that is, breaking up the original one piece into several local ITSs and correspondingly introduces location parameters to primitives that facilitates control of system in a finer-grained level. Additionally, LIME provides an effective mechanism of reaction to context changes. LIME defines its semantics precisely with Mobile UNITY (Roman, 1997) which is not discussed deeply in this section. LIME actually offers a framework capable of dynamically configuring architecture. Although some problems of high level dynamic architecture, such as component type runtime creation, are beyond the scope of LIME, it is so handy to be applied which makes programmers concentrate on their business. Besides, it gives a new design paradigm for distributed systems in mobile environment.

8.3   Flexibility: Beyond the Dynamism

Flexibility appears far more in the world, for example, in the manufacturing field, physics, or even management area. The extensive application of this term does not mean that flexibility has been deeply researched or analyzed. In the contrary, this case indicates that it is still in the status of chaos without precise definition or framework guiding people to understand it. In the software architecture area, even the proposals titled with this term always mix it with other features of software, such as extensibility, characters that helps rapid development or dynamism. In this concern, we should clarify what is flexible software architecture.

8.3.1   Concept of Flexible Software Architecture

The flexibility of an object is its ability to perform deformation under external strength. If it is too hard, deformation is impossible; if it is too soft, it cannot maintain its shape and recover when external force is removed. Both cases will tremendously increase the cost of object's usage. A flexible object can adapt itself to fit for its external world, which reduces the price of using it, although building or purchasing it may consume more. Imagine the case of waistband. For example, we have four kinds of it:

- **Rope as waistband (long enough for most people):** even though it is feasible to use a rope as the waistband which can adapt for almost everybody, few people use it because it is too difficult to manipulate and rather unstable.
- **Waistbands with a fixed length:** People who buy it cannot use it any longer if their waistlines change. Or they can buy many waistbands with different lengths. Therefore, too much will be spent on it.
- **Waistbands with a buckle and several holes (additional holes can be drilled):** People like the waistbands of this kind because it can adapt to a range of waistline only through simple manipulation. When people take exercise, they can set it tightly; when taking dinner, they can set it loosely. This is termed "user-oriented flexibility". If existing holes are not enough, people can drill more of them, termed "developer-oriented flexibility".
- **Elastic as waistband:** This kind of waistband has no buckle, and does not need any manipulation. But the ease is brought with price: its effective range reduces and it is not so firm as conventional waistband. In short, it is suitable for special purposes only.

From the waistband example, we can see that flexibility brings convenience and promotion of cost performance. Besides, we can find some tips help to establish the concept framework of flexible software architecture (FSA). This introduces issues that should be taken into account around flexibility itself. First of all, FSA should employ the architecture capable of changing during runtime. This is the key point of dynamic software architecture, the subject of Section 8.2. Compared to FSA, the architecture featuring rigidity never changes its shape no matter how the environment evolves over time. But it is so hard that when it is unsuitable completely, it possibly cannot work continually, but stay in a crash or suspend state. And the architecture organized in a loose style is so soft that it cannot be directly used to support a particular system, but normally offers styles, patterns or paradigms that just have meaning of guidance.

Secondly, FSA should be able to feel its context. During runtime, the main triggers includes users' direct instructions, user patterns of operations, networking issues, working load, natural factors and user customized factors, all of which can be referred to the context in FSA. It is the external aspect that should be viewed as a necessary part of FSA.

Thirdly, FSA needs to leave an interface through which users or developers can activate the change process, similar as the buckles and holes in waistband. A direct effect of this point is to separate the FSA control part with computing part that is to handle the job. Although it is possible to mix them up, it is not a good design strategy which will almost, if not for sure, lead to a chaos when scale gets larger and new functions are added.

Fourthly, the ultimate goal of FSA is cost performance centered, or say, to maximize the proportion of benefit to cost. FSA tends to be available in a more generic range in the case that more additional effort should have been paid. This is specially important to introduce FSA into current business built on software system to meet the changes that get faster and faster, from years level to less than several seconds. Essentially, FSA is benefit-driven. Even there is an architecture able to change dynamically, to collect information from its context, and to provide an interface for manipulation by users or developers, it is nonsense if it is weak in increasing cost performance, and thus cannot be identified as FSA. Sometimes, however, even the effective range and interface seems not so powerful, an architecture may be a suitable infrastructure to a special project in that it shows its remarkable capability in some aspects, just as what the elastic waistband does. FSA should not be a concept-limited in the technology world only, but is an effective solution for the areas where business drives should be taken into account.

This four interrelated points construct the concept framework of FSA, and shown in Fig.8.17.

Therefore, we give the following definitions:

> Flexible Software Architecture is the context-driven dynamic software architecture which can be explicitly controlled to achieve certain business goals, especially the cost performance.

8. 3. 2   Trade-off of Flexibility

Compared to conventional software architecture, FSA indeed introduces additional overhead to the software. They are often brought about to enlarge its effective work range, that is, to handle more situations that are only expected possible or even unknown in the design phase. More particularly, the price comes from two aspects:

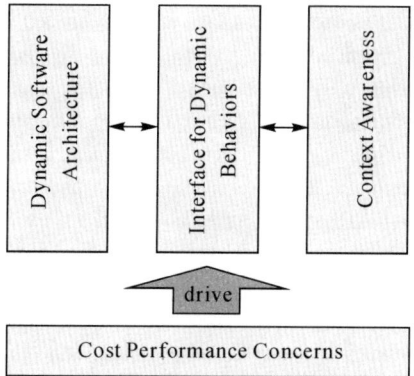

Fig. 8. 17   Concept framework of flexible software architecture

price of FSA development which means the time, effort and economic consumes by adding extra functions and indirect layers; and price of FSA adaptation, which includes the operations to trigger the change and the runtime overhead, such as maintaining the meta-information and dynamic component loading or disposing. Under the cost performance concerns, trade-offs should be taken in the benefits and cost of flexibility, the primary issue in the design of FSA.

The most important of benefits brought by FSA is its effective work range, or *adaptive range*. The *absolute adaptive range* is the set of functionality that an architecture can support by adaptation. It is highly related to the granularity of software constructs: the fine-grained constructs are the critical elements in meeting users' exquisite requirements, but consume much more than the coarse-grained ones. For example, to build a house, we have two choices. The first one is building it with fine-grained constructs, such as rocks, sands, water and the like. Through this method, you can build a house of any style that you like. Another method is to use build-in components, such as bricks, roof frameworks, tiles and so on. By making use of them, you can proceed much faster and easier. However, your creativity may be limited. If the *absolute adaptive range* is the sole target to pursue, the first choice undoubtedly is the best one. However, in fact, very few people make this choice in that it arouses too much trouble. Thereby, blindly enlarging the absolute adaptive range is not the target of trade-off. Normally speaking, a right combination of fine-grained and coarse-grained software constructs is the solution, by which most parts of a system can be assembled with existing components while their seams are filled by fine-grained constructs. The developing of programming language proves this point. Even in the time of object-oriented and component-oriented languages getting rather popular, the low level languages such as assembly or C still can get their positions. And Java still reserves the mechanism of JNI [1] until today.

Further more, *absolute adaptive range* is not the direct factors deciding the experience of users. To compound the problem, we introduce *relative adaptive range*,

---

[1] Java Native Interface, a mechanism allowing Java programmers to use functions written in C.

indicating the set of user requirements that can be achieved via adaptation. *Absolute adaptive range* does not concern the price brought by adaptation, while *relative adaptive range* believes that only those functions which users need is necessary. For example, to provide a general enough system, the development team implements a programmable API, which can help users customize almost every detail of the system's behaviors. However, for users, especially the ones who are not familiar with programming, this API is completely useless, which only increase the complexity and this the cost of that system. A typical example of it is Microsoft Office, which offers the VBA APIs. Besides, general adaptive range often incurs overhead, which may slow down the execution speed and increase the memory occupation. This is evaluated by users. After evaluation, they decide whether they feel good and whether they will continue to use them. In these concerns, *relative adaptive range*, not *absolute adaptive range* should be considered carefully during trade-off.

At last, *profitable range* is the adaptive range leading to the best commercial profit. Software development organizations or companies prefer this range in that *relative adaptive range* does not focus on the cost and risk introduced by developing flexible software. Developing is a kind of business whose success determines its life. The profit of developing flexible software can be split into two kinds: the visible profits (comes from incoming of software sale and saving in software maintenance) and the invisible profits (comes from users' satisfaction and thus software's competivitiness). Obviously, the *relative adaptive range* and the cost spent on developing flexible software is mutually excluded, and the trade-off point is definitely where the profit can be maximized. FSA is a panacea to improve this situation by tremendously reducing the cost of flexible software development. Just like a template, FSA can be used as a reference framework which then is fine-tuned to meet various flexible requirements. In this way, cost, time-to-market, and the quality of flexible software, corresponding with the explicit application of FSA, can be optimized.

It is a common belief that software development is risky and flexible software development holds this. Therefore, before burying head into the design activities, estimation about the expected adaptive range, complexity, approximate cost and benefits should be taken first, all of which are beyond the technologies but more important. This is called the phase of decision making on general strategies. Here is an illustrative economic model of flexible software development.

The cost of first development of flexible software is obviously higher than that of conventional software. But since its flexibility, in the subsequent development and maintenance, flexible software costs less and finally proves its advantages. Corresponding with increase of the amount of requirements, its marginal cost gradually becomes smaller, approaching to zero, that means during some period, the flexible software can adapt itself (within the adaptive range). Here, even no additional development is needed, and software changes dynamically. Conversely, conventional software requires additional iterations, including requirements collection, redesign, implementation and deployment, which force the

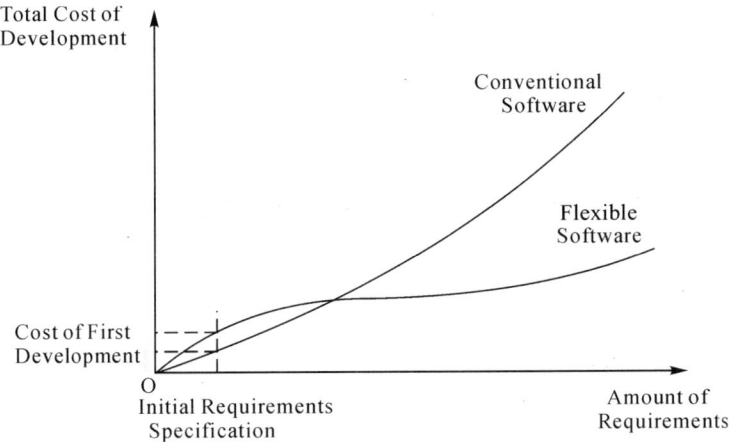

Fig. 8. 18   Economic model of flexible software development

software to stop working, and thus incurring more loss which is added in its marginal cost. Therefore, the curve of conventional software owns a scope increased along with more and more requirements. However, if requirements experience few changes, so that flexibility does not fully make contribution, it is the time to hold a conference to discuss whether the adaptive range should be reduced. For users, *relative adaptive range* improves its usability and applicable area; for developers, *profitable range* avoids the waste of cost, effort and time incurred by blindly seeking for flexibility. In conclusion, trade-off between *relative adaptive range* and *profitable range* is necessary to find the most ideal flexibility.

8. 4   Study Cases

In this section, we will give a brief introduction of two proposed (prototype) systems that employing the FSA. They are self-adaptive and self-managed systems with different focuses. By the way, not all the self- system can be considered as the flexible software because some of them never touch architecture, but achieve those changes via simply invoke those functions that are always standby since their start. In other words, the layouts of their structures remain the sample and their behaviors do nothing to affect their architecture. The cases in the following explicitly put their software architecture on the front page, rather than a ghost like abstraction behind the system. Thanks for the architecture-based flexibility, they achieve the tasks which seems difficult, if not possible, in those conventional software systems.

8. 4. 1   Rainbow

Rainbow (Garlan, 2004) is a self-adaptation infrastructure aiming at solving two problems that harasses developers in building adaptive systems for a long time: the wide variety of systems that a general self-adaptation infrastructure has to face, considering their different domains and specific concerns; and the overhead that may be incurred by adding external control components. Rainbow includes a runtime global model of architecture, represented by a structure of interconnected components and connectors, attached with system-level exposed behaviors and important properties. Besides, a set of constraints and strategies are also maintained in the model, help to ensure the validity of changes. Fig.8.19 is Rainbow's overall framework (Garlan, 2004).

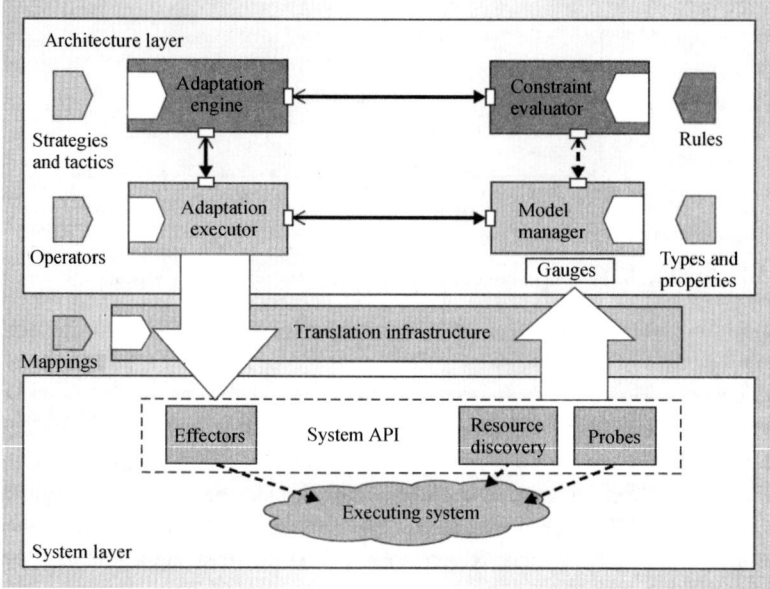

Fig. 8. 19   Overall framework of Rainbow

Rainbow separates the system into the adaptation infrastructure and system-specific adaptation knowledge part. The former contains the system, architecture and translation layers, facilitating the general functions of self-adaptation systems. More particularly, the system layer defines an interface to manipulate Rainbow. Additionally, *Effectors* are constructed for performing the actual system modification. *Probes* and *Resource Discovery* are employed to query system's properties and resource respectively. In the architecture layer, *Model Manager* holds the runtime architecture model, which updates itself with new property values collected by *Gauges*. The *Constraint Evaluator* periodically checks the validation of constraints and triggers adaptation. The *Adaptation Engine* and *Adaptation Executor* together determine the detailed actions of adaptation and start that course. And the translation layer maps the architectural elements into the concrete elements of the system.

The system specific knowledge means to tailor the adaptation infrastructure to adapt itself to one certain system. The specific knowledge includes the set of valid adaptation operations under an architectural style and corresponding strategies. The valid adaptation operations mean those actions that can be correctly applied to a style, commonly implemented as methods of the style or component representing types. A sample code of strategies is shown in Fig. 8.20. The keyword invariant specifies an "action-reaction" relationship, where the adaptation behavior is set after the "! (" mark. A strategy is defined in the function like style. In this case, when memory occupation of the SampleComponent c is too high, it then checks every sub-component typed ServiceProvider. If one service is not used currently (when its access count is 0), it is removed followed by the update of runtime architecture model. Finally the architecture gets changed by the actions specified in the method removeServcie.

```
invariant (self.memOccupation > maxMemOccupation)
    ! ( memControlStrategy(self);

strategy memControlStrategy(SampleComponent c) {
    foreach ServiceProvider s of c {
        if(query("access—count", s) == 0) {
            c.removeService(s);
        }
    }
    return true;
}
```

Fig. 8. 20   Sample code of Rainbow strategy

Systems that want to make use of Rainbow should access its interface and provide system specific knowledge by following Rainbow's guide. Rainbow essentially is a two-layer reflective system but leaves plenty of hook points for customization. But the distributed systems built on Rainbow will notice that the Rainbow infrastructure actually plays a role of coordinator that is capable of boosting the system toward overall adaptation goals.

8.4.2 MADAM

MADAM (Mobility and ADaptation-enAbling Middleware) (Floch, 2006) is an adaptive middleware for mobile computing. The middleware has three functions: collecting information from context, reasoning about the adaptation behaviors and implementing those actions.

The mobile environment faces frequent variety, coming from the users, the natural factors and the mobile applications themselves. Under such circumstances, it is common to adapt to various context. The ultimate objective of MADAM is to realize runtime self-adaptation in mobile devices. As the computing and memory resource is restricted, MADAM attempts to reduce the overhead as much as possible and ensures the quality of services.

The architecture model of MADAM is described as a composition of component types which specify the behaviors for communicating. The variants of runtime components are achieved as distinct component implementations which conform to those types. The components types construct application's framework. And during runtime, application chooses the best implementations and activates them according to runtime status and selection rules. The type-implementation relationships can be nested, that is, a type may contain several implementations; and an implementation is defined as a sub-framework composed of types. An illustrative example is shown in Fig.8.21.

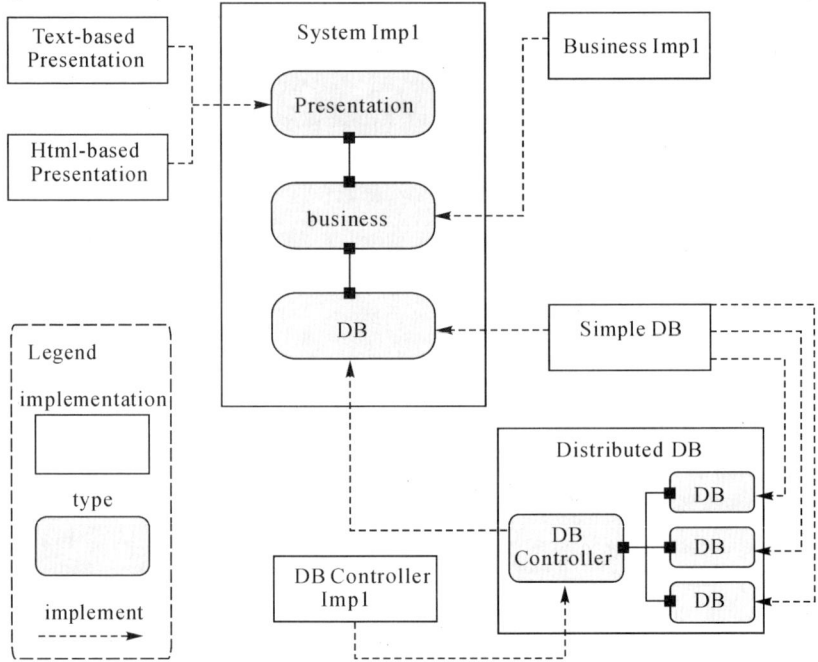

Fig. 8. 21   Sample MADAM framework

Associated with the framework, the implementations contain properties defined by their types and corresponded with the ports which regulate the calculation rules. For example, the memory occupation of a SimpleDB is calculated according to all its records; and that of a DistributedDB may be calculated via the summation of each contained sub DB implantations. For achieving this task, each implementation employs *property predictor functions* to calculate the property values in a given context. During the "choose" phase, MADAM uses the *utility functions*, which associate one weight value to each kind of property, to generate the final *utility* values for architecture candidates combined by an arbitrary set of implementations. MADAM aims to adapt the application to the architecture candidate with the highest *utility value*. In this mechanism, those weights reflect users' needs and concerns, and can be adjusted if they wish to.

An implementation of MADAM in the form of middleware has been published in http://www.ist-madam.org, whose work flow is shown in Fig.8.22. The Context Manager initializes, aggregates and predicts the context relevant properties and notifies their changes to Adaptation Manager, who subsequently takes the reasoning and evaluating job with framework architecture model, and finally generates the valid reconfiguration solution. And Configurator is responsible of comparing the input reconfigured model and current instance architecture model, the representation of current application architecture with concrete implementations. When appropriate (the new model owns a higher utility value, for example), Configurator executes the reconfigure steps.

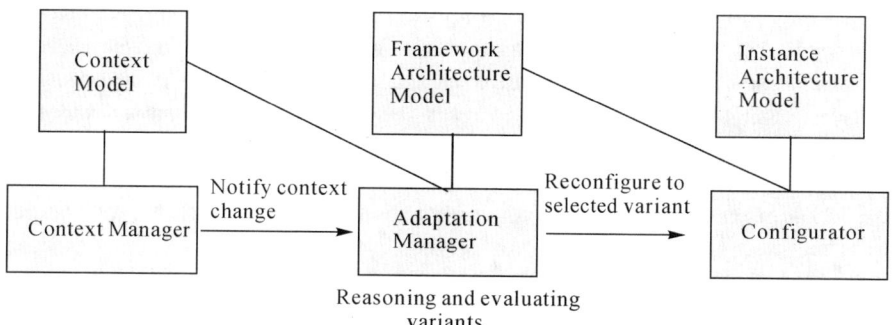

Fig. 8. 22   MADAM Middleware

MADAM seems similar to Rainbow. They both maintain the runtime architecture models; both reflect the context through properties; both separate the adaptation and computing parts. However, they are different in those aspects of their specific concerns. Rainbow is a general infrastructure attempting to suit for a variety of systems. The result is it is split to the common adaptation modules and system specific knowledge part. Meanwhile it adopts a complicated architecture model facilitating the increase of its adaptive range. What's more, it defines a language to specify the adaptation strategies. In the contrary, MADAM is designed for mobile devices. It has to simplify everything to accelerate the process of reasoning and adaptation. Its framework architecture model is rather concise, only suitable for the actions such as component replacing. The adaptation rules in MADAM use the simple utility functions, effectively reducing the overhead incurred by reasoning.

There are many other examples of flexible software. (Yang, 2006) introduces mobile agent into the architecture-based self-adaptation. (Zhang, 2006) establishes runtime architecture model with Petri Net. (Mun, 2006) brings flexibility into the fractal manufacturing system (FrMS). And (Kim, 2005) integrates architectural self-management with software product lines.

8. 5   Summary

This chapter discusses a new branch of research on software architecture. Flexible software architecture is alive. They can feel and take some responses, during which the change behaviors may be validated and ensured as harmless. This capability is a natural extension of the change forms of software, from the maintenance of software's extensibility with such as encapsulation and decoupling, to the manual reconfiguration by writing configure files or changing settings of preference, and finally to the self-behaviors. This is an evolution triggered by faster and faster changes of context, which are driven by business objectives, such as commercial benefits or promotion of competitiness.

Flexible software requires the support of dynamic software architecture, represented by a model or a language that explicitly focuses those behaviors performing the changes in architecture level and the consequence of their executions. The great thing about this is that it restricts the dynamism under control before the implementation dependent model is created, which lets you focus on the issues of highest risk brought by dynamic behaviors. We mention four kinds of formal foundation in the dynamic architecture area, and all of them have their own features. Graph-based approaches are easy to handle, but only concentrate on structures; Algebra Process based models emphasize on behaviors. It is an elaborated method which enables reasoning and validating in a punctilious manner, and thereby evokes too much trouble for practice use. Some ADLs based on them are trying to make the trade-off between formal features and usability. Reflection theory extends the deepness of dynamism. With an infinite number of meta-layers, it is possible to create new component or connector types or even their meta-types if one wishes to. But it has to cooperate with other models together to specify a concrete project. In this perspective, it should be viewed as an infrastructure to describe dynamic software architecture. And Coordination Model provides an abstraction of communication in distributed systems which are very easy to use. But it does not explain how the dynamic behavior happens, but only solves the problems assuming dynamism is given. And it has to define semantics with the help of other formal languages, for example, UNITY.

Flexible software architecture is beyond dynamic architecture, by combining the context awareness and explicit maintenance of runtime architecture model. To apply a flexible software architecture, pre-planning is necessary. This allows people to choose suitable adaptive range, more particularly, taking trade-off among absolute adaptive range, relative adaptive range and profitable adaptive range.

Finally we give brief introduction to several typical examples based on flexible software architecture, which follow the general idea of flexible software architecture, and start the initial stage of software of the next generation.

References

(Ahuja, 1986)   Ahuja, S., Carriero, N. & Gelernter, D. Linda and Friends. Computer 1986(19): 26-34.

(Allen, 1998)   Allen, R. J., Douence, R. & Garlan, D. Specifying and Analyzing Dynamic Software ArchitecturesLncs 1382, Fundamental Approaches to Software Engineering. Springer.1998.

(Anreoli, 1996) Anreoli, J. M., Hankin, C. & M tayer, D. L. *Corrdination Programming: Mechanisms, Models and Semantics*: Imperial College Press. 1996.

(Arbab, 2004) Arbab, F. Reo: A Channel-Based Coordination Model for Component Composition. *Mathematical Structures in Computer Science* 2004 (14): 329-366.

(Banville, 1996) Banville, M. *Sonia: An Adaptation of Linda for Coordination of Activities in OrganizationsLncs* 1061, *Coordination Languages and Models*. Springer.1996.

(Barbacci, 1993) Barbacci, M. R., et al. Durra: A Structure Description Language for Developing Distributed Applications. *Software Engineering* 1993(8): 83-94.

(Bradbury, 2004) Bradbury, J. S., et al. A Survey of Self-Management in Dynamic Software Architecture Specifications. *Proceedings of the 1st ACM SIGSOFT workshop on Self-managed systems* Newport Beach, California.2004:28-33.

(Carriero, 1989) Carriero, N. & Gelernter, D. Linda in Context. *Communications of the ACM* 1989(32): 444-458.

(Carriero, 1994) Carriero, N., Gelernter, D. & Zuck, L. D. *Bauhaus LindaLncs* 924, *Selected Papers from the Ecoop'94 Workshop on Models and Languages for Coordination of Parallelism and Distribution, Object-Based Models and Languages for Concurrent Systems*. Springer.1994.

(Chapman, 1997) Chapman, B., et al. Opus: A Coordination Language for Multidisciplinary Applications, *Techincal Report*, TR-97-30, 1997.

(Chaudet, 2001) Chaudet, C. & Oquendo, F. (2001). Pi-Space: Modelling Evolvable Distributed Software Architectures. In: Arabnia, H. R., (Ed) *Pdpta'2001: Proceedings of the International Conference on Parallel and Distributed Processing Techniques and Applications*. Athens: C S R E a Press.

(Cimpan, 2005) Cimpan, S., Leymonerie, F. & Oquendo, F. *Handling Dynamic Behaviour in Software ArchitecturesSoftware Architecture*, Proceedings. Berlin: Springer-Verlag Berlin.2005.

(Clemens, 2006) Clemens, S. *Modeling and Analyzing Mobile Software Architectures*.2006.

(Cuesta, 2001) Cuesta, C. E., Fuente, P. d. l. & Barrio-Solarzano, M. Dynamic Coordination Architecture through the Use of Reflection. *Proceedings of the 2001 ACM symposium on Applied computing* Las Vegas, Nevada, United States.2001:134-140.

(Cuesta, 2005) Cuesta, C. E., et al. An "Abstract Process" Approach to Algebraic Dynamic Architecture Description. *Journal of Logic and Algebraic Programming* 2005(63): 177-214.

(Floch, 2006) Floch, J., et al. Using Architecture Models for Runtime Adaptability. *Software, IEEE* 2006(23): 62-70.

(Fuggetta, 1998) Fuggetta, A., Picco, G. P. & Vigna, G. Understanding Code Mobility. *IEEE Transactions on Software Engineering* 1998(24): 342-361.

(Garlan, 2004) Garlan, D., et al. Rainbow: Architecture-Based Self-Adaptation with Reusable Infrastructure. *Computer* 2004(37): 46-54.

(Gelemter, 1992)   Gelemter, D. & Carriero, N. Coordination Languages and Their Significance. *Communications of the ACM* 1992(35): 96.

(Georgiadis, 2002)   Georgiadis, I., Magee, J. & Kramer, J. Self-Organising Software Architectures for Distributed Systems. *Proceedings fo the first workshop on self-healing systems*, Charleston, South Carolina.2002:33-38.

(Gruhn, 2004)   Gruhn, V. & Schafer, C. An Architecture Description Language for Mobile Distributed SystemsSoftware Architecture. Berlin: Springer-Verlag Berlin.2004.

(Hirsch, 1998)   Hirsch, D., Inverardi, P. & Montanari, U. Graph Grammars and Constraint Solving for Software Architecture Styles. *Proceedings of the 3rd Inernational Software Architecture Workshop* (ISAW-3).1998:69-72.

(Kim, 2005)   Kim, M., Jeong, J. & Park, S. From Product Lines to Self-Managed Systems : An Architecture-Based Runtime Reconfiguration Framework. *ACM SIGSOFT Software Engineering Notes* 2005(30): 1-7.

(M tayer, 1998)   M tayer, D. L. Describing Software Architecture Styles Using Graph Grammars. *IEEE Transactions on Software Engineering* 1998(24): 521-533.

(Maes, 1987)   Maes, P. Concepts and Experiments in Computational Reflection. *Conference Proceedings on Object Oriented Programming Systems, Languages and Applications*, Orlando, Florida, United States.1987:147-155.

(Magee, 1995)   Magee, J., et al. Specifying Distributed Software Architectures. 1995.

(Maloe, 1994)   Maloe, T. W. & Crowston, K. Interdisciplinary Study of Coordination. *ACM Computing Surveys* 1994(26): 87-119.

(Minsky, 1994)   Minsky, N. H. & Leichter, J. Law-Governed Linda as a Coordination Model. *LNCS 924, Selected papers from the ECOOP ' 94 Workshop on Models and Languages for Coordination of Parallelism and Distribution, Object-Based Models and Languages for Concurrent Systems* 1994.

(Mun, 2006)   Mun, J., Ryu, K. & Jung, M. Self-Reconfigurable Software Architecture: Design and Implementation. *Computers & Industrial Engineering* 2006(51): 163-173.

(Murphy, 2006)   Murphy, A. L., Picco, G. P. & Roman, G.-C. Lime: A Coordination Model and Middleware Supporting Mobility of Hosts and Agents. *ACM Transactions on Software Engineering and Methodology* 2006 (15): 279-328.

(Oquendo, 2003)   Oquendo, F. The Archware Architecture Description Language: Turorial, *Techincal Report*, Report R1.1-1, 2003.

(Oquendo, 2004)   Oquendo, F. Π-Adl : An Architecture Description Language Based on the Higher-Order Typed Π-Calculus for Specifying Dynamic and Mobile Software Architectures. *ACM SIGSOFT Software Engineering Notes* 2004(29): 1-14.

(Oreizy, 1999)   Oreizy, P., et al. An Architecture-Based Approach to Self-Adaptive Software. *IEEE Intelligent Systems* 1999(14): 54-62.

(Papadopoulos, 1998)   Papadopoulos, G. A. & Arbab, F. Coordination Models and Languages *Techincal Report*, SEN-R9834 1998.

(Parrow, 2001)   Parrow, J. To an Introduction to the *Π-Calculus Handbook of Process Algebra*. Elsevier.2001.

(Picco, 1999)   Picco, G. P., Murphy, A. L. & Roman, G. C. *Lime: Linda Meets Mobility*.1999:368-377.

(Picco, 2000)   Picco, G. P., Murphy, A. L. & Roman, G.-C. Developing Mobile Computing Applications with Lime. *Proceedings of the 22nd international conference on Software engineering*. Limerick, Ireland.2000:766-769.

(Picco, 2005)   Picco, G. P., Balzarotti, D. & Costa, P. Lights: A Lightweight, Customizable Tuple Space Supporting Context-Aware Applications. *Proceedings of the 2005 ACM symposium on Applied computing Santa Fe, New Maxico*.2005:413-419.

(Roman, 1997)   Roman, G.-C., McCann, P. J. & Plun, J. Y. Reasoning and Specification in Mobile Computing. *ACM Transactions on Software Engineering and Methodology* 1997(6): 250-282.

(Sangiorgi, 2001)   Sangiorgi, D. & Walker, D. *The Π-Calculus: A Theory of Mobile Processes*: Cambrige University Press.2001.

(Schmerl, 2002)   Schmerl, B. & Garlan, D. Exploiting Architectural Design Knowledge to Support Self-Repairing Systems. *Proceedings of the 14th international conference on software engineering and knowledge engineering*, Ischia, Italy.2002:241-248.

(Sommerville, 1996)   Sommerville, I. & Dean, G. Pcl: A Language for Modeling Evolving System Architectures. *Software Engineering* 1996(11): 111-121.

(Taentzer, 1998)   Taentzer, G., Goedicke, M. & Meyer, T. *Dyanmic Change Management by Distributed Graph Transformation: Towards Configurable Distributed SystemsLncs 1764, Theory and Application of Graph Transformations*. Springer.1998.

(Tolksdorf, 1996)   Tolksdorf, R. Coordinating Services in Open Distributed Systems with LauraLncs 1061, *Proceedings of the First International Conference on Coordination Languages and Models*. Springer.1996.

(Wermelinger, 1998)   Wermelinger, M. Towards a Chemical Model of Software Architecture Reconfiguration. *IEE Proceedings-Software* 1998(145): 130-136.

(Wermelinger, 2001)   Wermelinger, M., Lopes, A. & Fiadeiro, J. L. A Graph Based Architectural (Re)Configuration Language. *Proceedings of the 8th European Software Engineering Conference and 9th ACM SIGSOFT Symposium on the Foundations of Software Engineering (ESEC/FSE 2001)*. Software Engineering Notes, 2001(26): 21-32.

(Yang, 2006)   Yang, Q., Yang, X. & Xu, M. A Mobile Agent Approach to Dynamic Architecture-Based Software Adaptation. *ACM SIGSOFT Software Engineering Notes* 2006(31): 1-7.

(Zhang, 2006)   Zhang, J. & Cheng, B. H. C. Model-Based Development of Dynamically Adaptive Software. Proceeding of the 28th international conference on Software engineering Shanghai, China.2006:371-380.

9

A Vision on Software Architecture

In this chapter, we summarize software architecture in modern software industry; we mainly describe the importance of SA in the whole software engineering circle. In its following section, we list the main research areas of software architecture in future. After reading this chapter, readers will know the position of SA in software engineering, and what we can do about software architecture.

9.1 Software Architecture in Modern Software Industry

In modern times, the software industry has become the main force which impulses our economy. At the same time, software industry is the important guarantee that keeps our nations independent. In the following sections, we will introduce the categorizing of software and software product line.

9.1.1 Categorizing Software

Software can be classified as package, embedded software and software services. In the following paragraphs, we will take China as example.

In China, the earning of package in 2004 is 47.8 billion. In this earning, 8.996 billion is system software, middleware is 698 million, and application software is 3.0453 billion. The earning of embedded software is 67.4 billion, and the earning of software service is 93.7 billion.

According to the data above, we can find:

- The global market of software is continually increasing, especially in China. But the quotient of China is still so low. In 2003, the increase ratio of global software industry is 7.39%, the whole scale is 749 billion dollars. It keeps on making great contributions to the development of world's economy. In China, the increase ratio is even higher. For instance, the whole earning is 160 billion in 2003, which is about 19.3 billion dollars, and increases about 45.45% to the 2002. Within this 160 billion, the export earning is 2 billions, which increases about 33.33% to 2002. Although we make great improvement, the global quotient of China is only

2.5% . Compared with the U.S. (about 39.67%) and Japan (about 10.22%), we are still so small. But this fact also indicates that we have large space to develop our software industry.

• The application software develops quickly, but system software develops a little slowly. At present, 11 software industry bases, 6 software export bases and 172 key enterprises are built. In 2003, the earning of application software is 59.5 billion, which increases 85.5% by last 2002 and is about 74.2% in all the earnings of software products. In the same time, the system software develops slowly, the earnings in 2003 is about 7.8 billion, increases by 14.7% , and is about 9.5% in all the earnings of software products. Many foreign products still keep high market lot.

• If we take stock of international market, we can find in the post PC times, the development of information electric fitment, mobile telephone and PDA provides wide market for the development of embedded software. In 2004, the earning of global embedded software reaches 200 billion dollars. In recent years, the embedded software in China also develops quickly, and the ratio of embedded software in software industry is increasing, especially in communicating areas. In a lot of communication devices, the value of embedded software is about 30% － 40% in the whole device. In mobile device, digital fitment, digital machine tool, automobile electronic, medicine electronic, aviation and spaceflight, entertainment facility, the earning of embedded software is about 10% － 30% in the total value of device. The digital content industry is developing dramatically, especially network games. In 2003, the earning of global network game is about 30 billion. The earning of network games in America and China has already exceeded the earning of movie industry. People's culture is not only cartoon, games, but also the applications based on digital content process and service technology which are involved into education, culture and science. In 2003, the market of digital content industry is about 1.5% in international market. In China, the market of digital content industry will develop rapidly in 5 to 10 years, maybe will increase about 30% every year. The market requirement is bloom.

• The software industry is to be of network, of service, and globalization. Network is the most powerful development trend. The regulation of software industry is changing: software is changing from product to service; software industry turns into service industry.

The second class of software is system software. System software can control and harmonize computer, communicate devices and other external devices, can make them work so as to facilitate users. This software can provide middle support and run-time environment. System software can be classified as operating system, database management system and sustain software.

As computed, in 2004, the market scale of system software in China is 8.996 billion, among which market of operating system is 4.419 billion (about 49% in all the system software market); the market of database management system is 2.006 billion, the market of sustain software is 2.571 billion.

After several decades, system software has become a large industry; the Unix/

J2EE, Windows/Net/ and Linux/OSS are formed. Unix/J2EE is good at its techniques; Windows/Net strengthens its monopolization position. The Linux/OSS system is developing under the banner of open source.

With the rapid development of information technology, technique of system software is changing and developing. The trends of system software are systematization, network and high reliability.

- systematization. At present, competition of software is not only product competition, but also system competition. Operating system, database management system and middleware software is merging, software development toolkit is integrated with software runtime toolkit, forming a uniformed basic software toolkit. For example, in the product of "NET", operating system, database system, component runtime toolkit and other related software development environment are included.

- Network. With the coming of network period, information techniques are facing the change from "machine-centered" to "network-centered". Because it is system software, but not users that accomplish the performance optimization, the code which can be written once, but run anywhere is the necessity trends.

- High reliability. The large hardware resource and complicated software hierarchy make information system face a challenge of controlling complexity. Society are dependent more and more on software. Once the national defense and commercial sustain software systems are damaged, the result is calamity. Information society is based on service and dependents more on service's time and availability. High reliability techniques which have high availability and QoS are the main research content of future system software.

Of course, Internet is the greatest technique development in the 20th century; its popularization and development provide us a global scale information base establishment.

How to provide available software techniques and products for a number of network resources is an important requirement and this requirement makes the middleware appear as a new type of software. From its original function, we can find that middleware is a distributed software which is in the middle of system software and application software and link system software and application software on the internet, this kind of software mainly solves the interconnect and interoperation problems of distributed software on the heterogeneous network environment.

With the rapid development of internet, middleware has more and more connotation, becomes the middle place software. Its main goal is to meet the requirement of large scale application software that runs on different platforms in the network distributed computing environment. This kind of software can shield the heterogeneity of computer's hardware and software, and is the platform which sustains the application software

Because of the importance of middleware, the main computer enterprises all make their own middleware software platform strategic plans and application solutions. The main research plan includes: Sun's SUN ONE plan, IBM's WEB SERVICE strategic plan, Oracle's network software platform develop plan based on Oracle 9i, Microsoft's Microsoft Net plan, BEA's WEBLOGIC, etc. At present, three main distributed computing standards are formed, which are CORBA, J2EE and DCOM. At the same time, W3C provides the network information change criterion and XML standard.

At present, the main development trends of middleware includes: (1) Middleware techniques directly support component's deployment and running at the implementation level, and object middleware are developing towards the component middleware. (2) Internet's dynamic and open characteristic and the industry patterns requires that systems based on different middleware are capable of interoperating on internet, so the web service appears as "middleware's middleware". (3) Because of its low band and low availability, wireless network makes a challenge for the middleware techniques, generating a new research hotspot—mobile computing middleware. (4) The requirements for opening the inner detail of middleware and reusing middleware's functions in a manner of "white box", lead to the research of reflective middleware. (5) The function's Quality of Service for the high level application provided by middleware has been attached much importance. (6) For a middleware, how to support a number of resources becomes an important application fields we must face.

In 2003, the market of global middleware software increases quickly, the total turnover is about 7 billion dollars, increased by 27% compared with the last year. The earning of middleware product in America market is 4.8 billion, which occupies about 68.6% in the global middleware market. As computed, in 2004, the scale of middleware market in China is 0.698 billion, the increase rate is 30.5%, which is higher than the whole increase rate of China's IT market. The main enterprises such as BEA, IBM, Oracle, Microsoft and SUN always dominate China's middleware market, and has main market lot.

In this part, we will discuss the trends of application software. Application software can implement a concrete application, but not need users to program again. This kind of software can be classifies as general application software and special application software. Generally speaking, general application software includes security software, office software, management software and game software. Special application software is customized for a special use of a special industry, which can meet special requirement. This kind of application includes finance, telecom, government, education, scientific research, energy sources, traffic, etc.

In China, the application software develops especially quickly; the techniques improve fast, especially industry application software.

In this paragraph, we will discuss the development trends of embedded software. Embedded software includes embedded operating system, embedded software develop tools and embedded middleware.

In recent years, the embedded software industry develops quickly in China; the proportion is increasing in the software products. As computed, in 2004, the market scale of embedded software in China is 67.362 billion, which is beyond the suit software, and becomes the second largest earning of software industry. At present, the market of embedded software is being divided. Products facing different fields appear, including intelligent cell phone, digital devices, automobile electronic and traditional industry alteration. The research and application of embedded software has become the main techniques for "information bring along industry", and became the important force of software industry developing in China.

In recent five years, embedded software has the following developing trends:

• The core of embedded operating system is getting smaller, more reliable, more available, higher in performance and better constructed in structure. The operating system begins to support integrated development and debug. More over, Model Driven Development (MDD) provided by embedded operating system is also entering the period of getting mature. Wireless communication and power management is becoming more and more important.

• Open source in the industry level is becoming popular, especially in the area of domain specific embedded operating system. Different enterprises make up their own standards and platforms, which share something in common: these standards and platforms support system open, share of design technology, reuse of software and hardware and compatible application. With the help of them, maintenance and collaboration are more convenient, which is critical and effective to increase capability of competition.

• Technologies in those free open source software are extraordinarily favored in embedded applications. For example, Linux for embedded devices is on the way of becoming the mainstream. Linux is excellent in its characters of open; modularity, high execution performance and reliability, accepting technique support from the software development enthusiasts around the world. And J2ME/JINI, the representative of embedded software development technologies, is another case of open source's influence to embedded area.

• The trend of integration between embedded software and System On Chip (SOC) is more obvious. The quick development of SOC forces the amalgamation. In this case, the edge between these two areas becomes more blurry. Embedded software is often existed in the form of hardware Intellectual Property (IP), which helps to improve the performance in real time, and to enhance the maintainability. The component library technology based on embedded IP is creating a growing up software industry.

• The "deep connection" of Internet and the "dynamic reconfiguration" of sensor networks improve the tight combination between the embedded and the Internet technologies. Thus, the embedded products and the Internet applications promote each other. Finally the former will become the primary terminals of Internet. And its soul, embedded operating system will help to improve the experience of Internet.

• The ubiquitous embedded software will get the crucial position in the trend of embedded software development. Its ubiquitous, self-adaptive, nomad and permanent features will bring creative development to the embedded area. Wireless communication products based on it will get the importance in the area of embedded software. This kind of software enables that anyone can access any information anywhere at any time.

In this paragraph, we will discuss the development trends of software service. Software service industry is all the software researches and relevant activities except producing application software, including system integrated, software contract, consultation, software customization, data processing and machining, system maintenance, management, etc. In short, software service is an important modern service industry.

As computed, in 2004, the earning of software service in China is about 93.7 billion, which is about half of the total software industry earning, and is the largest module of the software industry, which attracts most people. Software processing service is about 20 billion, which is one of the most important industry trends of software service.

The software industry is one of the fastest growing industries in the world. Even companies that have been associated largely with hardware in the past, estimate that $80\% \sim 90\%$ of their engineers are involved in software development. As a consequence of this rapid expansion there is a serious worldwide shortage of software engineers who are able to deal with the complexity of developing high quality software systems.

9.1.2 Software Product Line

Developing software architecture needs plenty of time and money, it also needs intelligent personnel to take part in. Therefore, we hope to reuse the architecture in different systems so as to get the most return. An organization which is good at architecture treats its architecture as the most valuable fortune, and is searching the best methods to generate extra earning and debase its cost through using its architecture. Generating extra earning and debasing its cost both can be implemented through reusing architecture.

In this part, we will discuss how to reuse software architecture explicitly after programming in relative systems. When an organization develops many similar systems and uses the same architecture, it can get more advantages, including cost debasing and time-to-market shortening. This is just what the advantages of software product line. We can define it as:

> A set of software-intensive systems sharing a common, managed set
> of features that satisfy the specific needs of a particular market segment
> or mission and that are developed from a common set of core assets in a
> prescribed way. (Clements, 2001)

After finishing the software product line, we can save every reusable asset in the "core asset base", because we can apply it in many systems, the reusable asset is more to our profit. In the ideal case, the core assets have variation point, that is to say, we can delete it quickly. In a successful product line, system architecture turns into getting proper asset from the core asset base, then we can adapt it according to the requirement of the current system we will build, then we can combine them to form an integrated system.

Of course, the product line has nothing new the manufacturing. At present, every company use different method to reuse the common things sufficiently. The "software" product line based on the common things of products represents a creative, development concept in software engineering. Every user has its own requirement, and this demands the flexibility of every company. The software product line simplifies the creation of system aiming at special user and user group.

The successful use of product line brings cost debasing, time-to market shortening, the benefit is so great. We will give two examples:

- After using product line, Nokia produce 25 — 30 telephone models from 4 in the past.
- After using product line, Cummins Company can produce software about diesel engine in 1 week for 1 year in the past.

Creating a successful product line depends on the software engineering, technique management, and organization management's corporation. We will mainly discuss software architecture in software engineering.

The essence of software product line is: when producing product family, we reuse asset in a canonical, politic way. The companies and development personnel think product line is so useful, because we can use the common characteristics through reusing, so as to realize the product value. The factors of software product line includes:

- Requirement: most requirements are similar to the systems developed earlier, so we can reuse it, not needing analysis of requirement.
- Architecture design: when designing software architecture, the most intelligent personnel must put much time in the process. We have found that, after establishing architecture, the quality aim is diminished in much degree (such as performance, reliability, modifiability, etc.). If the architecture is not proper, the system development for sure is not successful. But, for the development of a new product, we can jump over this step through reusing architecture.
- Element: software elements are useful in single product. In general, it is only code reuse. The element reusing includes: reusing original design work, capturing and reusing the redeeming feature of a design, avoiding the bad designs. The element mainly includes: interface, document, test plan and any model design to estimate and measure its action. A collection of reusable element is the user interface of a system; this represents many key design strategies.
- Modeling and analysis: the performance analysis, distribute system problems, processing assignment can all be reused.
- Test: after using product line, all of the test plan, test process, test case, test data and test tool need to exist.
- Project programming: we can use experience to forecast the future work,

including budget and schedule. We need not build our work breakdown structure. So we can easily establish team, team scale.

- Process, method and tool: the configuration control rule, application program, document plan and authorization process, tool environment, system generation and distribute rule, code standard and other project plan support activities can all be reused in product. The whole software development process is ready, and is being used all the time.
- Personnel: the applications developed must have common characteristics, so we can translate personnel among projects. So the special techniques of these personnel can be used in the entire product developing of the whole family.
- Sample system: treat the products as high quality demo antitypes and high quality engineering design antitypes.
- Diminishing bug: using product line can improve quality, because every new system benefits from the old system's success of diminishing bug, and the old system already uses the product line. The self-confidence of developing personnel and customers is increasing. The more complicated the system is, the higher return can be got when the project design problems are solved.

The software product line depends on reuse, but just as described in the beginning of this chapter, in the software engineering, reuse has a long history, but is not resplendence. The return of reuse is always not so good as we expect. Why? The reason is that in all the time, we build the reuse based on the theory that "if you have built reuse base, you can get product line". The reuse base saves the elements of the previous project, and we expect the development personnel check this reuse base before coding new elements. It is almost likely that we produce any product according to the model. If the information in the reuse base is small, developing personnel can get little useful information, at last he gives up; if the information in the reuse base is large and abundance, it is hard to get the useful information we need. If the element is too small, it is easier to develop new element rather than using the existing one; but if the element is too large, it is hard to understand the functions of these elements, so development personnel can hardly reuse it in any case. In most reuse bases, the families are often mistiness. The requirement of new application can hardly match with the quality attributes of elements provided in the reuse base.

In any cases, these elements are possible not proper for the architecture model used by the new system. Although an element can work well, has proper quality attributes, is it the required architecture? Has it the proper alternant protocol? Dose it adhere to the new application's mistake processing? It is worthy of doubting.

Software product line is useful through building a context for reuse. Define architecture, specify function, and comprehend its quality attributes. Only these elements which are considered for reuse when to be produced can be put into the reuse base.

Like any other architectures, it is necessary to evaluate the software product line. In fact, many systems use architecture; as a result, the evaluation of software product line is important.

The evaluation skills are very good for the evaluation of software product line. It is necessary to evaluate the architecture's robust and general attributes, so as to make sure it can be treated as the base of products in the software product line. To make sure the architecture satisfy the requirement of products' action and quality, evaluating architecture is necessary. We first discuss the content and method of evaluating, then discuss the evaluating time.

What and how to evaluate.

We must mainly evaluate the variation point, so as to make sure: they are proper; they provide adequate flexibility, so that they can occupy the estimated scale of product line; they support quick construct product; they will not generate any performance cost that can not be accepted. If the evaluation is based on scene, we must get the different scenes related to architecture instantiate to support different products in the family. Besides, the different product in the product line may have different quality attribute requirements, we must evaluate the combining ability of architecture. At present, we also need different scenes.

In general case, at the primary time, the hardware and other factors that effect performance are unknown. In this case, evaluation can fix on the boundary of performance, and can postulate a boundary for hardware and other variation factors. This evaluation can fix on the potential conflict, so that you can make strategies and policy solve these conflicts.

When to evaluate.

We must evaluate the instance and variation of the architecture that build one or more products in the software product line. Whether to evaluate the product's architecture in a single, special way depends on the differences between this architecture and product line. If there is no difference, we can simplify the evaluation of product line architecture, because we will solve the problems generated in the evaluation of a problem. In fact, just as product architecture is a variation of product line architecture, product architecture is a variation of product line architecture evaluation. Therefore, depending on the evaluation method, evaluated products have the potential of reuse, so we must memorize it when creating these products. In general case, the result of product architecture evaluation can provides useful feedbacks for the product line designers, and improves the architecture.

When the new product proposed to develop is not in the scope of the original product line, we can evaluate the product line architecture, to find whether this architecture is enough for the new product to be developed. If it is enough, we can extend the scope of product line, so that the new products are included, or we can generate a new product; if it is not enough, we can know how to modify the architecture through evaluating, so that the product line architecture accepts the new product to be developed.

To use product line successfully, the development organization must have ample experience. Techniques are not the only obstacle; organization, process and commercial problems are equally important to get the dominance in getting software product line methods.

For any project, architecture definition is an important activity, but just as we have seen, we must emphasize the variation points of software product line. For any project, configuration is also important, but for software product line, configuration management is even more complicated, because every product is the result of binding many variations. The configuration management is to copy the products' all versions that have been delivered to end-users. The product here refers to code and sustain product, including requirement standardization, test cases, user handbook, and installation guide. The configuration management includes: find which version in the reuse base is used, how to reduce the product line asset, and what special code and document are added.

Analysis of every aspect of product line is beyond the scope of this book, but we will analyze the key aspect, so that you can know the difference between the product line and single system development. These problems must be faced when the organization considers whether to use product line.

Just like using any other new techniques, it is difficult to make the organization use the product line. How to solve this problem depends on the organization's culture and context.

When the managers decide to use the product line, it is using product line top-down. When using this method, it is necessary to change the work style of the personnel who are hard working. When the designers and development personnel recognize that they need not do the same things each other, start to share resource and develop the common core asset, it is using product line bottom-up. When using this method, we must find a manager who supports using product line, and can make other department's personnel use the product line too. These two methods are both available: they both need a person who supports product line and can give plenty of help. This person absolutely believe the great use of product line, and can share the believable thought with other personnel.

Independent with the problems of techniques development orientation, the problem is how the product itself to develop. As following, we will give two models:

In a proactive product line, the organizations use a broad scope to define the product line family. They use the experience, their comprehension of market and technique development trends and excellent commerce sense, not crystal ball to build the proactive product line. In this two product line development model, the proactive model is stronger, because it can make the organization constitute the most far-reaching strategy. Explicitly fixing on the boundary of product line, you can find what new products are needed in the market, but they are not produced, so that you can extend the product, quickly fill up this gap. In a word, proactive product line scope can make the organization hold its own fortune.

In some time, the organization can not use the hint confirmation of proactive product line model to forecast the market requirement. Maybe because this is a new field, or the markets are in variation, or the organization does not have enough fund to construct a core asset base that covers the whole product line scope. In this case, the organization is more likely to use a reactive model. In this model, organization constructs the product family's one or more members according to the former products. With the development of every new product, the architecture and design blue prints are extended according to the requirements and the core asset base is constructed with the elements which are "proved" but not "planed". The reactive model does not emphasize the advance plan and strategy orientation. On contrast, the organizations operate under the market's baton.

Understanding various models is good for the organization to choose their proper model. The proactive model requires initial investment, but spends hardly on the poor work; the reactive model almost has no initial investment, but need to do much poor work over again. For a special organization, how to choose model depends on the idiographic case of the special organization.

The organizations who own the product line have a architecture and a related set of elements. The organization often can create a new member of the product line; it not only has the common characteristics with other products in the product line, but also has its special characteristics.

A problem related to the product line is how to manage its evaluation. With time going, product line—especially the core asset that is used to construct product— also needs evaluating. This evaluation is forced by external and internal source.

External source

The element created by external source can be added to the product line. For instance, some functions finished by internal elements must be finished by external source. Or the future product must use new techniques, but these techniques are included in the external developed elements. New characteristics can be added into the product line, so as to satisfy the user's requirements or adapt the competition.

Internal source

It is necessary to make sure whether the new functions added to the product are in the scope of product line. If yes, we can simply finish the development of new product using the product line reuse base. If not, we must make decision: we can depend upon the improved product from the product line to evaluate, or enlarge the asset base, so that the reuse base can include these new functions. If these new functions are likely to be used in future products, updating the product line is the most intelligent choice, but updating the core asset base needs time. If the product line's asset has changed, though the organization can withdraw the constructed products, and can change the product according to the newest asset base, it can not do so. Making product and product line compatible needs time and energy, but if it does not do so, the updating of future product will take more time and energy. This is because product must be consistent with the newest product line elements, if not do so, we can not add new functions to the product line.

In the rest of this part, we give the organization structure. The asset base product has its own evaluation way, it requires the organization to decide how to manage it and how the products develop. Jan Bosch searched the product line organization model, and identified four types as following (Bosch, 2000):

Developing department

All the software developments are concentrated in a unit. We expect every member in the unit is almighty, and can do field project design and application project design. Small organizations and organizations that provide consultation usually use this model. Although this model is quite simple, and convenient to communicate, but only owning a unit may has many problems.

Operation unit

Every operation is in charge of a subset of the products family's system. These subsets are gathered according to their similarity. The shared assets are developed by the units that need them, and provide it to the organization; the operation units that are developing new assets can cooperate with each other. This model has variation, and it depends on the flexibility of the operation unit when developing new assets. If has no restriction, the products will be different on its evaluation way, so that making the software product line can not achieve its targets.

Fields project unit

We must specify a special unit that is in charge of the core assets' development and maintenance, thus the operation unit can construct products according to these core assets. Bosch points out, if the number of personnel of the organization beyond 100, the single communication channel between operation units can not accept the work strength, and building a shared asset communication channel is necessary. In this model, we must have a strong, standard process, to manage the communication between units, so as to make sure the good operation of product line is the main goal of every department.

The layered fields project unit

We must treat the large or complicated product line as a layered system. That is to say, the product line can be made up of sub-cluster. Compared with other members in the product line, these sub-clusters have more common characteristics. In this case, a field's project unit develops shared assets for the whole product line; another field's project unit develops shared assets for the special sub-cluster. This instance has two layers, but if the sub-clusters have their own special sub-clusters, this model can be extends infinitely. The layered fields unit is proper for the large organization to construct large product line. The main disadvantage is the model is too large, so the response of organization to new requirement is slow.

Because more and more organization find that using product line can improve the products' cost, process and quality, this method become more and more popular.

But, just as other new fields, this technique is unknown in many aspects. Considering from the architecture aspect, the key point is to fix on and manage the common characteristics and variation point, but we must solve the non-technique problems at the same time, including how to use this model, how to arrange the organization's structure and how to maintain the external interfaces.

9. 2   Software Architecture Used in Other Fields

9. 2. 1   The Outline of Software Architecture Application Practice

From the date that SA is put forward, the theory research and industry practice are both attached much importance. In a word, the application and generalization of SA are incarnated in these several aspects:

- The establishment of industry standards

For instance, IEEE established the international standards which are related to software architecture (IEEE, 2000); SAE established the standards of ADL, which is called AADL; in the UML standards established by OMG, the 4+1 views defined by (Kruchten, 1995) are also used; the UML 2.0 standards absorbed the research achievement of software architecture, the concept of connectors, combined components which are brought in from SA as new notion is also absorbed; in many industrial frameworks, the notion of connector is also explicitly brought in, such as JSR 112 standards, the J2EE Connector Architecture is established, which is used to connect heterogeneous systems.

- The development of real product

For example, the Bell Laboratory enforces the application of SA in real software products development, and through the form of projects unite, entering into science, the experiences of industry practice are contributed to the software architecture researcher. For instance, the SEI in CMU owns lots of research personnel from industry. In software enterprise, software architects are independent as a special profession, and become a technology leader of a software project. The most typical instance is Bill Gates, who treats himself as the chief software architect.

- The relative books and courses

The SA is attached with much importance, it is also incarnated in publishing of related books and the setting of related sources. The software architecture technology boost community was founded in CMU-SEI. This organization published a set of books, courses, and products related to software architecture; the Worldwide Institute of Software Architects and International Association of Software Architects are also founded, and they enforce the education and application of SA through book publishing and community member activities.

9. 2. 2   The Development Trends of Domain-Specific Software

The software architecture is the new theory arisen in recent years. The Domain-Specific Software Architecture (DSSA) is one of its trends. Because of its accordance with engineering requirement, it develops quickly.

For the design of any large scale software, the key aspect is to organize its main architecture, because the architecture represents the computing elements and their relations on a high level, and this is just the design of architecture. For a long time, software architecture is an important content in the software engineering, and in the recent years, software architecture appears as a dependent field. In nowadays, this trend has the following characteristics: much work is done in the module interfaces; Domain Special Architecture, Architecture Description language. Design handbook, and architecture design environment, these all belong to the software architecture level design; the others include the whole general outline design, the global control structure design, communication, synchronism, protocol design of data accessing, constitution of the balance of scale and performance for the design element, and the choice of design methods.

Although software architecture has already been a main content in software engineering, many scholars bring forward their own viewpoint. But up to now, there is no universal accepted definition. The earlier researcher such as Garlan defined software architecture as "the structure of program and system component, their relationship, and the principle and guidelines that govern their design and evaluation". This definition describes the main aspect of architecture, but the concrete content must be designed and implemented in research and development.

These two development trends must be attached much importance, and worth a lot of thought. One trend is that, after many years, the development personnel start to recognize that we must develop some shared method, techniques, normal formula, and conventional grammar to construct some complicated systems. And in nowadays, many research articles come out. For instance, the rectangle and line graph accompanying with high level system description normally hint the "pips" and "Server/Client system". They permit the designers to use this simple and abstract method that makes the system easy to understand to describe the complicated systems. Again, they provide effective semantic content to tell others the special characteristics that this system owns, for instance, the desired evaluation ways, the whole computing normal formulas and the relationship with other similar systems.

The other trend is: the more and more attention to the supply of reusable framework for the products used in special fields. These developments are based on this thought: we can distill the common aspect of related systems, so as to construct new systems through instantiating the common design in low cost. The familiar example is the standard decomposition of compiler. With this method, people can construct a new language compiler in shorter time. The second example is the standard communication protocal, which makes manufacturers be able to provide services in different abstract level. The last example is GUI tool kits and frameworks, such as menu or dialog box, with which we can create rich client with much less effort.

The architecture design of large scale software always plays an important role in the process which determines whether the system is successful or failed. This is because, if we choose an unsuited architecture, the result is a disaster. The recognition and comprehension of architecture are more and more important. This will lead to the appearance of more regular architecture design, and this architecture design will improve our abilities to effectively construct our software system efficiently. Especially, using software architecture in principle will bring much benefit in the following five aspects:

- Comprehension

Software architecture can simplify the understanding of the system through building abstract description on high level of systems. In addition, the software architecture description opens out the system constraint on high level and the basic principles which determines the special architecture.

- Reuse

The architectural description supports reuse in multiple levels, and the current reuse research is mainly on component lib. The architecture design can support reuse of large component and multiple component integration. The DSSA, framework and normal formula for design already have these trends.

- Evaluation

The software architecture can reveal the orientation of system evaluation. System maintenance personnel can better understand the offshoot of system modification, so that we can estimate the modification cost more accurately.

- Analysis

The architecture description provides new artifice for the analysis, including the high level check of system obdurability, the consistence of architecture styles, the consistence of quality attributes, the special fields' architecture analysis which conform to the special form.

- Management

The successful of software architecture will be the main milestone of software industry processing. The architecture must satisfy the requirement of system initialization and the desired development orientation. When starting to develop the product, developers do not consider to satisfy the condition, as a result this system will not be fit or not modifiable.

The software architecture is a framework that helps to understand the system component and the relationship between them, especially the attributes which always span time and implementation. This comprehension is very necessary for the current system analysis and future system integration. On the support of analysis, architecture holds the consistence of fields' knowledge and the real circumstance, enforces the evaluation of design and the actualization of component, and reduces the emulator and antitype construction. On the support of integration, the software architecture provides the basis for building the product family, using domain knowledge construct and maintain module, subsystem and system.

In the constraint of reducing budget and shortening development time, and under the continual requirements of system's complication and extendedness, the reuse attribute becomes more and more important. In the document of "Software reuse estimation and strategy" by Department of Defense, the DOD emphasized the importance of using architecture as the center reuse techniques to develop and sustain the whole software cycle. To reach this goal, DOD sponsored many researches which treat the architecture as the focus. These research include: STARS, CARDS, DSSA, Prototech and software engineering foundation, the SATI in SEI, CMU, etc. As the reusable framework, architecture's availability can be seen from the similarity between civil engineering and chemical engineering. Secondly, the effort from distinct and applied architecture techniques, can be considered as one part of entering the mature software engineering law.

The software architecture techniques are implemented in the STARS and DSSA plan. The double life cycle model as shown in Fig.9.1 and the three level system model of DSSA as shown in Fig.9.2 can be treated as the different views on the same processing which is architecture-centered.

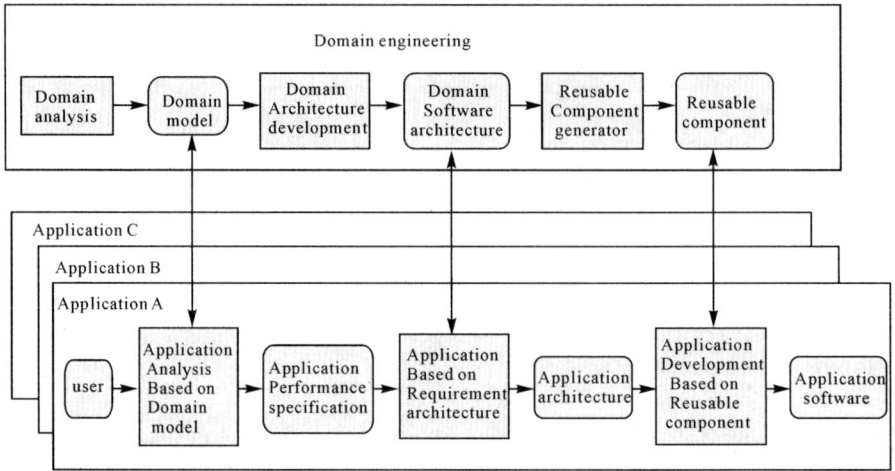

Fig. 9. 1   STARS' double life cycle

Essentially, DSSA is a collection of software component. It is written in standard structure and protocol, and it is for special task, then is generalized, used for the whole similar problems.

DSSA provides a omnibus software design method for a kind problems in a large range. It concentrates the designer's interests on the special requirement of current problems, and the common problems judged by DSSA are omitted. If the designer wants to use DSSA method, software engineer must provides descriptions of special requirement to the special problems, then the solution to a special problems can be generated from the whole design according to the DSSA. The system checks the consistence of the problems description, and the generated software guarantees the solution of this problem.

In the process of designing universal components for large, middle commercial systems, we can use DSSA method. To build domain model, we must know customers' requirement, decompose scene, and make the problem domain dictionary, so as to make the E-R graph, the dataflow graph and state transition graph. Then, we can bring forward the object model, generate domain model according to object model. This is a general method. The Unified Model Language is recommended. The

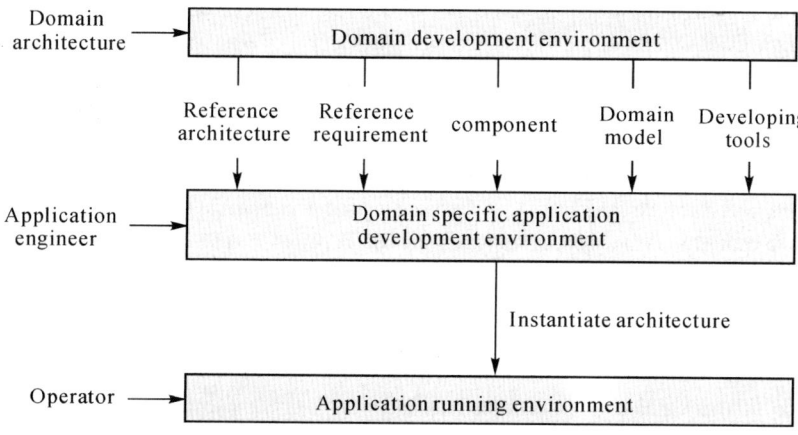

Fig. 9. 2   DSSA's three-level system model

UML is a language that mainly refers to the OMT and Booch method, inosculates other object-oriented analysis design method. UML is convenient to describe and assist the analysis and design work of software system. Using DSSA also has the following requirement: in the complicated constructing process, we must use the increment method smartly. In the linear documents, we must provide domain architecture descriptions that have different complication, so that users can modify the connotative domain knowledge, and add them to their own description.

Most of the complicated problems can not be solved directly, hence we decompose them into several simpler problems, and these simpler problems can be decomposed into basic ingredient. For example, developing a new compiler for the new language on new machine can be treated as an instance of complier construction problem. We know, a compiler construction problem can be decomposed into scanning, parsing, name analysis, and code generating by special method. Problems which can be decomposed using this method are called "composite problems". After analysis, composite problems can be decomposed into "ingredient problems".

The comprehension of composite problems and their solutions include three aspects: how to decompose a composite problem into ingredient problems; how to solve each ingredient problem; how to composite these independent solutions for the ingredient problems into a solution for the composite problems. The method that can be used to solve DSSA problems can only be used to solve the problems whose domain are recognized clearly, whose basic requirement can be modeled. Only to these problems, the advantages of DSSA can be incarnated. We take the compiler software as example. After several decades' research, it is considered that DSSA is the proper solution. For example, Colorado University used the DSSA methods constructed the compiler Eli, and this compiler can be used in a variety of environment, including FORTRAN, C, PSDL, etc. The especially important characteristic is that it can construct a new compiler for a new language quickly. The success of Eli directs the orientation of DSSA developing, using this thought and method; we can provide good help for the software development's velocity and quality.

In the process of practice, the solutions of real problems have many similarities, and the commercial systems are a good example. The operations of commercial systems have many similarities, and are easy to distill domain model. How to combine the real conditions, use these advanced thoughts and method such as software architecture and DSSA, help development personnel to produce plenty of software quickly, is becoming the main research target in the future.

9.3   Software Architecture's Future Research

Because of the hard work of researchers and practicers, in nowadays, the research of SA has already filtered into all the phases of software lifecycle, and has got plentiful research results. Being similar with other fields (such as structured method, object-oriented method) in software engineering research, the research of software architecture first puts attention to one phase of software architecture (design), then transits to the phases after design (implementation, deployment, post-development), at last we again put attention to the phase before design (requirement), so that a set of methods that overlay every phases are formed.

With the enlargement of software system's scale, the application of software architecture in real software development is more and more important, so we must research and practice more about SA in every phases of software lifecycle. On the other hand, the development of Internet technologies enforces the appearance of new software conformation—network-based software. To adapt the open, dynamic and variable running environment, the network-based software appears the characteristics of flexible, multiple goals and continual reaction. This will lead to the continual adjustment and adaptation of network-based software's architecture and its composed components, so it brings the requirement of researching new SA in the new environment. We think it is necessary to research these four aspects about SA:

• The further research about traditional SA's research areas and the further research about unsolved problems. For instance, the automation and semi-automation from requirement to SA, the uniform software architecture structure description method based on meta-model, the style of mixed architecture, the more applied architecture's evaluation and analysis methods, the transmission method from design to application system combined with component pack and model transmission, the pack and deployment of automation component based on architecture, the representation of run-time architecture and system platform support, the rebuild and reuse for legacy system, the traceable support of software architecture in the whole software lifecycle, the architecture design, analysis and evaluation tool support, etc.

• The role of SA in software lifecycle. Compared with traditional software, the networking software is more complicated, variable and open; these enhance the comprehension, analysis and development's difficulty for network-based software. How to define the role of SA in the network-based software's lifecycle? This will be a problem that worth researching and attending. The main researching areas include: the description and analysis methods for networking, the quality attributes and guarantee mechanism of network-based software based on architecture.

- The software developing methodology based on architecture. The development of software involves many aspects, through displaying the core functionality of SA in the software lifecycle; we can efficiently organize software's development, deployment, maintenance and evaluation.

- The software architecture's support to real software development. How to apply the scientific research results to real software development is always the problem that puzzles the researchers. In nowadays, though the practice of architecture has got elementary result, but in the real practice, we still mainly depend on the experience of software architect. There is no successful method and case that systematically use architecture to guide the software development. We still have to do much on the method to apply architecture to real software development. For instance, to integrate the relative concepts and workflow of software to software development environment, to research the methods of merging and integrating software architecture with the existed software development; to hold the education and training relative to architecture, etc.

9.4 Summary

This is the last chapter of this book. In this chapter, we first describe software architecture's position in modern software industry. We categorize software into package, embedded software and software services, and describe each type of software's characteristics and its developing trends, we list much data to show the software market scale and increasing rate, so as to describe the whole visage of software.

After describing the classification of software, we introduce the concept of software product line. Software product line is used to improve software's production rate and quality. Its main principle is to create and maintain a "core asset base". We save the reusable components in this base, so if we need some components that have the same or similar function with component in the core asset base, we need not build new component from nothing. The only thing we need to do is to pick up the component in the base. But the technologies of software product line is not mature. It is still in developing and attracts many researchers.

It is well know that Domain-Specific Software Architecture (DSSA) is one of software architecture's developing trends. So we take much attention to the software architecture used in other fields. We first summarize software architecture application practice, and then introduce the development trends of Domain-Specific software.

In the third part, we talk about software architecture's future research. We think these four aspects are worth researching and have much to do: The further research about traditional SA's research areas and the further research about unsolved problems; the role of SA in software lifecycle; the software developing methodology based on architecture; the software architecture's support to real software development.

We hope this chapter can give a guideline and direction for architecture's researchers and users.

References

(Bosch, 2000)   Bosch, J. *Design and Use of Software Architecture: Adopting and Evolving a Product Line Approach*: Addison-Wesley.2000.

(Clements, 2001)   Clements, P., Northrop, L. & Northrop, L. M. *Software Product Lines: Practices and Patterns*: Addison-Wesley Professional.2001.

(IEEE, 2000)   IEEE. IEEE Recommended Practice for Architectural Description of Software-Intensive Systems.2000.

(Kruchten, 1995)   Kruchten, P. B. The 4+1 View Model of Architecture. Software, IEEE 1995(12): 42-50.

Index